Oklahoma
Gardener's Guide

Steve Dobbs

COOL SPRINGS PRESS
A Division of Thomas Nelson Publishers
Since 1798

Published by Cool Springs Press, a Division of Thomas Nelson, Inc., P. O. Box 141000, Nashville, Tennessee, 37214.

Dobbs, Steve, 1959-
    Oklahoma gardener's guide / Steve Dobbs.—[Rev. ed.]
        p. cm.
    Includes bibliographical references and index.
    ISBN 1-59186-124-1 (alk. paper)
1. Landscape plants—Oklahoma. 2. Landscape gardening—Oklahoma. 3.
Gardening—Oklahoma. I. Title.
    SB407.D63 2004
    635.9'09766—dc22
                        2004026262

First printing 2005
Printed in the United States of America
10 9 8 7 6 5 4 3 2 1

Managing Editors: Bryan Norman
Editorial Assistance: Allan Storjahann
Designer: Sheri Ferguson Kimbrough
Production Artist: S.E. Anderson

On the Cover: Coreopsis verticillata, photographed by Neil Soderstrom

Cool Springs Press books may be purchased in bulk for educational, business, fundraising, or sales promotional use. For information, please email SpecialMarkets@ThomasNelson.com.

Visit the Thomas Nelson website at www.ThomasNelson.com and the Cool Springs Press website at www.coolspringspress.net

Dedication

In loving memory of my dad:
Orville Harold Dobbs
July 4, 1928–March 5, 1992
Memories grow more precious still when loved ones have to part,
and remain forever blooming in the gardens of the heart.
— *author unknown*

Acknowledgements

My hope is that as you use this book, it will enable you to truly enjoy the beauty in your garden and that your lives will be touched by the Creator of that beauty.

And to our Creator, the original gardener, the giver of life, who grants daily miracles in our gardens and landscape for all to enjoy. Thank you for these life-inspiring marvels where we can learn of ourselves and be closer to you!

Thank you Jo Alice and my family for the sacrifices you have made during this book update and revision. To my mom, Alma, thanks for your continued example of courage, faithfulness, and devotion. I love you all!

Thanks to all the many friends and gardeners along my horticulture journey who have planted inspiring and encouraging seeds in my life!

And lastly I'm very grateful for the support and opportunities to work with the great folks at Cool Spring Press. In particular Bryan, I sincerely appreciate your patience, endurance, and devotion to this project!

Table of Contents

Featured Plants *for Oklahoma*

Annuals
Begonia, 24
Bidens, 25
Copper Plant, 26
Esperanza, 27
Firebush, 28
Globe Amaranth, 29
Impatiens, 30
Joseph's Coat, 31
Lantana, 32
Licorice Plant, 33
Melampodium, 34
Mexican Bush Sage, 35
Mexican Heather, 36
Million Bells, 37
Ornamental Sweet Potato, 38
Pansy, 39
Periwinkle, 40
Persian Shield, 41
Pinwheel Zinnia, 42
Plectranthus, 43
Princess Flower, 44
Purple Heart, 45
Scaevola, 46
Shrimp Plant, 47
Starflower, 48
Summer Snapdragon, 49
Sun Coleus, 50
Swiss Chard, 51
Twinspur, 52
Waffle Plant, 53

Bulbs
Autumn Crocus, 58
Bearded Iris, 59
Blazing Star, 60
Bysantine Gladiolus, 61
Caladium, 62
Canna, 63
Crinum Lily, 64
Crocosmia , 65
Daffodil, 66
Daylily, 67
Elephant Ears, 68
Lily, 69
Oriental Hyacinth, 70
Ornamental Onion, 71
Oxalis, 72
Oxblood Lily, 73
Surprise Lily, 74
Tulip, 75

Ground Covers
Archangel, 78
Blue Plumbago, 79
Blue Star Creeper, 80
Bugleweed, 81
Creeping Euonymus, 82
Creeping Phlox, 83
English Ivy, 84
Hardy Ice Plant, 85
Moneywort, 86
Pachysandra, 87
Peacock Moss, 88
Stonecrop, 89
Sweet Box, 90
Vinca, 91

Ornamental Grasses
Bushy Bluestem, 94
Fountain Grass, 95
Inland Wild Oats, 96
Japanese Blood Grass, 97
Lily Turf, 98
Maiden Grass, 99
Mondo Grass, 100
Muhley Grass, 101
Plume Grass, 102
Reed Grass, 103
Ruby Grass, 104
Sedge, 105
Sweet Flag, 106
Switch Grass, 107

Perennials
Barrenwort, 110
Beebalm, 111
Black-eyed Susan, 112
Blue Mist Spirea, 113
Butterfly Weed, 114
Cardinal Flower, 115
Catmint, 116
Coneflower, 117
Coral Bells, 118
Coreopsis, 119
Cupflower, 120
Dianthus, 121
Elderberry, 122
False Indigo, 123
Foamflower, 124
Gaura, 125
Goldenrod, 126
Hardy Hibiscus, 127

Welcome to Gardening
in Oklahoma

Gardening and landscaping in Oklahoma is both rewarding and challenging at the same time. Native landscapes and beautiful gardens abound across the state. We are a land of magnificent forests, mountains, lakes, and rivers as well as diverse ecoregions. Of course, there is heat, humidity, heavy soils, drought, pests, and a range of mind-boggling temperatures to contend with! But even with these challenging conditions, our versatile landscapes are filled with a natural beauty that can be easily duplicated in our own backyards.

Gardening Where You Live

Know your growing environment. The fact that you reside in Oklahoma is not enough information. No other state is as ecologically diverse as ours. Learn about your specific cold hardiness zone, ecoregion, planting location, basic plant needs, soil type, rainfall, and unique microclimates to better help you understand and prepare for the challenges at hand and rewards that will follow.

Hardiness

A cold hardiness zone is defined by the northernmost boundary in which plants can grow when the weather is at its coldest. In Oklahoma these zones vary north to south, from 6a to 7b (see page 21). The majority of the state is Zone 7a, with another large area of 6b. In Zone 6 the coldest temperatures can range from 0 to -10 degrees Fahrenheit. The range for Zone 7 has lows somewhat less severe, from 10 to 0 degrees. Winters vary from year to year, some mild, some very cold. So knowing which plants are more cold-tender and their cold hardiness zone is valuable information when selecting plants for your landscape or garden. Many plant entries in the book indicate cold hardinesss zone or the likelihood of overwintering in a particular area of Oklahoma.

Many plants are affected not only by freezing temperatures, but also by the range of heat extremes experienced throughout the year. Coupled with this is humidity. If the cold of winter does not kill something, sometimes the heat of summer will. If you have spent a summer in Oklahoma, you know it is hot. A recently released Heat Plant Zone Map by the American Horticultural Society shows Oklahoma as heat zones 7, 8 and 9. I did not include this map however since Oklahoman's know that gardening in the summer has two phases - hot and hotter. Until plant distributors start putting heat zone information on tags, it will continue to be trial and error figuring out which plants take our Oklahoma summers, wind, humidity, and periodic drought.

Ecoregions

Mostly you will hear our state referred to as Eastern and Western growing regions due to notable differences in soil type, wind, altitude, temperature, and moisture. But in all actuality, our state should be

Visit Botanical Gardens for Landscaping Ideas

divided into quadrants when it comes to gardening. This is best depicted by an ecoregion map from the USDA Forestry Service. It shows our state divided into four distinct ecoregions: the Great Plains (the Panhandle), the Desert Southwest (southwestern Oklahoma), the Continental East (the northeastern counties), and the Humid South (southeastern Oklahoma). (See map on page 238.) As a longtime resident of the state, this map better sums up our diverse gardening regions. If you reside in the panhandle or northwestern Oklahoma study resources and select plants adapted to the great plains. Blue Spruce and other conifers perform better in this quarter of the state. The same goes for the southwestern corner. Choose plants that are more suited to arid conditions similar to New Mexico, Arizona and West Texas. Gardeners in eastern Oklahoma have more success with plants that grow from Missouri to Philadelphia. I reside in the southern part of the state, so I seek out plants similar to those along the gulf coast but more cold, heat, and humidity tolerant.

Microclimates

Microclimates are areas of the landscape or yard that deviate from the normal climate or growing zone. For instance, areas sheltered by masonry walls, trees or hedges may typically be warmer in the winter than the yard as a whole. Areas on the southeast side of a home or fence in particular that are more protected from winter conditions may also create microclimates. It is in these areas that gardeners try to fool nature by growing plants that are not as cold hardy in hopes that they will overwinter. Extra pampering with winter mulch, watering during winter droughts, and planting early in the spring are all practices to better help ensure that your plants make it through their first winter.

Plant Needs

Plain and simple, to grow and thrive plants rely on soil, water, air (both around the plant and in the soil), food, light, temperature, and protection. Learning the basic requirements and meeting those needs is the key to successful establishment and longevity. Some plants prefer full sun, some full shade and some a combination of both. Part-sun is intended to mean that a plant requires lightly filtered, dappled, or afternoon shade in the heat of the day. Full sun in neighboring states, however, is not the same as it is in Oklahoma. In Oklahoma, plants marked for full sun oftentimes do better in part shade, which is afternoon shade. Those guidelines are also dependent on where the plant is to be grown as far as soil type and wind. Determining whether your planting site is north, south, east, or west of structures in your yard will help you identify sun, shade, and wind patterns. Changing sun angles and deciduous leaf drop in the winter also impacts the shade patterns. For example, the north side of a house or structure will get more shade further out because of the sun's change in angle during the winter and summer. In the summer a northwest corner is very hot in the afternoons and should be treated as full sun locations when selecting plants.

Soil Type

Great soil grows great plants! Be patient and prepare you site properly ahead of time.

It is extremely important to know your soil type, whether it is clay, sand, loam, silt or a combination. Most soils in Oklahoma contain some percentage of our "State Soil," Port Silt Loam. Port Silt Loam is a highly productive soil component that is found in thirty-four of Oklahoma's seventy-seven counties. But in reality most of our urban garden and landscape soils are compacted and non-productive thanks to pre-construction practices. The compacted soils can even equal that of bricks. And remember that many a brick has been made from Oklahoma clay. These compacted soils frequently lack oxygen and hold either too much water or keep water from penetrating. These characteristics easily suffocate plants or cause them to succumb to disease. Amending the soil prior to planting, planting in raised beds, or planting above the soil grade can help, though you may sometimes find it easiest to grow plants that prefer heavy, waterlogged soils.

Regardless of soil type, it is always best to incorporate organic materials into the existing soil. Great soil is typically rich, productive, high in organic material (also known as humus) and well drained. Therefore improving soil is an ongoing process and starts with adding humus whenever possible. It is an investment that will pay off with big dividends. Organic matter is basically decaying plant and animal debris. Manure, compost, sawdust, roots, leaves and grass clippings are some of the most common forms of organic garden materials. Organic material helps to enrich and loosen the soil, improve drainage, hold water and nutrients, furnish some slow release fertilizer, decrease erosion and provide a favorable environment for earthworms and beneficial microorganisms.

Daylilies and Purple Coneflower

Plant Selection

The statement, "the right plant in the right place," is not just a saying but a fact. Trying to grow a plant in the wrong location is trouble in the making. Yet, as gardeners we constantly try to push the limits, which is part of the fun. Just because I brag about a plant does not mean it will perform the same way for you if you neglect the plant's needs. In each chapter, I have listed a few plant recommendations. This is by no means an all encompassing list, but instead some underused or tried and true favorites. I have listed even more plant recommendations in the back that should also be considered when landscaping in Oklahoma. If a plant is not on the list, ask garden centers, gardening friends, gardening club members, master gardeners or the extension service for more information on how it performs in our state.

Things to know in addition to the basics of soil, light, temperature, air, food and water requirements are mature plant height, width and if the plant is prone to particular pest problems. Be careful when plants are described as fast spreading, quick to fill, or fast growing. Clarify if they mean invasive or aggressive instead. Of course the best knowledge is personal experience; in other words try it and see what happens. There are numerous plants in my landscape that I have moved several times, either because of stress from being in the wrong location, I did not like the look, or aggressive spreading tendencies. Do not give up too early however because most plants need at least two growing seasons to get established. And remember "you are not stretching yourself as a gardener if you aren't killing a few plants", as the late J.C. Raulston, a good friend, fellow "Okie", and renowned horticulturist, would often remind me.

A few of the plants in this book may be somewhat difficult to find, but I feel it is better to provide information on additional tried-and-true plants for our state than to limit our choices. Frequent requests to retail suppliers will often bring about better plant offerings. Thanks to an active wholesale and retail nursery and garden center industry, plant selection in Oklahoma is growing. The launch of mail-order and Internet sales has further expanded plant choice and availability.

Know the plants botanical name even if it is just on paper. Common names are often interchangeable among different plants and species. This can cause unfortunate cases of mistaken identity. Confirm the genus species to ensure that you have the plant you want. When you have located the proper plant, look for healthy, pest-free specimens to take home.

Twinspur 'Ruby Field'

Ornamental Onion and Daylily

When to Plant

We are fortunate to have a growing season that lasts for seven or eight months, depending on the region. Planting times are determined by frost or freeze dates particularly with tender plants. The last frost in spring generally occurs sometime between March 31 and April 25; the first frost in fall usually takes place between October 15 and November 3. Milder air temperatures and natural rainfall make spring, early summer, and fall plantings the most successful. Fall plantings in many cases can be even better than spring. The air temperatures are milder, there is typically good soil moisture, plus the soil temperatures remain quite warm sometime up until January. Even though the top may not be growing the roots are. Summer plantings however, mean greater risk as hot soil and air temperatures, as well as drought, can make establishment difficult.

Planting

Leave enough room between plants so they can easily grow to their mature size. That is unless you can afford to put in an instant landscape. Then there will be more crowding and pruning to contend with in a very short time. Proper spacing can actually save you money in the long run because you will not have to buy as many plants. Though they may look lonely at first, the plants will quickly grow into the allotted space.

Most plants are available either as container grown, bare root or ball and burlap. Plants like fruit trees and roses are typically sold as bare root. There are no real advantages over one or the other especially if you follow proper planting procedures and give them ample water until they are established. Nonetheless, I lean toward container grown plants. The risk with container grown plants would be pot bound roots that eventually cross each other, sometimes even girdling the plant near the trunk. Gently loosening and pulling the pot bound roots apart is an important part of planting container grown plants. If you do go with balled-and-burlapped specimens try to take the burlap off when planting. I have seen many stunted trees or their root formation delayed because the burlap did not rot as quickly as you would think. Though it decomposes quickly when the plants are stored above ground, burlap buried in the soil decomposes much more slowly, and often limits root penetration. If the rootball is firm, place the plant in the hole and remove all of the burlap. If the rootball seems loose, place it in the hole and roll the burlap down to the base of the hole; cut off and remove the excess. Always remove any string from around the trunk. Wire cages should also be cut back to avoid later girdling of the trunk as it matures.

When planting in singular holes (as with trees), it is not recommended that you amend the soil with peat moss, root stimulator, or other products. Trees and shrubs are better planted in holes that are as deep as and two to three times as wide as the rootball, using the existing soil as backfill.

Japanese Blood Grass and Sedge

It is best to mix products into the existing soil ahead of time rather than to apply soil amendments as backfill to a small hole, which could cause the roots to grow only in the hole, creating a rootbound plant. High-nitrogen fertilizer and root stimulators may burn the roots when placed in direct contact with them, especially when used at higher-than-recommended rates. It is best to dig wide holes, and backfill with soil that is loosely dug and has plenty of moisture. Unless a soil test shows a significant need for phosphorus and potassium, wait until plants are established to fertilize. When necessary, phosphorus and potassium products can be placed in the bottom of the planting hole and covered with a layer of soil to avoid direct contact with plant roots.

Mulching

There is probably not a better or more effective maintenance practice in the landscape than mulching. Mulch minimizes weed control, holds in soil moisture, regulates soil temperature, provides slow-release nutrients, and helps stop erosion. It is true that it sometimes increases insect populations, inviting moles and armadillos; and despite mulching, weeds can still be problematic thanks to windborne or bird-scattered seed (though mulch keeps the amount of sun light germinating seed to a minimum). Still, the benefits of mulching far outweigh the disadvantages.

Many different kinds of mulch are available; I am particularly fond of cottonseed hulls, pine straw, and wood chips. Cottonseed is perfect for annual plant beds or vegetable garden, where after a couple of seasons it can be tilled into the ground for organic soil improvement. I also use it with shrubs, trees and the entire landscape. However, coarse, slower-degrading products are typically more appropriate for trees, shrubs, and other perennials. Apply two to four inches of organic mulch, depending on the site and the plant's size. Avoid placing mulch on a plant's trunk or stems, which is often referred to as volcano mulching that can harbor insects and promote disease.

I do not recommend weed barriers. The organic mulch used to hide it weathers away exposing the black fabric. Bermuda can grow through many brands and eventually the organic mulch decomposes and weed seed germinate on the surface of the fabric. Omitting it also allows for better oxygen and water penetration to the plant roots.

Though mulch is an added expense, I encourage gardeners to cut back on the size of the landscape bed or number of plants before they cut back on mulch. It can be more affordable by mulching plants in landscape project stages. The job is not finished until the mulch is applied.

Roots on some plants may grow up into the mulch itself; deep and infrequent watering will encourage deeper root growth. Because most mulch is organic and breaks down after a few years, it should be reapplied periodically (every couple of years). An inexpensive source of mulch is from tree-trimming companies. Expect large quantities that are great for trees, shrubs, and walkways, even though the mulch may contain some "trash" and weed seed.

Watering

Rainfall is important for plant establishment and growth. See page 237 for a map of average rainfall for our state. The Panhandle generally receives some 20 inches of rainfall a year, while southeastern Oklahoma receives over 50 inches, as much annual rainfall as in some parts of Florida. Much of our rain however is seasonal, and supplemental irrigation is often needed.

Choose plants based on their water needs and group accordingly. Cluster water-loving plants near the home where there is greater access to supplemental irrigation. Annuals typically require more water throughout the growing season and need to be easily accessed for supplemental irrigation. Drought-tolerant or arid plants can be located at distances farther from the home. A plant must be established first however before it can be drought tolerant. You may ultimately find it best to invest in an irrigation system; many of the newer designs are water efficient and pay for themselves in just a few seasons of saved water and time.

The preferred method for watering plants is to water deeply and infrequently. In other words, really soak the plants down to the root system and wait a few days before the next application. This encourages roots to grow deep. Watering every day for just a few minutes at a time encourages roots to remain shallow, making plants more susceptible to drought, freeze, and stress. In general, plants thrive on one to two inches of water a week, including rainfall. And do not forget that drought occurs in winter just as readily as in summer. Just because a plant is dormant does not mean it will not need an occasional soaking if rainfall is deficient. Plant roots are still

Santolina, Lavender, and Daylily

functioning and active even during the winter. Lack of winter watering following fall planting can cause poor establishment and even death.

Fertilization

The basic plant nutrients (referred to as macro nutrients) are nitrogen, phosphorous and potassium or N-P-K on the fertilizer bag. Many of the major nutrients, such as phosphorus (P) and potassium (K), are best incorporated into the soil before you plant so that the slow change of soil chemistry in the root area has time to occur. Nitrogen (N), on the other hand, is more water-soluble and can be applied as topdressing on an as-needed basis. Micro-nutrients are equally as important but are not as common in plant deficiencies as the major three.

Water-soluble, slow-release, controlled-release, and organic (natural) fertilizers release nitrogen over a longer period of time. They are often more expensive but well worth the added expense. I find my self using slow release organic products applied at the appropriate time under my mulch which seems to help with a more consistent dissemination of the nutrients.

The best advise is to do a routine soil test from a qualified lab to provide a starting point for figuring soil nutritional inadequacies and plant needs. The Oklahoma Cooperative Extension Service County Offices are accessible locations with such soil-testing services.

Fertilizer rates are based on 1 lb. of actual nitrogen per 1000 sq. ft. To determine how much fertilizer to apply, you first have to determine how much nitrogen is in the formulation you are using. For example: 13-13-13 is a common granular landscape fertilizer that is 13 percent nitrogen. To calculate how much fertilizer you need for 1000 sq. ft., you divide 1 (for 1 lb. nitrogen) by .13 (the

Roses and Irises

13 percent nitrogen in the fertilizer). The result is 7.7, which means you should apply 7.7 lbs. of 13-13-13 fertilizer for every 1000 sq. ft. Refer to the fertilizer chart in the book's appendix for additional information.

Plants, especially those growing in poor soil or that show signs of nutritional deficiency, may require supplemental feeding either by sidedressing or with soluble types of fertilizers mixed and applied with water. Just because a plant is sickly does not mean it needs fertilizer. Applying additional fertilizer in cases where root problems exist from compaction, damage or drought can burn or further stress the roots.

Soil pH

Plant growth is impacted by the degree of alkalinity (sweetness) or acidity (sourness) of the soil. Soil pH is the mechanism upon which this scope of soil alkalinity and acidity is measured. The pH scale ranges from 1-14, with 7 being neutral. Anything below 7 is acidic and above is alkaline or basic. The scale is also logarithmic; the distances from one number to the next is compounded. For example a pH of 5 is 10 times more acidic than a pH of 6 and 100 times more acidic than a pH of 7.

An Arbor with Annuals

Plant sensitivity to soil pH depends on many factors like the type of plant, its pH preferences, soil type, and environmental conditions. A soil test to determine the existing pH of the soil is crucial so plants can maximize soil nutrients and future fertilizer applications. If the soil pH is not in check with the particular plants growing range it can interfere with uptake of particular nutrients to the plant. Extreme pH ranges beyond a plants tolerance level can also weaken the plant making it more susceptible to disease, insect and environmental stresses.

Grasses in Autumn

The pH is typically raised by applying liming materials or lowered by applying sulfur products. The amount should be based on a soil test that identifies the current soil pH. Soil type and amount organic matter also influences the quantity to be applied. The process of changing the soil pH typically takes months to correct.

Pruning

Pruning, deadheading, trimming, and pinching are often-necessary maintenance practices that help train plants, control their growth, and initiate additional growth. These methods should be performed in accordance with a plant's growth period and flowering.

Pruning cuts should be made at the branch collar of the trunk limb. This is typically a swollen area where the limb emerges from the trunk. The branch collar is more noticeable on older trees and some particular species. Cuts made further out on branches should be made slightly above any buds or branches. Observe the direction the branch or bud is facing which determines the direction of growth. Avoid leaving stubs which eventually deteriorate further back into the plant's heartwood. Most plants do not heal from improper cuts or damage from weedeaters or lawn mowers. They just cover up the damage and the plants may be weakened. Never remove more than one-third of a plant's canopy at a pruning time. Pruning paints or sealers are optional.

Deadheading has to do with removing flowers that are spent or past their peak. Trimming is loosely used to tidy up shrubs or plants throughout the growing season. Pinching often refers to removing the central growing point of a plant to either make it bushier or to remove an unsightly flower spike like in the case of coleus.

The general rule is to prune deciduous trees in the winter, evergreen trees in the spring, flowering shrubs as soon as they are through flowering, evergreen shrubs in the spring, and perennials, annuals and others as needed through the growing season. And most things can be pruned at any time throughout the year when it comes to safety. Just make sure the proper pruning cut is made.

Pest Control

Inspecting landscape plants routinely is the best method of insect and disease management. Early detection and identification make for more effective management. Think of diagnosing pest problems as a process of elimination based on symptoms and maintenance practices, such as proper site selection, soil preparation, plant selection, placement, planting method, and maintenance practices. Stressed plants are more susceptible to insects and diseases.

Before you pull out the chemicals, try to work with nature to keep the problems in check. This philosophy includes making educated decisions regarding management techniques; incorporating pest-resistant plants, encouraging natural predatory insects, choosing natural or synthetic chemical controls based on toxicity, effectiveness and the least potential impact on the environment.

Rely on gardening friends, the Extension Service, and full-service retail garden centers for help with proper pest identification and control.

Common Gardening and Landscaping Mistakes

- Using poor quality plants
- Wrong plant, wrong place
- Restricted planting hole
- Shallow watering
- Plants too close to each other and structures
- Not keeping Bermuda out of landscape beds
- Not Mulching
- Expecting instant success
- Not monitoring for pests routinely

Book Layout

There are 10 different plant categories covered in the book in alphabetical order. The plants showcased throughout these chapters demonstrate nature's wondrous beauty, which we can have right outside our doors. Everything from annuals, shrubs, trees, vines, groundcovers and more will guide you as you find a solution for your landscaping needs that not only respects a budget but also respects your time. So peruse the book and gain from the years of personal experience within to make your landscaping project exactly what you imagine and more. Whether you are new to Oklahoma, new to gardening, or an experienced gardener, it is my hope that this book will help make your plant selection and maintenance more manageable and enjoyable. Happy gardening!

How to Use the Oklahoma Gardener's Guide

Each entry in this guide provides you with information about a plant's particular characteristics, habits, and its basic requirements for active growth, as well as our personal experience and knowledge of the plant. I include the information you need to help you realize each plant's potential. Only when a plant performs at its best can one appreciate it fully. You will find such pertinent information as mature height and spread, bloom period and colors, sun and soil preferences, water requirements, fertilizing needs, pruning and care, and pest information.

Sun Preferences

Symbols represent the range of sunlight suitable for each plant. Full sun means eight hours or more, including midday. Part sun means six to eight hours, not midday. Part shade means three or four hours, preferrably morning. Shade means less than two hours of sun. Some plants can be grown in more than one range of sun, so you will sometimes see more than one sun symbol.

 Full Sun   **Part Sun**   **Part Shade**   **Shade**

Additional Benefits

Many plants offer benefits that further enhance their value. The following symbols indicate some of the more important additional benefits:

 Attracts Butterflies

 Attracts Hummingbirds

 Produces Edible Fruit or Foliage

 Has Fragrance

 Produces Food for Birds and Wildlife

 Suitable for Cut Flowers or Arrangements

 Long Bloom Period

 Native Plant

 Supports Bees

 Provides Shelter for Birds

 Good Fall Color

 Drought Resistant Once Once Established

 Season-Long, Colorful Foliage

Landscape Merit/Companion Planting and Design

For most of the entries, I provide landscape design ideas, as well as suggestions for companion plants to help you create pleasing and successful combinations—and inspire original compositions of your own. This is where I find much enjoyment from gardening.

My Personal Favorite

With so many plants coming into the trade, I use this section to recommend those that show great promise for Oklahoma.

USDA Cold Hardiness Zones

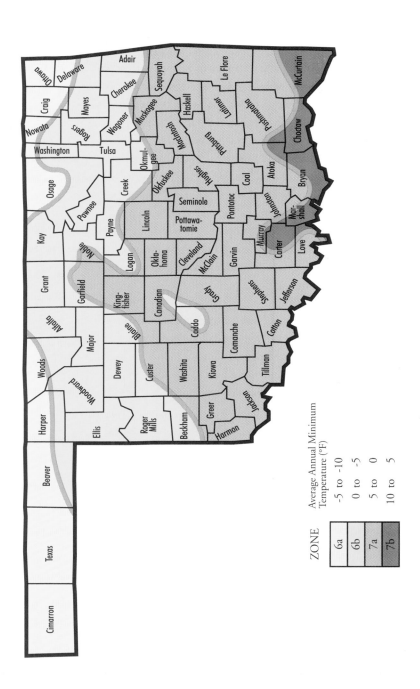

Cold Hardiness Zones

Cold-hardiness zone designations were developed by the United States Department of Agriculture (USDA) to indicate the minimum average temperature for an area. A zone assigned to an individual plant indicates the lowest temperature at which the plant can be expected to survive over the winter.

Annuals *for Oklahoma*

Warm-season annuals are not cold hardy or tolerant of freezing temperatures. Gardeners plant them every year after the last frost in the spring or early summer. The first frost or freeze in the fall then puts an end to their temporary, but rewarding, growing season. Some tender perennials, such as lantana and Mexican bush sage, which are not always cold hardy in parts of our state, are often grown as annuals. The annuals highlighted in this chapter provide impressive color throughout the growing season, tolerating the summer heat and requiring minimal care. Gardeners can choose from a wide variety of annuals to suit their individual tastes and draw attention to their landscape beds and containers.

Use annuals in the landscape in locations where you need your greatest show of color, such as near the mailbox or a prominent entrance to your property. Annuals are perfect for container gardening in apartments, on patios, or in that spot in the landscape where nothing else seems to grow. Annuals are even good companions for the perennial garden. Achieving continuous bloom in a perennial bed is hard to accomplish. Fill the empty space with a few annuals to brighten up the spot between those perennial flowering voids. Annuals with prominent foliage color like coleus, copper plant, and Persian shield are also good choices for summer-long color.

Match the height of the annual to the scale of your garden layout. In other words, use smaller plants around the border in front and keep mid-sized and taller plants in the middle and back respectively. Or keep it simple and use plants all the same height, although uniformity is sometimes influenced by the type of soil you have and your fertilizing and watering habits. The layering of plants should be based on how you view the bed or container. Is it viewed from one side or all the way around? Layer plants accordingly.

Give Them What They Need

Annuals perform best in fertile, moist, well-drained soils. Mulch is vital to retain soil moisture and reduce weeds. Crabgrass, knotweed, and purslane can be easily managed with the simple addition of mulch. The weeds germinate when the seed becomes exposed to sunlight. Mulch acts as a barrier to block out the sun and keep them from germinating. The mulch should be applied two to three inches thick and kept away

from the stem of the plant to avoid rotting. Some weed seed will still manage to germinate around the base of the plants and near the sidewalk or landscape edge. But it is much easier to pull and manage weeds with mulch than without it.

Most of the annuals featured in this chapter actually thrive in our hot, humid Oklahoma summers. Many of them prefer being planted in May, when the temperatures are warmer, instead of in April. The timing works well for gardeners who like to plant cool-season annuals such as pansies, which grow in the fall, winter, and early spring. Pansies will often be at their peak in March, April, and sometimes early May. After the cool-season annuals decline from the heat, summer-loving annuals can be planted in their places.

Globe Amaranth

Impatiens Border

Room to Breathe

Spacing plants is a little tricky to get the best coverage for your investment. Follow proper spacing recommendations to keep plants from becoming overcrowded. Many of the larger plants, such as sun coleus, lantana, and esperanza need to be spaced about two to three feet apart. With this spacing, not many plants will be required to fill a landscape bed. Even though newly placed transplants look lonesome with all the space between them, in no time they will fill in the extra room. Allow for that growth, but make sure the expected height will fit your particular spot and not hide any other plants that might be planted behind. You can use the "Calculating Plant Quantities" guide in the introduction for ground covers to figure out the number of annual bedding plants needed for a particular area.

Once the annuals are planted and mulched, they respond favorably to starter solution of water-soluble fertilizer. To ensure consistent growth and flowering, you can routinely use water-soluble fertilizer applied during watering throughout the growing season. Most of the annuals discussed here are fairly drought tolerant; however, there can be a lull in the flower production if the plants become too drought-stressed.

Pests and Pruning

Annuals, especially if they are actively and healthily growing, are somewhat resistant to pests. Yet you should always keep an eye out for aphids and spider mites. Rotating annual flower plantings every couple of years is a good idea. Periwinkles, for example, are known to get a soil root-rot disease when they are planted too early under cool, moist conditions. The pathogen will build up its population when the host is planted in the same site year after year.

Some annuals require deadheading, pinching, or shearing throughout the season to initiate more blooms. Others are self-cleaning, needing no extra work. Some need to be pruned to keep them within their allotted space. After pruning is a good time to side-dress with fertilizer.

Annuals are perfect for island beds, display beds, mailbox planters, windowboxes, and containers of any shape and size. You will not find any traditional marigolds and geraniums in this chapter. There are far too many other excellent and underused choices for our crispy Oklahoma summers. All of the entries are warm season except for Swiss chard. Also, see the Appendix for more great annuals for Oklahoma.

Begonia

Begonia Semperflorens-Cultorum Hybrids

Begonias are popular summer bedding plants, but most gardeners are still afraid to try them in hot, full sun. These succulent-type plants are truly tough annuals. The plants are known for their bronze, green, or variegated stems and foliage. The flowers are either single or double blooms. Most of the bronze foliage selections seem to do the best in full sun. I have also had success with the green-leaf types in full sun. 'Cocktail', 'Wings', 'Pizzazz', 'Vodka', and 'Excel' are popular series of this annual. The 'Lotto' series is known for larger flowers on compact plants. 'Frilly Dilly' has wavy leaf petals. 'Pink Charm', 'Red Charm', and 'Lois Burke' are variegated foliage selections. 'Cherry Blossom', 'Sunbrite Red', 'Lady Frances', 'Lady Carol', and 'Lady Snow' are double-flowering types.

Other Common Names
Wax Begonia, Fibrous-Rooted Begonia

Bloom Period and Seasonal Color
Red, pink, or white blooms in summer.

Mature Height × Spread
8 to 15 in. × 6 to 12 in.

When, Where, and How to Plant
Plant transplants in April or May. Begonias like fertile, moist, sandy loam soils with good drainage, and they prefer full sun or afternoon shade. The plants thrive in partial shade but become leggy with too much shade. The bronze foliage types are paler in color when grown in heavy shade. Plant begonias at the same depth as their containers and dig the holes wider than the rootballs. Mulch them and keep them watered but not soggy. Space begonias 6 to 8 inches apart if you want the plants to eventually touch. A 10- to 12-inch spacing cuts costs and still offers quite a show.

Growing Tips
Irrigation is needed in severe drought conditions; otherwise, plants fail to bloom consistently. Too much water and cooler soil temperatures early in the spring cause the plants to rot. Avoid mulching up on the plant stems. Mulch in between and angle down to the base of the stem; mulch retains soil moisture, which is needed especially later in the season, The plants fill in nicely with supplemental feedings using a slow-release product prior to planting or a water-soluble application every two to three weeks.

Care
Begonias seldom need pruning. Botrytis blight, leaf spots, stem rot, and powdery mildew are potential disease problems in wet sites with too much shade or when begonias are planted too early. Mealybugs and thrips are possible insect threats and can be easily managed with over-the-counter labeled products or organic treatments.

Companion Planting and Design
These compact plants are perfect as potted plants for colorful bowls, containers, or windowboxes. They also make perfect border plants. Plant them in clusters for a more impressive display. Begonias are so compact in their growth that you can use million bells, scaevola, or verbena as ground cover color in front.

My Personal Favorite
You can't beat the colorful bronze leaf varieties for full sun. Most any cultivar series will work.

When, Where, and How to Plant

Place container-grown plants outside after the danger of frost has passed in the spring. Occasionally, seed is available for direct planting in well-prepared beds or in containers. Plant seeds directly into the landscape bed in mid to late April when soil temperatures begin to warm. Plant seeds in containers indoors in bright light starting in late February. Buying container-grown plants is a better choice. Full-sun locations are best; however, the plants tolerate a half-day of shade. They like rich soil but accept poor soil as long as it is not waterlogged. Container-grown plants from the garden center provide instant and nonstop color. Space the plants 18 to 24 inches apart. Mulch them to minimize weed growth and to hold in soil moisture for the summer. Water them after planting and on a regular basis for the first three to four weeks.

Growing Tips

Once plants establish, they tolerate dry soils; however, a severe drought shuts down the plants completely. Consistent watering and good drainage usually prolongs flowering. Fertilize a couple of times throughout the growing season and especially after shearing the plants.

Care

This lovely blooming plant is self-cleaning and requires no deadheading of spent blooms. Occasionally, gardeners choose to trim overgrown, leggy plants in mid to late season, but it is not necessary to maintain flowering. Pests are of minimal concern, but in case spider mites occur spray them sharply with water.

Companion Planting and Design

Use bidens in annual beds by themselves or in combination with other annuals. Plant them among shrub and perennial beds. Allow some selections to cascade over walls, windowboxes, or hanging baskets. Add them to container displays as companion plants. Bidens makes an excellent companion plant with the even lower-growing purple or pink verbena.

My Personal Favorite

The abundant flowers and compact growth of 'Solaire™ Yellow' has been a favorite in my landscape.

Bidens brightens up any garden spot for the entire growing season, and it has a mild, sweet fragrance. The golden-yellow flowers float atop feathery, vigorous foliage from planting time until frost. The plants grow upright and eventually fall over, giving a cascading effect. The plants thrive in our hot Oklahoma conditions and are fairly drought tolerant. Some cultivars are more prostrate in growth while others reach two feet in height. 'Golden Eye' has a darker greenish-brown center but is prostrate. 'Golden Goddess' is more upright and airy with solid-yellow flowers. 'Golden Falls' has almost cosmos-like flowers on taller foliage. 'Gold Marie' has smaller flowers on cascading foliage. 'Goldie PPAF' is a Proven Winners selection with tiny, bright-yellow flowers on the most compact plant to date. 'Snow Falls' is a white selection.

Other Common Name
Yellow Bidens

Bloom Period and Seasonal Color
Yellow blooms throughout the season.

Mature Height × Spread
1 to 2 ft. × 1 to 2 ft.

Copper Plant

Acalypha wilkesiana

Copper plant is a prime example of a plant that can offer knock-your-socks-off color with its foliage. It is a tropical plant and loves the hot, humid Oklahoma summers. This majestic plant takes up quite a bit of space as the season progresses, which means you do not need many to fill an area. This carefree charmer offers landscape color without a showy flower from spring until frost. 'Macafeana' is a common selection with creamy, copper-variegated foliage. 'Louisiana Red' is a selection with glossy foliage and red undertones in its variegation. 'Kilauea' has narrower foliage. 'Haleakala' and 'Marginata' have uniquely curled foliage with finely cut margins. 'Macrophylla' has heart-shaped leaves. 'Chocolate Thunder' offers earthtone colors. 'Java White' is variegated with green and yellowish-white shades, and it prefers afternoon shade.

Other Common Name
Acalypha

Bloom Period and Seasonal Color
Green, red, and copper foliage

Mature Height × Spread
2 to 3 ft. × 2 to 3 ft.

When, Where, and How to Plant

Plant container-grown plants any time after the last frost from mid-April through May. Planting copper plants in full sun produces magnificent foliage colors. They prefer well-prepared, rich soils. The plants can grow in poorer soils but typically are not majestic. Container-grown, vegetatively propagated plants are sold in assorted sizes up to 1 gallon specimens. Watch for potbound roots, and butterfly them before planting. Set the plants at the same depth that they were grown in their containers, but dig the holes slightly wider than the rootballs. Mulch after planting. Particular selections vary in size, but you should typically space 2 feet between plants.

Growing Tips

Water copper plants on a regular basis, but avoid waterlogged, heavy soils. Copper plants respond well to supplemental feedings throughout the season using a water-soluble product. Supplemental feedings are seldom needed if a slow-release product is incorporated into the soil ahead of planting or placed under the mulch.

Care

Pruning is rarely needed. Pinch the plants shortly after planting to encourage more branching and bushy growth. There is never a need to deadhead since the flowers are discreet, cascading plumes among the foliage, taking second stage to the showy foliage. Other than an occasional mealybug or spider mite, pests are rare.

Companion Planting and Design

The height and boldness of the copper plant are used to good advantage as background for other annuals in beds. It also makes an attractive display all by itself or in a container. Coleus, dwarf purple fountain grass, and Joseph's coat as well as plants with yellow, pink, or red flowers complement the colors of copper plant foliage. Arrange the plants in relation to their height so that one does not hide the other.

My Personal Favorites

'Mardis Gras' is absolutely one of my favorites, maturing around 2 feet with narrow, strap-like leaves resembling confetti. 'Firestorm' and 'Cypress Elf' are different names for 'Mardi Gras'.

When, Where, and How to Plant

Plant this tender herbaceous annual after the last chance of frost, from April through June. Plant seeds in sandy, well-drained soil about $1/2$ inch deep. Seedlings need protection during the winter in a greenhouse or bright sunroom. Esperanza likes full sun in fertile, organic sites, but it accepts a half-day of shade in sandy and limestone conditions. Loosen the roots of any potbound plants before planting. Set the plants at the same depth that they were grown in their containers, but dig the holes slightly wider than the rootballs. Mulch esperanza in landscape beds and containers. The mulch is decorative and beneficial in both cases. Allow 2 to 3 feet between plants.

Growing Tips

Esperanza responds to supplemental feedings of water-soluble fertilizer. Slow-release products are also a good choice. Do not overfertilize, or you can get all foliage and few flowers. Water the plants 2 to 3 times a week when rainfall is not present to get them established. They are relatively drought tolerant, but supplemental irrigation will be needed in severe dry periods or the plants will stop blooming.

Care

Pruning is not needed unless you want to control plant height or direct its growth. Old flowers can be trimmed off or left alone, in which case they often produce dangling, legume-like seedpods. Keep the seeds once they are dry and try to start seedlings next year. Potential pests include mealybugs, spider mites, and aphids.

Companion Planting and Design

Use esperanza as a background plant for low-spreading lantana, periwinkle, Joseph's coat, and summer snapdragon. In a larger container, it can be a center or background plant with duckfoot coleus, verbena, and Mexican heather. Always match companion plant site preferences with those of esperanza. In other words, do not mix shade-loving plants with sun-loving ones, especially in containers.

My Personal Favorite

Tecoma stans 'Lonesp' is a summer-long blooming favorite.

I have grown this trumpet-shaped flowering beauty. I am amazed at its fortitude. It gets bigger and better as the season progresses. Esperanza blooms the entire season as long as supplemental moisture is provided. The fragrant, large, showy flowers are tubular and formed in large clusters above glossy green foliage. It is a perfect choice as a seasonal container or herbaceous bedding plant. Its lush bushy appearance adds to any container display by itself or in combination with other plants. Tecoma stans var. stans, T. stans var. angustata, and Tecoma alata are the three primary species used for breeding these delightful plant introductions. Named cultivars include 'Lonesp' (yellow), 'Orange Jubilee' (orange), and 'Burnt Out' (burnt-orange flowers).

Other Common Name
Yellow Bells

Bloom Period and Seasonal Color
Yellow and orange blooms in summer.

Mature Height × Spread
2 to 4 ft. × 2 to 4 ft.

Firebush

Hamelia patens

This plant is so rugged that I sometimes think it could grow in concrete. Firebush is native to Mexico and grows as an evergreen large shrub or small tree in milder zones. In Oklahoma, it is grown as a tender perennial or as an annual. It blooms nonstop from May until November in hot, full sun and dry conditions. Firebush also works well as a warm-season bedding or container plant. The most frustrating part about promoting this plant is its appearance early in the spring when there are seldom any blooms; the foliage is not showy due to cooler temperatures. Plant it in warmer temperatures, and firebush will get better and better as the summer progresses.

Other Common Names
Mexican Firebush, Scarlet Bush

Bloom Period and Seasonal Color
Scarlet and yellow-orange blooms in summer; green foliage with hues of red.

Mature Height × Spread
2 to 3 ft. × 1 to 2 ft.

When, Where, and How to Plant
Plant firebush as soil and air temperatures warm up in late April, May, or June. Full-sun locations are the most desirable. It accepts a half-day of shade, but the plant foliage loses its red color and the blooms are more sporadic. Though firebush tolerates alkaline and clay soils as long as they drain well, for the best results amend your plot with organic material. Dig a planting hole that is wider than the rootball and as deep as the container. Space plants 1 to 2 feet apart; the bigger the plants, the farther apart they should be planted. Mulch to retain moisture and to minimize weed growth.

Growing Tips
Although the plant is drought tolerant, it displays better with supplemental irrigation throughout the season. Mix in slow-release fertilizers during planting. Give supplemental feedings when the temperature warms up and the plant is sending out new growth. Do not fertilize during cool wet periods. With heavy mulch, firebush occasionally overwinters in the southern parts of the state.

Care
Firebush needs no pruning or deadheading. Potential pests include fungal leaf spots and spider mites. Once the temperatures warm up and the sunshine kicks in, the plant will outgrow the leaf spots. Spider mites need to be monitored routinely and treated when the population is small. Healthy plants with good air circulation are less likely to succumb to disease or mites.

Companion Planting and Design
Plant it as a bedding plant in large groups or in combination with other annuals. The manageable growth makes it a good choice for container or patio displays. Use it as a warm-season annual to follow cool-season pansy removal in May or early June. Verbena, petunia, and million-bells are great companion plants, especially in white or pink.

My Personal Favorites
Improved cultivars are rare in the trade. Anything you can find will perform well. Occasionally you will find a dwarf or compact selection. There is also one sold as an African firebush, which displays an orange-golden flower.

Globe Amaranth

Gomphrena globosa

When, Where, and How to Plant

Start indoors from seed six to eight weeks before transplanting outside. Soak seed in water a couple of days prior to planting in a container and at least six weeks before planting outside. Harden off transplants before their journey to the garden. Direct-sow seeds in the planting site after frost. Seed germination takes anywhere from fourteen to twenty-one days at temperatures around 70 degrees Fahrenheit. Plant container-grown plants outdoors after the last chance of frost is past. The plants prefer rich, well-drained garden soil but tolerate poorer sites. Check the plants for potbound roots, and loosen the roots if necessary. Plant them at the same depth that they were grown in their containers. Space plants 1 to 2 feet apart, with more compact plants spaced on 1-foot centers.

Growing Tips

Once established, the plants are fairly drought tolerant. Mulch them to minimize weed growth and retain moisture. Slow-release fertilizer applied at planting keeps the plant fed most of the summer. Otherwise, apply water-soluble products every couple of weeks to keep the blooms coming all summer long.

Care

Gomphrena seldom needs pruning or deadheading. Taller varieties are the best choices for arrangements (cut in the morning). Pest outbreaks are rare but watch for an occasional spider mite.

Companion Planting and Design

The uniquely shaped flowers are a nice change in texture for the annual garden. There is quite a bit of variation in size. Taller plants make better background plants, and shorter ones are suitable for the front of borders. The plants complement other annuals or do well in beds by themselves. They are also frequently found near fencerows, in the vegetable garden, or in containers. Mass plantings make the best display. 'Evergold', Joseph's coat, or scaevola make nice companions.

My Personal Favorites

I like the "Gnome" series for the landscape and 'Strawberry Fields' for cut flowers, fresh or dried.

Gomphrena is an annual that even the non-green-thumb gardener can successfully grow. This old-fashioned flower is tolerant of hot weather, loaded with color, and virtually pest free. The clover-like flowers are stunning in numbers and appearance. The flowers are produced throughout the summer and make great fresh cut and dried arrangements. Able to hold their color after they are dried, they are often referred to as "everlasting." The flower heads hold up through heat, wind, and rain and require practically no care through the growing season. If you want a truly low-maintenance plant, gomphrena is the one. The Buddy and Gnome Series with assorted colors are compact, maturing at six to eight inches. Taller series include Woodcreek, and assorted mixes. Specific cultivars include 'Strawberry Fields', 'Bicolor Rose', 'Lavender Lady', and 'Aurea' (orange).

Other Common Names

Gomphrena, Clover Amaranth

Bloom Period and Seasonal Color

White, red, purple, rose, or pink blooms in summer.

Mature Height × Spread

1/2 to 3 ft. × 1 to 2 ft.

Impatiens

Impatiens walleriana

Impatiens is popular, dependable, and shade tolerant. Mounding plants provide color throughout the summer if they do not get too much sun or become too dry. They are available in numerous solid, blushed, or swirled colors. There are many variations in size as well as double- or dwarf-flowering forms. Impatiens are usually sold as hybrid series with assorted colors, such as 'Dazzler', 'Accent', 'Mini', 'Elfin', 'Tempo', 'Mosaic', and 'Splash'. For a dwarf flower on a somewhat compact plant, consider the tiny, vivid flowers of the Firefly Mini Impatiens Series. Double impatiens do not have the bloom coverage of singles, yet their rose-like or camellia-like flowers are absolutely beautiful. New Guinea impatiens (I. hawkeri) are somewhat more tolerant of sun, although all day in Oklahoma's hot, scorching sun is not suggested.

Other Common Name
Busy Lizzie

Bloom Period and Seasonal Color
Red, pink, white, lavender, orange, or salmon blooms in summer.

Mature Height × Spread
6 to 18 in. × 6 to 18 in.

When, Where, and How to Plant
Plant impatiens from after the last chance of frost is past until early June. Impatiens prefer moisture-retentive, well-drained, humus-rich soils. Mulch is essential to keep these beauties from wilting frequently in the hot summer weather. Try cotton-seed hulls. Do not allow the mulch to touch the plant stems; angle it down toward the base of the stem but keep it about 2 to 4 inches thick between plants. Space plants 15 to 18 inches apart. Water them after planting and then regularly thereafter.

Growing Tips
Although impatiens prefer moist soils, they quickly die in heavy, waterlogged sites or when overwatered. Impatiens are notorious for wilting in the heat of a summer day. Wilting is not always caused by lack of water but by scorching air or soil temperatures. At the end of the day when the temperatures begin to break, the plants perk up. Gage your watering by pulling back the mulch and checking to see if the soil feels moist at 2 inches deep. Impatiens respond nicely to supplemental feedings with a soluble brand fertilizer applied during watering.

Care
Other than infrequent aphid, thrip, or whitefly, or spider mites, pests are usually of no concern. In cases where high populations of pests are found, control is needed. Pinching is occasionally needed to keep the plants shapely and uniform. Other than that, the flowers are pretty much self cleaning. Impatiens occasionally reseed from year to year. Learn to identify the young seedlings so you don't mistake them for weeds. Germination usually occurs in May.

Companion Planting and Design
Impatiens are favorites around trees, in planters, hanging baskets, window boxes, and as bedding plants in shaded sites. Waffle plant and Persian shield are other good shade-loving companions.

My Personal Favorite
I love the intense bold colors of the cultivar 'Wild Thing'. They brighten up any shady spot.

Joseph's Coat
Alternanthera species

When, Where, and How to Plant
Plant this tender annual in the spring after the last chance of frost is past. Plant container-grown Joseph's coat in full sun or in sites with no more than three or four hours of shade. Soil type is not critical as long as it drains well. Dig planting holes that are wider than the rootballs and as deep as their containers. Space plants 1 to 2 feet apart for the larger cultivars and 8 to 10 inches for the more compact selections. Mulch, water, and fertilize them with water-soluble product after planting.

Growing Tips
A good soaking twice a week suffices in drought periods, depending on your soil type and mulch. This plant responds well to additional water-soluble fertilizer applications mixed with water and applied a couple of times a month. Incorporating slow-release or organic fertilizers at planting is also a benefit.

Care
Joseph's coat needs occasional shearing for bushy and compact foliage. Shear the plants at an angle so that the base is slightly wider than the top, allowing for more exposure to the sun. The ghost caterpillar favors Joseph's coat foliage. It is a larva that feeds on the foliage at night, causing unsightly holes and damage; they can easily defoliate the plant in a few days. Look for black droppings on the ground and foliage. Control them with organic and synthetic insecticides once the feeding frenzy begins. Expect 2 to 3 insect life cycles a summer.

Companion Planting and Design
Use pink Tapien verbena or pink million bells as a border plant with the pink variegated Joseph's coat as a mid-level bedding plant. In larger beds, use purple-blooming princess flower and sun coleus 'Fancy' or 'Eclipse' as taller background plants. The same combinations work well in container plantings.

My Personal Favorite
My favorite is 'Ruby Amaranth' (or giant Joseph's coat), also sold as 'Purple Knight', with bushy, 3-foot growth and brilliant, large, purple-wine foliage.

This annual is known for its dependable, glistening, colorful foliage. It is truly tough, growing in full sun and fairly tolerant of dry soils. One of its best features is its resilience after shearing. Joseph's coat provides an ever-changing display. Variegated Alternanthera often becomes various color shades throughout the summer, thus the name "calico plant." Some variegated yellow-green selections turn more solid green in the summer while others get more yellow. The same plants often revert to their original colors in the fall. There are named cultivars such as 'Aurea Nana', with green and yellow variegation, and 'Haantze's Red Sport', with pink, yellow, and green colors. Leaf shapes vary, with some selections having spoon-like shapes, others very narrow and almost strap-like, and some shaped like a parrot.

Other Common Names
Garden Alternanthera, Calico Plant, Parrot Leaf

Bloom Period and Seasonal Color
Non showy clover like flower grown instead for the green, copper, yellow, pink, rose, white, gray foliage

Mature Height × Spread
6 to 15 in. × 8 to 24 in.

Lantana

Lantana camara

Lantana is one of the most durable, heat-tolerant annuals for Oklahoma. This plant is fast growing with showy blooms throughout the summer and until frost. Its cascading nature and rugged growth quickly fill large flower beds with color. The color spectrum is phenomenal with many vibrant choices. 'Confetti' (yellow and pink), 'Gold Mound' (yellow-orange), 'Irene' (rose, orange, and yellow), 'New Gold' (golden yellow), and 'Radiation' (red-orange) are popular hybrid cultivars sold as "patio tree" specimens. Trailing ground cover types—L. sellowiana (L. montevidensis)—include 'Trailing Purple', 'Trailing White', and 'Lavender Swirl' (purple and white). The Patriot Series includes assorted award-winning varieties with numerous showy flowers. Variegated foliage selections include 'Lemon Swirl', 'Lemon Marble', and 'Samantha'. L. trifolia, sold as 'Lavender Popcorn', is better known for its colorful purple fruit than its flowers.

Other Common Name
Mexican Lantana

Bloom Period and Seasonal Color
Yellow, white, pink, red, lavender, or orange blooms in summer.

Mature Height × Spread
2 to 5 ft. × 3 to 6 ft.

When, Where, and How to Plant
Plant after the chance of frost is past. In many cases, it is wise to plant lantana in May or early June. Plant lantana in almost any soil as long as it drains well. It prefers full-sun sites, although it tolerates two to three hours of shade. Loosen the roots of potbound plants prior to planting. Plant them at the same depth that they were grown in their containers, but dig the holes wider than the rootballs. Spacing should be 18 to 36 inches from the center of one plant to another. Mulch to minimize weeds and to retain soil moisture.

Growing Tips
The plants are drought tolerant after they are established but bloom more consistently with supplemental irrigation. Plants are less likely to flower and often succumb to powdery mildew when grown in too much shade. Routine feeding ensures continuous bloom. Some selections have a lull in flowering as berries are produced. Trim off any berries and fertilize the plants to stimulate quicker repeat flowering. The berries can be left alone, however, and in two to three weeks new growth will emerge and produce more flowers.

Care
Shear larger selections to keep plants under control anytime it is needed. Potential pests include white flies, spider mites, and the occasional lacebugs.

Companion Planting and Design
The lower-growing, more prostrate selections do well in hanging baskets and containers. It is a great rotational plant to follow cool-season plants like pansies, which start to decline in the heat. Grow it in large groups as a bedding plant or in combination with other plants. Use this tough, brilliantly flowering annual as a specimen plant, especially in patio pots. Esperanza, sun coleus, and princess flower are good companions with similar growing heights.

My Personal Favorite
'Patriot™ Cowboy' is a great one developed by an OSU alumnus in honor of his alma mater. It has very compact growth and prolific "cowboy" orange flowers with a hint of yellow.

Licorice Plant

Helichrysum petiolare

When, Where, and How to Plant

Licorice plant is a warm-season annual. Plant it outside after the last chance of frost has passed. The plants actually do best with afternoon shade, though full-sun locations are acceptable. Soils amended with organic matter that are fertile and well drained provide the right conditions for plenty of showy foliage growth. With too much shade, the plants lose their unique coloration patterns. Space plants in landscape beds 15 to 24 inches apart and mulch after planting.

Growing Tips

Overwatering causes rotting, especially in poor soils. Overly dry situations cause the plant foliage to scorch. Be aware of moisture conditions and try to keep soil consistently moist but not waterlogged. I have found that licorice plants require more frequent amounts of water than most annuals. Supplemental feedings initiate vigorous growth whether by slow-release applications incorporated at planting or by water-soluble feedings every couple of weeks during watering.

Care

Prune any time to control size. Other than occasional white flies, pests are rare. Some helichrysum varieties are favorite hosts for the larval stage of butterflies. Expect some foliage feeding from the larva, followed by the pupal stage, and shortly thereafter fluttering butterflies. Live happily with this pest because you get beautiful butterflies afterward. Besides, the plants quickly grow back their colorful foliage once the life cycle is complete.

Companion Planting and Design

Licorice plant is a designer's dream come true! Combine gray licorice with purple verbena in a hanging basket or lemon licorice with 'Fancy' sun coleus and pink million bells. The nice blend of colors and textures appears almost like a living bouquet, and *H. petiolare* is the right ingredient for a tasty display of brilliance.

My Personal Favorites

There are two that I use often in my container gardening displays. 'Icicles' has gray, narrow, almost strap-like foliage, and 'Limelight' is a vibrant chartreuse color.

Licorice plant sounds good enough to eat, and when you see the striking foliage combined with other plants, you may be tempted—although it would not be recommended. If the genus Helichrysum sounds familiar, it is the same genus as strawflower, just a different species. The related licorice plant is grown strictly for its soft, colorful foliage rather than for its flowers. This lively plant can be used as a component plant in combination with other flowering annuals in ground beds or containers of all shapes and sizes. Cultivars include 'White Licorice' (gray-green foliage with a silvery-white fuzzy lining), 'Petite Licorice' or 'Dwarf Licorice' (same as 'White Licorice', just smaller foliage and growth), 'Licorice Splash' (variegated yellow and green), and 'Limelight' and 'Lemon' (chartreuse).

Other Common Name
Velvet Plant

Bloom Period and Seasonal Color
Gray-green, white, yellow and green, and chartreuse foliage.

Mature Height × Spread
6 to 28 in. × 12 to 24 in.

Melampodium
Melampodium paludosum

This bright golden-yellow, daisy-like, flowering plant blooms throughout the summer and loves the heat and humidity, making it a perfect choice for our gardens. Even better is the fact that melampodium is fairly drought tolerant. The flowers typically have yellow petals with yellow centers, or eyes, emerging from pleasant green foliage. The newer releases are more compact in growth; the original species and named cultivars were more upright. Probably the hardest part of growing melampodium is learning to say the name. Try this easy, beautiful plant and see if it does not rank as a top performer in your garden and landscape. 'Derby' is a compact release. 'Million Gold' is one of the most compact, growing to an 8-inch mound.

Other Common Name
Showstar

Bloom Period and Seasonal Color
Yellow blooms in summer.

Mature Height × Spread
8 to 24 in. × 8 to 24 in.

When, Where, and How to Plant
Start seeds indoors six to eight weeks prior to planting. Expect seed to germinate in fourteen to twenty-one days. Harden off seedlings before placing them in the garden or landscape. Set out container-grown plants after the last chance of frost has passed. Melampodium prefers fertile, well-drained soils but grows in almost any well-drained site. The plants prefer full-sun locations but tolerate two to three hours of shade. Space plants 1 to 2 feet apart, depending upon the cultivar. Angle mulch down toward the base of the plant, but keep it 2 to 4 inches thick between plants.

Growing Tips
Melampodium are fairly drought tolerant but won't thrive through severe drought. They prefer drier soils. Do not overwater. Allow the plants to dry between waterings. Do not over-fertilize melampodium. With high-nitrogen blends, the plants reward you with more foliage and fewer flowers.

Care
This floriferous plant typically is self-cleaning and requires no deadheading of spent blooms. Occasionally, the plant blooms its heart out and then rests a little while before starting again, especially on the more upright, older cultivars. During this break, shear the plants, fertilize, and water to initiate more growth and flowers. Pests most likely to favor melampodium are spider mites. With high populations, control is necessary. Powdery mildew can become a problem during consistent cloudy or wet conditions or when the plants are grown in too much shade.

Companion Planting and Design
Use this compact plant among perennials and shrubs or in containers and patio planters. The vivid yellow color goes well with purple, pink, or white flowers. Plants with colorful foliage such as sun coleus, Joseph's coat, and dwarf purple fountain grass are good background companions.

My Personal Favorite
'Million Gold' lives up to its name and is relatively compact (12 to 18 inches) depending on the soil type and moisture conditions.

Mexican Bush Sage
Salvia leucantha

When, Where, and How to Plant

Plant this herbaceous tender perennial from after the last chance of frost through June. Plant in areas protected from north winds when trying to grow as a perennial. The lush plants perform well in rich garden soil with good drainage. They thrive in hot, full sun but will grow in partial shade (three or four hours sun). Space plants 3 to 4 feet apart. Dig planting holes that are wider than the rootballs and as deep as their containers. Loosen potbound roots before planting. Mulch them for moisture conservation and weed control.

Growing Tips

Even though the plants are drought tolerant, they bloom best if supplemental irrigation is provided, especially later in the summer and early fall. Supplemental feedings are not needed with good soil preparation. Too much fertilizer and the plants become too tall and risk blowing over. When fertilizer is needed, stick with slow-release products. Mulch these beauties with about 6 inches of compost, leaf litter, cottonseed hulls, grass clippings, or wheat straw for winter protection in areas with marginal cold hardiness.

Care

No pruning is necessary; leave the dead tops in place as good insulation and winter protection. In spring, around late March, remove the mulch and dead tops to allow for new growth. In Zones 6a, 6b, and sometimes 7a, the plants are hard to overwinter—even with protection. Other than an occasional spider mite, pests are rare.

Companion Planting and Design

Use *Salvia leucantha* as a background plant in the perennial garden or annual landscape bed or as a nice specimen plant among shrubs. I like to use it as a hedge or screen along fencerows or to hide eyesores. It can be a single specimen in a container where it is moved front and center in the fall, although it will be smaller grown in a pot.

My Personal Favorite

'Santa Barbara' is a compact variety maturing to about 3 feet, which is more to scale in my perennial garden.

Mexican bush sage is, without a doubt, one of my favorite fall-flowering plants, and the hummingbirds love it too. The velvety purple-and-white flowers form on elongated stems from tall, bushy plants in late summer or early fall and continue until frost. This Mexican native loves the heat and is occasionally grown as a perennial in the southeastern quadrant of Oklahoma. For the rest of the state, though, it is best grown as an annual and well worth the investment each year. Mexican bush sage is occasionally categorized as an herb, although it is not typically used for culinary purposes. Instead, the flowers are used for fresh cut and dried arrangements. 'Midnight' is a solid purple selection.

Other Common Name
Mexican Salvia

Bloom Period and Seasonal Color
Purple blooms in fall.

Mature Height × Spread
4 to 6 ft. × 3 to 5 ft.

Mexican Heather
Cuphea hyssopifolia

Mexican heather is a tough perennial of the southeastern United States grown as an annual in Oklahoma. The lacy plant offers a texture like a fern but with tiny flowers. Occasionally, the plant overwinters in southern Oklahoma during mild winters, but it does better as a seasonal bedding plant or as a container companion plant. Even though the flowers are fairly small, they provide continuous bloom for a charming display of color throughout the summer. Named cultivars include 'Allison' with rose-purple flowers; 'Alba' and 'Linda Downer' with white blooms; 'Palest Pinkie' with pale pink; and 'Rosea' with a magenta color. 'Hanging Basket' has a weeping growth habit with lavender flowers. Golden Mexican heather has chartreuse foliage. Cuphea × glutinosa is a University of Georgia hybrid selection, hardy in Zone 7 with some winter protection.

Other Common Names
False Heather, hawaiian Heather

Bloom Period and Seasonal Color
Purple, pink, or white blooms in summer.

Mature Height × Spread
8 to 15 in. × 10 to 15 in.

When, Where, and How to Plant
Plant Mexican heather after the temperatures begin to warm in the spring and after the last chance of frost has passed. Fertile or poor soils are acceptable as long as they do not hold water. Like most plants, they grow more vigorously in loosely prepared organic sites with a top layer of mulch. The proper spacing is 12- to 15-inch centers if you want the plants to touch at their maturity and fill up the bed.

Growing Tips
Blooms are more consistent with irrigation during severe drought. Side-dressing with a fertilizer is rarely needed unless the plants are a chlorotic yellowish color or planted in very poor sites. Supplemental water is needed during drought periods. A good soaking every week—maybe twice a week during severe drought—is ideal.

Care
The dainty flowers are definitely self-cleaning, so no deadheading is needed. Because their natural growth habit is compact and somewhat flat, additional pruning is seldom needed. I have seen Mexican heather spaced close together and sheared as a hedge. The formal appearance made quite an impact. Remember when trying this method to trim the plants so that the base is slightly wider than the top to allow better penetration of light for more uniform growth.

Companion Planting and Design
Cuphea hyssopifolia is a great choice for a uniform border plant in a special annual bed or even for seasonal color in the perennial landscape. The compact growth and fine texture make the plants candidates for container combinations, rock gardens, walkways, windowboxes, mailboxes, and just about any place you need a plant. Verbena, calibrachoa, and scaevola are nice, low-growing companions.

My Personal Favorite
My favorite is 'Batface Cuphea' (*C. cyanea*) with purple, slender flowers and orange-red petals making the bat's ears.

Million Bells™

Calibrachoa hybrids

When, Where, and How to Plant

Plant them in spring after the chance of frost has passed, just about any time from April to June. Full-sun sites are best as long as irrigation is provided during dry times. The plants accept partial or afternoon shade, but with too much shade, the plants become spindly and bloom sporadically. They perform in almost any soil type as long as drainage is satisfactory. Moisture-retentive soils that drain well are ideal. Space plants at least 2 feet apart in nutrient-rich soils.

Growing Tips

Moisture seems to be the key to growing these delightful plants. Without supplemental irrigation, the plants stop blooming. Moisture-retentive sites or locations with irrigation proved best for continuous bloom throughout the summer. In some locations, the plants overwinter; survival depends on the severity of the winter, the condition of the plants, and the site. Supplemental feedings with a slow-release product or water-soluble brand even more flower power.

Care

The plants seldom need pruning and no deadheading. Occasionally the plants creep onto my sidewalk and need a little trimming. They grow from the crown and sprawl along the ground, seldom rooting into the soil and never suckering. White flies would be the pest most likely to watch for.

Companion Planting and Design

Calibrachoa does well in containers and baskets but is even better as a bedding plant or ground cover. The plants truly have a ground cover growth habit, not reaching more than 4 to 6 inches high but easily spreading 2 feet. Visitors to my garden complimented my seasonal designs with Million Bells as a front border in combination with periwinkles in the middle and sun coleus in the background.

My Personal Favorite

I've tried many, but one of the originals, 'Trailing Pink', seems to always surface as my favorite.

Million Bells™ is a registered trademark of the Proven Winners™ plant cooperators and is named after its hundreds of bell-shaped blooms that appear throughout the season. I had reservations at first about the promotions touting their tolerance to full sun. I expected them to melt down in our hot, humid summers. Boy, was I wrong! They bloom in full sun all right; as a matter of fact, on cloudy days the flowers close up. They need supplemental moisture, though, to thrive in the heat. Million Bells™ have received accolades from various state university horticulture trials and have earned their keep as bedding plants in Oklahoma's hot summers. 'Cherry Pink', 'Trailing Blue', 'Trailing Pink', and 'Trailing White' are releases from Proven Winners™. 'Liricashower Blue' and 'Liricashower Rose' are two similar releases from Flower Fields.

Other Common Name
Miniature Petunia

Bloom Period and Seasonal Color
Pink, rose, yellow or white blooms both in solids and in various shades in summer.

Mature Height × Spread
4 to 6 in. × 24 to 36 in.

Ornamental Sweet Potato

Ipomoea batatas

Ornamental sweet potato is a true sweet potato, just like the traditional baking sweet potato. The biggest difference is the colorful foliage of the ornamental. The best part of using ornamental sweet potato in the landscape is that few plants are needed to fill a large area. If you do not trim the vines to make them bushier, they easily grow 6 to 8 feet long—and longer during the summer. 'Margarita' or 'Marguerite' is a lovely chartreuse color. 'Terrace Lime' has a similar lime-yellow color. 'Blackie' is a dark purple, almost black, with finely lobed foliage somewhat resembling a star. 'Black Beauty' or 'Ace of Spades' is the same deep purple but with unique, heart-shaped leaves. 'Tricolor'—also sold as 'Pink Frost'—has gray, pink, and creamy-white variegation.

Other Common Name
Sweet Potato Vine

Bloom Period and Seasonal Color
Chartreuse, purple, gray, or pink variegated foliage.

Mature Height × Spread
1 to 1 1/2 ft. × 4 to 6 ft.

When, Where, and How to Plant
Ornamental sweet potato is a heat-loving plant; plant it in May or June when the soil temperatures begin to warm. Full-sun locations are best, though they will take two to three hours of shade. Rich garden soils usually produce aggressive vines. Ornamental sweet potato does not tolerate wet feet. Space the plants in ground beds a minimum of 3 feet apart. In a container, one plant is enough.

Growing Tips
Mulching the ornamental sweet potatoes controls weeds and retains soil moisture. Sweet potato is relatively drought tolerant once established. In severe drought, it will need an occasional drink, or the foliage will wilt, scorch, and burn. Do not overfertilize the plants; they will take over. I seldom feed mine unless the foliage is not vigorous or is pale in color.

Care
Tip-pruning keeps the plants compact and bushy, forcing side shoots back along the foliage. White sap will ooze from the wound, which is characteristic of this genus. Potential insect threats are spider mites and aphids. Any sweet potato may become the prey of the sweet potato weevil, although to date it is not commonly found.

Companion Planting and Design
This somewhat aggressive annual grows perfectly as a ground cover. Its vining and cascading growth is also impressive where it flows over a wall or planter. Use it as a border plant or among taller annuals. Be careful not to use it around short annuals, or the vines quickly overgrow and consume the smaller plants. It is better to go with tall growing annuals like esperanza, lantana, or coleus.

My Personal Favorites
I typically use a combination of either 'Blackie' or 'Ace of Spades' planted with 'Margaruite'. The purple-chartreuse color is quite showy.

Pansy

Viola × wittrockiana

When, Where and How to Plant

Plant pansies in late September or early October in northwestern Oklahoma. October to early November is best for the remainder of the state. Organic, well-drained soils are a must. Waterlogged sites spell certain death. Mulch 2 to 3 inches deep with pine straw, cottonseed hulls, or pine bark immediately after planting to help insulate the roots for overwintering. Keep mulch from directly touching stems. The mulch also smothers henbit, chickweed, and other cool-season annual weed seed. Soak the plants, and water in all the mulch to help settle it for better insulation.

Growing Tips

Pansies are relatively drought tolerant once established. Supplemental rainfall throughout the fall and winter is typically sufficient. Be observant, though, and water if drought occurs. Slow-release fertilizers low in nitrogen and high in phosphorus and potassium work to help establish roots during the cooler months. Feed pansies again in early spring with a water-soluble fertilizer in early to late March. This helps provide continual bloom until the heat kicks in sometime in May.

Care

Insects to watch for are the occasional spider mite or white fly and the more frequent caterpillars. The flowers are typically self cleaning. The plants may become leggy and stretch from prolonged heat in the fall and benefit from trimming the foliage back a quarter to half way, helping initiate more growth and flowers.

Companion Planting and Design

Follow pansy plantings, as they decline, with heat-loving plants like sun coleus, lantana, firebush, sweet potato, and scaevola that actually prefer being planted later. As a cool-season companion, try acorus (sweet flag), cool season snapdragons, or tulip bulbs. In a container, plant a few bulbs in the soil for an extra surprise next spring.

My Personal Favorites

I like them all and usually plant a couple of different color combinations each year. Ask your local garden center for input on which varieties are cold hardy for you area (such as the "Fama" series).

If you are not planting pansies, you are missing an entire season of color. Many gardeners hesitate to plant pansies because their peak bloom is in late April or May – the most popular time to plant summer color. Never fear, there is plenty to plant that actually do better when planted later. No other plant performs as well as pansy in cool-season flower beds. These cold-hardy annuals thrive in the fall, routinely overwinter for most of the state, and provide unmatched early season color. Color assortment and intensity help bring life to a typically drab time of year. Flower size ranges from large to small. The pansy cousins known as Johnny-jump-ups are the smallest of the cool-season violas and have a greater tendency to reseed in the flowerbed.

Other Common Name
Viola

Bloom Period and Seasonal Color
Shades of purple, pink, maroon, orange, yellow, blue, white, and assorted combinations that bloom in the fall, winter, and early spring.

Mature Height × Spread
6 to 12 in. × 10 to 12 in.

Periwinkle
Catharanthus roseus

The popularity of vinca almost always puts it in the top ten best-selling bedding plants from year to year. Thanks to their heat tolerance, vincas are dependable bloomers from spring to frost. The colors go with almost any annual display. Many selections are sold in a series with assorted colors. Heat Wave, Peppermint, Pretty In, Tropicana, Pacifica, and Cooler series are some of the most popular. The Little series is more compact in growth, averaging about ten inches in height. 'Passion', 'Blue Pearl', and 'Caribbean Lavender' are in the race for a bluer flower. 'Santa Fe' and 'Terrace Vermilion' are uniquely salmon-colored with large flowers. Low-growing, more prostrate periwinkles to consider for hanging baskets or front border plants are the Mediterranean series, 'Cascade Appleblossom' and 'Vining Pink Star'.

Other Common Name
Vinca

Bloom Period and Seasonal Color
Pink, white, or lavender blooms in summer.

Mature Height × Spread
8 to 18 in. × 12 to 18 in.

When, Where, and How to Plant
Annual vinca is notorious for rotting in cool, damp soils early in the season when it is planted too early. Plant in late April in southern Oklahoma and in May in the rest of the state. Fertile organic soils with good drainage are a must. Vincas prefer full-sun locations and tolerate no more than a half-day of shade. Space plants on 12- to 15-inch centers. Do not mulch these plants too thickly around the stems, or root rot occurs. Mulch more thickly between plants and with finer products. Water them after planting, but allow the planting sites to dry between waterings.

Growing Tips
Overwatering early after planting is detrimental. As the soil and air temperatures begin to sizzle, water the plants on a more consistent schedule. Supplemental feedings are not needed unless they are grown in poor soils or they show symptoms of nutrient deficiency.

Care
Planting vincas in the same site year after year builds up root rot pathogens. Rotate vincas from the same planting site at least every couple of years to avoid this misfortune.

Companion Planting and Design
Annual periwinkle is a great rotational plant with pansy plantings. As soon as the pansies are removed in May, the vincas take their place. Border or mass plantings suit these plants perfectly. Vincas, especially the trailing types, are even adapted to containers and hanging baskets. One of the most commented-on annual beds at our display gardens included annual vinca 'Raspberry Red' as the mid-level plant with *Calibrachoa* 'Trailing Pink' as the low-growing border and 'Ruby Giant' Joseph's coat as the background plant. The various shades of violet and purple made for a truly stunning summer-long display.

My Personal Favorites
I'm using more of the trailing selections for border plants in my color beds or in container displays. I particularly like Mediterranean 'Deep Rose' and 'Punch'.

Persian Shield
Strobilanthes dyerianus

When, Where, and How to Plant

Plant Persian shield as the soil temperatures begin to warm up and the chance of frost is past. Set out plants in late April or May. The foliage intensity is best achieved in organic soils in partial shade. Space the plants 18 to 24 inches apart in groups. Diagonal planting offers better design and allows the plants to fill in the space. Check for potbound roots before planting and loosen them if necessary. Plant Persian shield at the same depth that they were grown in their containers but slightly wider than the rootballs. Water them after planting. Mulch to retain soil moisture and to minimize weeds.

Growing Tips

Persian shield starts a little slow in the spring after planting, but once the temperatures heat up, it grows fairly rapidly. Water on a regular basis throughout the growing season. Avoid getting mulch angled up on the plant stem because rotting can occur. The plants tolerate heat and humidity. Persian shield responds well to supplemental fertilizer applications, especially in poor soils. Occasionally you will get small purple flowers in late summer but nothing compared to the intensity of the foliage.

Care

Once the plants are placed outside, it is a good idea to pinch them to initiate more compact, uniform growth. There are no particular diseases or insect problems other than an occasional white fly when the plants are grown in a greenhouse. The prominent foliage and strong stems require no staking.

Companion Planting and Design

Use Persian shield as a specimen or background plant. It is also appealing massed in ground beds. Flower colors of purple, pink, and white are perfect companions. For lower-growing, ground cover-type, sun companions use petunia, *Calibrachoa*, Mexican heather, ornamental sweet potato, purple heart, scaevola, and verbena. Summer snapdragon, plectranthus, coleus, princess flower, purple fountain grass, and lantana are taller sun-loving companion annuals. Impatiens are perfect shade-loving companions.

My Personal Favorite

The species is pretty much all that is available in the trade.

Foliage color has always been important; just look at the breeding done with bronze- or variegated-leaved flowering plants. Persian shield has outstanding color but not from a flower—it comes from its silvery-purple metallic foliage. The bold coarseness of the foliage in combination with the unique color scheme makes for a brilliant display. In most of Oklahoma, this foliage beauty is best grown in afternoon or partial shade. In rich, moist soils with mulch, it can tolerate full sun. Persian shield is an old-fashioned plant, which has not changed much over the years. It is often sold as a houseplant in the foliage section of the garden center, but thanks to creative and open-minded gardeners, Persian shield is now making its way into the nursery trade as a bold, beautiful, seasonal bedding plant.

Other Common Name
Metallic Plant

Bloom Period and Seasonal Color
Silvery-purple metallic foliage all summer.

Mature Height × Spread
15 to 36 in. × 18 to 32 in.

Pinwheel Zinnia

Zinnia angustifolia

Mention the name zinnia, and many gardeners run the other way—thanks to a notorious disease called powdery mildew. Pinwheel zinnias, however, are tolerant of this dreaded foliage pathogen. The flowers of pinwheel zinnia are not as large as the standard, upright-growing selections, but the season-long blooms make up for their size in other ways. Most of the flowers are self-cleaning and require little or no deadheading. Because they are shorter, they do not require staking. Zinnia linearis 'Starbright Mix' is another variety that is more spreading with the same positive attributes. Look for the disease tolerant, compact hybrid "Profusion" series. "Dwarf" describes zinnia's plant and flower size. It does not mean it is disease tolerant like the pinwheel varieties, so read the fine print.

Other Common Names
Dwarf, Narrow-leafed, or Spreading Zinnia

Bloom Period and Seasonal Color
Yellow, white, or rose blooms all summer.

Mature Height × Spread
8 to 12 in. × 12 to 15 in.

When, Where, and How to Plant
Start seed indoors in February or eight to twelve weeks before the last frost. Direct seeding into the ground is risky because of competition from weeds, but it can be done in April. Set out container-grown plants after the last frost. Plant in full sun for the best display or in no more than a half-day of shade. They prefer rich, fertile garden soil, but the plants perform in poorer soils. Good drainage and air circulation are essential. Space plants 12 to 15 inches apart.

Growing Tips
Mulch the plants after planting or when the temperatures warm up. Avoid getting the mulch too thick near the delicate plant stems, or rotting occurs. Water on a regular basis throughout the summer. Supplemental feeding is beneficial occasionally during the growing season, but don't overdo it or you will initiate too much lanky growth that tends to fall over. Slow-release or organic mixes are best.

Care
Pests are seldom a problem. Powdery mildew is not likely on these tolerant selections unless they are stressed and planted in too much shade. Occasionally caterpillars, flea beetles, and lacebugs can be found.

Companion Planting and Design
Pinwheel zinnias make nice border plants in the annual flower bed or even work as accent plants in the perennial or shrub landscape. Grow these colorful beauties in borders of the vegetable garden for color and for their use as cut flowers. Pinwheel zinnias also do well in containers and windowboxes when sufficient sun is available. Lower-growing plants like scaevola, verbena, and calibrachoa are nice plants for layering in front of pinwheel zinnias, or consider coleus, lantana, and firebush for taller background plants.

My Personal Favorite
'Profusion Orange' has a nice mounding habit and a vibrant color that does not fade.

Plectranthus

Plectranthus species

When, Where, and How to Plant

As with most tropicals, plant plectranthus in late April, May, or June after the last chance of frost is past. It accepts organic soils but may have overly vigorous foliage. Space plants 18 to 24 inches apart. Loosen potbound roots before planting. Plant them at the same depth that they were grown in containers, in holes slightly wider than the rootballs. Mulch them for moisture retention and weed control. Water them after planting.

Growing Tips

Water as needed throughout the growing season, especially during periods of drought. Fertilize only when the plants show obvious signs of non-productive growth. Too much tender loving care and the plants get lanky.

Care

Depending on the species, plectranthus sends out unappealing flower spikes. Trim them during the season to keep the plants more presentable. Also, like sun coleus, the plants achieve more uniform and bushy growth when pinched at planting and throughout the growing season. There is no pest of significant harm, although white flies are a problem in the greenhouse. Caterpillars and grasshoppers are possible.

Companion Planting and Design

Use many of the *Plectranthus* species as companion contrast plants in patio container displays, or plant them in landscape beds. Most *Plectranthus* species have aromatic foliage, making the plants good choices in herbal gardens. The gray foliage of many of the plectranthus varieties makes it a perfect contrast plant for white-, purple-, and pink-flowering plants. Even foliage companions like Persian shield and sun coleus make great companions.

My Personal Favorite

I love the color combination of Plectranthus 'Quick Silver' (a.k.a. silver leafed tropical mint 'Silver Seas'), especially when planted with Persian shield.

Most plectranthus selections are grown more for their foliage than their flowers. Most gardeners are familiar with the houseplant Swedish ivy (P. coleoides) and its trailing, variegated, waxy foliage. Numerous other species have upright foliage instead, which is useful as a bedding plant and as an impressive container companion plant. Many of the Plectranthus *species grow in shade or sun. P. argentatus, or silver plectranthus, is a soothing, velvety blue-gray; 'Quick Silver' is one named selection. P. mboionicus, or oregano plectranthus or Cuban oregano, is a variegated green and creamy yellow with prostrate growth. 'Athen's Gem' is an outstanding landscape bedding plant. P. coleoides, P. madagascarienses, and P. minimus are trailing prostrate types with assorted variegated foliage colors of green and white or yellow; some have a strong menthol scent.*

Other Common Names

Velvet Plant, Tropical Mint, Swedish Ivy

Bloom Period and Seasonal Color

Silvery gray, green with yellow foliage through summer.

Mature Height × Spread

4 to 36 in. × 12 to 24 in.

Princess Flower

Tibouchina grandiflora

This plant's royal presence comes from its purple flowers that have an average diameter of 2 to 3 inches. The vibrant purple blooms form all season long on a shrubby plant with velvety foliage. There is nothing quite like its dynamite flower color, especially when used in beds or containers adjacent to yellow- or white-flowering or variegated companions. T. urvilleana is the most commonly sold species of princess flower with medium-sized foliage and lavender flowers. T. grandiflora is harder to find but has larger, bolder, even fuzzier leaves. T. granulosa has darker purple flowers and narrow, sandpaper-like foliage. Most selections sold on the market at this time are the species, but it will not be long before improved cultivars or hybrids are offered.

Other Common Name
Glory Bush

Bloom Period and Seasonal Color
Purple blooms all summer.

Mature Height × Spread
2 to 4 ft. × 2 to 3 ft.

When, Where, and How to Plant

Because of its tropical background, set this plant outside in late April when temperatures begin to steadily warm. Do not subject this plant to frost. Consistently moist but well-drained soils are best for this plant. When repotting or planting it in the ground, check for potbound overgrown roots. Loosen the roots by severing the sides and, in worst-case scenarios, cutting off the bottom 2 inches. Plant princess flowers at the same depth that they were grown in the containers but dig the holes wider than the rootballs. Mulch is beneficial to keep the plant roots moist in both ground beds and containers.

Growing Tips

Water princess flower on a regular basis after planting throughout the growing season. Severe drought and wind will scorch the foliage and abort the blooms. It responds to frequent feedings throughout the growing season with water-applied fertilizers high in phosphorus and potassium and low in nitrogen.

Care

The bushy growth seldom needs staking. Pruning is generally needed only to keep plants in a manageable shape. The flowers are produced in clusters opening a few at a time throughout the summer. Insect pests are ones that typically attack tropical flowering plants, primarily spider mites and aphids. Budworm is fairly easy to control with either organic or synthetic insect sprays. I have had success with using Di-Syston insecticide granules in the container.

Companion Planting and Design

Princess flower is elegant enough to be a specimen plant by itself in a container or in a landscape bed. In larger containers, it does well in combination with other colorful and textured plants. Ground bed plantings in masses are absolutely breathtaking. It looks especially nice when combined with Persian shield or 'Dark Star' coleus. Verbena and million bells are nice cascading companions.

My Personal Favorite

I've never met a princess flower that I didn't like, but I typically use *T. urvilleana* 'Athen's Blue' because of its medium size that is more compatible with most of my designs.

Purple Heart
Setcreasea pallida

When, Where, and How to Plant

Plant purple heart in late April or early to mid-May after the chance of frost has passed. It likes full-sun locations but tolerates a half-day of shade. Full-sun locations intensify the purple foliage. Well-drained soils are a must. The foliage readily rots in waterlogged or over-watered sites. Soil type is not crucial since the plants grow in poor or fertile soils. Space plants on 15-inch centers. Use fine-particle mulch such as small pine bark, cocoa beans, pecan hulls, or shredded leaf mold. Heavier mulches often hold in too much moisture.

Growing Tips

Even though the plants prefer dry soils, they need an occasional watering during a severe drought. Waxy coating on the foliage forces the water to run off into the crotch angles until it evaporates. Supplemental feedings are seldom needed unless foliage appears nutrient deficient.

Care

The sprawling habit of the plant rarely needs pruning. If you are going to try to overwinter it in Zone 6b, be sure to plant it in the spring, and once the foliage dies back from a hard freeze, cut it back and mulch the crowns with about 4 to 6 inches of leaf compost or cottonseed hulls. Pests are rare, although a fungal leaf spot can occur in very rainy conditions. Pulling off the infected foliage or trimming back the vines helps control the spread.

Companion Planting and Design

The low-growing nature of this plant makes it a perfect border plant near sidewalks or in front of low signs. The vibrant purple foliage works as a specimen. I have used the plant as a companion in containers with yellow-flowering esperanza, pink Tapien verbena, purple angelonia, yellow bidens, and gray plectranthus. In ground beds, pink or white begonia, vinca, sun coleus, scaevola, melampodium, Mexican heather, and pink million bells complement purple heart.

My Personal Favorite

Named varieties are few and far between, but one sold as 'Purple Queen' is occasionally found in the trade.

Purple heart will melt your heart with its violet-purple fleshy stems and foliage. This lovely spreading plant is proof that breathtaking color can come from foliage as well flowers. The flowers of setcreasea are not very showy, but bees love them. The pinkish-white, sometimes pale-lavender, flowers are borne in the branch terminals, or leaf axils. The flowers bloom most of the summer, but the blooms definitely take a backseat to the vibrant foliage. This tropical plant thrives in the heat and humidity of our Oklahoma summers. It is often confused with a houseplants (T. pallida and Zebrina pendula) sold with the some of the same common names; these are not cold hardy. Setcreasea is best described as a noninvasive annual ground cover and overwinters as a perennial in Zones 7a and 7b.

Other Common Names

Setcreasea, Tradescantia, Moses in a Boat, Purple Jew

Bloom Period and Seasonal Color

Purple foliage with pinkish blooms throughout summer.

Mature Height × Spread

6 to 12 in. × 15 to 18 in.

Scaevola

Scaevola aemula

This tough, heat-loving plant thrives in Oklahoma as an annual bedding plant. The flower is unique—almost fan-shaped with purple flowers and a yellow eye. Several species of scaevola are on the market, including S. aemula, S. albida, S. striata, and S. serica as well as many named hybrids. 'Blue Wonder', 'New Blue Wonder', 'Mauve Cluster', 'Petite Wonder', 'Blue Shamrock', and 'Fan Falls' are just a few of the recently introduced cultivars. Read the fine print for the growth habit and flower size of these selections. 'Mini Pink' and 'Pink Fan' are pink introductions. 'Alba', 'White Charm', and 'White Fan' are white-flowering types. There is even a new purple-and-white striped flowering form sold as 'Zig Zag', but in the Oklahoma heat it turns more white than striped.

Other Common Name
Fan Flower

Bloom Period and Seasonal Color
Purple and yellow, pink, or white blooms in summer.

Mature Height × Spread
4 to 6 in. × 10 to 15 in.

When, Where, and How to Plant
The temperatures need to warm up for this plant. Plant it in May or June. Poor or average soils are preferable for this seasonal plant. Rich, humus soils are acceptable, but they definitely need to drain well. Waterlogged sites mean sure death for this succulent plant. Dig planting holes that are wider than the rootballs and as deep as the plants were growing in their containers. Plant them on 12- to 18-inch centers. Mulch with finer products such as small pine bark and shredded leaves.

Growing Tips
Occasionally, the plants become yellowish or chlorotic in really poor soils. Correct the condition by using a fertilizer dissolved in water applied when watering. The growth of this plant is in direct correlation to hot temperatures. After planting in the spring, the plants tend to sit until the soil and air temperatures rise. The plants decline in the fall when cooler, wet conditions arrive.

Care
Scaevola is a low-maintenance plant. The flowers are self-cleaning, so no deadheading is needed. Trimming or pruning is seldom required. Other than an occasional spider mite, pests are rare. The biggest problem is rotting as a result of over-watering or poorly drained sites.

Companion Planting and Design
I have found scaevola to be the perfect rotational plant for cool-season annuals. Once pansies start to die out in early summer, plant scaevola in their place. The low growth is perfect for a border or a filler plant. It cascades over rocks or walls and even in hanging baskets. Plant in masses in ground beds, in containers, and in hanging baskets. Fan flower is brilliantly displayed when planted in masses in front of yellow lantana, bidens, melampodium, pinwheel zinnia, or sun coleus.

My Personal Favorite
'New Wonder' with its violet blue flower and taller height (10 to 14 inches) fits the bill for most of my uses, whether in the landscape or in a container.

Shrimp Plant

Justicia brandegeana

When, Where, and How to Plant

Plant these heat-loving plants from the time that the danger of frost is past through late May and early June. These high-performing plants will produce abundant flowers in full sun or even partial or filtered shade. Fertile, organic soils are perfect for this tropical beauty; however, shrimp plant tolerates poor or sandy soils with good drainage. Space plants 18 to 24 inches apart. Set the plants at the same depth at which they were grown, in holes slightly wider than the rootballs. Mulch and water them after planting.

Growing Tips

Although the plants are somewhat drought tolerant, provide supplemental irrigation in a severe drought to keep the foliage and blooms from dropping. Feed them occasionally during the growing season. A water-soluble brand high in phosphorus and potassium and low in nitrogen applied with supplemental irrigation throughout the season works well.

Care

This tropical plant is a dependable bloomer all summer with whimsical upright flower spikes that later droop with weight. Deadhead unsightly flower spikes throughout the growing season to ensure even more vigorous blooming. Prune the plants early on to encourage branching and a denser appearance, and anytime needed during the summer. Spider mites and white flies are the most common pests to watch for.

Companion Planting and Design

Shrimp plants are considered mid-level plants when used in combination with other annuals. In large ground beds, plant them in masses or in smaller groups of four or five. Plant them so that the flower colors complement other blooming plants of yellow, red, pink, or white. Colorful foliage plants such as sun coleus are good background choices for shrimp plants. Plant them by themselves or in combination with other container patio displays.

My Personal Favorite

You can't beat the display of the most commonly sold variety *J. brandegeana* with big yellow flowers.

Shrimp plants, with their tubular flowers, are a favorite of hummingbirds. Hot, humid summers never seem to faze these nonstop bloomers. In Oklahoma, they are used as warm-season annuals providing rapid growth and season-long color. The unique flowers are composed of colorful bracts from which the true flower emerges. In addition to J. brandegeana with its golden-bronze flower spikes, there is a variegated foliage version sold as 'Variegata'. A bedding plant, Brazilian plume (J. carnea), displays pink flowers. J. carnea 'Alba' has lovely creamy-white flowers. J. candicans, known as red justicia or hummingbird bush, has a more compact branching habit with red, more distinct, tubular flowers. Mexican honeysuckle, or J. spicigera, is the most shade tolerant of all the species and has golden-orange tubular flowers.

Other Common Names

Hummingbird Bush, Brazilian Plume

Bloom Period and Seasonal Color

Red, orange, yellow, or white blooms in summer.

Mature Height × Spread

2 to 3 ft. × 1 1/2 to 2 ft.

Starflower

Pentas lanceolata

Pentas has always been a star in my garden with dainty-pointed, star-shaped flowers that last until frost. Starflower has deep-green velvety foliage that shows the colorful blooms to advantage. The plants thrive in heat and are fairly drought tolerant. The New Look series in assorted colors is a compact variety, reaching 8 to 10 inches tall. The Starburst series, semi-dwarf at 12 to 18 inches, is a bicolor form with vivid colors. 'Cranberry Punch' is a cranberry red of medium height, near 18 to 24 inches. 'Alba' or 'White' matures near 24 inches. 'Pink Profusion' is semi-dwarf, averaging 12 to 15 inches. 'Orchid Illusion' is orchid-lavender, also of medium height. 'Pearl White' is semi-trailing and good for hanging baskets. 'Ruby Glow' is brilliant red, and 'Blushing Beauty', maturing near 18 inches, is light pinkish white.

Other Common Name
Egyptian Starflower

Bloom Period and Seasonal Color
Pink, red, white, or lavender blooms in summer.

Mature Height × Spread
$3/4$ to 2 ft. × 1 to 2 ft.

When, Where, and How to Plant
Plant this warm-season annual after the chance of frost is past, any time throughout April or May. Start pentas from pelleted seed. The seed needs light to germinate and should not be covered with soil; just sprinkle soil on top and water. The seed germinates within ten to twenty days. It takes ten to twelve weeks before the plants are ready to go outside. Harden off transplants prior to planting. Starflower thrives in full sun and prefers organic, well-drained, rich soils. Space the plants 8 to 24 inches apart; the bigger they are, the farther apart they should be planted. Check for potbound roots, and loosen them as needed before planting. Water pentas after planting. Mulch keeps soils moist in the summer and minimizes weed growth.

Growing Tips
Water on a regular basis. The foliage occasionally becomes chlorotic in poor soils; the evidence is a yellowish color and green veins. Supplemental feedings throughout the season invigorate plants. Slow-release applications at the time of planting are beneficial. Pentas is a high-nitrogen feeder.

Care
Starflower is typically self-cleaning, so pruning or deadheading is seldom needed. Pinch the taller selections back next to a leaf node after planting to keep the plants more compact. Trim them as needed throughout the season. More compact or dwarf cultivars require little pruning. Potential pests are spider mites, white flies, and aphids.

Companion Planting and Design
Any of the sizes or selections work well planted in masses. The taller versions are perfect as background plants in the annual flowerbed. For containers, plant compact versions in windowboxes, patio pots, or mailbox planters. There are foliage color cultivars of coleus, Joseph's coat, and plectranthus that match up nicely with any color of starflower.

My Personal Favorite
The variegated green and yellow foliage of 'Stars and Stripes' accents the ruby red flowers on this taller growing selection that the butterflies and hummingbirds adore.

Summer Snapdragon
Angelonia angustifolia

When, Where, and How to Plant
Place this tropical plant outside after the last chance of frost is past, typically anytime from mid-April through the end of May and even in early June. It performs best in full sun or a half-day of shade. Too much shade or filtered continuous shade causes the plant to get leggy with sporadic bloom. It accepts average, well-drained soil. Like most plants, the tropical beauty performs even better in rich, fertile soils. Angelonia is primarily vegetatively propagated or pot-grown instead of seed-grown. Space plants on 15- to 18-inch centers. Mulch them after planting, and water.

Growing Tips
Provide irrigation during drought conditions to keep the blooms coming. Additional fertilizer is generally not needed if fertilizer is applied at the time of planting.

Care
The blooms are self-cleaning and need no additional deadheading or pruning. The plants have strong growth but do not require staking. Pinching the plants early forces bushier growth. Pests are of minimal concern; however, watch for aphids and spider mites. Virus problems with distorted yellow foliage are also problematic as a result of heavy thrip and white fly infestations, especially in a greenhouse environment.

Companion Planting and Design
Angelonia is absolutely intriguing as a bedding plant in masses. It is so unusual that it works well as a single specimen plant. The lovely upright and slightly cascading appearance complements container combination plantings. I have had success combining it with sun coleus, purple heart, plectranthus, verbena, million bells, dwarf purple fountain grass, and ornamental sweet potato.

My Personal Favorites
It is a toss up between the pastel color choices, so I typically go with the purple and white striped cultivars like 'Angelface™', 'Blue Bicolor', or 'Tiger Princess'.

If you like the shape and look of snapdragon flowers, you will absolutely love summer snapdragon, which thrives in the heat. The showy, orchid-like flowers are 1/4 to 1/2 inch in diameter and are produced in elongated spikes, opening from the base to the tip while sending up new blooms for an airy display. The colors complement almost any flower in the landscape. I used them in masses by themselves in ground beds, in containers, and even in the garden. Angelonia easily gives your garden a hint of the tropics with interesting and colorful blooms. 'Hilo Princess' and 'Lavender Princess' are purple forms. 'Blue Pacific' and 'Tiger Princess' are bicolored with purple and white. 'Alba' and 'White Princess' are white. 'Pink Princess', 'Pandiana', and 'Pink' are, as you might guess, pink.

Other Common Names
Angelonia, Angel Flower

Bloom Period and Seasonal Color
Purple, white, or pink blooms in summer.

Mature Height × Spread
18 to 24 in. × 10 to 15 in.

Sun Coleus
Solenostemon scutellarioides

Sun coleus selections are vegetatively propagated to ensure consistent foliage color and minimal seed formation. And to top it off, the foliage colors are traffic-stopping. Sun coleus is perfect as a specimen, contrast, or texture plant. The magnificent foliage is long lasting in arrangements and adds color and texture in combination with flowers. There are hundreds of named selections. 'Plum Parfait' and 'Burgundy Sun' are the most sun and heat tolerant. 'Rustic Orange', 'Purple Emperor', and 'Dark Star' are great for Halloween container displays. Duckfoot coleus is available in colors of purple and green, green, yellow and purple, and red. They are somewhat more compact and prostrate in growth, making better front or mid-level plants and good choices for containers and hanging baskets.

Other Common Name
Painted Nettle

Bloom Period and Seasonal Color
Red, purple, pink, green, chartreuse, and color combination foliage.

Mature Height × Spread
18 to 24 in. × 10 to 15 in.

When, Where, and How to Plant
Plant sun coleus after the last chance of frost is past, any time throughout June. Full sun is best to get the most brilliant color display. They accept a half-day of shade, but more shade means less color. Rich garden soils provide more vigorous growth, but these tough plants tolerate poor or average sites. Space plants 2 to 3 feet apart. Loosen the roots of potbound plants before planting them. Place them at the same depth that they were grown in the containers, in holes 2 times wider than the rootballs. Mulch them to keep the soil moist and weed free.

Growing Tips
The plants wilt slightly, due to heat instead of moisture stress, as impatiens do. Provide supplemental watering during prolonged dry times. Supplemental feedings are generally not needed (or the plants become too overgrown) unless they are planted in poor soils.

Care
Sun coleus sends up flower spikes but not as frequently as the old seed types. The flower spikes are usually formed later in the season or under stress. Some cultivars have showy flowers that attract hummingbirds. Most folks trim them out to give the plants a more manicured appearance. Pinch the plants at planting and throughout the season to keep them more compact and neat. Other than an occasional mealybug, pests are rare.

Companion Planting and Design
Use sun coleus as background plants in combination with other annual bedding plants or in masses by themselves for a brilliant display where it does not take many to fill a large area. Even a single plant speaks for itself as a specimen. They grow in patio displays, in the cutting garden, and as a small hedge when alternately planted for late-season coverage. Plant them in the fall as complementary black-and-orange autumn colors for container displays. There are so many coleus colors that you are guaranteed to find a match to complement any summer flower.

My Personal Favorites
'Fancy', 'Eclipse', 'Spectrum', and 'Japanese Giant' are some of my favorites.

Swiss Chard

Beta vulgaris

When, Where, and How to Plant

Plant seed indoors in containers in late January or early February for transplanting outdoors around March, or direct-seed into the ground in early March. Plant seed approximately 1/2 inch deep and in rows 18 to 24 inches apart. Later, as the seedlings emerge, thin the plants to 4 to 6 inches apart. Plants are grown in the fall as well for a cool-season autumn display. Start fall transplants four to five weeks earlier around mid-August, or direct-seed in September. Plant container-grown bedding plants at 18- to 24-inch spacing. Full-sun locations are best, although these succulent plants also tolerate some light or afternoon shade. As is true for any vegetable or bedding-type plant, good, rich, fertile, well-drained soils are best.

Growing Tips

In the fall, Swiss chard tolerates some light frost once established and even survives the entire winter during mild years. The plants respond to an occasional side dressing of fertilizer through the growing sseason.

Care

Cut the outside leaves near the ground. This allows the center of the plant to continue its display of non-stop color. The plants grow up until the temperatures begin to get scorching hot in July or August or in afternoon shade during normal summers. In milder summers, Swiss chard grows all season long. Potential pests include aphids and an occasional spider mite.

Companion Planting and Design

The brilliant rainbow of colors brightens up any landscape as a border plant or in groups as a focal planting. The plants are nice when used as background in association with pansies, tulips, or other cool-season bedding plants. The towering cluster of color nicely emerges through pansies when used as a ground cover. Swiss chard is also suitable for containers.

My Personal Favorite

'Bright Lights' has so many delectable colors that make quite a show in the landscape and are tasty to boot.

This lovely, textured plant is a cool-season vegetable grown during the same seasons as spinach, lettuce, and broccoli. When used as an ornamental, it is grown during the same time as pansy, dianthus, snapdragon, and calendula—although it is not as frost tolerant. It is available in a mix of colors including pink, red, violet, yellow, gold, and creamy white. As the plant grows, the erect stems sport luscious green foliage highlighted with colorful veins. 'Bright Lights' is an All-America Selections winner with a rainbow mix of colors. There are varieties with single colors like 'Bright Yellow', 'Vulcan Red', 'Lucullus' (lime green), and 'Ruby Red'. 'Fordhook' or 'Giant Chard' is the standard green Swiss chard with larger stalks and crinkled, green, glossy foliage. The flavor of the cultivar 'Bright Lights' is especially mild.

Other Common Names

Ornamental Chard, Leaf Beet

Bloom Period and Seasonal Color

Pink, red, violet, yellow, gold, or white foliage in fall, spring, or early summer.

Mature Height × Spread

1 1/2 to 2 ft. × 1 to 1 1/2 ft.

Twinspur

Diascia hybrids

This dainty, cascading plant has masses of tubular flowers borne throughout the summer. The plants are perfect for flower beds, windowboxes, containers, and hanging baskets. 'Ruby Field' (pink) was the first introduction into the United States. 'Pink Queen' and 'Elliot's Variety' (peachy pink) soon followed. More recently released are 'Summer's Dance' (salmon) and 'Strawberry Sundae' (strawberry pink). Several species of Diascia as well as hybrid crosses are used in the landscape trade. D. barberae, D. rigescens, and D. vigilis are the most commonly sold seasonal plants. D. vigilis selections and crosses are thought to be more tolerant to summer heat but prefer afternoon or dappled shade in the southern part of the state. Some selections overwinter in southern Zone 7b of Oklahoma.

Other Common Name
Diascia

Bloom Period and Seasonal Color
Pink, rose, or salmon blooms in summer.

Mature Height × Spread
10 to 14 in. × 10 to 14 in.

When, Where, and How to Plant

Plant twinspur in the spring after the last chance of frost is past. Start seed indoors ten to fourteen weeks before planting outside. Twinspur likes a site that receives afternoon shade. Filtered or dappled sun is acceptable, but it does not like full shade or full sun in Oklahoma. Good, rich garden soils are ideal. The soils should be somewhat acidic and moisture retentive but not waterlogged. Dig a planting hole that is slightly wider than the rootball and as deep as the plant was grown in the container. Space plants 12 to 14 inches apart. Mulching is essential for twinspur to retain soil moisture, to moderate hot summer temperatures, and to minimize weed growth.

Growing Tips

Supplemental moisture is required during a drought. Like most annuals, diascia responds well to supplemental feedings throughout the season. Water-soluble fertilizers applied on a regular basis at the time of watering work nicely.

Care

Twinspur seldom requires attention. The flowers are self-cleaning and bloom all season without shearing or trimming. Heat, drought, and full sun will most likely shut the plants down from flowering and occasionally scorch the foliage under severe conditions. Other than the possibility of aphids and spider mites, pests are not a major concern.

Companion Planting and Design

The plants have a tendency to cascade as they grow without becoming invasive. Plant them in any container setting or in the front of a partially shaded flower bed. The bold colors of coleus and Persian shield help bring out the delicate flower colors of twinspur.

My Personal Favorite

'Flying Colors™ Trailing Red' is a hit when planted with dragon wing red begonia or bronze leaf red begonias.

Waffle Plant
Hemigraphis alternata

When, Where, and How to Plant

Plant it in beds outside after the chance of frost is past in late spring. Humus-rich, moisture-retentive soils are perfect. When planted in more sun, waffle plant frequently wilts in the heat of the day. Space plants on 12-inch centers. Mulching is a must with this plant to keep the soil moist.

Growing Tips

The plants require quite a bit of moisture, especially during drought periods. Place the plants where there is easy access to water. They respond to supplemental feedings, especially in poorer soils.

Care

The plants are truly striking, and the small flower is self-cleaning. The plants are trouble free; they need very little attention. Insect pests include white flies, primarily in the greenhouse, and an occasional aphid. Occasionally they may need trimming back to keep the cascading foliage in bounds.

Companion Planting and Design

The low-growing prostrate growth makes a nice ground cover, and it often roots along the purple stems as it spreads. It is by no means invasive and works great in borders or as filler. One plant easily fills a 10-inch hanging basket. Use waffle plants as companion plants in container displays with other shade-loving plants. The purple and dark-green colors are perfect for pink or white color combinations. Shade-loving impatiens, Persian shield, and plectranthus are excellent companions for waffle plants.

My Personal Favorite

I really like the trailing form with metallic purple maroon foliage sometimes sold as 'Red Equator'.

Most shade gardens are somewhat limited when it comes to annual flower color. Waffle plant is a nice foliage plant with small, white, tubular blooms tolerant of most shade garden sites. I first became familiar with this plant at Cypress Gardens in Florida. The colorful plant was being grown as a bedding plant in partially shaded sites and occasionally in full sun with mulch and moisture-retentive soils. The burgundy-green foliage is quite striking, especially with white-flowering companions. The foliage is showy for both its color and its crinkled or twisted texture, thus the name waffle plant. In Oklahoma, this plant prefers afternoon or filtered shade. It is stunning in hanging baskets. Waffle plant is often sold as a houseplant and is available also as trailing and narrow leafed varieties.

Other Common Names

Red Ivy, Red Flame

Bloom Period and Seasonal Color

Burgundy-green foliage with white blooms in summer.

Mature Height × Spread

6 to 8 in. × 8 to 12 in.

Bulbs *for Oklahoma*

Most gardeners never know what to call this group of plants. The tendecy is to refer to them all as "bulbs." But it is not that simple. Bulbs can actually be divided into more specific botanical categories: tubers, tuberous roots, rhizomes, corms, and true bulbs. Regardless of what you call them, they function in very similar ways; modified stems and roots both store food and propagate the plant.

Tubers are plant storage organs consisting of a thick underground stem called the "stem tuber." Caldium is the most common of this type. Axillary growth buds (or eyes) along the surface give way to new plants. Propagate new plants by cutting tubers into pieces containing at least one eye; place them in well-drained soil.

Tuberous roots are different from tubers in that the storage area is actually root tissue. When propagating tuberous roots. the root portion must include stem and bud tissue as well. Oftentimes, depending on the species, the bud's stems and roots form at opposite ends of the root. For this reason, lay tuberous roots horizontally when planting. Dahlia, daylily and tuberous begonia are well known tuberous roots.

Rhizomes are stems that grow horizontally below the soil surface forming both shoots and roots at its nodes. Bearded Iris, calla lily, and canna are great examples because their thick, fleshy rhizomes are easily recognized. Mint and bermudagrass, known for their aggressive growth, are vigorous thanks to small rhizomes.

Corms (often mistaken for bulbs) are short, swollen, food storage stems below the ground. They are usually more flat than a bulb but also contain a papery-like covering. Roots develop from the sides and bottom while the plant shoots come from a pointed apex, or top. As the plants develop the original corm shrivels and a new one is formed on top of the old one for next year's plant. Tiny corms (cormels) form around the base of the parent corm, on the roots or between the old and new corm on some species. This

typically occurs after the plant blooms. Plant corms with the larger end facing down and the pointed end where the buds will emerge facing up. Crocus, freesia, gladiolus, and crocosmia are started from corms.

A true bulb is comprised of modified leaves (or scales) and the actual flower all in a neat little package. Tulip, daffodil, Dutch iris and hyacinth are some of the most common "true" bulbs. Bulbs should be planted with the pointed side up and the broader side down. New bulbs develop each year from old ones to provide next year's plant. Some bulbs, such as lilies, form new plants from tiny bulbs called "bulblets" at their base (bulbils) in their stems.

Daffodils

Tulipa 'Hans Anrud' (dark purple) and 'Peer Gynt' (pink)

For convenience, I will refer to the group "as bulbs" throughout the chapter though we now know the truth.

Some bulbs are very cold hardy and can be left in the ground well into the northern U.S. Others need to be dug for indoor storage each winter. Microclimates, mild winters and thick layers of mulch (once the plants have died back from freezing temperatures) can help some so-called tender bulbs to overwinter in colder growing zones.

Bulbs are also classified by the time of year they bloom, spring, summer or fall. Flowering time helps with planning especially if bulbs are intended to fill a space in the perennial garden particularly void of flowers. Bloom time usually indicates specific needs in planting time. For example, bulbs that flower in the spring or early summer typically have a chilling requirement that must be met before they will flower. They must experience cold for germination to occur and to send out a healthy root system. Fall planting will satisfy this cold requirement. The chilling requirement varies from 6 to 16 weeks depending on the plant. Plant spring flowering bulbs in the fall when the soil temperatures are around 60 degrees Fahrenheit and before the ground freezes. The optimum bulb planting time in Oklahoma is October through December. Summer and fall flowering bulbs are best planted in the spring after the last expected freeze.

The flowering time, as in the case of tulips and some other bulbs, is broken down into early, mid or late season bloomers. Make sure to pay attention to these guidelines particularly if you want them to all bloom at the same time or if you want to stagger the blooms over a longer period of time. These are relative bloom categories and cannot anticipate the exact bloom time, which varies slightly depending on air and soil temperatures and planting depth.

Planting Bulbs

Bulbs are planted in different ways. Some folks remove several inches of the soil coinciding with the planting depth, keeping it off to the side or in buckets. Several bulbs are then placed at the proper spacing and the soil put back over the top, mulched and watered thoroughly. Others plant one hole at a time. Phosphorous and potassium are best applied at planting time with a few inches of soil between the fertilizer and the bulb. This practice is not needed every time you plant however. A soil test to determine deficient nutrients is well worth the effort, especially before starting a new landscape bed.

Once the bulbs finish flowering, be sure and leave their foliage on until it starts to die. The foliage is crucial for the growth and multiplication of the bulbs, providing nutrients to the new modified stem for next year's flower. Cutting the foliage off too soon diminishes the flower size and can even reduce flowering all together. Generally the bigger the bulb the bigger the flower.

It is commonly thought that all bulbs have uniform soil and light requirements. This is not true though some of the most popular bulbs, such as canna, Dutch iris, water iris, summer snowflake, spider lily, and rain lily, tolerate wet feet. All other bulbs benefit from adding organic matter to the planting bed. If you are planting bulbs under trees, be careful not to till up the soil and damage the roots of the tree.

Proper planting depth is another crucial step in successful bulb growing. Depth is key to future bulb development. Bulbs planted too deeply may rot, not form flowers or bloom sporadically. With shallow plantings, bulbs freeze or have leggy foliage that breaks off. Here's a little piece of gardening wisdom if no planting guidelines are provided: plant bulbs three times deeper than its size measured from top to bottom.

Some bulbs prefer shade while others do best in sun. Crocus, squill, wood hyacinth, caladiums, and elephant ears are some that can tolerate part or dappled shade. Sun loving daffodils can be planted under deciduous trees as well. Daffodils bloom early and their foliage dies and droops down fairly quickly; it often coincides with leaves emerging out of the trees in spring. Remember that inadequate light for sun loving bulbs can cause poor flowering and leggy plants. As a general rule, six hours of sun is adequate for most bulbs.

Getting the Most Color

If you want a spectacular color show, plant bulbs in groups and at the proper spacing. You can even plant several different plants in the same sites at different layers. This will result in continual and variegated color. Bulbs grown as perennials often become overcrowded and will need thinning every three or four years. Clumps can be dug and divided and replanted at the appropriate time, which is opposite their blooming season. As with daffodils, this may mean that no foliage will be present at dividing time. Plan ahead if you are going to dig up bulbs and use stakes, flags or row markers at flowering time to identify clumps that will need later replanting.

Perennial vs. Tender Perennial

Perennial bulbs can stay in the ground and don't have to be dug out each winter to flower year after year. Most bulbs qualify as perennial; however, some perennial bulbs are treated as annuals in Oklahoma and must overwinter indoors. These are called "tender perennials," and though they will return year after year they are sometimes not hardy enough to withstand cold winters. When planning a bulb bed, make sure you know your hardiness zone (see map in "Welcome to Gardening in Oklahoma") and whether you'll need to dig up bulbs and bring them inside during the winter. Some bulbs not only last the winter season after season but also spread on their own, naturally colonizing the area around their original planting.

Tulips seem to have a class of their own. Some hybrid tulips are developed to give a burst of color the first spring after planting and are basically made to be grown as annuals. Even if tulips overwinter, the bulb size diminishes each year until there is no plant at all. This is sometimes caused by mild winters, warm summer nights, and soils that retain too much moisture in the summer when the bulbs are dormant.

Watering and Fertilizing

Water new beds thoroughly after planting. Since there is no initial root and top growth to drink up the moisture, do not water frequently until plant growth emerges. Fall planted bulbs typically receive enough natural rainfall during the winter months to get them established. However, droughts can still occur during the winter; in this case, supplemental irrigation is necessary. Bulbs planted in spring and summer will need supplemental irrigation during the growing season if rainfall is deficient. In both cases, water deeply and less often to get a good soaking down to the bulb and roots. Mulching two to three inches deep after planting also helps hold in soil moisture, minimize weeds, and provide cold protection.

Let the plants tell you whether they need fertilizer or not. Feed bulbs that flower in spring the previous fall or during the moment in spring when growth emerges but flowers have not formed. Bulbs flowering in summer and fall can be fed as soon as growth emerges in the spring. Robust, healthy, blooming plants in organic, rich soils seldom need additional feedings. Always water after applying fertilizer. Slow release or organic fertilizers applied at planting time reliably supply small, consistent amounts of nutrients. Seek out those high in phosphorus and potassium like 5-10-10. As a general rule you do not want to feed bulbs when they are flowering. High-nitrogen formulations can burn the flowers, encourage disease, and possibly cause premature petal drop.

Fungi, bacteria and viruses can affect the flowers, foliage and buds. Bulb rot, gray mold (botrytis), leaf spot, and powdery mildew are the most common disease problems. Good drainage and air circulation between plants drastically reduces the onset of these pathogens. Preserve the health of your plants by removing diseased leaves or flowers as soon as you recognize the problem. In severe cases, you might need the appropriate natural or synthetic fungicide or bactericides.

Insect problems include spider mites, aphids, and in the case of flowering bulbs, thrips. Thrips are yellow or brownish black, very small, and hard to see. They feed with rasping, sucking mouthparts on plant foliage, flowers and buds. Damaged tissue develops yellowish or silvery blemishes. Heavy infestation and feeding cause discoloration and deformities that oftentimes prevent the flower bud from opening.

Your preventative action depends upon the severity of the infestation. A few spots or critters here and there are not necessarily problems. In fact, most times natural predators tend to keep pests in check. You should be concerned if you plan on entering your prized beauty in a flower show or if a new plant's establishment is threatened. Mechanical, organic or synthetic products may be required. Always follow the label. The best pest control is not only paying attention to your garden and fostering a healthy plant, but also knowing the bad pests from the good insects.

Voles, deer, gophers, moles and armadillos are other common bulb pests. Spring flowering tulips are especially tasty to deer. Gophers and voles actually feed on the bulbs. Armadillos and moles do more harm by digging them up as they go about their search for soil insects. Fences, wire barriers and traps are about the best methods of prevention. Repellants help some but only for short periods of time. If the problem doesn't go away, some prized bulbs can be planted in large containers and then the entire container can be placed in the ground. Make sure the container's drainage holes are small enough to allow water to settle out and keep critters from getting in. Some gardeners successfully deter these garden critters by enclosing small-holed wire or hardware cloth around the bulb or placing crushed chiten, shells, or pea gravel in the planting hole with the soil.

This chart helps you determine the number of bulbs needed for recommended spacing between plants.

Total square footage of planting bed	4 in.spacing	6 in. spacing
	(width × length)	
25	225	100
50	450	200
100	900	400
150	1350	600
200	1800	800
250	2250	1000

Autumn Crocus

Colchicum autumnale

Typically, when we think of bulbs we think of fall planting not blooming. But Autumn Crocus does just that—it provides showy flower color in a time typically known for bulb planting. Autumn Crocus sends up surprise blooms on leafless stems as the nights begin to cool in September and as summer droughts come to a close. Although called a crocus, this member of the lily family is not a true crocus like the common spring flowering form, Crocus vernus. *The goblet-shaped flower is similar to* Crocus vernus *but much larger. Autumn Crocus grows low to the ground but not as low as the true crocus. When planted in large groups they are quite a site and last two to three weeks depending on weather conditions.*

Other Common Name
Fall Crocus

Bloom Period and Seasonal Color
White, lavender or pink in September or October

Mature Height × **Spread**
4 to 6 in. × 4 to 6 in.

Cold Hardiness Zone
6a, 6b, 7a, 7b

When, Where, and How to Plant
Plant the corm in mid to later summer. Don't delay planting or they will bloom whether in the soil or not. Plant 3 to 4 inches deep and 6 to 8 inches apart. For an ideal site, simulate woodland sites with rich, fluffy, organic, well drained soils. Dig individual holes verses rather than tilling the entire drip zone, which can harm vital tree roots. If you do not want to risk digging, layer soil and compost over corms on top of the soil without getting higher than 6 inches. Lightly mulch and water after planting to discourage weeds, settle the soil, and help the plant roots establish.

Growing Tips
Once established, little care is needed, especially if these plants are in organically rich soil. If the plants are not vigorous from year to year, apply organic fertilizer in late fall as the foliage emerges and after the flowers have faded.

Care
Autumn crocus sometimes sends up foliage after blooming; some species send up foliage in spring and bloom in fall. Shortly after emerging, the foliage will turn yellow and die. Leave the foliage on the plant since this is what feeds the corms for fall bloom. The bulbs can be left undisturbed for several years. Dig bulbs in late spring or early summer to thin overcrowding bulb beds. Labeling the bulbs will help during digging time if your autumn crocus is a tender perennial in your hardiness zone.

Companion Planting and Design
Bulbs in large groups are great for perennial garden borders. Since the foliage is unsightly in the spring, plant things that will take away from the fading foliage but not over power the compact blooms in the fall. Groundcovers like ajuga, mondo grass, compact sedums, and low growing veronica are nice companions. Put autumn crocus in a rock garden where companion plants are lower growing. They also can complement sidewalks, pathways, and garden art.

My Personal Favorite
'Album' is a nice bright white.

Bearded Iris
Iris germanica hybrids

When, Where, and How to Plant

Plant in spring or summer in sites with full sun and well drained soil. Iris blooms and thrives in most any soil as long as it drains. Too much shade and poorly drained soils minimize bloom, increase disease and shorten the plant's life. Plant the rhizomes 1 in. deep; any deeper and they will not bloom well. Mulch in between rhizomes to discourage weed encroachment; do not mulch atop the rhizomes.

Growing Tips

Provide plenty of moisture during bloom time to ensure healthy blooms that are longer lived. Once they are through blooming the plants are remarkably drought tolerant. Fertilizer in the spring as soon as growth emerges or several weeks after blooms fade if supplemental feedings are needed as evident by non vigorous blooms or foliar growth.

Care

Overcrowded plants bloom poorly; divide immediately after flowering up until July. When dividing, make sure there is at least one set of leaves and some roots on each rhizome section. Discard old, damaged or decayed rhizomes. Trim the foliage back to 6 inches during transplanting but not as a regular maintenance practice. Small foliage tips of transplants should face up and away from each other. Iris borer is the most common insect pest feeding. Most iris insecticides, if applied according to directions during spring, will control pests. Old fall foliage can harbor eggs so be sure to remove it. Bacterial soft rot can occur in plants set too deep or in poorly drained, heavy soils.

Companion Planting and Design

Mix iris with perennial gardens to stagger the color of the sporadic blooming plants. Mass plantings look good for a time, but the texture of iris foliage does little for the landscape after the bloom season. Match heights to avoid hiding plants.

My Personal Favorite

The nice dwarf habit of 'Baby Blessed' offers several periods of yellow blooming throughout the season and fits in to almost any perennial garden without overpowering its neighbors.

Bearded Iris is so resilient you can almost throw it on top of the ground and it will live. Of course, proper planting brings about the best show of color. It is drought tolerant and does not even flinch when divided in the heat of the summer. The range of colors is mind boggling. If you can describe a color there is probably a hybridized match. Size also widely varies with dwarf, standard, intermediate, and tall selections ranging from 8 inches to over 2 feet. Many of the flowers are fragrant and some even bloom continually throughout the season. A close cousin and a great plant for perennial gardens is I. pallida, variegated iris, that retains its visual intrigue after blooming thanks to variegated white or creamy yellow stripes.

Other Common Name
German Iris

Bloom Period and Seasonal Color
Late spring to early summer in assorted colors

Mature Height × Spread
8 to 32 in. × 15 to 24 in.

Cold Hardiness Zone
6a, 6b, 7a, 7b

Blazing Star
Liatrus species

Oklahoma is home to several species of this perennial with a perpendicular growth habit. This native loves well drained soil and summer heat, and will brighten any perennial display. L. spicata *and* L. scariosa *are the most frequently used species in the landscape. Improved or named selections include 'Silver Tip', which is very tall with lavender flowers. 'Alba' is white', and 'August Glory' blooms earlier with bluish-purple flowers. 'Floristan Violet' has more violet flowers, and 'Floristan Weiss' has cream-white blooms.* L. aspera var. intermedia *(eastern Oklahoma) has pink, late-summer blooms. Dotted snakeroot* (L. punctata) *has purple blooms in fall (western Olkahoma). Elegant blazing star* (L. elegans) *is found in purple or white (northeastern). Prairie button snakeroot* (L. pycnostachya) *blooms purple flowers in late summer (central and eastern).*

Other Common Names
Gayfeather, Button Snakeroot

Bloom Period and Seasonal Color
Purple, pink, white blooms in summer

Mature Height × Spread
2 to 4 ft. × 1 to 3 ft.

Cold Hardiness Zone
6a, 6b, 7a, 7b

When, Where and How to Plant
Plant blazing star in spring, early summer, or fall. Seed can be used to start this perennial native, but it will take two years to see flowers. This plant thrives in full sun in moist, loamy native soils. As a landscape plant, it is not too picky about soil as long as it has good drainage. Blazing star accepts sites with no more than three or four hours of shade. Plant container-grown blazing star at the same depth as it was growing in its container and slightly wider than the rootball. Plant bare-root blazing star at a depth of 4 to 6 in. and 3 ft. apart. Water the plants regularly after planting until they are well established. Mulch to keep the soil moist and weed-free.

Growing Tips
Many times the roots rot during the winter in sites that hold too much winter moisture. Leaving the tops on often diverts water. Plant them somewhat shallow in heavier soils, similar to the way iris is planted. Supplemental feedings are seldom needed in nutrient-rich soils. Poor soils occasionally need sidedressing, especially when plants begin to look chlorotic, or yellow.

Care
Cut back dormant growth each spring before the new growth emerges. Stake the flower spikes or allow the to cascade along the ground during the bloom period. After flowering, the foliage of some species dies back. Trim off the dead stalks late in the season or early next spring.

Companion Planting and Design
It is often used in perennial flower beds or in wildflower meadows. Mix and match heights based on location in the perennials garden. Taller species are best used in the back or center, while smaller ones can be used towards the front of the garden. Mass plantings also work in naturalized settings.

My Personal Favorite
L. spicata 'Kobold' (gnome) makes its home in my perennial garden with mauve-pink flowers on compact 2 ft. spikes.

Bysantine Gladiolus
Gladiolus byzantinus

When, Where, and How to Plant
This cold hardy "glad" is best planted in the fall. This allows the corm plenty of time for the roots to establish before sending up foliage in early spring. Plant the corms 4 inches deep and 4 inches apart. Well drained organically amended soils are ideal for vigorous growth. They can also naturalize in compacted soils, but the plants don't get nearly as big. Mulch after planting to help keep weed competition down and hold soil moisture in.

Growing Tips
Mix slow release organic fertilizers into the planting bed in the fall. Every couple of years, apply additional organic or slow release fertilizer on top of the ground and before you reapply withering mulch. If rainfall is lacking, the most crucial time for supplemental irrigation is during spring while foliage emerges up until the foliage dies in early summer.

Care
Plant foliage will die down on its own after blooming. As with most bulbs, allow foliage to turn completely brown before removing; this ensures a healthy flower crop the following year. When using glads as cut flowers, leave some of the foliage to form new corms and growth for future flowering. Propagate by digging the corms as soon as the stalks die down. Pests are of minimal concern. Heavy shade and poorly drained soils encourage rotting, lanky growth, foliar disease, and few to any flowers.

Companion Planting and Design
Cornflower is an ideal companion for the perennial garden. The corms should be planted close together to form a larger flower display. Plant them among ground cover or mid-size plants that are late to emerge like 'Moonbeam' coreopsis, trailing lantana, or purple heart. The companion plants will grow and fill in the voided spot once the bysantin foliage dies and is removed in mid summer.

My Personal Favorite
The most commonly available is the luminous fuschia colored selection.

I'm always tempted to buy Glad corms each spring due to their vibrant, almost velvety flower colors. But as I pick up the package I remember that they always flop over and I never get to enjoy the blooms in the perennial garden. I'm too lazy to stake them, so I just skip them all together. Then I tried Bysantin Gladiolus, which are now a prominent part of my early spring perennial garden. The compact stalks seldom flop over and provide weeks of vibrant magenta color. The compact flowers have the same characteristics as the standard Gladiolus. The fuschia flowering selection is most common with an occasional rare white flowering form found among collectors. This tough garden beauty is also considered an heirloom dating back to the early 1600's.

Other Common Name
Hardy Gladiolus, Cornflowers

Bloom Period and Seasonal Color
Spring with magenta color

Mature Height × Spread
15 to 20 in. × 4 to 6 in.

Cold Hardiness Zone
6a, 6b, 7a, 7b

Caladium
Caladium bicolor hortulamum

I've been a fan of foliage color plants for a long time. Their nearly tropical foliage offers instant season-long color, and they are great companions with annual flowers. Caladium is no exception. The big flashy colorful foliage is truly traffic stopping. They are one of the few seasonal plants to grow in shade. The plants are primarily available in fancy leaf, strap leaf, and more recent sun tolerant selections. Be careful on the sun tolerant cultivars, since they can scorch in hot afternoon sun in Oklahoma especially in windy sites. Caladiums do flower but all the attraction is from the flamboyant leaves. Caladiums are grown as an annual in the state with a few rare stories told of the tubers overwintering in milder winters in far southeastern Oklahoma.

Other Common Name
Fancy-leafed Caladium

Bloom Period and Seasonal Color
Red, burgundy, green, pink and white colored foliage from summer to frost.

Mature Height × Spread
1 to 2 ft. × 1 to 2 ft.

Cold Hardiness Zone
Grown as an annual in Oklahoma in Zones 6a, 6b, 7a, and 7b

When, Where, and How to Plant
Plant caladiums in late spring after the chance of frost has past and the soil warms. Plant tubers indoors 1 in. deep in a soil-less mix several weeks before planting outside; do not direct seed. The indoor site must be warm and bright; a greenhouse is best. Water sparingly until foliage emerges and roots form. When transplanting, place caladiums in fertile, highly amended, fluffy organic soils that drain well. Once in the ground, they like a lot of water and humidity but cannot tolerate heavy water logged soils.

Growing Tips
Mix controlled-release fertilizers into the soil at planting to provide consistent amounts of nutrients. For supplemental feedings use soluble fertilizer applied with water. Mulch the plants to hold in soil moisture but keep the mulch away from the plant stems or crown. Water as needed especially during drought conditions.

Care
Remove the white cone-like flowers as they emerge by cutting them back to the ground. This practice keeps all the energy going to the leaves to ensure constant foliage growth and beauty throughout the entire growing season. Dig caladiums in October as they begin to go dormant. The tubers need four to five months of dormancy prior to spring planting. Allow the plants to dry, remove the foliage and store the tubers in peat moss in a dry, cool frost-free location. Larger tubers can be divided immediately prior to planting with at least two buds (eyes) per section. Pests include critters like slugs, snails and grasshoppers. There may be occasional leaf spot or rotting due to poorly drained soils.

Companion Planting and Design
Caladiums are great with impatiens whether in beds or containers. Mass plantings of caladiums are also showy when spaced 18 to 24 in. apart. Use them as a background plant, near a sidewalk, in containers or by themselves.

My Personal Favorites
I love the two complementary colors of 'Gingerland' and 'Rosebud' when together. 'Florida Sweetheart' and 'Florida Sunrise' are also favorites.

Canna
Canna hybrids

When, Where, and How to Plant
Plant in spring or summer in organically rich soil. Space container-grown plants 2 to 3 ft. apart in a hole wider than and at the same depth as the container. Plant rhizomes 6 to 8 in. deep. Mulch to conserve moisture and to discourage weeds. Water to settle the soil and as needed thereafter.

Growing Tips
Cannas are heavy feeders and like supplemental feedings, especially in poor soils. Slow release organic products applied at planting time are also good. Light green, chlorotic foliage indicates a sure need for fertilizer. Avoid excessive nitrogen feedings, which cause accelerated growth and floppy plants. Thin beds after three of four years when they become too crowded. Dig rhizomes of non-hardy plants after the first light frost and store in peat moss or sawdust in a cool, dry location. Do not let the rhizomes dry out during storage. Check routinely for rotting rhizomes, and discard them immediately.

Care
If foliage becomes ratty, cut the plants literally to the ground during the growing season to force new, healthy foliage. Cannas are prone to caterpillar damage, but most insecticides control these critters and prevent further damage. Japanese beetles and cucumber beetles may eat cannas planted in the vegetable garden. Root rot occurs in poorly drained soils. Potential, but infrequent, problems are rust and mosaic or aster yellows virus. Cannas are generally tough plants, though, and can weather most pest problems.

Companion Planting and Design
Cannas are perfect background plants in the perennial garden, but they make a statement in a bed all by themselves. Cannas are popular as container plants, requiring large pots. 'Knock out' rose and Salvia greggi are great companions both in size and flower color.

My Personal Favorites
I especially like two dwarf cultivars available by seed or rhizomes called 'Tropical Rose' and 'Tropical Red'. I also like 'Intrigue' for the burgundy staplike foliage.

These tough plants have lush, tropical looking foliage sporting vivid flowers all summer. If you think cannas are boring, recondiser new selections with incredible foliage and a kaleidoscope of bloom color. Some cannas are not cold hardy in Oklahoma winters, but many make it through winters without special care especially in zones 7a, b and occasionally 6b with protection. These beauties thrive in our hot summer heat, however. 'Tropicanna' ('Phaison)', 'Bengal Tiger', 'Minerva', 'Pink Sunburst', 'Stuttgart', 'Durban', and 'Kansas City' are popular variegated foliage cultivars. 'Miss Oklahoma', 'President', 'Black Knight', and 'Wyoming' are some of the "oldie goldie" favorites. The Liberty Series are relatively new dwarf hybrids bred for tolerance to heat and resistance to leaf roller worms, and for self-cleaning flowers.

Other Common Name
Canna Lily

Bloom Period and Seasonal Color
Yellow, pink, red, orange and mixed blooms in summer

Mature Height × Spread
2 to 7 ft. × 2 to 3 ft.

Cold Hardiness Zone
7a, 7b

Crinum Lily
Crinum spp.

Travel farther south and you'll see large clumps of this southern heirloom. You can bet this plant is easy to grow when you see it thriving in abandoned home sites and cemeteries. In early summer, the clumps of straplike foliage send up elongated spikes of fragrant Easter lily-like flowers. Rebloom occurs in late summer and fall. The plants adaptability to arid and boggy soils makes them a favorite to share with gardening friends. Crinums can be safely grown in zones 7a and 7b with cold hardy species like C. bulbispermum (*whitish or stiped color*), Crinum × powellii (*pink or white*), and Crinum × herbertii (*striped wine and white*). Occasionally gardeners can overwinter these species in southern locales of zone 6b with protection.

Other Common Name
Milk and Wine Lily

Bloom Period and Seasonal Color
Summer blooms in white, pink, and rose.

Mature Height × Spread
2 to 4 ft. × 2 to 4 ft.

Cold Hardiness Zone
7a, 7b

When, Where, and How to Plant
Plant the large bulbs in spring or early summer in sandy loam or organically rich soils. They will tolerate heavier soils, but multiply best in loose soils. Plant the bulb below the soil surface with the neck slightly above. In group plantings, space the plants 3 to 4 ft. apart. Mulch to help hold in soil moisture.

Growing Tips
The plants appreciate supplemental feedings and irrigation, though they will survive without hardly any care once established. But for the best foliage and flowering display, water weekly during drought conditions and fertilize with a slow release product each spring. If your plants seldom bloom and have chlorotic foliage apply a light application of higher nitrogen fertilizer to stimulate repeat blooms and healthy lush foliage.

Care
The plants seem to perform best when left alone and not disturbed. Some gardeners even suggest that they resent being disturbed. Propagate plants by dividing them in early spring with a sharp tool and good strong back. Pests are primarily aphids and leaf hoppers and occasional leaf spots. If the foliage gets too unsightly, cut if off at the base and it will quickly grow healthy foliage.

Companion Planting and Design
Crinums are so big and bold they make great focal specimen plants. They work well in the perennial garden when planted with other big foliage plants like canna and daylily. Ornamental grasses are also nice companions with the different foliar textures. Or mix them in with seasonal color displays of coleus, copper plant or most anything tropical looking. I've used them to provide a taller border zig zagging along a walkway. They can also be planted in larger containers especially in colder climates and brought into the garage during the winter.

My Personal Favorites
Crinum × 'Ellen Bosanquet' is one of the most colorful, but I also like the old *Crinum* × *herbertii* with its fragrant white and pink striped flower.

Crocosmia

Crocosmia × crocosmiiflora

When, Where, and How to Plant

Container grow plants can be set out in the spring or early summer. Plant the corms in spring; 5 to 10 corms per sq. ft. at 2 to 3 in. deep produces a quick, full display. Space container grown plants 2 ft. apart. Moist, well drained soils are best. Add organic matter and slow release fertilizer prior to planting into the site. Water and mulch afterwards.

Growing Tips

The plants will need supplemental irrigation during drought. Supplemental fertilizer is seldom needed unless planted in poor soils. In most cases, the plant's vigor, foliage color, and bloom will tell you if additional feeding is needed. Some crocosmias wait until the second season to bloom. Once established the plants and blooms will get bigger and better each year.

Care

The plants are pretty cold hardy throughout most of Oklahoma. However, in the panhandle you should mulch the plants once they are dormant in the winter. Propagate or thin crowded beds in late summer or fall as the foliage goes down and the corms are easier to find. You can divide in spring too if you can find the corms without the foliage. In southern Oklahoma, replant corms in the fall. In northern Oklahoma store them in a cool, dry place and plant again next spring. Spider mites like crocosmia, especially in sites stressed with drought, poor soil, and poor circulation.

Companion Planting and Design

The upright, spiky foliage with arching flower stems provides great texture in the perennial garden. Nice companions are daylily, coneflower, and salvias. The plants are tall enough to plant in the back or middle of the perennial garden. They also work as a border plant when planted in large groups. Also, plant these in the cutflower garden since they last long in arrangements.

My Personal Favorite

I love the hot red color of 'Lucifer', but hate the name. Go figure it is also one of the more cold hardy cultivars.

I first became familiar with this plant while touring a botanical garden in Missouri. The massive planting of upright foliage and brightly colored flowers was truly traffic stopping. The sword-like foliage resembled gladiolus, but the flowers were one of a kind. They emerged from the erect stalks with zig-zag clusters of trumpet shaped flowers blooming from the base up. The stems weeped and dangled in the wind due to the heavy clustering of buds and blooms at tips end. Yet the foliage added linear accents to the perennial border without being too overpowering. Before I knew it there were others standing around me also in awe of this daring perennial that seemed to demand all the attention in the garden.

Other Common Names
Sword Lily, Montbretia

Bloom Period and Seasonal Color
Orange, yellow, red and scarlet flowers in mid to late summer

Mature Height × Spread
2 to 3 ft. × 1 to 2 ft.

Cold Hardiness Zone
6a, 6b, 7a, 7b

Daffodil
Narcissus species

The most common and popular of all bulbs is the daffodil. Or is it called jonquil or is it narcissus? Botanically they are all narcissus, but from garden standpoint you can keep it straight this way. Narcissus are typically the early blooming powerfully fragrant, cluster flower types also known as paperwhites. Jonquils are also cluster flowering types that are mostly yellow and sweetly fragrant. Daffodils are the large solitary trumpet shaped flowering (one per stem) types with little to no fragrance that are mostly yellow. Of course there are other classes and hybrids but these are the three basic that most folks get mixed up. Whatever you call them, they are a nice welcome of color in very early spring after the winter doldrums.

Other Common Names
Buttercups, Jonquil, Narcissus

Bloom Period and Seasonal Color
Yellow, white, orange, salmon and bi-colored in early spring to late spring.

Mature Height × Spread
6 to 24 in. × 4 to 12 in.

Cold Hardiness Zone
6a, 6b, 7a, 7b

When, Where, and How to Plant
Plant bulbs in October through early November 4 to 6 in deep with the pointed tip up. Mulching insulates bulbs during the cold winter, helping the plants establish roots and minimizing weeds. Daffodils like well drained soils; they like drier soils during dormancy. Mix in special bulb fertilizers 6 in. deep ahead of planting to enrich the phosphorous and potassium in the soil. Or, mix fertilizers in single holes two inches beneath the bulb.

Growing Tips
Water after planting to settle the soil and help the bulbs establish roots. Water the bulbs periodically during dry winters, especially the first few months after planting. Supplemental feedings are seldom needed when soil is amended at planting. In the case that plants lack vigor and bloom, add slow release products in early spring or synthetic or water soluble fertilizers when the plants finish flowering.

Care
Allow the foliage to die on its own. There is a great debate on whether a gardener should neatly fold unsightly foliage after blooming. It doesn't seem to hurt next year's blooms as long as it is done once foliage starts to yellow. When completely brown, cut foliage off at ground level. It is during this time that the plants prefer dry soils. Wet, heavy, water logged soils year round result in minimal flower set or even bulb rotting.

Companion Planting and Design
Group plantings give the best color. Some species, particularly heirloom types, naturalize, spread, and colonize on their own. The drier, root-inhabited soils of the trees complement daffodils. Do not disturb trees' feeder roots by tilling the soil. Instead, scatter individual holes throughout the site and use naturalizing selections that will spread without harming roots.

My Personal Favorite
Choosing a favorite daffodil variety is not only difficult but almost impossible since my preferences change from picture to picture. But in my garden, I like the old fashioned *N. jonquilla* that naturalizes readily and is sweetly scented.

Daylily
Hemerocallis species

When, Where, and How to Plant

Plant containers in spring or summer. Plant the tuberous root or bare-root daylilies in early spring, late summer, or early fall. Divide overgrown daylily clumps every three to five years in early spring, late summer, or early fall. Daylilies respond to well-drained, fertile soils; however, they adapt to a wide range of soil types. Incorporate a balanced fertilizer with phosphorus and potassium into the bed before planting. Place containerized plants in holes 2 to 3 times wider than and the same depth as the rootballs. Set bare-root plants in wider holes but the same depth that they were previously grown. Place the crown at the soil line. Space 15 to 24 in. apart, depending on the plant maturity size. Apply mulch and water after planting.

Growing Tips

Daylilies are considered drought tolerant once established. Provide supplemental water to keep plants flourishing. Provide supplemental feedings in early spring and at least once again during the growing season.

Care

Most daylilies are deciduous in Oklahoma. Remove dead foliage any time during the dormant period or leave the foliage until early spring and cut it back as soon as new growth emerges. Remove spent flower stalks to encourage more growth and repeat blooms. Insect pests are spider mites, aphids, thrips, and slugs. Potential diseases are fungal leaf streak, bacterial soft rot of the roots, and rust.

Companion Planting and Design

This clump-forming plant is great filler in perennial gardens, and the restricted growth makes daylily a natural choice for borders. The cascading foliage is a nice contrast for placement near rocks, garden art, and other hardscape features. The most dramatic display is a group planting. But some cultivars are so unique that they stand alone as a specimen. Use daylilies as container plants for a patio display.

My Personal Favorites

'Eanie Weanie' (yellow), 'Pardon Me' (red), and 'Happy Returns' (yellow) are some of my favorite repeat bloomers.

One of the top-selling perennial plants year in and year out is daylily. It is no wonder, either, because they are beautiful, drought-tolerant, and pest-tolerant. There are literally hundreds of hybrid cultivars when you consider both the numerous professional breeders and backyard breeders. If there is a shortcoming, it is one day blooms. But successive blooms stretch the season out four to six weeks. Even more exciting is the trend in daylily production to release "repeat bloomers," providing more abundant color throughout the season. 'Stella de' Oro' (yellow) and 'Black-Eyed Stella' (yellow with dark eye) are two of the most widely sold repeat-blooming cultivars. 'Miss Mary Mary' (yellow gold), 'Raspberry Pixie' (pink), 'Lemon Lily' (yellow), and Luxury Lace (purple) are fragrant.

Other Common Name
Hemerocallis

Bloom Period and Seasonal Color
Yellow, red, pink, purple blooms in early and late summer

Mature Height × Spread
10 to 36 in. × 12 to 24 in.

Cold Hardiness Zone
6a, 6b, 7a, 7b

Elephant Ears
Colocasia spp.

If you like bold, robust, tropical foliage then elephant ears will surely fit the bill. The standard green foliage selection, however, is quickly being upstaged by the newer, more exciting color choices of solid burgundy, white, yellow or bi-colored foliage selections. Some selections even have uniquely colored stems. Elephant ears generally are not cold hardy for most of Oklahoma and are grown as annuals. Surprisingly, a few of these newer burgundy foliage colored selections like C. antiquorum 'Illustris' and C. esculenta 'Ruffles' are cold hardy through most of zone 7. And there are quite a few that will overwinter in zone 7a.

Other Common Name
Taro

Bloom Period and Seasonal Color
Showy foliage from spring until fall.

Mature Height × Spread
2 to 6 ft. × 2 to 6 ft.

Cold Hardiness Zone
7, 7a (depending on species and selection)

When, Where, and How to Plant
Plant the tubers in late spring after frost danger has past or in early summer. Cover them with at least 2 in. of soil. Elephant ears love rich organic soils. They tolerate wet soils and some can grow in bog conditions. Mulch after planting to help conserve moisture and discourage weeds. For mass planting, space 3 ft. apart. When choosing a selection, find out if it sends out runners. This would require more spacing, though most elephant ears not invasive.

Growing Tips
Elephant ears are not drought tolerant. They need irrigation during dry periods of at least 1 gallons a week, even more during peak summer months. The massive plants are heavy feeders and respond to any fertilizer. I use slow release products for a gradual boost throughout the growing season. If your plants are not growing enough, you either need warmer soil temperatures or more fertilizer. The plants also tend to emerge later in the spring or early summer so don't give up too early.

Care
If attempting to overwinter the more cold hardy selections, plant in spring or early summer on the southeast side of a structure, which provides more winter protection. Mulch 4 in. thick in the fall after the first frost to insulate. Elephant ears perennialize best in soils that are drier during the winter. Many newer types do not form large tubers like the old favorite, so digging and overwintering them is tough due to insufficient food reserves. Ones with large tubers can be stored indoors in a cool, dry location in peat moss or sawdust.

Companion Planting and Design
The large dramatic leaves provide great backdrops for other perennial plants. Use large foliage plants like canna, coleus, and even ornamental grasses as companions. They also make nice container garden plants or water garden bog plants.

My Personal Favorites
I like a combination planting of *C. antiquorum* 'Illustris' (variegated purple and green) and *C. esculenta* 'Black Magic' (solid purple almost black).

Lily

Lily species and hybrids

When, Where, and How to Plant

Plant bulbs in spring and container grown selections in late spring or early summer in well drained, sandy loam soils. Bulb size varies so apply the general rule to plant twice the depth of the bulb. Too much tender loving care in loose, fluffy soil and the plants can flop over or uproot. Typical spacing is 12 to 18 in., but the tall varieties can be planted 2 ft. apart. Mulch for moisture retention.

Growing Tips

Most lilies like their heads warmed by the sun and their feet cooled by the shade. Achieve this using low-growing companion plants or mulch. If you mulch, cottonseed hulls are a great choice. Keep lilies moist during the growing season. Irrigation is necessary during prolonged winter drought. Most lilies are best undisturbed for several years. When thinning is needed, dig and divide bulbs in the fall or early spring. Some species form bulblets along the stem or adjoining the bulbs. These can be removed and planted in containers or in the ground with protection.

Care

Summer care varies depending on the species and bloom time. Some types keep their foliage until frost, while the foliage of others yellows and dies soon after flowering. Allow the foliage to die on its own. Supplemental feeding is not needed unless chlorotic foliage and non-vigorous growth indicates nutritional deficiencies. Apply slow release fertilizers in fall or early spring. Insects to watch for are aphids. Basal root rot can occur in soils with poor drainage.

Companion Planting and Design

Design definitely depends on the species and its height. Plant towering varieties in large groups or in the back of a layered perennial bed. Interplant mid-size types in the typical perennial garden. Lilies make great choices for cutflower gardens. Lower growing plants, such as million bells, salvia, liriope, and verbena, help shade the lily roots.

My Personal Favorites

You can't beat the long-lived Asiatic hybrids. The Pixie series is especially nice because of its dwarf size.

Lilies are perhaps the most historic bulbs. There are well over eighty species and even more hybrids. They add wonderful fragrance and architectural drama to the garden thanks to their coarse stems and horizontal foliage. Sadly they get a bad reputation for being difficult to grow. But on the contrary, ones like L. lancifolium are easy to naturalize in the perennial garden. The hard part is picking a particular color or size because of the many choices. They make great cut flowers, but can be sometimes messy indoors. A trick I learned years ago from a gardening buddy was to cut off the stamens and anthers as soon as the flower opens to keep from getting the staining pollen on your clothes, cabinet tops, and tables.

Other Common Name
Garden Lily

Bloom Period and Seasonal Color
Assorted colors with varieties varying in bloom from spring to fall

Mature Height × Spread
1 to 7 ft. × 1 to 3 ft.

Cold Hardiness Zone
6a, 6b, 7a, 7b

Oriental Hyacinth
Hyacinthus orientalis

Hyacinths have a historic, romantic quality about them. They are picturesque, fragrant, and offer a softening array of pastel colors in early spring. They are great for the perennial border in the short term and even better as an indoor forcing flower. Hyacinth's are quite expensive and oftentimes don't last that long in the perennial garden. With time, many of the hybridized flowers seem to get smaller and smaller, almost disappearing from the garden. The old fashioned naturalizing "French Roman" types are seldom available anymore except through heirloom sources and collectors. The "Festival series" is easier to find and works as a substitute with dainty multi-flowering stalks that are quite showy and very fragrant. They also naturalize well. Double flowering hyacinths are also available.

Other Common Name
Dutch Hyacinth

Bloom Period and Seasonal Color
White, yellow, pink, rose, purple or red flower in the spring.

Mature Height × Spread
8 to 12 in. × 4 to 6 in.

Cold Hardiness Zones
6a, 6b, 7a, 7b

When, Where, and How to Plant
Hyacinth are true bulbs planted in October, November or early December about 5 in. deep and 6 in. apart in sandy loam soils. To avoid staking the flowers, plant them closer at 5 per sq. ft. Avoid highly organic soil and amend the planting site with a complete fertilizer low in nitrogen and high in phosphorus and potassium. The site needs to be well drained, particularly once the plants go dormant. Mulch 2 in. thick for weed control.

Growing Tips
Water the bulbs in fall during dry periods to establish roots. Provide intermittent, supplemental irrigation during foliage and flower display, but allow the soil to dry in between watering. Spring rains are typically sufficient. Watch for aphids in early spring. Use slow release organic fertilizers applied each fall.

Care
Allow the foliage to yellow and die on its own before removing like with tulips and daffodils. Hyacinths make great bulbs for forcing indoors. Plant the bulbs practically touching in a shallow container and keep in a cool dark place while the roots form typically two to three months. As foliage spikes emerge gradually expose them to warmer conditions and more indirect light. Watering is seldom needed until the foliage starts to elongate.

Companion Planting and Design
Because they like drier soils after they go dormant, hyacinths are not good companions for plants that require excess or frequent supplemental irrigation during the summer. They are better fit in perennial gardens that get minimal irrigation. Daylily, Russian sage, sedums, and iris are nice companions. Their compact size makes them perfect for borders and rock gardens.

My Personal Favorite
Call me old fashion, but I like the old southern roman hyacinth with a wild flowering look that is delightfully fragrant and naturalizes well in drier parts of a tough lawn.

Ornamental Onion
Allium spp.

When, Where, and How to Plant
Plant bulbs October or November at 5 to 6 in. deep in well drained sandy loam soils slightly amended with organic matter. Giant flowering types are planted at 1 per sq. ft. Mid-size (softball sized) flowering types are planted closer at 5 per sq. ft., and smaller types (golf ball sized) are even closer at 10 per sq. ft. Container grown plants are occasionally available for spring planting. Mulch to retain moisture and minimize weeds.

Growing Tips
Fall applications of slow release fertilizers work well. Supplemental fertilizer during the growing season may be needed if growth is non-vigorous. Avoid high nitrogen fertilizers that can stimulate too much growth and floppy foliage. Ornamental onions are relatively drought tolerant and don't need to be pampered once established. In severe droughts, supplemental irrigation is recommended.

Care
Thrips are the most likely insect to attack. Root rot or bulb stem rot can occur in heavy, poorly drained soils. The flower stalks can be cut back to the plant crown once it begins to yellow or become unsightly. Allow foliage to die back on its own before removing. The plants form clumps and can be easily lifted and divided in fall or early spring. Individual bulbs or the entire clump can be divided to start new plants.

Companion Planting and Design
Ornamental onions are perfect for the perennial garden as a border plant, background plant or even combined specimen plant. They are perfect in the cutflower or butterfly garden. Plant early-blooming alliums in the fall in containers with pansies. Ornamental onion fits well in rock gardens because of their drought tolerance. Russian sage, salvia, lilies, and daylilies, which also tolerate drier soils, are all good companions.

My Personal Favorites
If you can imagine a round, rose-colored flower the size of a softball stuck on a stick, then you c an imagine the uniqueness of *A. giganteum.* Even easier to grow and naturalize is Drumstick Ornamental Onion *A. sphaerocephalon.*

These onions bring a smile to your face instead of tears to your eyes. Related to the edible onion, these easy-growing ornamental types provide consistent showy flowers year after year. The color, size, height and foliage vary immensely among species. To most gardeners' surprise, there are well over 30 species and named cultivars and certainly more to come. Most have ball or globe-shaped flowers emerging high above the linear foliage on a single leafless stalks. The flowers last two weeks while the seed heads last even longer. When the foliage is bruised, it resembles the scent of other allium family members, such as onions, chives, garlic and shallots. Only these beauties are low maintenance and offer plenty of charm for the perennial garden.

Other Common Names
Flowering Onion, Allium

Bloom Period and Seasonal Color
White, yellow, pink, or rose blooms in late spring, early summer

Mature Height × Spread
1/2 to 3 ft. × 1 to 2 ft.

Cold Hardiness Zone
6a, 6b, 7a, 7b

Oxalis
Oxalis spp.

Like with so many other plants, negative species give a bad name to the whole group. For example, O. stricta (yellow woodsorrel), is a pesky container and flowerbed week. However, many oxalis are well behaved plants with long- blooming, showy flowers and a clumping growth habit ideal for landscape borders. The clover like foliage offers a nice design element with colorful white, pink or rose blooms at various times throughout the growing season. Some of the more popular landscape species are the ones with vibrant purple or burgundy foliage that makes a statement with or without the flowers. One that is most common in the trade is Oxalis crassipes with vibrant pink flowers.

Other Common Names
Woodsorrel, Shamrock

Bloom Period and Seasonal Color
White, pink or rose in spring, early summer and fall

Mature Height × Spread
1 ft. × 1 ft.

Cold Hardiness Zone
6b, 7a,7b

When, Where, and How to Plant
The tiny true bulbs can be planted in the spring 1 in. deep. Container grown plants are also frequently available for spring or summer planting. Fall planting is not recommended in most of Oklahoma since the plants need several months to get established before an Oklahoma winter. Woodland type settings are best in Oklahoma with dappled or afternoon shade. Moisture retentive, well drained, organic, slightly acidic soils are ideal. Adding peatmoss to the planting site at a 50/50 ratio with the soil will help.

Growing Tips
Mulch after planting and reapply mulch as needed every couple of years. Supplemental irrigation is a must during drought periods. The plants do respond well to supplemental feedings during spring or early summer. Slow release fertilizers applied at planting and then reapplied each spring provide small amounts of nutrients over a longer period of time.

Care
Some species go dormant in the heat or drought times of the summer. They reappear in the fall or early spring. Most ornamental types seldom seed and are clump forming. Few spread by forming new adjoining bulblets enlarging the clumps; these are not invasive. The plants can be dug and divided in early spring to start new clumps or share with gardening friends. Watch for occasional spider mites. Also, bulbs can rot in water-logged sites.

Companion Planting and Design
The nice compact growth is perfect for borders in perennial shade gardens or along a garden path. They also work in container gardening combinations and a few will even overwinter as a houseplant. They are often touted as a good "shoes and socks" plant for other bulbs that can easily emerge through the more compact oxalis foliage. Good companions are ajuga, moneywort, dwarf Solomon's seal, and barrenwort.

My Personal Favorite
The brilliant purple foliage and light pink flowers of *O. regnellii* 'Triangularis' (a.k.a. Purple Leaf False Shamrock) are real show stoppers.

Oxblood Lily
Rodophiala bifida

When, Where, and How to Plant

Plant the bulbs in the middle of summer when foliage goes dormant. Dormant mail-order bulbs are often shipped in August. These tough perennials thrive under deciduous trees where the bulb foliage gets winter sunlight. The plants adapt to almost any soil—clay, rocky, or sandy loam—as long as it drains well. The bulbs are best planted in combinations or sites that remain dry in the summer. Like most plants however, they are more vigorous in better soils. Plant the bulbs 3 to 4 in. deep and 8 to 12 in. apart. Oxblood lilies are no different from any other perennial; they get better with age. Adding light organic mulch consisting of shredded leaves, pine bark, or compost rewards you with more beautiful color.

Growing Tips

In heavy, water-soaked soils the bulbs rot. Oxblood lily is quite drought tolerant once established. The lilies respond to early-spring and summer feedings, but these are not necessary in rich, humus soils.

Care

Pruning is not necessary. Allow the foliage to turn yellow and die on its own to feed the bulb for its grand finale of color. You can remove withered flower stalks, although they fade out of sight quickly on their own. Pests are of no concern.

Companion Planting and Design

Oxblood lilies are tough and easily naturalize in perennial beds, through groundcovers, in lawns, and by traffic-congested thoroughfares. Planting them in rows or drifts where they fill in with time makes for the most spectacular display. Do not forget to put a few in permanent patio containers for an added late-summer surprise. For season-long bloom, plant daffodils for spring flowers, crinums for summer, and oxbloods for fall.

My Personal Favorite

The species is the most commonly available and well worth the time in finding mail order sources.

If you are looking for a naturalizing bulb that thrives in the Oklahoma heat better than tulips, consider oxblood lily. Oxblood lily is more common in neighboring Texas, although it does quite well in the southern zones of our state. It does not need chilling hours to prosper and bloom. The other difference from tulips is that Rodophiala species bloom in late summer/early fall. The primary color available is intense red. The strap-like foliage emerges in late fall after it blooms and is semi-evergreen through winter. The foliage dies in early to midsummer. The flower stalks later burst through the ground after the first good rain usually in August, producing vivid color. After two or three weeks of blooming, the flower stalks wither, starting the process all over again.

Other Common Name
Schoolhouse Lily

Bloom Period and Seasonal Color
Red, pink coral blooms in fall

Mature Height × Spread
12 to 15 in. × 15 to 24 in.

Cold Hardiness Zone
6a, 7a, 7b

Surprise Lily
Lycoris species

Now you see them, now you don't. There are many stories associated with the common names of this popular pass-along plant. My favorite is a former pastor who proclaimed a first sermon was his first in front of "naked ladies." He was talking about the cut flowers in front of his podium. It didn't take long for him to learn some more "orthodox" gardening names. The names are often used interchangeably among several species that bloom in late summer or early fall. L. radiata is called the red-flowering "spider lily" because of the spider-like flowers; it is also called hurricane lily in the south because its bloom period aligns with hurricane season. L. squamigera is the traditional pink surprise lily, and a rare yellow form, L. africana, is best in southeastern Oklahoma.

Other Common Names
Hurricane Lily, Spider Lily, Naked Lady, Magic Lily

Bloom Period and Seasonal Color
Red, yellow, or pink in August or September

Mature Height × Spread
12 to 18 in. × 6 to 8 in.

Cold Hardiness Zone
6b, 7a, 7b

When, Where, and How to Plant
Plant in spring or early summer at 3 to 4 in. deep. Digging and planting a pass-a-long plant in late summer is the optimum scenario. The plants thrive and multiply best in slightly acidic, organically fertile soils, but are generally not very picky about soil types as long as they drain well. Slow release fertilizers mixed into the soil at planting time is ideal. Like most perennials, the plants get better with time.

Growing Tips
The plants are fairly drought tolerant once established; they actually like to be left alone. Lycoris is seen thriving in abandoned sites. Some attest that they prefer drier soils during summer, which is their dormant period. Mulching to suppress weed competition, and water after planting and during drought periods when the foliage is present.

Care
The bluish green foliage that occurs in the winter and spring feeds the bulb and helps develop the flower that blooms in late summer; let the foliage die down on its own. *L. squamigera* is more cold hardy and the best choice for zone 6b while *L. radiata* is ideal for zone 7. Pests are rare. In the case of overcrowding or diminished flower prominence, dig and divide the bulbs in late summer.

Companion Planting and Design
These plants are great to use in among ground covers like Asiatic jasmine, moneywort, million bells, ajuga and vinca. They also can naturalize in lawns. Mass plantings are a sure joy seeing them lined up like soldiers each fall spaced about 4 to 6 in. apart. Random plantings in groups of 3 or 5 are also common under deciduous trees. The Lycoris foliage grows during the time of year when the deciduous companion has dropped its leaves.

My Personal Favorites
Both *L. squamigera and L. radiata* are favorites in my garden. Improved hybrids or selections are not that common.

Tulip
Tulipa species and hybrids

When, Where, and How to Plant
Plant tulips in October or November at a depth 4 times the size of the bulb. This is usually 8 to 10 in. for regular bulbs and 5 to 6 in. for smaller bulbs. Always place the pointed side up. Well drained, sandy loam soils are a must. Mix organic material and fertilizers with phosphorus and potassium into the site prior to planting. Cover fertilizer in a site with soil to avoid direct contact with the roots. Water and mulch after planting.

Growing Tips
To perennialize tulips, place them in location with dry summer conditions. In addition to the well drained, organically amended soils, full sun and regular feeding during the growing season is recommended. Let the foliage die on its own. Planting deeper still has mixed reviews but plant at least 8 in. Again, some varieties just last longer like single early species, single late species and lily flowered types, on other words the old time heirloom types that were bred for gardens and not for pot or cut flower production are best.

Care
Pest problems are minimal in good air circulation and full sun sites. You might see the occasional aphid. Early spring winds and rains can tatter flower petals and shorten color display. Most every rodent, as well as deer, favor tulip bulbs, so mechanical barriers of some kind are the best deterrent.

Companion Planting and Design
Tulips are ideal for mass planting (4 bulbs per sq. ft.) in seasonal color displays. Good companions are pansies, violas, and variegated sweet flag. Don't forget to put a few tulips in fall container plantings for added spring color. In perennializing, consider full sun sites and plants that tolerate drier summer conditions like sedum and and moss rose. Dry, non-irrigated rock gardens or lawn areas without summer irrigation are best.

My Personal Favorite
I like the species *T. tardiva*. It is a good naturalizer with bicolor yellow/ white flowers and nice compact growth.

Tulip bulbs are another one of those mesmerizing, spring-flowering bulbs. But like hyacinths, many of the new hybrids do not provide color year after year. If you can get two to three years of enjoyment count yourself lucky. Of course, even one season of color is worth the time and money. As a result, many gardeners use tulips as annuals. They plant them in the fall, enjoy the brilliant spring bloom and then pull them to make space for summer annual displays. There are tulip species, however, more inclined to perennialize but they are typically the shorter flowering species types. Tulips are categorized many ways and there are hundreds of choices. Watch for bloom times when mixing and matching if you are trying to achieve uniform flowering sequences.

Other Common Name
Garden Tulip

Bloom Period and Seasonal Color
Assorted solid or mixed colors and shapes blooming in spring.

Mature Height × Spread
6 to 36 in. × 10 to 12 in.

Cold Hardiness Zone
6a, 6b, 7a, 7b

Ground Covers *for Oklahoma*

With only a few plants and a little time, ground covers can easily fill large, vacant landscape spaces. Because, as the name implies, ground covers are plants growing and spreading along the ground. I have been using more ground covers lately since they do not require a large initial investment. Another nice thing about ground covers is that they work as living mulch. Organic mulches need to be replaced every couple of years, but ground covers are permanent once established.

Ground covers can be herbaceous (soft-stemmed) or woody. Some spread by underground stolons, others root along their stems, and a few vine up nearby objects. Ground covers are evergreen (retaining most leaves year-round) or deciduous (losing leaves in the winter). Turfgrass is also a ground cover. Most gardeners have finally come to the realization that grass, although very important to the landscape, does not often thrive in shade. Many ground covers, on the other hand, serve the same purposes as turf and tolerate various levels of shade. As result, they are perfect understory companions for trees. Ground covers help in erosion control and are often planted on sloping sites or allowed to cascade over walls. Many of these prostrate growers are gaining in recognition as container or windowbox companion plants.

Slow Growth Is Good

Incorporating organic materials and slow-release nutrients into planting beds ahead of time is always a good idea, except when planting ground covers around trees. The products can be applied on top of

the ground but no thicker than four to six inches. Do not till or mix the materials with the existing soil, or the tree's fibrous roots may be readily damaged, shortening its life. Instead, plant the ground cover plants singly at the proper recommended spacing where they can later spread. Following this method does minimal damage to tree roots.

Spacing is determined by the spread of the particular plant. Measure from the center of one plant to the center of the next plant for proper placement. Arrange plants diagonally to get a quicker fill. Avoid planting too close to borders. Buy ground cover plants in smaller containers. They are easier to plant, cheap, and quickly catch up to a larger-sized plant.

The chart on page 77 will help you determine the number of plants needed for a bed. Do not overcrowd ground covers because they will spread and mature as the season progresses.

A Ground Cover Landscape

Pachysandra Edging a Walkway

Calculating Plant Quantities

1. Determine planting bed area: _____ (width × length = sq. ft.)
2. Recommended Spacing

Recommended Spacing	Number of Plants Per Sq. Ft.
6 inches	4.00
8 inches	2.25
10 inches	1.44
12 inches	1.00
18 inches	0.44
24 inches	0.25

3. Multiply the number of plants for the recommended spacing by the square footage.
4. Example: 125 sq. ft. with 10-in. spacing = 180 plants needed (1.44 × 125 sq. ft. = 180).

Mulch two to four inches deep between plants to minimize weed growth until the plants spread and fill the bed. Pine bark, cottonseed hulls, shredded leaves, compost, and pine straw mulches are best for ground covers. It usually takes two to three years for ground covers to completely fill in a landscape space, so reapplication of the mulch will likely be needed during this time. Weeding, mulching, fertilizing, and watering speed up the establishment process. Apply slow-release or organic products in early spring or fall, but let the plant's performance tell you when to feed it. If you fertilize ground cover underneath a tree, it also feeds the tree and vice versa. Pinching or tipping the vines or branches throughout the first couple of growing seasons will promote thicker growth.

Archangel
Lamium maculatum

Archangel has colorful flowers and glistening foliage. The flowers are borne in whorls on small, upright stems. The foliage is shaped like a spade and covered with fine, downy hairs. Foliage colors range from gray to yellow to light green. The plant is deciduous in most parts of Oklahoma, although occasionally semi-evergreen in mild winters. A cultivar known for its silver leaves with narrow, green edges and pink flowers is 'Beacon Silver'. 'White Nancy' looks like 'Beacon Silver', but it has white flowers. 'Pink Pewter' and 'Shell Pink' have pink flowers. 'Chequers' has uniquely marbled foliage with rose-pink flowers. 'Aureum' has golden foliage with pink flowers and is not as aggressive. Lamium galeobdolon (Lamiastrum galeobdolon), known as yellow archangel 'Herman's Pride', is noninvasive with attractive yellow flowers on silver-flecked foliage.

Other Common Name
Spotted Deadnettle

Bloom Period and Seasonal Color
White, pink, or yellow blooms in late spring to early summer.

Mature Height × Spread
8 to 12 in. × 12 to 24 in.

Cold Hardiness Zones
6a, 6b, 7a, 7b

When, Where, and How to Plant
Plant archangel in spring, early summer, or early fall. This plant definitely needs afternoon shade or dappled sun. Planted in hot, scorching sun, *Lamium* will live up to its other name of deadnettle. It prefers fertile, moist, well-drained soils. Archangel is not likely to survive severe heat and drought. Planting it in afternoon shade, mulching it, and providing supplemental irrigation will help keep it thriving. Plant archangel in groups 15 to 18 inches apart. Be careful not to set them too deep when planting. Divide these plants in the spring or early fall when they become overcrowded. This perennial responds well to fertile, organic soils that retain some moisture yet drain well.

Growing Tips
Mulching is almost a necessity to keep the soil moist. Water during dry conditions. If the plants are healthy and vigorous, do not worry about supplemental feedings especially in well prepared garden soil. Non-vigorous plants will respond well to supplemental feedings. Remember, fertilizer does not fix other causes of poor performance like pests or heat scorch. Fertilizer that dissolves and is spread via water gives the quickest response. Slow release fertilizers are also beneficial.

Care
Pruning is seldom needed because of their low-growing habit. Trim taller selections back after flowering to keep them orderly. Spider mites and heat scorch are occasional problems in sunnier locations. Fungal leaf spots and powdery mildew are not common but do occur.

Landscape Merit
Use it as a border or foreground plant in perennial shade gardens, or use it as a companion plant with shade-tolerant perennials, especially ones with white, purple, or yellow flowers. Use archangel as colorful filler in container displays or in hanging baskets. Hostas are good companions but can overgrow Lamium. Other shade-loving plants similar in size include coral bell, foam flower, and Solomon's seal.

My Personal Favorite
One of my favorites is 'Beedham's White' with wonderful chartreuse foliage and white flowers.

Blue Plumbago
Ceratostigma plumbaginoides

When, Where, and How to Plant

Plumbago is typically sold in 4^1/2-inch, 1-quart, or 1-gallon containers. Plant in April, May, or June. It prefers afternoon shade or sites with dappled sun. It occasionally takes more sun if it is in moist, well-drained sites. Moist, fertile soils provide the best growth, although leadwort takes drier conditions once established. Soggy, compacted soils put a quick end to this plant. Set the plant's rootballs at the same depth as in the original containers. Space plants 12 to 18 inches apart. Mulch to prevent competition from weeds until it is established. Divide and move leadwort in spring.

Growing Tips

Water as needed and especially during drought. Fertilize once the new growth has started to emerge in the spring and possibly again in late June or early July. Do not fertilize any later, especially with high-nitrogen fertilizers, so that the plants harden off before the onset of winter. Always water after granular fertilizer applications to rinse foliage and avoid burning.

Care

Plumbago is slow to emerge in the spring. Flowers are formed on new growth. Once in a while, blue plumbago thins in the center of the initial planting. Shear the plant to the ground in early spring. Other than that, pruning is seldom needed. There are no reports of significant pests.

Landscape Merit

Use blue plumbago as filler in front portions of landscape beds or as a border along sidewalks. Plumbago's low-growing habit makes it a suitable plant for companion bulb plantings. Leadwort is an effective companion plant with yellow-flowering Asiatic lilies and other yellow-flowering, partial-shade perennials. It is often used in combination with chartreuse or variegated shade plants. Pink-flowering plants are also a good combination with leadwort.

My Personal Favorite

The species is the most commonly found and well worth the investment.

Gardeners really get their money's worth with this plant. Blue plumbago offers unique landscape appeal from May until November. This outstanding deciduous ground cover emerges late in the spring with shiny, ovate foliage forming along small, woody stems. It soon sports some of the bluest flowers I have ever seen, which mature into attractive, coppery seedheads persisting into early fall. As the days get shorter and cooler, the foliage turns a bronzy-red color. Be careful not to select Chinese plumbago (C. willmottianum) for a perennial in Oklahoma. This similar-looking species will not tolerate our winters and is hardy only through Zone 8. Be patient with plumbago. It takes a couple years to start spreading as a ground cover and rewarding you with an ever changing seasonal display.

Other Common Name
Leadwort

Bloom Period and Seasonal Color
Blue blooms in June and July with bronzy-red fall foliage.

Mature Height × Spread
8 to 12 in. × 12 to 18 in.

Cold Hardiness Zones
6a, 6b 7a, 7b

Blue Star Creeper
Laurentia fluviatilis

This ground cover has spreading speed and flower power to boot. The delicate, star shaped, purple flowers are quite prolific in late spring and early summer. The round, green foliage seems even more delicate. But do not let that fool you because this little beauty tolerates foot traffic fairly well. It forms a one- to two-inch tall mat and spreads twelve to eighteen inches the first year. Even with that growth rate, it is not considered invasive. In southeastern Oklahoma, blue star creeper can occasionally exist in winter as an evergreen, keeping its greenish foliage all season. A close cousin, L. axillaries, grows taller with bigger flowers, making it a better selection for the part sun, part shade perennial garden rather than a ground cover.

Other Common Names
Fairy Creeper, Solenopsis

Bloom Period and Seasonal Color
Blueish flowers in May and June, with sporatic blooms throughout the summer and fall.

Mature Height × Spread
1 to 2 in. × 12 to 18 in.

Cold Hardiness Zones
6b, 7a, 7b

When, Where, and How to Plant
Plant in early spring to early summer. Fall plantings are okay in southeastern Oklahoma. Even when planted 15 to 18 inches apart, small containerized plants quickly fill in their allotted space. Moist, well drained soils rich with organic material provide the best growth and landscape display. However, I have seen them do well in drier sites with supplemental irrigation. The plants can tolerate some morning sun in moist sites. Full sun sites with poor soils typically result in scorched, non-vigorous plants.

Growing Tips
Mulch 2 inches thick between plants to squelch weed competition. The rhizomatous (rootstock) spreading plants easily emerge through most mulches at that thickness. Leaving fertilizer on wet foliage can burn the delicate foliage. Rather, incorporate slow release fertilizers at planting time. Otherwise, an occasional water-soluble mix during early summer speeds the spreading process.

Care
Once they are established, divide the plants to share with your friends or fill in your landscape. To do this, dig 2- to 4-inch sections out of the established plant. Be sure to include some roots. Set them out in other landscape sites in early spring or replant them in small containers to plant later. Pruning is seldom needed. Edging or adjoining turf manages the plants. Pests include an occasional white fly or spider mite. Poorly drained sites are an invitation to rotting.

Landscape Merit
The quick, low growth makes for great ground cover in shaded rock gardens or around stepping stones. It also becomes nice living mulch around shrubs and herbaceous perennials in partially shaded locations, adding texture and color during the growing season. It works well as a border plant by adjoining sidewalks or water gardens. Although the plant tolerates some foot traffic, it will not hold up to constant traffic by pets or people.

My Personal Favorite
No improved cultivars are sold, so look for the species *Laurentia fluviatilis.*

Bugleweed
Ajuga reptans

When, Where, and How to Plant

Plant ajuga in spring or early summer. Optimum growing conditions cause some cultivars to grow vigorously and benefit areas in need of thick ground cover. Adequate moisture factors big in the plant's success. Drainage is important, though, or the plant succumbs to crown rot. It prefers dappled or afternoon shade. In full-sun sites, the plant needs good, moist soil and wind protection. Plant on 1- to 2-foot centers at the same depth as the rootballs. Mulch until the plants are established to minimize weed growth. The ajuga runners easily emerge through the mulch as it spreads. Divide plant clumps before temperatures become too hot.

Growing Tips

Ajuga succumbs to drought and heat, so provide supplemental water to avoid leaf scorching. Many cultivars retain their foliage during mild winters; most are deciduous in severe winters. Spring fertilizing with slow-release organic or synthetic products promotes quick growth and spread. Wash granular fertilizer off the foliage to prevent burning. Fertilizers that dissolve in water give a quick surge of growth.

Care

Ajuga is typically not aggressive, though after a few years it may creep outside its designated space. Occasionally, plants will melt down from fungus during prolonged wet periods, especially in poorly drained soils in heavy shade. Fungicides applied according to directions help the problem as does cleaning out the infected areas.

Landscape Merit

Use bugleweed in beds adjoining sidewalks, in borders, and containers to keep the plant bounded. Make it a companion plant for low-traffic areas between shrub beds in moist, partially shaded sites. I have seen ajuga uniquely placed on a nonfunctional wooden bridge topped with soil and compost. Ajuga was planted in the shallow soil and mulched to hold it in place. The planting established and completely carpeted the bridge. The flower display in the spring was one of a kind.

My Personal Favorite

I like the cultivar 'Chocolate Chip' (Ajuga × tenorii 'Valfredda') for the wonderful erect flower display and narrow foliage.

Ajuga is a longtime favorite ground cover with creeping stems. Certain cultivars are vigorous and cover large areas fairly rapidly. Most selections send up spikes of whorled flowers in late spring, purple being the most common color. In some cultivars the colorful foliage is showier and longer lasting than the actual flower. More unusual colors include 'Alba', a white-flowering selection, and 'Pink Beauty', with pink flowers. 'Burgundy Glow', 'Burgundy Lace', 'Jungle Beauty', and 'Silver Beauty' are all cultivars with foliage variegation. 'Bronze Beauty', 'Gaiety', and 'Braunherz' have varying shades of purple foliage. 'Cristata' probably has the smallest foliage and is strongly crinkled, and 'Catlin's Giant' has the largest foliage. For less aggressive species, consider A. pyramidalis and A. genevensis, which have more clumping forms. 'Metallica Crispa' is a popular cultivar of the pyramidal type.

Other Common Names
Carpetbugle, Ajuga

Bloom Period and Seasonal Color
Purple, pink, and white blooms in early to late spring.

Mature Height × Spread
6 to 9 in. × 5 to 10 in.

Cold Hardiness Zones
6a, 6b, 7a, 7b

Creeping Euonymus
Euonymus fortunei

Wintercreeper euonymus is a great evergreen plant for a ground cover, with a deep forest-green color during the growing season, topped off with a violet-purple fall color. This plant is more woody than herbaceous but makes a thick cover fairly quickly. Some of the shrubbier cultivars of this species have clinging characteristics and grow up trees, walls and other structures with time. Creeping euonymus is probably the ground cover to plant when tying a group of trees together to form one landscape bed. As it matures, its vines mat together and form a thick, six- to eight-inch living mulch to keep weeds in check. Creeping euonymus needs plenty of space for its greatest impact. The 'Emerald' selections of wintercreeper are more upright in growth and come in a wealth of foliage colors.

Other Common Name
Wintercreeper

Bloom Period and Seasonal Color
Violet purple fall foliage.

Mature Height × Spread
4 to 12 in. × 12 to 24 in.

Cold Hardiness Zones
6a, 6b, 7a, 7b

When, Where, and How to Plant
Plant creeping euonymus in spring, early summer, or fall. The plants prefer afternoon shade, although some can adapt to full sun. These plants are very adaptable to soil types and pH. They cannot tolerate waterlogged soils, however. Dig planting holes at least 2 times wider than and the same depth as the roots. No organic amended backfill is required. Space wintercreeper euonymus at least 2 to 3 feet apart, 5 feet if you are patient. Add mulch to prevent weeds until the plants spread.

Growing Tips
Supplemental fertilizer applications speed growth of non-vigorous plants. Typically, however, the plants grow quickly on their own. The plants are also fairly drought tolerant when established. Water weekly and deeply the first few months after planting if rainfall is not present. Once established, just water to keep leaves from dropping in severe drought.

Care
These tough plants respond well to pruning just about any time of the year. On newly planted sites, tip the ends of the elongated runners to encourage spreading and bushy, uniform growth. Shear mature or well-established sites of creeping euonymus to keep a uniform height and edge on the sides of the beds. Euonymus scale is a problem on some cultivars of the *E. fortunei* species, especially in stressed situations. Powdery mildew and other leaf diseases threaten this plant when in heavy shade.

Landscape Merit
Size depends on the cultivar and determines placement in the landscape. Most are considered foreground plants or mid-level shrubs. They are often used for erosion sites and even for cascading wall plants. Due to their vigorous spread, euonymous work best in large plantings by themselves.

My Personal Favorites
My favorite cultivar is the low-growing 'Coloratus' because of its superb fall color. Use it for large areas. 'Coloratus' is often substituted in Oklahoma for Asian (Asiatic) jasmine (*Trachelospermum asiaticum*). For smaller, delicate plantings use 'Kewensis', which literally hugs the ground at only a couple inches tall.

Creeping Phlox
Phlox subulata

When, Where, and How to Plant

Plant in spring in order to know the plant's colors. They need at least four to five hours of sun for the best growth and bloom. Planting in too much shade causes tall, leggy, and sparse growth with few flowers. Creeping phlox prefers well-drained, fertile soil, though the plant is adaptable. Diagonally space plants 12 to 18 inches apart to get the best fill. Divide mounded plants in early spring after flowering. Many times the plants have sporadic blooms again in late summer or early fall.

Growing Tips

During drought conditions, supplemental water is recommended. Flower blooms are formed later in the season, and drought affects the flower set. Fertilizing stimulates healthy growth. Slow-release products incorporated at planting is best. Broadcast applications are tough because the fertilizer catches in the foliage and can burn the plants if not watered in thoroughly. Brands that dissolve and are applied with water work well for supplemental feedings during the growing season.

Care

Plant growth is typically mounded and compact. However, the center tends to thin out as plants mature. Shearing plants after blooming promotes more mounding growth in leggy plants and rejuvenates new growth. Spider mites are a potential threat in drought-stressed, full-sun locations.

Landscape Merit

Creeping phlox with its evergreen foliage is a great plant to use in the foreground of deciduous, sun-loving perennials. Full-sun locations are best for border or edging plants. Plant them on slopes or near walls where they are allowed to cascade. Plant them in groups of at least five to make a more dramatic impact with color. Spring flowering bulbs are a nice companion. The bulb growth and bloom will emerge through the phlox foliage for an added surprise each spring.

My Personal Favorite

'Candy Stripe' with its pink- and white-striped bloom seems to go with almost any landscape color design.

Creeping phlox brings a breath of freshness each spring, thanks to its spectacular color display. Few plants start off the season with such a bang. There is something rejuvenating about a landscape filled with the magical colors of phlox, daffodils, dogwoods, and redbuds after a winter's rest. I wish their flowers lasted longer, but at least the foliage remains somewhat evergreen, providing filler for the remainder of the year. Many cultivars have a center or "eye" of a different color. White, pink, and blue (purple) are the most popular cultivars. 'Crimson Beauty' is closer to red. 'Candy Stripe', the pink-and-white-striped cultivar, blooms later than other cultivars. Planting 'Candy Stripe' with the solids will extend the bloom period. 'Nettleton's Variation' is a highly variegated foliage selection with pink flowers.

Other Common Names

Flowering Moss, Moss Phlox

Bloom Period and Seasonal Color

Pink, purple, and white blooms in early spring.

Mature Height × Spread

3 to 6 in. × 24 in.

Cold Hardiness Zones

6a, 6b, 7a, 7b

English Ivy

Hedera helix

Most gardeners are familiar with this lustrous evergreen ground cover or vine. The stems easily form roots along leaf nodes, transforming the plant into a true clinging vine that attaches itself to trees, brick walls, and utility posts. 'Bulgaria' is a tough, cold-hardy variety and is tolerant of heat and drought. 'Baltica' with its unique, smaller leaves is fairly hardy through Zone 6. Quite cold hardy is '238th Street', which has heart-shaped leaves. 'Gold Heart' has dark-green foliage with a gold splash down the center of the leaf, and 'Thorndale' is a small, variegated leaf selection—both significantly cold hardy. 'Pixie', a white-veined selection with crinkled leaves, is hardy for most of the state, and 'Buttercup' is a lime-green cultivar tolerating a little more light, but not full sun.

Other Common Name
Ivy

Bloom Period and Seasonal Color
Evergreen foliage.

Mature Height × Spread
6 to 10 in. × 4 to 6 ft., or as permitted

Cold Hardiness Zones
6a, 6b, 7a, 7b

When, Where, and How to Plant
Plant English ivy in spring, early summer, or fall. This plant can grow as a ground cover or as a vine and favors partial shade in moist, fairly organic sites. It tolerates acid or alkaline soils. English ivy transplants easily and roots fairly quickly. Space plants 1 to 2 feet apart in holes that are slightly wider than and as deep as the rootballs. Mulch until the plant establishes.

Growing Tips
Supplemental moisture is necessary until plants are well established. Supplemental feedings encourage quick growth and cover. Granular fertilizer left on the foliage burns the leaves, so water the plants immediately after fertilizer application to wash it off.

Care
Pruning early on promotes more uniform, bushy coverage. Once established, they require minimal care. Leaf diseases are possible in environments with poor air circulation. Spider mites are potential pests. Be careful to keep ivy off weaker trees since it can eventually shade them out. If allowed on a mature tree, prune and maintain about head high. The same holds for growth up buildings. The plants can beautify multiple story homes, but the fibrous roots can penetrate into mortar depending on the home's construction.

Landscape Merit
Plant ivy as a groundcover to tie trees together in island bed designs, or use it as a green barrier, adding texture and color to fences and trellises. Just a few plants can be placed without damaging too many tree roots and will fill in an entire bed within a couple of growing seasons.

My Personal Favorites
I particularly like the creamy variegated cultivars that brighten up shady spots, such as 'California Gold' and 'Peppermint'. Of course, the variegation tends to fade with age, but continued new growth exhibits the variegation making for a continual display of color. If you want them to act as a perennial, check for cold hardiness characteristics.

Hardy Ice Plant

Delosperma cooperi

When, Where, and How to Plant

Plant hardy ice plant in early spring or summer. This plant does well in sandy loam, well drained soils; waterlogged sites cause quick death. Plant it at the same depth as the rootball in a hole twice the width. Space plants 12 to 18 inches apart. Hardy ice plant is easy to divide in early spring and summer. Extract clumps 3 to 4 inches in diameter from the outer edges of the existing plant mass. Don't worry, it won't leave gaps; fill the holes with soil and ice plant quickly grows back.

Growing Tips

Occasional watering is needed while the plants are getting established; otherwise, they are very drought tolerant. Hardy ice plant is semi-evergreen and dies back to the ground in cold, wet winters. It usually emerges the following spring as soil temperatures begin to warm. Cool, damp conditions in early spring delay the emergence of this plant, but do not give up on it. As soon as the temperatures rise, so does the succulent foliage of hardy ice plant. Few supplemental feedings are needed.

Care

This trouble-free plant seldom needs additional care. There are no serious insect or disease problems, though spider mites occasionally occur. Hardy ice plant makes many xeriscape (drought-tolerant landscaping) lists touting its minimal care. Rotting is typical in poorly drained soils.

Landscape Merit

Plant *Delosperma* in full sun in a rock garden, or use it as a border plant near sidewalks. Hardy ice plant spreads but is noninvasive. It is easy to pull up if it grows out of its designated area. Bulbs and other perennials readily grow through hardy ice plant. Match yellow-and-purple-flowering perennials with the violet-magenta color of this brilliant-flowering ground cover.

My Personal Favorite

'Starbust' has nice design features because of its lilac flowers highlighted with a distinct yellow and white center.

If you are looking for an extremely low ground cover that loves the heat and full sun, look no farther. This succulent plant thrives in harsh conditions and rewards gardeners with bright, daisy-like, eye-catching flowers most of the summer. This native of South Africa loves our Oklahoma summers. Most Delosperma species are hardy through Zone 6, and D. cooperi is the most common. Even though this plant has a succulent appearance, it offers glistening blooms. The plant slowly spreads by underground runners and occasionally reseeds, making it a manageable ground cover. There are other hybrids and species with white, pink, or yellow flowers. There are also some differences in the coarseness of the succulent foliage. Not all ice plant varieties are hardy in Oklahoma.

Other Common Name

Ice Plant

Bloom Period and Seasonal Color

Purple blooms in June through fall.

Mature Height × Spread

2 to 12 in. × 8 to 24 in.

Cold Hardiness Zones

6a, 6b, 7a, 7b

Moneywort

Lysimachia nummularia

Moneywort is one of my favorite truly low-growing ground covers. It is evergreen in most seasons and produces a thick, lush, green growth, seldom growing taller than four inches. The carpet-like growth is a perfect living mulch that rarely allows weeds through it. Easily grown, it is used to cascade over walls, banks, or slopes. It is a perfect border plant, too. This beauty is grown primarily for its ruffled, lush foliage, but it occasionally blooms with yellow flowers. Moneywort is adapted to and thrives in full shade. It is the perfect plant for moist, shaded sites where nothing else seems to grow. In addition to the solid green species, a cultivar with light green, almost yellow foliage is sold as 'Aurea' and sometimes as 'Goldilocks'. Occasionally, it reverts to solid green.

Other Common Name
Creeping Jenny

Bloom Period and Seasonal Color
Yellow blooms in spring.

Mature Height × Spread
2 to 4 in. × 12 to 24 in.

Cold Hardiness Zones
6a, 6b, 7a, 7b

When, Where, and How to Plant
Plant it in spring, summer, or fall. Moneywort will not tolerate dry soils. It must have consistent moisture. The soil quality is not as important as the moisture. It prefers afternoon shade but tolerates full shade as long as there is good drainage. It readily establishes when it is planted in loosely dug holes the same depth as the roots. Space plants 12 to 18 inches apart. Water is a necessity to establish moneywort. Mulch after planting to hold in soil moisture until the plant spreads and acts as its own mulch.

Growing Tips
Supplemental feedings help establish the plants, but be careful not to burn the foliage with granular fertilizers. Always water after granular feedings to wash the fertilizer from the foliage. In severe winters, expect the foliage to scorch and return the next season. Ideally the plants respond best to consistently moist soils that are well drained. That means good organic matter and supplemental waterings during drought.

Care
This plant requires little maintenance other than an occasional trimming when it grows beyond its borders. It does not tolerate heavy traffic. There are no serious pest threats.

Landscape Merit
The low-growing nature of moneywort makes it a perfect choice for sidewalk and landscape borders. Many gardeners plant it to cascade over walls and out of containers, patio bowls, hanging baskets, and windowboxes. Its low-growing habit makes a nice plant for flowering bulbs to emerge through each spring. It is also a nice ground cover to fill in around hosta, coral bells, cardinal flower and other shade-loving perennials. Use it too as a companion with impatiens in container gardening as a cascading plant.

My Personal Favorite
Golden Moneywort or 'Aurea' is my favorite. The chartreuse color brightens shady spots and contrasts nicely with purples, pinks, whites, and almost any flowering companion.

Pachysandra
Pachysandra terminalis

When, Where, and How to Plant
Plant container-grown pachysandra in spring or early summer. Do not plant in high-traffic areas since it does not withstand heavy foot traffic. Pachysandra must grow in moist, fertile soils with a slightly acidic pH. It will not tolerate dry, sunny locations. Space plants about 15 inches apart. Mix in soil sulfur and organic matter into your planting site. The extra effort will reward you with a uniform, glistening ground cover.

Growing Tips
Once planted, water on a regular basis at least weekly when rainfall is lacking. Once it is established, do not forget to give the planting a good soaking during severe drought or the plants will wilt and thin out.

Care
Overall growth is more upright than spreading but still appears very compact. Pachysandra generally does not need pruning. The almost succulent-looking stems are low growing and spread with underground stolons. Pachysandra is not generally considered invasive and stays fairly well within its boundaries. Pests include spider mites and scale. Pests are also more likely on drought-stressed plants. Fungal leaf diseases and root rots are possible in heavily shaded sites that are poorly drained, especially during prolonged periods of wet cloudy weather.

Landscape Merit
Pachysandra spreads by stolons and is a great filler plant in shade gardens. It also offers a coarser texture than some other ground covers. Pachysandra is useful in combination with shade-loving deciduous perennials. Use pachysandra as a border plant. It is not as good a cascading plant as some other ground covers included in this chapter. Gardeners like to plant it in shaded courtyard areas, around trees, and in shade rock gardens.

My Personal Favorite
'Green Sheen' pachysandra is one of the glossiest green-leaved plants I have ever seen. It almost looks as if someone has sprayed and cleaned the foliage.

Pachysandra is another evergreen ground cover that prefers shade. The wedge-shaped foliage is arranged in whorls along the stem. When pachysandra is planted in and around deciduous plants, the evergreen foliage commands attention, especially in dormant winter landscapes. Plants are typically evergreen in the southern counties of the state and semi-evergreen in the northern locations. It has a place in our landscapes in appropriate sites, and some of the new cultivars should be considered more often in areas that need a ground cover. 'Green Sheen', a lustrous, shiny-leaved selection, is probably the best choice for our hot and humid conditions. It is also disease tolerant and hardy through Zone 5. 'Green Carpet' is the old standard, and 'Silver Edge' has a variegated, creamy-white leaf margin.

Other Common Names
Japanese Pachysandra, Japanese Spurge

Bloom Period and Seasonal Color
White blooms in early spring.

Mature Height × Spread
6 to 8 in. × 12 to 18 in.

Cold Hardiness Zones
6a, 6b, 7a, 7b

Peacock Moss
Selaginella uncinata

One of the most unusual ground covers I have ever grown is peacock moss. The delicate, iridescent foliage is so flat it almost forms a mat. The various shades of blue and green glisten in dappled light. I have used peacock moss next to a rock sidewalk leading into a shaded area by a water hydrant. The moist, shady site seems to be perfect for this one-of-a-kind ground cover. Another species, Selaginella pallescens, is commonly called arborvitae fern because the foliage resembles arborvitae (only without the bagworms!). The flat foliage is a deep green and softer to the touch than arborvitae. It gets a little taller, maturing at fifteen to eighteen inches. Arborvitae fern is primarily deciduous in the winter but cold hardy in Zone 6.

Other Common Names
Spike Moss, Peacock Fern, Rainbow Fern

Bloom Period and Seasonal Color
No bloom; grown for the fernlike foliage.

Mature Height × Spread
3 to 5 in. × 12 to 24 in.

Cold Hardiness Zones
7a, 7b

When, Where, and How to Plant
Plant it in late spring or early summer. It tolerates full shade, but the various displays of colors are sometimes lost. Peacock moss suffers in a site with heavy foot traffic. It prefers fertile, moist, and well drained soils. Where possible, amend the soils before planting time. Place the rootball in a hole 3 times the width of the rootball and the same depth that it was grown. Plant 15 to 18 inches apart from center to center of each plant. Mulch the plants to preserve moisture.

Growing Tips
Peacock moss requires minimal maintenance. Fertilizer is seldom needed if an organically rich soil is prepared before planting time. Mulching conserves moisture and minimizes weed growth until the plants are well established. To avoid smothering this delicate plant, be careful not to get the mulch more than 2 to 3 inches thick.

Care
Peacock moss is late to emerge in the spring, sometimes not growing until late April or early May. Remove dead foliage in late spring as the new growth emerges. Do not give up on it or forget where it is planted. Reapply mulch as the new growth emerges. Pests are minimal, but spider mites are possible like with most any other stressed plant. Leaf scorch is likely in dry windy spots that get too much afternoon sun.

Landscape Merit
This low-growing ground cover is definitely a border plant in partial shade. It works well in shaded rock gardens and as a lower foreground plant in combination with ferns, hostas, and other shade-loving plants. Planting the lower-growing peacock moss in front of the taller *Selaginella pallescens* (arborvitae fern) makes for a refreshing, almost tropical look in the summer.

My Personal Favorite
A unique one called *S. kraussiana* or 'Gold Tips' is very dainty and can be used in moist sites as a delicate ground cover. 'Gold Tips' works in terrariums, too. They both have different uses in the landscape because of their height differences.

When, Where, and How to Plant

Plant sedum in spring and summer in full-sun sites. Well drained soils are key in growing sedum. They accept heavy soils, rocky soils, sandy soils, and just about anything in between as long as they are not waterlogged. Plant sedum at the same depth as the rootball in loosely dug soil 15 to 18 inches apart. No amended backfill is needed. Pampering the soil and plants too much can cause leggy plants that flop over. Sedums are easy to divide any time during the growing season. Divide and replant clump-forming sedums in very early spring before the shoots emerge from the winter mound.

Growing Tips

Fertilize only if the plants demonstrate deficiency symptoms. Sedums can burn easily if the fertilizer gets trapped in the foliage and is not watered in well after applying. Overfertilizing can also cause plants to become leggy and fall over. Most sedums are drought tolerant. Over-watering can cause rotting. There are some exceptions, however; selections that take more shade will also tolerate moist, well drained sites.

Care

Sedum generally takes care of itself. Some cultivars need to have the dead flower stalks removed once a year. There are seldom disease problems. Black aphids favor some sedums early in the spring, but they are easily controlled.

Landscape Merit

Plant dwarf types in the front and taller ones in the middle or back of the site. Sedum is a great companion plant for bulbs planted in fall or as an accent in rock gardens. The bulbs easily emerge through the low-growing sedum foliage in early spring. Arrange taller clumping types in groups of three or five. Cascade the more spreading, prostrate forms over rock walls. Combine with hardy ice plant, which produces blooms longer in summer.

My Personal Favorite

In the winter, 'Angelina' takes on an almost coppery orange hew that is unmatched by any plant. Its 6 inch growth habit and trailing form makes a great ground cover.

Sedum is one of the best choices for hot-sun landscape beds. It thrives in heat. Some cultivars take partial shade, but most sedums display best in the sun. Height variation and foliage texture vary, depending on the species. The showy blooms occur in spring, summer, or fall, depending on the cultivar. Many times the best display comes from combinations of sedum textures and colors. 'Autumn Joy' sedum is an example of a mounding form often compared to cabbage in its early stages of growth. 'Rosy Glow' grows to six to eight inches but does not spread well, so plant a prostrate, more spreading cultivar like 'John Creech' to fill in around it. 'Vera Jameson', 'Elizabeth' ('Red Carpet'), 'Dragon's Blood', and 'Purple Form' have reddish-purple foliage in addition to their flowers.

Other Common Name
Sedum

Bloom Period and Seasonal Color
Red, pink, and yellow blooms in spring, summer, or fall.

Mature Height × Spread
4 to 24 in. × 12 to 24 in.

Cold Hardiness Zones
6a, 6b, 7a, 7b

Sweet Box

Sarcococca hookerana

This shade-loving, drought-tolerant plant has glossy, year-round evergreen foliage. Sweet box does not have showy flowers, but when it blooms some time between February and April, you know it! The name "sweet" is bestowed because of the sweet smelling flowers. Occasionally, small black berries develop as the season progresses, but they are hidden in the foliage. The most notable feature of this plant is the consistent, green, lustrous foliage, a trait important in landscape design, especially in winter settings. S. hookerana var. humilis has low-growing ground cover traits. Slightly taller is S. hookerana var. digyna, which has narrower, lighter green foliage with purplish stems. S. confusa and S. ruscifolia are less cold hardy and recommended for Zone 8 or in protected areas of Zone 7.

Other Common Name
Himalayan Sweet Box

Bloom Period and Seasonal Color
Evergreen foliage with non-showy white blooms in late winter, early spring.

Mature Height × Spread
1 to 1½ ft. × 1 to 3 ft.

Cold Hardiness Zones
6b, 7a, 7b

When, Where, and How to Plant
Spring planting of sweet box is better since it helps it establish before winter. This plant prefers sites with afternoon shade and somewhat acidic soil. It tolerates alkaline soils but is not as prolific. Sweet box grows in protected areas of Zone 6, but the risk of winter injury is great. Loosely dig holes 2 to 3 times wider than the rootballs and the same depth. Water is essential during the establishment period. Mulch is vital in any landscape bed, especially with this tough shrub. Space plants about 15 to 18 inches apart when planting. The plants are very slow growing, so if you want an instant filled look consider planting them a foot apart.

Growing Tips
Supplemental water is needed during drought periods until plants are established. Once it is established, sweet box is quite drought tolerant and prefers somewhat drier shade. Supplemental fertilization is usually not needed unless the foliage shows nutrient deficiencies. Reapply mulch to keep weeds at bay until plants are well established.

Care
Some selections spread as a result of stoloniferous growth but are not aggressive. The spreading growth easily emerges through any mulch. Pruning is seldom needed, other than to keep the plant in specified areas. Pests are not serious concerns. Drought tolerance is relative with this plant. It takes less water than most ground covers and will tolerate drier soils. However in severe drought, supplemental watering is beneficial for the livelihood of the plant.

Landscape Merit
Use dwarf sweet box as a border plant near sidewalks or for the front of landscape beds. Because of its spreading nature, it is a great filler plant, reaching only 12 to 18 inches

My Personal Favorite
For a ground cover selection, the species form *Sarcococca hookerana* is the only way to go.

Vinca

Vinca minor

When, Where, and How to Plant

Plant vinca in spring, early summer, or fall. Vinca likes partial dappled or afternoon shade. Full sun has a tendency to scorch the leaves. The plants are considered fairly quick growers, especially when planted in moist, fertile soils. Space plants 12 inches apart from center to center to get the quickest fill. If spaced wider apart, they take longer to grow together. Dig holes wider than and the same depth as the rootballs of the plants.

Growing Tips

Supplemental water is needed during drought conditions. Mulch keeps weeds in check and retains moisture during the establishment period. The vines easily grow through the mulch as they mature. Fertilizing speeds up the growth for a quicker fill. Be careful not to overdo it and burn the foliage, especially with granular fertilizers. Slow-release products, whether organic or synthetic, work well to feed the plants over a longer period of time.

Care

Pruning is seldom needed other than to trim back growth escaping from the border. Occasional leaf and stem diseases occur as well as powdery mildew in heavy shade with poor air circulation. Watch for occasional scale insects. Most over-the-counter products labeled for the appropriate pest will maintain the problem.

Landscape Merit

Use the plants as fillers for borders and landscape beds or as a quick-growing ground cover under trees. Plant vinca so that it cascades over walls. Vinca is a great cascading plant to use in color bowls or container displays as well as in window-boxes. I like to use it with Acorus 'Ogon'. The texture combinations are quite unique.

My Personal Favorite

'Illumination' does just that in my shade gardens. The variegated green and yellow shiny leaves are truly traffic stopping. The plants tend to revert back to solid green with age, so I have to keep the green growth trimmed out. The extra work is well worth the result.

This ground-hugging plant is widely grown and commonly used in landscapes. Most cultivars are evergreen; however, there are a few deciduous selections. Many perennial periwinkles have attractive flowers early in the spring with sporadic blooms through the summer and fall. The flowers are pleasant enough, but the plant is probably better known for its tough growth and attractive foliage. The perennial ground cover periwinkle should not be confused with the annual flowering periwinkle or vinca (Catharanthus roseus). Popular V. minor cultivars include 'Ralph Shugert', an elegant, white-variegated leaf form with colorful blue-purple flowers; 'Alba', 'Emily Joy', and 'Jekyll's White', with white flowers and green foliage; 'Bowles' ('La Grave') and 'Shademaster', with lavender flowers; and 'Rosea', with a violet-pink color. Double-flowering types are 'Mutliplex' and 'Rosea Plena'.

Other Common Names
Common Periwinkle, Trailing Myrtle

Bloom Period and Seasonal Color
Pink, purple, and white blooms in April and March.

Mature Height × Spread
3 to 10 in. × 12 to 24 in.

Cold Hardiness Zones
6a, 6b, 7a, 7b

Ornamental Grasses & Grasslike Plants *for Oklahoma*

Ornamental grasses are also considered perennial herbaceous plants, but because of their unique qualities and specific popularity, I have placed them in a separate chapter. Although pampas grass and maiden grass are the most well known, other landscape grasses have caught the attention of gardeners. Many of the grasses in this chapter are true prairie grass plants.

True grasses are members of the Poaceae, or grass family. Lawngrass typically comes to mind when we think of grass, but miscanthus, pennisetum, and panicum are also true grasses – just bigger and more ornate. Others in this chapter, like liriope, mondo, acorus, and sedge, are not really true grasses but are often categorized as ornamental grasses because of their growth habit and texture.

Ornamental grasses provide landscape intrigue, providing height, texture, softness, color and sound. Most are clump-forming and noninvasive plants send up flower plumes, known as "inflorescences," which later change to seed spikes. Some provide seed for birds; others are great additions to dried arrangements. Ornamental grasses often become the center of attention in late summer and fall. And like most perennials, they get better with age, almost doubling in size the year after planting.

On Home Turf

Oklahoma is known for its grasslands, particularly the tall grass prairie near Bartlesville. Visit in the fall and you will see why many of these beauties are making their way into the landscape as specimens. One way the state's eco-regions are divided is according to the different prairie grass plants with divisions of short, tall, or mixed prairie grasses. For example, short grasses cover the Panhandle, mixed grasses become more prominent east of the Panhandle, and cross timbers and southern tallgrass occupy the middle of the state. This goes hand in hand with our diverse climate, soil types, and rainfall detailed on the hardiness zone map in the book's introduction and other maps in the Appendix.

Ornamental Grasses Add Depth and Texture

Maiden Grass

You probably will not find ornamental grasses in the garden centers until late spring or early summer because they are slow to break dormancy in the spring. They lack eye appeal early on, but as the season progresses, their landscape brilliance and grandeur increase.

When to Prune

Most ornamental grasses go dormant in the winter. That is when some selections appear most spectacular with golden foliage, feathery seed plumes and the dried foliage rustling in the winter winds. You should leave the foliage in place all winter on most selections. Many grass species seedheads are also showy during the winter. Certain species tend to reseed easily, such as inland wild oats and 'Moudry' pennisetum. For such species, enjoy the seed plumes early on, but cut them off prior to ripening and falling on the ground.

The main maintenance chore is cutting back the dormant foliage in early spring to 4 to 8 inches from the soil just as the new, green growth begins to peek through. Ornamental grasses are truly multi-season plants. During the first few weeks of emergence, ornamental grass looks much like a typical grass. As it grows taller, the foliage starts to cascade, mound, or stand at attention, depending upon the species. The airy foliage softens harsh corners, provides dramatic contrasting texture, and offers subtle color choices for any landscape. As the summer progresses, the seed stalks emerge, further changing the appearance with assorted colors and shapes. When the flowers are pollinated and start to dry, they glisten in the sunlight, becoming almost translucent. In the fall, the plants will be at their peak for all to enjoy.

Warm-season ornamental grasses typically go dormant during the winter, emerge in the spring, and actively grow when the temperatures rise. They traditionally bloom later in the summer or fall and thrive in full sun. Cool-season grasses, on the other hand, put on their best growth when temperatures are cooler in the fall or spring. They ordinarily just sit there in the summer heat and perform better in Oklahoma with partial or afternoon shade. Most of the time, they bloom earlier in the year. Some cool-season grasses are semi-evergreen or evergreen during the winter, depending on the severity of the cold temperatures. Planting ornamental grasses with evergreen shrubs often intensifies the winter colors. The loosely textured grasses also are very compatible with coarser broadleaf plants and hardscape items such as rocks, birdbaths, and other garden art.

Ornamental grasses are moderate feeders and respond to supplemental fertilizer applications. Always wash off the foliage after applying granular fertilizer to avoid discoloration and never apply fertilizer to wet foliage or it can burn the plants. Ornamental grasses put on quite a show and perform best in fertile, moist soils. Mulching is always beneficial, and supplemental irrigation will be needed during severe dry spells. Pests are usually no threat. As the clumps mature, divide them in early spring prior to emergence for warm-season types or in fall or early spring for cool-season types. Replant smaller divisions, then share others with your gardening friends.

Bushy Bluestem
Andropogon glomeratus

Bushy bluestem is found in marshy, damp sites through-out eastern and southern Oklahoma. Its bushy, upright growth contrasts the compact, dense, feathery flower spikes sent up in the fall. When grown in clumps, the grass offers a wonderful texture to any landscape. Related is big bluestem (A. gerardii), a prairie native that makes a great landscape plant thanks to its blue-green foliage, purplish undertone flowers, and bronze-red fall color. 'Pawnee' is a robust, big bluestem variety with superior fall color. A. hallii, or sand bluestem, is a dry-land, upright, clumping grass with gray-green summer color and golden-red autumn color. A. capillipes 'Valdosta Blue' has chalky-blue foliage stretching four feet in height; its fall color is burgundy. Drought tolerant little bluestem (Schizachyrium scoparium) has delicate blue-green foliage and shorter growth.

Other Common Names
Bushy Broomsedge, Beardgrass

Bloom Period and Seasonal Color
Off-white blooms in fall with coppery gold or cinnamon fall foliage.

Mature Height × Spread
2 to 4 ft. × 2 to 3 ft.

Cold Hardiness Zones
6a, 6b, 7a, 7b

When, Where, and How to Plant
Plant bushy bluestem in the spring, summer, or fall. This beauty is hard to find in the nursery trade. You may have luck at nurseries in the state known for native plant material or specialty mail-order companies. Rich, moist garden soils often promote even more vigorous clumps. It prefers full sun but accepts a couple of hours of shade. Check container-grown plants for potbound roots; remove them, especially if there in a mesh. Place the plants in the ground at the same level that they were grown. Space the plants on 3- to 4-foot centers. Mulch them to hold in more moisture and minimize weed growth. Water at planting.

Growing Tips
Supplemental fertilizer is seldom needed, but slow-release products applied at planting time helps provide a steady supply of nutrition during the first few years. Supply non-vigorous plants with granular applications of fertilizer or use brands that dissolve and are applied with water for a quicker growth response. Do not overfertilize it or the plants will flop over.

Care
Since the plant is native to marshy conditions, it is important that supplemental irrigation be available during drought conditions. The grass is especially attractive during the winter. Leave the coppery foliage on until early spring then cut back 4 to 6 inches from the ground. Pests are rare.

Landscape Merit
Plant this unique native in groups of three or more for the best display in the landscape. Use it among colorful flowering perennial beds to offer eye-appealing texture and outline. The upright growth gives the appearance of height to shorter buildings and structures. Plant this deciduous native grass in combination with evergreen shrubs. The bushy plants are quite diverse, growing in moist or even waterlogged sites, and I have seen it grown in bog gardens.

My Personal Favorite
Named cultivars are rare in the trade. The species is most widely used in native landscapes, especially in poorly drained sites.

Fountain Grass
Pennisetum alopecuroides

When, Where, and How to Plant

Plant container-grown fountain grass in the ground in late spring or early summer. Fountain grass prefers full sun. Too much shade reduces flower spikes. Rich humus soils are perfect but not necessary; moisture retention and good drainage are more critical. The plants tolerate most soil types with a pH of 5.5 to 7.5. Trim root-bound plants by cutting off 2 or 3 inches of the mat and scoring the sides 3 or 4 times to promote more horizontal growth. Space the plants 3 to 4 feet apart.

Growing Tips

Though drought tolerant once established, you should water during severe droughts or the foliage tips will scorch and the blooms will not fully emerge. Fertilize the new growth once when 8 to 10 inches tall and again in midsummer before the flower plumes emerge.

Care

Trim the dormant growth 4 to 6 inches from the ground in early spring before new growth emerges. If you wait too long, new growth grows up into the old, making it hard to cut without damaging the new, lush foliage. Spider mites, a minimal threat, are the primary pest problem. Lace bugs pester *Pennisetums*, too, by sucking juices from foliage. Speckled foliage indicates spider mite and lace bug attack. Control by applying organic or synthetic materials at the first sign of the pest and repeat throughout the growing season.

Landscape Merit

Use 2- to 4-foot plants on landscape corners, near hardscape items, or as a background or border. Plant in groups of 3, 5, or 7 for an imposing display.

My Personal Favorite

I especially like 'Moudry' with distinct black seed plumes that resemble a bottle brush. Unfortunately, it reseeds aggressively in my adjoining flowerbeds and lawn. I learned to quickly remove seedheads before they begin to dry or turn brown. Even still, I get several weeks of enjoyment from plume-shaped bloom spikes.

Fountain grass is one of my favorites because the uniform cascading foliage looks like a fountain rising from the earth. In late May, June, or July, emerging flower plumes resemble a bottlebrush. Some are elongated and narrow while others are quite showy and wide. Pennisetum seed spikes do not hold up in the winter as well as Miscanthus spikes. But the foliage retains an attractive color and shape throughout the winter months. The soft foliage easily hides unsightly objects and softens landscape corners. P. alopecuroides is the standard species, maturing around four feet. 'Japonicum' is the tallest selection, reaching nearly five feet. 'Little Honey' grows to one foot with variegated foliage. P. caudatum and its cultivars have whiter seedheads while P. setaceum and its selections have pinker flowers.

Other Common Names
Hardy Fountain Grass, Chinese Pennisetum

Bloom Period and Seasonal Color
White, pink, and reddish-brown plumes in midsummer.

Mature Height × Spread
2 to 5 ft. × 2 to 5 ft.

Cold Hardiness Zones
6a, 6b, 7a, 7b

Inland Wild Oats

Chasmanthium latifolium

Inland wild oats are readily found in the shaded woods of Oklahoma. This ornamental grass is a good choice for the shade garden. The bamboo-like foliage is dark green, especially in shade. When it receives more sunlight, the foliage takes on a light green, almost yellowish appearance. The plants come back each spring from the crowns and even more so from the seeds. In late summer, the flower spikes shoot up from the foliage, turning into showy seeds that droop as they mature. The seed display becomes more prominent in the fall and winter as seeds turn a coppery color. The dormant, beige foliage and bronze seedheads make a wonderful winter display. They are also frequently used as a cut or dried flower. Inland wild oats is sometimes sold as Uniola latifolia.

Other Common Names
Northern Sea Oats, River Oats

Bloom Period and Seasonal Color
Green to bronze spikes in late summer through fall.

Mature Height × Spread
2 to 4 ft. × 2 to 3 ft.

Cold Hardiness Zones
6a, 6b, 7a, 7b

When, Where, and How to Plant
Plant inland wild oats seeds in the late fall or early spring, preferably ³/₄ deep in a container. Place them in a greenhouse or sunroom to avoid freezing temperatures. Be aware that many flowers are sterile and may not germinate. Set out containers in late spring or summer. Divide in the spring, planting these tough plants in their only special requirement, moist soil. Inland wild oats prefer sandy-type soils but tolerate heavier sites. Cut pot-bound roots of container-grown plants and score the sides before planting. Place container-grown plants at the same depth of their containers and two times wider than the rootballs, spacing plants on 2-foot centers. Mulch the plantings to minimize weed growth and to retain soil moisture. Water after planting.

Growing Tips
Water on a regular basis. Use slow-release or organic fertilizers only in poorer soils during late spring or early summer as new growth begins to elongate.

Care
Prune in early spring to remove last season's growth as the new foliage peeks through the soil. Pests are highly unlikely. In perennial gardens with loose exposed soil, the seed can readily germinate and become a nuisance. If seedlings become a problem, thickly mulch so the seeds are hindered from penetrating the soil. Also, trim the seedheads before they turn brown completely dry and ripen. Do not put them in the compost pile, or you will get seedlings there, too. Glyphosate herbicide spot treats unwanted seedlings, but don't spray other prized plants.

Landscape Merit
Use these upright plants as background or feature plants, grown in clusters of 3 or more, or plant them to give a hedge-like appearance. Choose inland wild oats for an edging plant near water or bog gardens.

My Personal Favorite
Improved or named cultivars are not readily found; the species is the most commonly available.

Japanese Blood Grass

Imperata cylindrica

When, Where, and How to Plant

Plant container-grown plants in spring or early summer in a place where the plants are backlit with filtered morning sunlight. Japanese blood grass prefers afternoon or lightly dappled shade. It prefers moist, humus-rich, organic soils, but it tolerates sandy loam soils. It accepts clay-soil sites as long as they drain well. Poor, unimpressive growth results from poorly drained soils or hot, dry areas. In rootbound container plants, remove the very base of the winding roots; score the sides to encourage horizontal growth and water penetration. Space the plants 10 to 12 inches apart. Set the plants at the same depth that they were grown and dig holes somewhat wider than the rootballs. Mulch for weed control and moisture retention. Dig out sections that try to revert to a green color, and retain the vibrant reds and purples.

Growing Tips

Drought conditions stunt this plant and scorch the foliage quite readily; supplemental irrigation is needed. Feeding is not necessary unless the soils are non-fertile from the start. Apply fertilizer when the growth begins to emerge and is 4 to 6 inches tall in the spring and again in midsummer.

Care

Each spring trim the old foliage back to the ground before any new, green growth emerges. This plant has no serious pest problems. In highly organic moist soils, the grass can slowly creep into unwanted areas. Avoid the invasive relative, Cogon grass.

Landscape Merit

Use this exciting grass as a mass planting near borders or edges of water gardens. Combine it with bolder, broader-foliaged plants and even variegated or yellow-leaved shrubs or perennials. Japanese blood grass impacts viewers when coupled with shade-loving miniature or dwarf impatiens in container or patio. I use it primarily in partially shaded areas that are framed with a building or sidewalks so as to keep the grass from spreading.

My Personal Favorite

'Red Baron' has even showier reddish foliage color that intensifies in the fall.

Japanese blood grass is wonderful because of its blood-red foliage and manageable size. Seldom reaching more than fifteen to eighteen inches tall, it spreads by rhizomes, forming colonies of brilliant color and adding texture to the garden and landscape. It is one of the few ornamental grasses without additional appeal like flowers and seed plumes. Once you see the magnificent color of the foliage, you will not care that it does not have showy flowers. The new spring growth emerges green with hints of red that increase with age. It achieves the best show of color and vigor in moist soils with partial sun, preferably in the morning. Choose appropriate planting locations since it can with time spread into adjoining flower beds.

Other Common Names
Red Baron Grass, Satin Tale Grass

Bloom Period and Seasonal Color
Red foliage in summer.

Mature Height × Spread
15 to 20 in. × 15 to 24 in.

Cold Hardiness Zones
6a, 6b, 7a, 7b

Lily Turf
Liriope muscari

Lily turf's lush, thick foliage is heat and humidity tolerant, making it a perfect plant for Oklahoma landscapes. The foliage ranges from deep, dark green to various shades of yellow or silver variegation. Many selections are evergreen. An added bonus in some selections is the flower spikes in May or June. The usually lilac-colored blooms are quite showy and seem to be more prolific when grown in sun. Harder to find are the white-flowering selections. Both produce small, dark-fruited berries late in the season. L. muscari improved selections are purple- or lilac-flowering forms and include 'Big Blue', 'Lilac Beauty', and 'Majestic'. 'Monroe White', 'Alba', and 'Traebert White' are white-flowering forms. If variegated foliage strikes your fancy, consider 'Variegata', 'Silvery Sunproof', 'Silvery Midget', 'John Burch', and 'Gold Banded'.

Other Common Names
Monkey Grass, Liriope, Blue Lily Turf

Bloom Period and Seasonal Color
Purple and white blooms in summer.

Mature Height × Spread
6 to 24 in. × 12 to 18 in.

Cold Hardiness Zones
6a, 6b, 7a, 7b

When, Where, and How to Plant
Start liriope in the landscape from container-grown or bare-root plants in the spring, summer, or early fall. Liriope prefers moist, organic soils, but this tough plant grows in almost any ordinary soil. Most liriope prefer afternoon shade, but some selections tolerate full sun sites. Pull apart pot-bound roots before planting. If exceedingly dense, cut the roots to loosen the rootball. Plant them in holes dug the same depth as the plant root system and somewhat wider. Space plants 8 to 15 inches apart, depending on the desired quickness of fill. Mulch them to minimize weed growth and retain soil moisture.

Growing Tips
Plants respond better to supplemental irrigation in severe droughts, although they accept somewhat dry conditions. Fertilize when the new growth begins to emerge. Water after fertilizing to prevent spotting of the foliage. Incorporating a slow-release fertilizer at planting time is also a practice worth the extra expense.

Care
Even though lily turf is often evergreen, it frequently succumbs to winter burn of the foliage. Each spring before new growth emerges, shear damaged foliage to the ground. In larger beds, it is a common practice to use a lawn mower, but mow high so you do not scalp the plant crown. Mealybugs, scale, and spider mites are occasional pests. Grasshoppers are pests in more rural areas. Fungal leaf spots and crown rot occur in wet, poorly drained sites.

Landscape Merit
The most popular use is as a mass planting for borders or fill. Its low-growing nature makes it compatible with sidewalk or edging locations. Liriope divides landscape sections where low-growing, contrasting plants are needed. It is perfect as an upright textured ground cover. It also adds texture in odd numbered groups when used in the partially shaded perennial garden.

My Personal Favorite
'Peedee Gold' (a.k.a. Peedee Ingot) is absolutely stunning. The chartreuse color brightens up my shady garden and makes a nice contrast plant with black mondo grass and *sedum makinoi* 'Ogon'.

Maiden Grass
Miscanthus sinensis

When, Where, and How to Plant

Plant containerized grasses in the spring or early summer. Plant bare-root plantlets in late spring. These grasses like moisture-retentive but well drained soils. Fertile soils will encourage vigorous growth; however, these elegant grasses tolerate most sites. They prefer full-sun locations. Trim a potbound rootball to better initiate horizontal root growth. Space plants 2 to 5 feet apart, depending on the selection.

Growing Tips

In severe droughts, the plants need supplemental irrigation so they will send up the beautiful flower plumes. Fertilizer is optional; the grassy plants respond to supplemental applications in late spring and early summer.

Care

Cut dormant foliage off in early spring to at least 6 to 8 inches from the ground before green growth emerges. Pests are generally of no concern; however, miscanthus mealybug can be a problem. Homeowners typically have nothing to worry about unless the bug is passed on at the point of purchase. Most miscanthus plants outgrow the pest with proper watering and fertilization. Remove the foliage when it is dormant in the winter.

Landscape Merit

Miscanthus cultivars make perfect singular specimen plants and do well in groups of three or more. I use them most often as upright, bushy specimens near corners of structures where they soften harsh angles. Their winter display has a lot of eye appeal, but planting them in combination with evergreen plants makes for an even better display. Interplant the narrow-leaved, textured grasses as companions to broadleaf, coarse foliage plants. Some of the taller and wider selections work as hedges to block unsightly views, but only later in the season. The graceful plants tone down vertical structures such as light poles, archways, and two-story homes.

My Personal Favorites

I like 'Adagio' and 'Little Kitten' because of their compact growth—4 to 5 feet 3 to 4 feet respectively. Both send up seed plumes earlier in the summer that hold up well all season long even into early winter.

These robust clumping grasses with narrow foliage and whimsical feathery plumes provide year-round excitement. The foliage emerges each spring, later sending up magical plumes. The plant holds up most of the winter, making for a lively presentation, especially when the winter winds bring the foliage to life. 'Gracillimus' is one of the tallest, maturing around eight feet and blooming late in the season. 'Adagio', 'Dixieland', 'Nana', and 'Nippon' are the smallest Miscanthus, reaching only three to four feet. 'Bluetenwunder' ('Flower Wonder') has a blue tinge to the foliage, and 'Purpurascens' ('Autumn Red') is more reddish, especially in the fall. Variegated types include 'Strictus' and 'Zebrinus' with horizontal gold bars across the leaf blades. 'Variegatus' has white-striped, arching leaves. 'Cabaret', 'Cosmopolitan', 'Silberfeder' ('Silver Feather'), 'Goldfeder' ('Gold Feather'), and 'Morning Light' are also variegated.

Other Common Names
Maiden Hair Grass, Miscanthus, Eulalia

Bloom Period and Seasonal Color
Yellow, pink, and red blooms in late summer and fall.

Mature Height × Spread
3 to 7 ft. × 4 to 6 ft.

Cold Hardiness Zones
6a, 6b, 7a, 7b

Mondo Grass

Ophiopogon japonicus

Mondo grass is often confused with liriope, but mondo has narrower foliage and metallic-blue fruit, is not quite as cold hardy, and prefers shade. The narrower and shorter foliage creates a slightly different texture from liriope. Mondo grass is evergreen in milder winters. In severe winters, the foliage has a tendency to burn, especially on the tips of the leaves. Mondo grass establishes slowly, but once it does, it makes a spreading groundcover, filling in and around shaded perennial and landscape shrub beds. I have even seen it grow into poorly established lawns in moist sites. In addition to the upright green species, 'Variegatus' has white margins. 'Nana' is the dwarf selection, reaching only two to three inches high. Flowing clumps provide a manicured appearance as mondo grass spreads.

Other Common Name
Dwarf Lily Turf

Bloom Period and Seasonal Color
Light blue blooms in summer.

Mature Height × Spread
6 to 12 in. × 4 to 18 in.

Cold Hardiness Zones
6b, 7a, 7b

When, Where, and How to Plant
Plant mondo grass in the spring or summer, placing it in a site with afternoon shade or dappled light. Avoid fall planting since there is generally not enough time for the plants to establish before winter sets in. Remove or loosen potbound roots for better horizontal establishment. Space plants 6 to 12 inches apart in fertile, moist soils. Plant them at the same depth that they were grown in their containers, but dig the holes somewhat wider than the rootballs. Mulch them with a light organic product, such as shredded leaves or fine pine bark, to keep weeds at bay until the plants are established. The underground stems emerge more readily through the lighter mulch.

Growing Tips
Watering during drought is essential. Side-dress the plants with a fertilizer in spring and again in early summer. Be careful not to burn the foliage. Reapply mulch as needed until the plants thickly fill the area.

Care
Trim foliage burned from winter close to the ground in early spring before new growth emerges. Trim the flower spikes and fruit in midsummer if they are not wanted. In the first year of establishment, remove the flower spikes to permit more energy to reach the leafy green foliage. Pests are not always problems, but slugs, snails, and grasshoppers occasionally chew the foliage. Spider mites accompany the plants home from the point of sale. Leaf spots and crown rot occur in sites that are poorly drained and poorly aerated.

Landscape Merit
Mondo grass is the ideal plant for edging sidewalks and borders. Because of its spreading nature, use it as a ground cover in larger landscape situations where filler is needed. Use as a textured plant in patio container displays.

My Personal Favorite
A truly spectacular mondo grass is black mondo (*O. planiscapus*) with deep-purple, almost black foliage. The very slow-growing species is available in several cultivars: 'Ebony Knight' ('Ebknizam'), 'Nigrescens', and 'Nigra'.

Muhley Grass
Muhlenbergia capillaris

When, Where, and How to Plant

Muhley grass can be planted in the spring or fall. Muhley grass is easy to start from seed and occasionally reseeds in landscapes where bare soil is exposed. Like most grasses, pot-grown plants tend to be rootbound and need to be teased apart before planting so the roots don't continue growing in a circle. The plants are native to moist habitats but also do well in drier soils. Organically amended soils provide the best growth and uniformity, but again the plants will tolerate poorer soils. Good drainage is a must.

Growing Tips

Muhley grass is somewhat drought tolerant once established, but in severe drought, supplemental irrigation is necessary. Drought-stressed plants tend to scorch, and the flower heads will be stunted, if they emerge at all. Supplemental feeding is typically not necessary in rich organic soils. In poorer soils, slow-release fertilizers help provide a steady supply of nutrition.

Care

Shear or trim last season's growth in early spring (typically late February or early March) before new growth starts to emerge. Mature clumps can be trimmed back to 5 or 6 inches, whereas younger plants can be sheared back as much as 4 inches. The plant clumps can be divided after several years as necessary.

Landscape Merit

Because of its tough nature, Muhley grass is a great choice for a low-growing grass near a driveway or street. It also a nice choice for island beds surrounded by concrete as long as supplemental irrigation is provided. Use it in large amounts for a magnanimous display. In perennial beds, single specimens work well to offer texture and early fall color from the flowers. The compact height blends in with most designs.

My Personal Favorite

Regal Mist™ is an improved selection with reddish-pink flowers.

Muhley grass is a wonderful southeastern U.S. native plant with a bad common name. It has wonderful airy, narrow, needle-like foliage all summer long that seldom cascades. Then in early fall, pinkish seedheads emerge like pink clouds of smoke rising from the plant. The inflorescence last about six to eight weeks, eventually turning brown as winter approaches. The foliage is a pale, grayish green which really compliments the late display of color. Compared to most ornamental grasses, it is tough, compact, and offers a lot of options in the landscape. The clumping growth is easy to manage— a brilliant addition to any landscape!

Other Common Names
Hairy Awn Muhley, Pink Puff Grass, Mist Grass

Bloom Period and Seasonal Color
Pinkish seedheads in late summer and early fall.

Mature Height × Spread
2 to 3 ft. × 2 to 3 ft.

Cold Hardiness Zones
6b, 7a, 7b

Plume Grass
Erianthus ravennae

Ravenna grass is an alternative to the coarse, overgrown appearance of pampas grass. Pampas grass has its place in wide, open spaces but rarely fits into most landscape situations. Ravenna, on the other hand, has the towering height without the coarseness, making it a perfect landscape ornamental grass. The typical growth habit of plume grass is clumping, with long, strap-like, greenish-gray foliage offset with a white stripe down the center of the leaf. The flower plumes (thirty or more per mature clump) emerge in late summer with silvery blooms changing to gray as they pollinate and mature. The glistening silver plumes (occasionally with a hint of purple) arise above the foliage starting in August or early September, creating an awesome, towering effect. The fall foliage usually turns from orange to beige to purple.

Other Common Name
Ravenna Grass

Bloom Period and Seasonal Color
Silver plumes in late summer with beige, orange, and purple fall foliage.

Mature Height × Spread
8 to 12 ft. × 4 to 5 ft.

Cold Hardiness Zones
6a, 6b, 7a, 7b

When, Where, and How to Plant
Plant ravenna grass in spring or summer. Divide ravenna grass in the spring. It prefers full-sun locations. Plume grass is truly an exception to the rule as far as typical soil type. Plant it in very fertile soil, and the foliage becomes excessive, sometimes falling over. It is more manageable in sites with poorer soils, but avoid poorly drained, heavy soils. Waterlogged sites usually mean certain doom for this rugged plant. For a potbound plant, cut off the lower few inches of roots and score the sides of the rootball. Otherwise, the container plant takes longer to establish and continues to be rootbound in its new home. In such cases, thorough water penetration is almost impossible. The sheer magnitude of the plant dictates the need for plenty of space, usually at least 4 to 5 feet square. Water the grass after planting and on a regular basis until it is established. Mulch it to keep weeds out and moisture in.

Growing Tips
Fertilizer is usually not needed because the plant becomes overpowering. In such cases, the foliage clumps open up and fall over. It is fairly drought-tolerant once established and does not need too much pampering except during severe drought. As with most grasses, severe drought will hinder the seed plume emergence.

Care
Cut the dormant foliage back in early spring as soon as the new, green growth emerges. It is often necessary to cut out the flower stalks in early winter before they fall over and mask the still attractive foliage. There are no serious pest problems.

Landscape Merit
It is often used as an accent plant, a specimen, or a screen. The graceful foliage is perfect for softening the harsh corners of structures or adding a lively element to formal designs.

My Personal Favorite
Named cultivars are rare. The species provides great landscape textural benefits.

Reed Grass
Calamagrostis species

When, Where, and How to Plant

Plant reed grass in spring, summer, or fall. It prefers full-sun locations; it accepts some shade, but no more than four or five hours. Planting reed grass in too much shade decreases flowering and causes lax, open foliage. Reed grass does well in fertile or average soils. It tolerates dry or moist sites as long as the soils are not excessively waterlogged. Attend to potbound plants before planting. Trim off the roots at the base, and score them on the sides to allow for more horizontal growth, spacing them 3 to 4 feet apart. Mulch plants for weed control and moisture retention of the soil. Water deeply after planting to encourage good root formation, and on a regular basis until plants are well established.

Growing Tips

Reapply mulch as needed. Water plants during extremely dry periods, especially the first year of establishment. Apply supplemental feedings in spring and again in early summer if needed. The plants respond well to feedings like most grasses and typically will let you know when it is time to fertilize based on the color and vigor of the plant.

Care

Occasionally, this cool-season grass overwinters as an evergreen in milder winters. The foliage is damaged during extremely cold periods. Remove damaged or dormant foliage in very early spring. Pests are typically not destructive. Rust is more likely in heavily shaded locations and affects stressed plants.

Landscape Merit

The upright form of the inflorescences makes reed grass an architectural dream. *Calamagrostis* is a medium-sized ornamental grass. Use it as a specimen or in clusters, especially on harsh corners or in blocky designs. The upright, vertical form gives height to smaller structures, even though the plant remains around 4 to 5 feet in height with its plumes. Use as a hedge or background plant with proper spacing.

My Personal Favorites

I really like 'Karl Foerster', especially when used in mass planting. It looks like soldiers all at attention. 'Overdam' and 'Avalanche' are variegated versions offering the same erect texture.

This glitzy cool-season grass is one of the earliest to bloom, usually around May. The dull-green foliage is somewhat rough to the touch and formed in a tight clump. The elegant flower plumes are some of the most erect of any ornamental grass. The three- to four-feet spikes emerge green with a touch of red. As they mature, they take on golden-wheat color that lasts most of the summer. With the approach of fall, the plumes turn a light straw color. Even though reed grass is considered a cool-season grass because of its early bloom, it performs throughout the hottest days of the summer. 'Stricta' and 'Karl Foerster' are the two predominant cultivars. 'Karl Foerster' is slightly smaller and blooms a couple of weeks earlier than 'Stricta'.

Other Common Name
Feather Reed Grass

Bloom Period and Seasonal Color
Pinkish-green plumes in early summer.

Mature Height × Spread
4 to 6 ft. × 2 to 4 ft.

Cold Hardiness Zones
6a, 6b, 7a, 7b

Ruby Grass
Melinis nerviglumis

There is probably not another ornamental grass that gets as many "oohs" and "aahs" as ruby grass. The compact, uniform plant, maturing to around two feet tall and two feet wide, offers grayish-blue foliage and pink seed-heads—a color display all by itself. It also works great to complement other annuals in the landscape or in container displays. Unfortunately, the plant is best used as an annual in Oklahoma but is well worth the investment each year. It is hard to overwinter even indoors, but the seed are fairly easy to save and start new seedlings the following spring. It is finally catching on in the industry and much easier to find at your favorite specialty garden center or via the internet.

Other Common Name
Crystal Grass

Bloom Period and Seasonal Color
Flower spikes emerge pink turning to white all summer long.

Mature Height × Spread
2 ft. × 2 ft.

Cold Hardiness Zone
Grown as an annual in Oklahoma in 6a, 6b, 7a, 7b

When, Where, and How to Plant
As with all other annuals, plant ruby grass in the spring after the last chance of frost. Start with healthy plants to get quicker growth and showy plumes. Starting from seed will also work but delays the showy color for a couple of months. Fertile, well drained soils provide the best growing conditions. Although ruby grass will grow in poorer soils, it is typically not as showy. Ornamental grasses tend to be potbound or root-bound when planting from a container. Loosen the roots before planting at the same depth as the rootball. Water and mulch to get plants off to a good start.

Growing Tips
The plants respond well to supplemental feedings, especially brands that dissolve and are applied with water. Slow-release fertilizers are also good when growing ornamental grasses. The plants do not require a lot of supplemental irrigation except under severe droughts.

Care
The seed plumes go from pink to white. You can deadhead declining plumes to tidy up the plants, but it is not necessary for continuous blooms. The plants typically send up new flower plumes throughout the year. Occasionally the plant will overwinter during a mild winter. It's more typical to get a scarce seedling here or there from previous year's growth and reseeding. Transplant any loners or pot them up to share with gardening friends.

Landscape Merit
The bluish color foliage and pink seedheads show all by themselves especially when planted in mass. I use them to add color and texture in annual gardens or as filler for voided spots in a perennial landscape. They are especially attractive in container-garden displays. They are the right size to blend with almost any scale, and the colors go especially nice with pastel type plantings or vibrant shades of purple, pink, and white.

My Personal Favorite
'Pink Crystals' is a delight, going from pink to a crystal white display all summer long.

When, Where, and How to Plant

Plant *Carex* in spring, summer, or early fall. The plants like rich, humus soils typical of many woodland gardens. If such planting sites are not available, prepare them well in advance before planting time. Be careful not to damage existing tree roots by tilling the soil. Add no more than 6 inches of organic material on top of the ground; do not mix it into the original soil. Place the plants 15 to 18 inches apart, directly into the top few inches of soil, then mulch. Water them after planting and regularly.

Growing Tips

Reapply mulch as needed to keep the soil moist and weed free. Drought conditions warrant supplemental irrigation. Apply supplemental feedings as soon as new growth reaches 3 or 4 inches. Water as soon as fertilizer is applied to wash off fertilizer trapped in or on the foliage.

Care

In mild winters, the plants remain green, providing winter interest. In harsh winters, the foliage occasionally burns. Remove it in early spring. Cut back heat-damaged foliage in the fall. Trim it close to the ground without damaging the plant crown. Other than an occasional leaf fungus or rust spot, there are not problems. In severe cases, trim the foliage back and spray the new growth with a labeled foliar-disease product.

Landscape Merit

Use the small mounding plants along shaded garden paths or as a border with sidewalks. Do mass plantings in groups of 3 or 5 to make eye-catching scenes. Enjoy the grassy texture with almost any companion plant. Some species are spreading in nature and can be used as a ground cover in moist sites; it is not invasive. Japanese sedge makes a nice border plant along shade-garden pathways.

My Personal Favorites

'Evergold' is a beauty with its illuminating, creamy, variegated foliage and weeping growth habit. 'Bowles Golden' has an even more golden display. Both are perfect for group plantings in the shade garden or as a companion to impatiens in container displays.

Carex is definitely grown and known for its colorful and versatile foliage, which enhances any garden. Japanese sedge is one of the few grassy plants to actually thrive in shade. Most Carex species are cool-season grasses and are semi-evergreen to evergreen with foliage potentially attractive year-round. Ornamental sedge even tolerates moist sites near the edge of bog or water gardens. The early-spring flower spikes are not showy. 'Bowles Golden', 'Frosted Curls' and 'Aurea Variegata' have variegated foliage. More unusual colors are 'Fox Red Curly' (reddish bronze), 'Hime Kansugi' (variegated white), 'Nigra' (black), 'Blue Gray', 'Orange Colored Sedge' (orangey bronze), and 'Evergold' (lemon yellow). For unusually shaped foliage, consider C. muskingumensis or C. phyllocephala (palm sedge grass), C. buchananii (leather leaf sedge), and C. ornithopoda (bird's foot sedge). C. muckingumensis 'Wachtposten' is somewhat more tolerant of dry soils.

Other Common Name
Japanese Sedge

Bloom Period and Seasonal Color
Tan to brown spikes in spring; colorful foliage most of the year.

Mature Height × Spread
1 to 2 ft. × 1 to 2 ft.

Cold Hardiness Zones
6a, 6b, 7a, 7b

Sweet Flag
Acorus gramineus

If you have a waterlogged or a poorly drained site, use sweet flag. This iris family member is best known as a water garden container plant but does well in the landscape. It is cold hardy and quickly fills such sites with colorful foliage. Sweet flag resembles Carex with colorful, variegated foliage. The biggest difference is the thick, clumping, upright growth of sweet flag. The flowers don't contribute much to the plant's decorative value. Many selections seldom bloom. When crushed, acorus leaves and rhizomes have a cinnamon-like, spicy aroma. Cultivars include 'Pusillus', a smaller version of the standard green species; 'Masamune', with white-striped leaves; and 'Yodonoyuki', with green-and-light-green variegation. 'Ogon', 'Oborozuki', and 'Variegatus' have various degrees of golden-yellow variegation. 'Minimus Aureus' is a dwarf, variegated golden form.

Other Common Names
Japanese Sweet Flag, Acorus

Bloom Period and Seasonal Color
Green spikes in fall.

Mature Height × Spread
10 to 15 in. × 12 to 15 in.

Cold Hardiness Zones
6a, 6b, 7a, 7b

When, Where, and How to Plant
Plant sweet flag in the spring or summer in wet or moist soil. Divide when needed in the spring. Sweet flag prefers afternoon shade but tolerates heavier, more dappled shade. Full-sun locations pose the risk of leaf scorching. Space container plants on 15- to 24-inch centers. Set the plants at the same level that they were grown in their containers, in holes slightly wider than the rootballs. Mulch plants to retain soil moisture. Water them after planting and routinely if moist conditions are not prevalent.

Growing Tips
Fertilizing is seldom necessary in bog settings. If supplemental feedings are needed, apply them in the spring when the new growth is 4 to 6 inches. When grown in regular garden soil, they respond to supplemental feedings like most ornamental grasses. Let the grass appearance dictate when fertilizer needs to be applied.

Care
Sweet flag is a semi-evergreen plant under mild winter conditions. When the foliage is burned during the dormant season, cut it to ground level in the spring before new growth emerges. The plants grow quickly into multi-clumped mounds resembling an iris but with finer foliage.

Landscape Merit
Acorus is useful as a container-grown water garden plant, bog plant, or landscape plant in moist sites. I have seen it at its best in morning sun in rich, constantly moist soils. With routine watering, the unusual foliage makes this a contrasting texture plant suitable for windowboxes and patio containers. Some species, such as *A. calamus*, spread with rhizomes and are somewhat invasive, which is an acceptable characteristic in certain bog settings. Otherwise restrict these species to a container as a water garden plant.

My Personal Favorite
'Ogon' without a doubt is my choice. I use it in shade perennial gardens, as a bedding plant in shady sites with impatiens, and in full sun with pansies in the winter both in the landscape and in container displays.

Switch Grass
Panicum virgatum

When, Where, and How to Plant

Plant switch grass from seed in the fall or early spring in a container. Many improved selections do not come back "true" from seed; therefore, divide clumps in spring to propagate. For a more consistent method, set out pot-grown plants in late spring, summer, or early fall. Switch grass accepts poor soils as long as they drain well. Richer, fertile soils generally produce a more vigorous plant, and full-sun locations are the most desirable. Trim the bottom of each potbound rootball, and score the sides of the roots to open up the rootball before planting. Space plants 2 to 3 feet apart. Place the plants at the same depth that they were grown in their containers, and dig the holes wider than the rootballs to allow for more horizontal root growth. Mulch the plants to minimize weed growth and retain moisture.

Growing Tips

Once established, the plants are drought tolerant. Do supplemental feedings as the new growth reaches 10 to 12 inches and again in midsummer. Do not overdo it on the fertilizer, or the plants will get too much growth and fall apart on you.

Care

Remove the dormant foliage in early spring as the new growth emerges. Seed plumes eventually bend from the winter weather. Cut stalks back to the foliage. Remove foliage in spring. Pests are minimal.

Landscape Merit

Use switch grass as a background plant in the perennial garden, cluster it in groups of three in the landscape, or plant it in double rows for a screen later in the summer. It is a natural companion choice for wildflower or meadow gardens or as a specimen. Color, height, and texture make switch grass selections excellent choices for the landscape. *Panicum* is a deeply fibrous-rooted grass, perfect for erosion control in problematic sites.

My Personal Favorites

I would have to lean towards 'Shenandoah' because of the purplish color in the foliage. But 'Dallas Blues' is a close second with its grayish foliage and pink seedheads.

Switch grass is a wonderfully wild-looking ornamental grass and is one of the earliest to bloom. The clumping foliage is either blue or green, occasionally with a tinge of red. Its appeal improves into late summer with upright flower plumes and later fall color. Switch grass is probably the most drought-tolerant ornamental grass available. 'Rubrum' and 'Rehbraun' have more reddish colors on the foliage and flowers. 'Heavy Metal' has metallic-blue, upright foliage. 'Cloud Nine' and 'Prairie Sky' have blue-gray foliage. 'Haense Herms', 'Warrior', and 'Rotstrahlbusch' have eye-catching red autumn color. 'Squaw' has pink inflorescences. 'Northwind' has erect foliage, yellow flowers, and golden fall color. 'Strictum' is a more upright grower known for its cold hardiness. 'Trailblazer' is a spreading, almost sod-forming selection, maturing to four to five feet.

Other Common Name
Panic Grass

Bloom Period and Seasonal Color
Purplish-red to beige plumes in mid to late summer with golden, bronzy, purplish-red fall foliage.

Mature Height × Spread
4 to 8 ft. × 2 to 4 ft.

Cold Hardiness Zones
6a, 6b, 7a, 7b

Perennials *for Oklahoma*

Soft-stemmed, herbaceous plants known as perennials are the hottest-selling plants in the nursery trade. Plant them and enjoy their beauty for years to come. That does not mean they are no-maintenance plants, which is often assumed. They frequently need deadheading to encourage more bloom. The dormant foliage should be trimmed each year. Many need dividing every few years. And there are fertilizing, mulching, watering, and pest patrol duties.

The flowers of some long-blooming perennials last six to fifteen weeks. But the majority bloom only a couple of weeks throughout the growing season. To maximize perennials' to advantage, plant several different kinds with various blooming times so that something will be in bloom from spring to frost. Do not forget to choose perennials that have colorful foliage as well. I've noted which ones in the chapter have cultivars with colorful foliage. Once the bloom is gone, you have eye-appealing foliage to catch your attention throughout the growing season. Using brilliantly colored foliage perennials and long blooming perennials makes your gardening experience more rewarding and enjoyable not to mention your landscape design continuously colorful.

Where to Plant Perennials

Perennial beds need to be big enough to accommodate numerous plants. Island beds are nothing more than large beds in the middle of a lawn. Flower beds adjacent to fence rows or corners of lots are conducive to a perennial garden. Near the home, perennials should be grouped among shrubs or made focal plants in clusters of three or more, again with assorted bloom periods. Design the landscape with at least half the plants composed of evergreen shrubs or specimens to offset the dormant periods of perennials and other deciduous plants. The ideal design includes assorted blooming perennials, deciduous and evergreen shrubs, and designated locations for annuals of various colors.

Before planting time, identify the sun and shade patterns to match the plant to its preferred growing site. Soil preparation is beneficial, although you can overdo it with many perennials. Too much organic matter and high nitrogen fertilizer can stimulate plants to the point that they flop over or spread aggressively. I typically encourage folks to use slow-release organic or synthetic fertilizers, depending on your preference, tilled into the landscape bed at planting time. This helps provide a small amount of fertilizer over a longer period of time without big spurts of growth. Then on a yearly basis, apply more amounts on the surface of the soil and under the mulch as you have to remulch your beds. Always watch your plants and let them be the gage of whether more fertilizer is needed. Stunted, non-productive, chlorotic plants are often signs of poor soil

Summer Phlox, Black-Eyed Susan, and Goldenrod

A Perennial Border

nutrition. Of course it is always wise to invest in a soil test from your County Cooperative Extension Office to find out which nutrients and pH adjustments need to be made. Then incorporate nutrients and organic material weeks, even months, before you plant, and kill weeds and grass. The time, money, and patience will pay off in the long run with healthy plants and eye-catching color.

Perennials may seem to just sit there the first year after planting. But the second and third years they get bigger and better. Follow recommended plant spacing to allow for future growth. Some perennials can be downright invasive. At the nursery or garden center, ask questions about their growth habits to avoid these problems. *Houttuynia cordata* (chameleon plant) and *Oenothera berlandieri* or *O. speciosa* (evening primrose) are overpowering plants.

The Importance of Mulch

Once the perennials are in the ground, mulch, mulch, and mulch some more to retain moisture, keep weeds at a minimum, and provide slow-release nutrients. Cut back on the size of the bed or the number of plants, but never cut corners on your mulch. Mulch should be two to four inches thick depending on the mulch. Never place mulch upon the plant stem. Mulching properly will mean less work over time, and the plants will reward you for the extra effort. Weed management will be a continual task until the plants have grown together and filled open areas. Bermuda grass is notorious for creeping in from the edges, and birds and wind distribute weed seeds in the beds.

How Much Water?

Provide supplemental irrigation at a rate of one to two inches per week, especially the first year of establishment. Know your plants' water preferences. Some like moist soil, others prefer dry soil, but most like well-drained soil. When watering, always apply enough to thoroughly soak the plants root system. Quick, shallow watering encourages shallow roots, which makes plants more susceptible to cold, drought, heat scorch, and overall stress causing more pest problems.

Gardeners often debate when to remove dormant foliage. I have found the following recommendations to be effective. Leave the old foliage in place to better insulate the plants throughout the cold months, especially the first winter after planting. The dead growth withers down eventually and traps fallen tree leaves to further insulate the plants. Every spring, around early March, pull the leaves between the plants that acted as mulch, remove any dead stalks, and wait for the perennial process to start again. Trim the foliage as soon as new growth emerges in the spring. Once the plants are growing, provide supplemental fertilizer to those appearing less vigorous. The only work left is occasional trimming or deadheading of the spent flowers to further extend the blooming season.

Barrenwort
Epimedium species and hybrids

Barrenwort is not an attractive name, but the plant is anything but ugly! The semi-evergreen, perennial ground cover emerges in spring with ruby-colored, heart-shaped foliage. In a short time, loads of attractive flowers, typically crimson, pink, or yellow, peek above the dainty foliage. The foliage on many others matures to a lime or dark green. Regardless of color, the noninvasive plant spreads slowly. There are more than twenty-five species of Epimedium and many improved hybrids. 'Rubrum' is most commonly found; it has red-tinged foliage in the spring and fall. The flowers are primarily yellow with crimson tones. 'Versicolor' has spectacular early-spring, ruby foliage with chartreuse veins and seems more tolerant of dry, shade conditions. The flowers of 'Versicolor' are yellowish pink. 'Niveum' has white flowers, and 'Roseum' has pink ones.

Other Common Names
Bishop's Hat, Fairy Wings

Bloom Period and Seasonal Color
Yellow, white, pink, and red blooms in early to mid-spring.

Mature Height × Spread
8 to 18 in. × 24 to 36 in.

Cold Hardiness Zones
6a, 6b, 7a, 7b

When, Where, and How to Plant
Spring planting is best for barrenwort. Planting it in early summer is second best, with fall planting as a last resort. These perennial beauties prefer moist, yet well drained, humus-rich soils that resemble established, slightly acidic woodland sites. Prepare the soil ahead of planting time if natural woodland conditions are not available. Incorporate peat moss, soil sulfur, and other pH-changing products into the existing soil according to package directions. Do not damage shallow tree roots during bed preparation. Plant dormant bare-root plants or container-grown plants at the same depth that they were previously grown. Dig the hole at least two times wider than the rootball. Space them about 12 inch apart and mulch 2 inches thick around plants with acidic organic products, such as pine straw, pine bark, or pecan hulls.

Growing Tips
Avoid dry conditions for this perennial ground cover. Providing supplemental moisture is essential during drought conditions. Provide additional feedings after flowering and once again during the growing season. Use products including iron and sulfur to keep soils acidic.

Care
Pruning is seldom needed. Occasionally, in milder winters the foliage does not go dormant. Prune the foliage and stems in early spring just above the ground to remove ragged or discolored leaves from the previous winter and summer. There are no major pests to consider. *Epimedium* defoliates in cold winters but readily reemerges in early spring.

Landscape Merit
Use as a border plant for shade gardens, rock gardens, or perennial beds. It is also compatible as a container plant. *Epimedium* is an excellent ground cover at maturity, but gardeners must be patient. There are not many compatible plants smaller than azaleas requiring acidic soil, but *Epimedium* is the perfect low-growing border plant for azalea beds. The blooms and foliage of barrenwort add to the display during the early azalea show of flowers.

My Personal Favorite
'Lilafee' is a dwarf selection about 10 inches tall with bronzy new foliage each spring that turns green followed by violet colored flowers.

Beebalm
Monarda didyma

When, Where, and How to Plant

Plant it in spring or early summer and allow plenty of room. *Monarda didyma* and many of its cultivars are controllable but become increasingly aggressive and susceptible to disease in heavier shade. Some of the newer cultivars are less aggressive. Dry, nonproductive soil restricts the growth of beebalm, and this can be used as a restraint. Beebalm prefers moist, fertile soils. Dig the planting hole two times wider than and the same depth as the rootball. Space plants 3 to 4 feet apart. Space dwarf selections 1 1/2 to 2 feet apart. Mulch plants to conserve moisture, and water them as needed.

Growing Tips

Use slow-release organic products to provide small amounts of nutrients over a longer period of time. Replace decomposed mulch as needed. Provide supplemental irrigation during severe drought periods, or the foliage can scorch.

Care

The blooms are produced on new growth, so deadheading the spent flowers ensures additional color. Prune only to remove the dormant foliage in the fall or early spring. Watch for yellow discoloration followed by a whitish-gray color, a symptom of powdery mildew. Spray with a fungicide according to directions and move the plants to sunnier locations with better air circulation and good soil moisture to treat powdery mildew. Remove and dispose of infected, dormant foliage. Plant disease-resistant cultivars.

Landscape Merit

The cultivar size and height dictate the placement of this perennial. Individual plantings work best in the perennial garden and will typically spread. Crowding them with other perennials tends to help keep them in their allotted space. I haven't seen too many successful mass plantings of beebalm because of disease and relatively short bloom period. Off their peak season, the plants can look a little ragged even with a few sporadic blooms.

My Personal Favorite

'Petite Delight', with its uniquely crinkled, dark-green foliage and attractive lavender-pink flowers atop compact growth, resists mildew and is not as invasive.

Bees and hummingbirds love the aromatic foliage of this native Oklahoma plant. The showy flowers bloom on and off through most of the summer. 'Cambridge Scarlet' is a taller cultivar but with poor resistance to disease. 'Snow White' and 'Alba' are popular white-flowering selections. 'Marshall's Delight' (medium pink), 'Gardenview Scarlet' (red), 'Jacob Kline' (dark red), 'Blaustrumpf' (purple), 'Scorpion' (red), and 'Aquarius' (light pink) are cultivars with various levels of disease resistance. Horsemint or prairie monarda (M. punctata) has pale-yellow flowers with purple spots later in the summer, and it is found growing in dry, sandy, western locales of the state. Russell's horsemint and wild bergamot (M. russeliana and M. fistulosa, respectively) are commonly found in the eastern half of the state with pale-lavender blooms from May to September.

Other Common Names

Horsemint, Bergamot, Monarda

Bloom Period and Seasonal Color

Pink, rose, purple, and white blooms in summer.

Mature Height × Spread

1 to 3 ft. × 2 to 4 ft.

Cold Hardiness Zones

6a, 6b, 7a, 7b

Black-eyed Susan

Rudbeckia fulgida

This native prairie plant in well-established sites is like a sea of yellow at the peak of its magnificent bloom. Black-eyed Susan is a no-fuss plant that brightens any perennial garden. The golden flower petals surround a dark-brown or black center, or eye, and range in size from 2 to 5 inches wide, depending on the species. The daisy-like flowers are long-lived. The grayish-green foliage has a coarse texture due to a covering of small, stiff hairs. Rudbeckia provides a wealth of showy color for years to come.

Other Common Name
Orange Coneflower

Bloom Period and Seasonal Color
Yellow blooms in late May, June, and July.

Mature Height × Spread
2 to 6 ft. × 2 ft.

Cold Hardiness Zones
6a, 6b, 7a, 7b

When, Where, and How to Plant

Plant seed in the fall or early spring. Plant bare-root plants in the spring. Set out container plants in spring or summer. The plants are not too picky about their soil as long as it drains well; well-worked soil permits better root development. They prefer full sun but accept partial shade. Dig the planting hole slightly wider than and the same depth as the rootball. Space plants 15 to 36 inches apart, depending on the cultivar. The plants fill in the space as they age. Divide every three to five years. Water as needed during the establishment period. Mulch to keep weeds under control.

Growing Tips

Water the plants as needed. Once they are established, they are relatively drought tolerant especially when mulched. Irrigate in prolonged droughts to keep them from scorching and thinning out. Sparingly feed nonproductive plants located in poor sites.

Care

Rudbeckia plants overwinter as rosettes of foliage close to the ground. Remove old foliage in the winter or early spring. Trimming spent flowers encourages more blooms. Apply organic products at the first sign of aphids and the nasty larvae of the sawfly, which quickly skeletonize foliage if not controlled. Powdery mildew occurs more often in shade or prolonged rainy periods. Fight mildew with fungicides or by cutting back ragged foliage. The regrowth quickly emerges typically later in the season when disease pressure is not as prominent due to drier conditions.

Landscape Merit

The most magnificent display of color results from planting these perennials in drifts or uneven groups because of their lengthy bloom period. In perennial beds, *Rudbeckia* is typically placed as a middle or background plant because of its height. Black-eyed Susan is also used in wildflower gardens and sold in wildflower seed mixes depending on the species.

My Personal Favorite

'Goldsturm' is a good one and is also the 1999 Perennial Plant of the Year.

Blue Mist Spirea
Caryopteris × clandonensis

When, Where, and How to Plant

Plant blue mist spirea in spring, summer, or fall. Blue mist spirea prefers well-drained, fertile soils, but it tolerates almost any soil type or condition. Dig a planting hole 2 to 3 feet wider than and the same depth as the container root system. Space plants on 2-foot centers. No amended organic backfill is needed. Water to settle the soil, and mulch to retain moisture and control weeds.

Growing Tips

The plants prosper with a yearly feeding in spring or early summer. Some reports list blue mist spirea as being drought tolerant, but I haven't found that to be the case. Supplemental irrigation is necessary during drought periods.

Care

Flowers are produced on new season's growth. Prune weakened twigs in late winter or early spring. Occasionally, the plants are killed to the ground by severe winters, but they readily rebound in the spring. In some years, the plants decline in bloom by the end of August or early September. In such cases, shear the plants for new growth and later blooms in the fall. There are no serious pests, although spider mites and lace bugs are possible. Both cause speckled foliage from their sucking feeding habits.

Landscape Merit

With its medium-sized, uniform foliage, blue mist spirea makes a great background in a perennial garden, especially when it is used in association with evergreen companions. Plant it as a border near fence rows. This interesting plant stands alone as a specimen or catches your attention in groups of three or more. Do not locate this plant next to a frequently used sidewalk or the entrance to a home unless you are willing to dodge the numerous bees attracted to this beauty. Use this plant among pink and other pastel colors for an eye-catching display.

My Personal Favorites

It is a toss up between the chartreuse foliage and blue flowers of 'Sunshine Blue'™ and the variegated white airy foliage of a related species *C. divaricata* 'Snow Fairy'.

Blue mist spirea is occasionally grouped with shrubs, but in my garden Caryopteris acts more like an herbaceous perennial, with tender, twiggy shoots, succumbing to winter and reemerging from the crown or base in the spring. It is without a doubt one of the few plants with nearly blue flowers. The fragrant flowers emerge along the stem and are a welcome sight later in the season until frost. The plant's flowers are arranged among grayish foliage for a perfect color combination. 'Blue Mist', 'Dark Knight', and 'Longwood Blue' are easily found in Oklahoma nurseries. Other hybrid cultivars that are well worth the hunt include 'Kew Blue', 'Azure', and 'Heavenly Blue'. 'Worcester Gold' has golden-yellow foliage during the summer with blue flowers in the late summer to fall.

Other Common Names
Blue Spirea, Bluebeard

Bloom Period and Seasonal Color
Blue-lavender blooms in August, September, and October.

Mature Height × Spread
3 to 4 ft. × 3 to 4 ft.

Cold Hardiness Zones
6a, 6b, 7a, 7b

Butterfly Weed

Asclepias tuberosa

This native is often found along roadsides, in pastures, and now frequently in the landscape. The showy flower clusters appeal to the home owner and the butterflies that frequently visit the blooms. They grow best in full sun and thrive in poor, dry soils. Butterfly weed is a good choice for a butterfly garden and perfect for hot, dry, perennial garden sites. 'Gay Butterflies Mix' is a selection with orange-red, pink, and yellow flowers. 'Hello Yellow' is a vibrant yellow, blooming a couple of weeks earlier than the original orange, native species. Swamp milkweed (A. incarnata) has two cultivar selections: 'Ice Ballet' (white) and 'Soulmate' (rose-pink flowers). Grow tropical butterfly weed (A. curassavica) as a beautiful annual bedding or container plant since it is not cold-hardy this far north.

Other Common Names
Silkweed, Milkweed, Indian Posey, Orange Root

Bloom Period and Seasonal Color
Orange, yellow, red, pink, and white blooms in late spring to midsummer.

Mature Height × Spread
2 to 4 ft. × 2 to 3 ft.

Cold Hardiness Zones
6a, 6b, 7a, 7b

When, Where and How to Plant
Plant butterfly weed in the spring or early summer. It prefers full-sun locations. In its native location, butterfly weed is most commonly found in dry, poor pasture or prairie soils throughout the state. Organic, humus-rich sites are not favorable to this plant unless they drain extremely well. Place the container-grown plants in medium-height garden spots. Seed or tip-cuttings easily propagate this native beauty. Start seed-grown plants in a container in late winter or early spring. Place the plant at the same depth that it was grown, in a hole several times wider than the rootball. Space butterfly weed 3 to 4 feet from center to center when planting it in groups. Mulching is beneficial to keep weeds in check.

Growing Tips
Butterfly weed is late to emerge in the spring. Avoid planting it in sites where there is frequent disturbance of the roots. In other words, planting it in an annual bed is not a good idea. Waterlogged soils mean sure death to this plant unless it is swamp milkweed (*A. incarnata*). Overzealous care and fertilization are not recommended.

Care
This plant is truly low maintenance when it is planted in the right location. Most of the time, butterfly weed produces long, pointy seedpods. Remove seedpods and deadhead the flowers to encourage more blooms later in the season. Generally, butterfly weed is pest free, but always watch for aphids and spider mites. Leaf spot and rust disease become nuisances when the plants are in too much shade.

Landscape Merit
Butterfly weed is a "natural" addition to wildflower meadow plantings. Use this colorful beauty as a component plant in the perennial garden where it can be left undisturbed. The showy, starlike flowers enhance this plant's usefulness by itself or in groups.

My Personal Favorite
You can't beat the resilience of the native species and the showy orange flowers.

Cardinal Flower

Lobelia cardinalis

When, Where, and How to Plant

Start it from seed in the early spring, preferably in a container or directly in a weed-free bed. Set out container-grown plants anytime in the spring or early summer. Divide plants in the spring or fall. Amend soils with humus-rich, organic material, and mulch the plants after planting to further simulate preferred growing conditions. Germinate seed at temperatures around 70 degrees Fahrenheit. These beauties naturally self-sow in the wild. When you plant cardinal flower directly in a bed, become familiar with the seedling plant appearance so that you will not confuse it with a weed. The seedling grows in a basal rosette form, which gives rise to the stout foliage and flower stalks. Plant container-grown plants at the same depth as the rootballs. Water and mulch after planting to keep soils moist and cool. Spacing should be about 18 inches apart for the best display.

Growing Tips

Supplemental feedings are not necessary in moist, nutrient-rich, organic soils. Reapply mulch in perennial beds as needed; do not mulch or cover seedling rosettes formed in the fall.

Care

The flowers are borne on new growth. Trim or deadhead spent blooms to initiate more flowering throughout the season. Leave the flowers intact if you want to collect seeds, or allow the plant to reseed. The plants go dormant in the winter. Leave the winter-killed foliage until the following spring then remove the foliage as new growth emerges. The plants come back from the root crown or reseed. There are no serious insect or disease problems.

Landscape Merit

Use cardinal flower as a border or background perennial for moist, woodland sites. If you duplicate this native's habitat in your landscape, it is perfect as a shade bog plant or water garden plant.

My Personal Favorites

For a vivid red flower, you can't go wrong with 'Crown Royal' which has burgundy foliage to boot. A more compact favorite is 'Grape Knee-Hi' with purple blooms.

If you've hiked near a woodland stream in the middle of the summer, you may have seen a brilliant-red-flowering native known as cardinal flower. The vibrant, scarlet-red flowers are quite powerful in these moist, shaded sites and are usually around through June. The plants are fairly narrow and erect with serrated, elongated, deep-green foliage. Named selections include 'Summit Snow' and 'Alba' with white flowers, 'Heather Pink' with medium pink, 'Rosea' with pink, 'Twilight Zone' with soft pink, 'Arabella's Vision' with brilliant deep red, and 'Angel Song' with salmon-and-cream flowers. Hybrid crosses include 'Oakes Ames' (scarlet flowers), 'Robert Landon' (cherry-red flowers), 'Wisley' (pale-red flowers), 'Brightness' (bright, glossy-red flowers), 'Ruby Slippers' (velvety-red flowers), and 'Fan Scarlet' (red flowers).

Other Common Names
Red Lobelia, Ruby Slippers, Indian Pink, Redbirds

Bloom Period and Seasonal Color
Orange, yellow, red, pink, and white blooms in late spring to midsummer.

Mature Height × Spread
3 to 4 ft. × 2 to 2¹/₂ ft.

Cold Hardiness Zones
6a, 6b, 7a, 7b

Catmint

Nepeta × faassenii

This herbaceous perennial provides summer-long color in the landscape. It is a wonderfully bright and long-blooming plant with grayish foliage compatible with many colors. Catmint impressively thrives in poor soils, heat, and drought. It is used as a border plant, with a tidy form. Unlike its cousin mint, which is so invasive, catmint grows in a mound or spreading clump. 'Blue Wonder' seems to be the best cultivar for compact, upright growth, especially in borders. 'Blue Wonder' seldom reaches more than 15 inches tall or 24 inches wide. 'Walker's Low' is more spreading, almost like a ground cover, maturing at 10 inches by 24 inches. 'Six Hills Giant' is more upright in growth, reaching 3 to 4 feet. 'Alba' and 'Snowflake' are white-flowering forms, and 'Dawn to Dusk' is pink.

Other Common Name
Catnip

Bloom Period and Seasonal Color
Violet-blue and pink blooms in summer and fall.

Mature Height × Spread
1 to 3 ft. × 2 to 3 ft.

Cold Hardiness Zones
6a, 6b, 7a, 7b

When, Where, and How to Plant
Plant catmint in spring or summer. It prefers full-sun sites in northern counties but likes afternoon shade in hot, humid locations. Do not fuss over the soil. The most important requirement is a well-drained site. Catmint is available as seed or as a container-grown plant. Plant seeds just below the soil surface. I recommend starting them in containers and transplanting them later. Divide in the spring. Place a container-grown plant in a hole dug wider than and the same depth as the rootball. Space grouped plants 24 to 30 inches apart. Water to settle the soil, soak the roots, and establish the plants. Mulch to keep moisture in the soil weeds in check.

Growing Tips
These tough plants are quite tolerant of most environmental stresses after they are well established, usually within a couple of years. Severe drought decreases the amount and show of blooms, so provide supplemental moisture. Mulch as needed.

Care
Pruning is seldom done except to initiate new growth and blooms during a lull in flowering periods. The only pest problems are occasional spider mites. Since catmint is related to catnip, keep cats from chewing the plants during the establishment period. The plants die if too much top growth is removed before they are well rooted with plenty of foliage (again, about the second season after planting). After that, cats can graze at will.

Landscape Merit
Use catmint as a border plant framing other, taller perennials. The showy plants do well as filler plants grouped in clusters of three or more. The violet blooms complement other plants with soft pink, yellow, or other pastel colors in the garden. Use the plant singularly as a specimen in combination with other broadleaf plants such as roses, hibiscus, or cannas. It is also a great landscape substitute for lavender.

My Personal Favorite
A nice color change is the cultivar 'Sweet Dream' with soft, two-tone pink flowers on upright, clumping plants.

Coneflower
Echinacea purpurea

When, Where, and How to Plant
Plant coneflower in spring or summer. It is available as seed, dormant-root cuttings, and container-grown plants. Coneflower accepts full sun or afternoon shade. *Echinacea,* though native to dry, prairie conditions, performs better in well-drained, fertile soils. Mix in slow-release or organic fertilizers at planting to provide a nutrients continuously over time. Plant them in loose soil in holes that are slightly wider than and the same depth as the rootballs. Space plants 18 to 24 inches apart. Mulch after planting, and water on a regular basis to establish the plants.

Growing Tips
Replace decomposed or weathered mulch to keep the soil moist and weed free. Fertilize early in the season as the dormant plants emerge from their winter's rest. Surface apply organic fertilizers every couple of years underneath a new application of mulch.

Care
Removing faded flowers ensures a longer bloom period. Remove dead, dormant foliage any time during the winter months or when growth emerges in the spring. I leave the seedheads through the winter for bird feeding and remove the stalks in early spring. If seedling invasion becomes a problem, cut off seedheads before they dry. Divide plants in early spring every three to five years to thin overgrown clumps. Coneflower is fairly disease tolerant, though mildew is a problem in shade. However, it succumbs to sawfly larvae feeding on the foliage.

Landscape Merit
These long-flowering beauties are perfect for sunny borders, prairie gardens, or wildflower meadows. I have seen this tall plant used as a single specimen near mailboxes or placed in the back of perennial beds in groups. Plant it near softer-textured plants such as fountain grass, coreopsis, and catmint.

My Personal Favorites
I cannot get over the new rusty orange color of 'Orange Meadowbrite'™ (a.k.a. Art's Pride). But I'm also fond of the large flowering 'Ruby Giant' that stands upright even with 5 inch diameter or more blooms.

This native prairie plant is a real showstopper in the perennial garden. The bold flowers perched on top of stately stems and foliage provide some of the most spectacular summer displays. The daisy-like flowers are 2 to 4 inches in diameter, with dark pink, ray petals and an orange cone in the center. Coneflower is considered a long-blooming perennial with flowers emerging for five to eight weeks in the middle of the summer. The long, dark-green, strap-like leaves have a rough, bold presentation and add coarse texture in the garden. 'Purpurea', 'Leuchtstern', 'Bright Star', and 'Bravado' are the most common purple cultivars. Coneflower is also available in white with cultivars such as 'White Swan', 'Alba', and 'White Lustre'. 'Crimson Star' is known for its more crimson-violet flower petals.

Other Common Name
Purple Coneflower

Bloom Period and Seasonal Color
Purple and white blooms in summer.

Mature Height × Spread
2 to 4 ft. × 2 to 3 ft.

Cold Hardiness Zones
6a, 6b, 7a, 7b

Coral Bells
Heuchera species and hybrids

As shade garden plants, coral bells are more forgiving of dry soils, wind and heat than other shady plants though they are not drought tolerant. These mounding perennials are best grown for their foliage; however, many produce colorful flower spikes. The plants get better with age and are long lasting with minimal care. Some varieties have bronze, purple, pink, orange, peach, and white foliage or various variegated combinations of each. A close relative of Heuchera is Tiarella species (foamflower). The two species are closely related and can be crossed. Such crosses are sold as Heucherella or foamy bells and offer the same foliage and flower attributes.

Other Common Names
Alumroot, Crimson Bells, Henchera

Bloom Period and Seasonal Color
White, pink, and coral blooms in late spring or early summer.

Mature Height × Spread
10 to 24 in. × 15 to 24 in.

Cold Hardiness Zones
6a, 6b, 7a, 7b

When, Where, and How to Plant
Set out containerized plants in spring or early summer. Coral bells needs good drainage. They are very showy in any soil type, but in highly organic, fertile sites, the foliage becomes even more colorful. Space plants 2 feet apart from center to center. Divide plants every four to five years when their centers become woody. Mulch the plants to retain moisture and to minimize weed growth. Water especially during the early stages of establishment and during severe drought. Heuchera responds well to slow-release organic fertilizers applied at planting.

Growing Tips
Plants are fairly shallow rooted. Reapply mulch as needed, and water during severe droughts to keep the plants from scorching and wilting. Supplemental feedings a couple of times throughout the growing season are recommended, especially during the first couple of years if slow-release products were not applied at planting.

Care
Coral bells are often touted as no-fuss plants. The routine chores consist of trimming the dormant foliage in early spring and removing the flower spikes after they bloom. In mild winters, the plants retain their foliage, but typically they are deciduous. Remove foliage in the spring if it is scorched or tattered. Deadhead the flowers for prolonged flowering. The flowers last only a couple of weeks, but the foliage remains appealing until frost. There are no significant pests.

Landscape Merit
Their low height makes them a nice choice for border plants in the front of the flower bed or next to sidewalks when planted en masse. Use coral bells as a border in afternoon or dappled shade, as a contrast when planted in groups of three or more to be fillers in the perennial garden, or as a display in a container.

My Personal Favorites
There are so many different colors that can be grown for their brilliant foliage alone. I particularly like the contrasts of 'Amber Waves' and 'Obsidian' that provide a fall Halloween display all season long.

When, Where, and How to Plant

Some species are planted as seed in the fall, but most coreopsis are container grown and are planted in spring or summer. This plant is not picky about soil type, but it requires good drainage. It demands full sun and grows more robust in moist, fertile soils. Space the plants 15 to 24 inches apart from center to center, depending on the cultivar. Water the plants as needed, and mulch them for weed control. Divide spreading forms of coreopsis every four to five years.

Growing Tips

The plants are considered drought tolerant, but you should irrigate in severe drought. Fertilize if the foliage appears nutrient deficient. Mulch as needed to replace decomposed or weathered mulch.

Care

Coreopsis is late to emerge in the spring. The new growth is somewhat delicate in appearance at first but later becomes sturdier. Trim dormant foliage in late winter or early spring as the new growth emerges. Some cultivars reseed themselves each fall. In such cases, do not trim so that seeds may mature and drop. Deadhead in the summer to force continued bloom. Pests most likely to watch for are an occasional caterpillar that chews on the foliage or spittle bugs that pierce and suck on the foliage. With severe infestations, cut foliage to the ground, dispose of it appropriately, and fertilize with a water-soluble brand as foliage regrows Watch for mildew especially during prolonged rain.

Landscape Merit

Depending on the size of the cultivar, use coreopsis as a border, background, or filler plant. It is a favorite in wildflower meadows. The delicate foliage of some cultivars softens harsh textures in landscape designs. With its long-blooming display, place it front and center for everyone to enjoy. Massed plantings are best.

My Personal Favorites

The old time cultivars 'Moonbeam' and 'Zagreb' continue to outperform in my garden.

If you are looking for a low-maintenance, high-performance plant, look no farther than coreopsis. The flowers offer a burst of bright color for most of the growing season. Coreopsis is a long-blooming perennial that thrives in the sun. This is another native of the prairie states, and it withstands poor soils, heat, wind, drought, humidity, and cold. Birds favor these tough natives for their seed. There are many species of coreopsis, so the number of selections is impressive. The height and flower sizes vary considerably depending on the cultivar. Some are clumping and some spread or colonize. Some even have variegated foliage.

Other Common Name
Tickseed

Bloom Period and Seasonal Color
Yellow, white, pink or rose blooms in May through frost.

Mature Height × Spread
12 to 32 in. × 15 to 24 in.

Cold Hardiness Zones
6a, 6b, 7a, 7b

Cupflower

Nierembergia hippomanica

Cupflower is an elegant, fine-textured perennial or annual bedding plant, depending on where it is grown in the state. The soft, delicate, threadlike foliage is semi-evergreen in the southern and east-central regions. In milder winters, the plant remains evergreen, but in extremely cold conditions it goes dormant, reemerging the following spring. In the colder, northwest locales, the plant is best used as an annual. Nierembergia is known for its cupped, star-shaped flowers 1/2 inch in diameter. Although the plants bloom until frost, the peak bloom time is June. Cupflower has the ability to thrive in heat, drought, and humidity, which makes it an impeccable selection for Oklahoma gardens. 'Purple Robe' and 'Regal Robe' are taller, upright growers with violet-blue flowers. Both hold their color well in full sun.

Other Common Name
Nierembergia

Bloom Period and Seasonal Color
Purple or white blooms in summer.

Mature Height × Spread
4 to 15 in. × 8 to 15 in.

Cold Hardiness Zones
7a, 7b (6b with winter protection)

When, Where, and How to Plant

Plant container-grown plants in spring or summer. Avoid fall plantings since the plant has marginal cold hardiness throughout all of the state. Start seed indoors in late January. Cupflower is not picky about its soil as long as the soil drains well. Rich, fertile soils encourage more vigorous plants. Dig the planting hole two times wider than and the same depth as the rootball. Space the purple cultivars 15 inches apart. The truly dwarf, white-flowering cultivar grows in a mound, reaching 4 to 6 inches in height and width. Space these plants 6 to 8 inches apart. Mulch and water at planting and as needed.

Growing Tips

Supplemental feedings throughout the season benefit this plant. Water weekly during drought periods. Mulch in the fall after the first hard freeze to help ensure root and crown protection from severe temperature drops.

Care

This free-flowering plant usually requires pruning only in early spring to remove winter-damaged foliage. Once the plants start flowering, pruning is not needed unless the plants stall out later in the season. Lightly shearing the spent blooms and then applying fertilizer sends out new growth and more flowers. Although pests are unlikely, watch out for spider mites. In severe outbreaks, apply a miticide or horticultural oil to control the pests.

Landscape Merit

Use the purple selections that are more upright in growth as fillers in the front of a perennial garden. Or plant the purple-flowering form as a border or in windowboxes, rock gardens, or patio containers. Use the dwarf, white-flowering cultivar as an edging plant in the front of perennial or annual beds and near sidewalks. All cupflowers make impressive displays in clusters of three or more or in double rows when used as edging plants. The soft texture of nierembergia is compatible with coarser-foliage perennials, such as daylilies, coneflowers, and cannas.

My Personal Favorite

'Mont Blanc' is the mounding, white-flowering dwarf cultivar with yellow eyes.

Dianthus
Dianthus species

When, Where, and How to Plant

Plant dianthus in early spring or early fall. These cool-season plants prefer dappled sun or afternoon shade but on occasion tolerate full sun with plenty of mulch and moisture. Soil should be fertile, moist, but definitely well drained. Waterlogged soils cause crown or root rot. Many of the plants prefer somewhat alkaline soils instead of acidic soils; they are suitable for northwestern Oklahoma. Dig the hole slightly wider than and the same depth as the rootball. Place dianthus slightly above soil grade in poorer soils. The spacing for dianthus is determined by the mature size of the species, from 8 to 24 inches. Do not overcrowd plants, especially in heavy shade, or disease is more prevalent. Mulch with shredded leaves, compost, or pinebark. Thick mulch smothers the plants if it is placed too close to the plant crown.

Growing Tips

Provide supplemental irrigation during drought times. Provide minimal fertilizations, usually in early spring as new growth emerges, with a complete fertilizer containing phosphorus, potassium, and low amounts of nitrogen.

Care

The severity of the winter temperatures dictates this plant's hardiness. For evergreen species, prune to remove flowers and stalks after they bloom. The peak blooming time is late March and April, but blooming recurs in the fall on some selections. Shearing the flower stalks after bloom ensures more vigor to the plants and possible rebloom again in the fall. Cut back foliage damaged by the winter in very early spring, usually February or early March. Other than occasional aphids, pests are not a concern; watch out for powdery mildew.

Landscape Merit

The small clumping and dainty height are perfect for borders, rock gardens, edging plants, or container patio displays. The grayish spike-like foliage on some selections makes a nice contrast plant in the perennial garden.

My Personal Favorites

'Bath's Pink' is an award-winning dependable choice, along with the double red flowers of 'Frosty Fire'.

Perennial dianthus is similar to annual dianthus, preferring cooler temperatures in partial or dappled shade. Dianthus flowers are fringed, single or semi-double, and are produced in masses for a brilliant early-spring display. The most popular colors are rose and pink, which add to the early flower show with redbuds, dogwoods, daffodils, and other spring bloomers. Some of the more heat-tolerant selections referred to as cheddar pinks include 'Bath's Pink', 'Firewitch' (magenta), 'Mountain Mist' (pink and taller), 'Spotty' (speckled red), and 'Tiny Rubies' (double pink, dwarf). 'Old Spice' is one of the most fragrant. Popular white-flowering cultivars include 'Aqua' (double) and 'It Saul White' (takes heat). The old-fashioned Dianthus barbatus (sweet William) is a favorite of cottage gardens but typically blooms biennially (every other year).

Other Common Names

Cottage Pink, Hardy Pink, Cheddar Pink, Hardy Carnation

Bloom Period and Seasonal Color

Rose, pink, white, or bicolor blooms in late spring and early summer.

Mature Height × Spread

10 to 15 in. × 8 to 24 in.

Cold Hardiness Zones

6a, 6b, 7a, 7b

Elderberry
Sambucus canadensis

In the landscape, this native is used as an ornamental or a small fruit. Ornamental elderberry has various foliage colors and fruit displays. Small fruit types are selected more for their production capabilities. In good soil, one plant has the potential to produce 15 pounds of fruit. Most plants will not set fruit the first year of planting. Because elderberries are poor self-pollinators, plant more than one cultivar to increase fruit production. Harvest ripe fruit clusters in August or September, depending on the cultivar. 'Adams' is one of the most publicized fruit-production cultivars. Canadensis selections for ornamental purposes include 'Aurea' (golden-yellow foliage), 'Maxima' (large flowers), and 'Rubra' (red fruit). S. nigra is the most widely used for ornamental purposes and includes a wide range of foliage colors and leaf shapes.

Other Common Names
American Elder, Sweet Elder, Pie Elder

Bloom Period and Seasonal Color
Greenish white blooms in late summer.

Mature Height × Spread
8 to 12 ft. × 6 to 8 ft.

Cold Hardiness Zones
6a, 6b, 7a, 7b

When, Where and How to Plant
Plant native elderberries in spring or early summer in rich, slightly acidic, moist soils. Though less vigorous, it tolerates heavy, compact, slightly alkaline, or poor sites. Some species and cultivars perform in full sun and others in more filtered shade. Attend to potbound roots before planting. Space plants for ornamental purposes 6 to 8 feet apart. For fruit production purposes, plant elderberries 5 to 6 feet apart and 10 feet between rows. Mulch the plants to conserve soil moisture.

Growing Tips
Irrigate during prolonged drought to avoid leaf scorch, leaf drop, and immature flower set or fruit drop. If the plants are non-productive, chlorotic, or stunted, I use slow-release products incorporated at planting and applied yearly for a steady nutrients supply without too much overgrowth. High nitrogen and water-soluble fertilizers cause leggy, droopy growth. Periodic reapplication of mulch preserves soil moisture.

Care
Fruit is borne on the previous season's growth or on current-season lateral growth on one-year-old wood. Take care to select older, weakened canes or trunks because dormant or an early-spring pruning reduces fruit. Prune ornamental plants as needed. Some folks like the plant's lacy foliage and prune them to 3 feet each spring to keep plants uniform and compact. In some of my landscape areas, I prune to the ground each year to get more of a bushy shrub-like growth. Potential pests include aphids and spider mites.

Landscape Merit
Elderberries' versatile growth makes them excellent summer screens or background walls. They can be grown in a row for production purposes. The native growing habit is somewhat stoloniferous, forming colonized groupings. Others grow as single or multi-trunked plants making perfect specimens. Where there are grown as an herbaceous perennial, some elderberry selections, including our native, are often killed back each year from cold.

My Personal Favorite
'Sutherland' (a.k.a. Sutherland's Gold) is a different species (S. racemosa) with cutleaf golden yellow foliage that takes a little more morning sun.

False Indigo
Baptisia australis

When, Where, and How to Plant

Plant seed in the fall, preferably in a container. Set out container-grown plants in late spring or early summer. Plant bare-root plants in the spring or fall. In its native state, *Baptisia* grows in dry, poor soils, typically in full sun. In the landscape or garden, keep *Baptisia* out of shady sites and extremely nutrient-rich soils, or the plants will sprawl. Good drainage is a necessity. Dig the planting hole at the same depth as and slightly wider than the rootball. Space the plants about 3 feet apart. Mulch the plants but do not get it overly thick, especially on the stems.

Growing Tips

Stake the plants when they are grown in too much shade and rich soils. The plants are very hardy and quite drought tolerant once they are established. Water them after planting to establish them but then reduce the amount of water as the plants mature. Baptisia is a legume plant forming nitrogen-fixing bacteria along the fibrous roots, so supplemental feedings are often not needed.

Care

Baptisia is often touted as a low- to no-maintenance plant. The unique flowers start to emerge in early summer and last for a couple of weeks. Some gardeners choose to cut back the flowers to encourage more blooms later in the summer. Wait to trim this dormant plant back in late spring to see where the new growth of the season emerges. Pests are of little concern.

Landscape Merit

Use this perennial garden plant as a specimen or background border plant. In the landscape, *Baptisia* is a delightful perennial offering a distinctive coarse texture, which complements finer-textured plants such as ornamental grasses, coreopsis, daylilies, and artemesia.

My Personal Favorites

'Purple Smoke' has blue gray foliage with elongated purple flower spikes. 'Screamin' Yellow' has vibrant yellow flowers. Both need plenty of space.

Blue indigo, a prairie native, has showy, pea-like flowers and coarse-foliage. The flowers are formed in upright spikes above the grayish-green, almost eucalyptus-like foliage. Black, pendulous seedpods follow the flowers. The winter color is a dark brown or grayish black. B. australis is the blue-flowering species, and the variety 'Minor' is a more compact version of the species. Nuttall's baptisia (B. nuttalliana) and golden wild indigo (B. sphaerocarpa) are yellow-flowering natives to the state. Other yellow types found in the nursery trade are B. perfoliata and B. tinctoria. White-flowering species include B. alba, B. leucantha (lactea), and B. pendula. There are very few named selections to date. 'Purple Smoke' is a North Carolina hybrid known for its dusty-smoke-purple flowers arising from charcoal-green foliage.

Other Common Names

Indigo Lupine, Blue Indigo, Wild Indigo

Bloom Period and Seasonal Color

Purple, yellow, or white blooms in spring or summer.

Mature Height × Spread

3 to 5 ft. × 3 to 5 ft.

Cold Hardiness Zones

6a, 6b, 7a, 7b

Foamflower
Tiarella cordifolia

This low-growing, clumping plant rewards gardeners with dainty, white flowers elevated above the lime-green foliage in mid-spring, in late April or May. In good soil, it spreads and forms a clumping ground cover. Consider foamflower for moist, woodland gardens. The maple-like foliage turns a reddish cast in the fall. Most species go dormant in the winter. A few species, especially in the T. cordifolia, retain a semi-evergreen appearance, depending on the severity of the winter. Some species are grown more for their colorful foliage or unusual-shaped leaves than for the flower. Some species are also better ground covers. Tiarella is very similar to Huechera and has even been crossed to form hybridized selections known as foamy bells or Huecheralla.

Other Common Names
False Miterwort, Allegheny Foamflower

Bloom Period and Seasonal Color
White and pink blooms in mid-spring; red fall foliage

Mature Height × Spread
6 to 15 in. × 12 to 24 in.

Cold Hardiness Zones
6a, 6b, 7a, 7b

When, Where, and How to Plant
Plant foamflower in early spring as a bare-root plant or in late spring and early summer as a container-grown plant. Divide overgrown clumps every four to five years. Partial or dappled shade cools the plants in harsh summers. They like woodland soil that is moisture retentive and high in organic matter. Dig the planting holes two times wider than and the same depth as the rootballs. Space the plants 18 to 24 inches apart. Mulch with an organic material such as compost, shredded leaves, or composted manure. Water routinely during the establishment period.

Growing Tips
Water on a regular basis, at least weekly if rainfall is absent. During prolonged droughts, supplemental irrigation is necessary to keep the plants from wilting and dying. Slow-release organic fertilizers help provide release of nutrients over a long period of time especially when applied at planting. Otherwise, side-dress with water-soluble fertilizer products applied with water.

Care
Trim the spent flowers after blooming, which usually lasts two to six weeks. Another flush of blooms can occur later in the season. Pests are of no concern.

Landscape Merit
This broadleaf, clumping plant is a good filler or border plant in shade gardens with moist soil. Plant foamflowers in groups of three or five for the best display. Use them in association with hardscape items such as rocks, yard art, birdbaths, and fountains. Foamflower is a good companion plant with astilbe, hosta, ferns, and other woodland plants.

My Personal Favorite
'Pink Skyrocket' has intriguing shape foliage and showy pink flowers. 'Heronswood Mist' could be grown for the mottled foliage alone.

Gaura
Gaura lindheirmeri

When, Where, and How to Plant

Plant container-grown selections in the spring or summer. Start seed indoors in a container during the winter. It prefers full sun. It tolerates partial shade but no more than four or five hours of dense shade. In its native setting, gaura is often found in loamy, moist sites. In the landscape, duplicate these conditions with good drainage, which is essential. Poor planting soils are acceptable but require additional feedings and care. Loosen pot-bound roots before planting. Dig the hole the same depth as and 2 times wider than the rootball. Space plants 3 to 4 feet apart. Mulch plants to control weeds and retain soil moisture.

Growing Tips

Supplemental irrigation is recommended during extremely dry periods. Do not overfertilize them, or the plants become more open and sprawling.

Care

The plants bloom most of the summer and require little pruning. Occasionally, there is a lull in flowering. Shear plants back to the leafy foliage to encourage more growth and blooms. Potential pests include spider mites and leaf spots. Planting sites with good air movement minimize pest problems and allow for more movement of the flowering spikes. Heavily shaded sites are more likely to be subject to leaf spots.

Landscape Merit

This tall, mounding plant is often used as a background border in the perennial garden. It is delightful in association with evergreen shrubs as well. Its unique growth habit and flowers make it a good choice for a singular specimen plant. In a patio or container display, the weeping, whirling appearance of gaura makes for quite a conversation piece. Grow the plants separately or plant in combination with other textured plants.

My Personal Favorites

One of my favorites is 'Crimson Butterflies' with its neat compact growth habit and burgundy foliage. 'Siskiyou Pink' is a close second.

Place this native roadside, pasture, and prairie wasteland in the landscape, and you will be amazed at its whimsical growth habit. The plant has nondistinct foliage, but in early summer the bushy growth sends up erect flower spikes full of white, butterfly-shaped flowers. At times there are so many that the flower stems begin to weep. Combine this with Oklahoma winds, and the plant literally comes to life with dangling and fluttering flowers, thus the common name of whirling butterflies. Most of the native species have white, creamy-white, or pale-pink flowers that bloom throughout the season. 'Franz Valley' has fragrant, white-flowers with more compact growth. 'Corrie's Gold' has variegated foliage with pink-and-white blooms. 'Whirling Butterflies' supposedly flowers more than the species with sterile white blooms.

Other Common Names
Whirling Butterflies, Wand Flower

Bloom Period and Seasonal Color
White and pink blooms all summer.

Mature Height × Spread
3 to 5 ft. × 3 to 4 ft.

Cold Hardiness Zones
6a, 6b, 7a, 7b

Goldenrod
Solidago canadensis

Contrary to popular belief, this native is not the source of your fall allergy problems. Goldenrod is often blamed for this allergy outburst because of its showy flowers that coincide with sneezing, sniffling, and headaches. The culprit is instead ragweed with not-so-showy flowers and wind-born pollen. Goldenrod on the other hand is insect pollinated. So relax, this native beauty has a lot to offer. The color yellow is said to soothe or invigorate people. Well, this fragrant, eye-catching bloomer does just that when given a chance in the landscape. The blooms last for several weeks in the late summer and fall with truly vivid-yellow or orange-yellow color. There is quite a diverse selection in height, flower, and foliage shape depending on the species.

Other Common Name
Solidago

Bloom Period and Seasonal Color
Yellow blooms in late summer and fall.

Mature Height × Spread
1 to 6 ft. × 2 to 4 ft.

Cold Hardiness Zones
6a, 6b, 7a, 7b

When, Where, and How to Plant
Plant container-grown selections in the spring or early summer. Divide overgrown plants every three to four years as needed. The native American species grows in well-drained soils in partial or full sun. Heavy or waterlogged soils mean sure death for goldenrod. Plant the container-grown herbaceous perennials in holes the same depth as and two times wider than their rootballs to allow for shallow root growth. Space plants on 3-foot centers when clustered. Mulch and water to establish plants. Avoid overwatering, especially during spring rains.

Growing Tips
Once plants are established, water them from time to time only during extremely prolonged dry spells. Overall, they are fairly drought tolerant. Supplemental feedings are not encouraged as the plants get too leggy and fall over. Apply slow-release organic fertilizer instead on a yearly basis.

Care
The plants bloom late July, August, or September until frost. They rarely need deadheading. Prune only in the spring to remove dormant foliage before the new growth emerges. Stake larger, upright-growing selections. As with any perennial, goldenrod gets better the second and third years after planting. Potential pests are spider mites, thrips, and leaf miners, and occasional diseases include leaf rust and powdery mildew. Properly spaced plants with good air circulation and afternoon shade are less likely to succumb to these problems.

Landscape Merit
Look for the appropriate plant height to match your particular planting site. Plant the taller selections at the back of the perennial bed. Use dwarf selections as border plants or in masses as a mid-level choice. The plants are interesting displayed in association with ornamental grasses, fall asters, and mums.

My Personal Favorite
I'm starting to sound like a variegated plant nut, but foliage color can be as enlivening as flower color. 'Gold Spangles' offers unique variegated foliage all season long in anticipation of the fall showy plumes.

Hardy Hibiscus
Hibiscus moscheutos

When, Where, and How to Plant

Plant dormant bare-root hibiscus in early spring and container-grown plants in spring, summer, or fall. The plants prefer moisture-retentive soils, but they tolerate dry sites once established. Rich, fertile soils accelerate growth and promote better blooms. Plant dormant bare-root plants in containers and plant later outside. Plant bare-root plants directly into well-worked soil in late spring at the same depth that they were grown. Place container-grown plants in holes dug two times wider than and the same depth as the rootballs. Do not crowd the plants unless they are to form a hedge. Spacing between plants should be about 4 to 5 feet. Mulch to conserve moisture, and water as needed.

Growing Tips

In Oklahoma's colder climates, such as the panhandle, mulch the roots during the winter months. They seldom need fertilizer unless the plants are stunted or chlorotic. Nitrogen-rich or excessive water-soluble fertilizer cause overgrown plants with few flowers. Hibiscus also works in the shallow part of bog or water gardens.

Care

The tall plants seldom need staking. Prune during summer to control growth. *H. moscheutos* is not as prone to litter the ground with old flowers as its cousin, *H. syriacus* (rose of Sharon). Other than an occasional aphid, spider mite, or chewing beetle on the flowers, pests are not a serious problem. Larvae feed through the flower bud before it opens, causing the bud to abort prematurely. Most labeled insecticides control this pest with thorough spraying on additional, newly formed buds. Foliar diseases are usually more of a problem in heavy shade with poor air circulation.

Landscape Merit

Use as single-plant specimens or in groups for even more breathtaking displays. The height naturally makes them background border plants in island perennial beds. I have seen them used as a hedge for a phenomenal summer exhibition.

My Personal Favorites

'Sweet Caroline' with pink rosebud-like flowers and 'Crown Jewels' with maple like burgundy foliage and white flowers are my two favorites.

If you want really big flowers, choose hardy hibiscus. This is one of the latest perennials to break dormancy, sometimes not until May or June. These cold-hardy plants go dormant after the first killing frost and emerge from the root crown with tall, sturdy stalks when soil temperatures warm. In just a few weeks, there is a spectacular display of flowers that lasts the summer. Each bloom lasts only a day, but the stalks form continuous buds and bloom until first frost. H. moscheutos flower size is often compared to dinner plates. Hibiscus is native to southeastern Oklahoma roadside wetlands, riverbeds, marshes, and shallow swamps. 'Blue River', one of the most popular white introductions, was discovered near the Blue River in Oklahoma.

Other Common Names
Rose Mallow, Swamp Rose, Wild Cotton

Bloom Period and Seasonal Color
Red, pink, white, and bicolored blooms in summer and fall.

Mature Height × Spread
3 to 8 ft. × 3 to 6 ft.

Cold Hardiness Zones
6b, 7a, 7b (6a with protection)

Indian Blanket
Gaillardia species

Proud "Okies" must include the state wildflower (G. pul-chella) in their landscape though it is a reseeding annual. You will be amazed by the intricate colors of the beautiful flower and its perennial cousins, truly a fine piece of work from our Creator. The large, showy flowers bloom around May and usually continue until September. The native species has named cultivars and selections, such as 'Butterscotch Bronze' (tricolor), 'Lollipops' (tricolor), 'Raspberry Red' (dwarf plant, scarlet flowers), and 'Red Plume' (double). Gaillardia × grandiflora is a hybrid cross noted for larger flowers. Look for powdery-mildew-tolerant selections, such as 'Baby Cole' (dwarf plant, bicolor), 'Bremen' (scarlet), 'Dazzler' (yellow flower petals, maroon center), 'Goblin' (dwarf plant, red flowers with yellow margins), 'Sun God' (yellow flowers with brown center), 'The Sun' (golden yellow), 'Tokajer' (rusty orange), 'Mandarin' (tricolor), and 'Yellow Queen' (solid yellow).

Other Common Names
Blanket Flower, Gaillardia

Bloom Period and Seasonal Color
Yellow and red, red, or yellow blooms in summer and fall.

Mature Height × Spread
1 to 2¹/₂ ft. × 1 to 2 ft.

Cold Hardiness Zones
6a, 6b, 7a, 7b

When, Where and How to Plant
Plant container-grown selections in the landscape in spring or early summer. Plant seed very shallow in the fall or early spring. Some growers scatter it on the surface of the soil in a container where it germinates under light in about two to three weeks at 65 to 70 degrees Fahrenheit. Dry, average soils in full sun describe gaillardia's native sites. Well-drained soils are the first priority. More organic soils usually produce vigorous plant growth, but flower production is evident in either soil type. The plants tolerate a pH range of 6.5 to 7.5. Plant Indian blanket on 12-to 15-inch centers when planting in masses.

Growing Tips
Moisture is crucial during the establishment period the first year, but allow the plants to dry out between watering. Once they are established, they are fairly drought tolerant but will grow and bloom sporadically during prolonged periods of drought. Apply slow-release organic fertilizer when planting and each spring.

Care
Gaillardia grows in small clusters. Deadheading spent flowers keeps the plants tidier and encourages rebloom, but it also limits plant perpetuation. Deadheading too much causes the perennial to be somewhat short-lived, lasting only three or four years in the landscape. At the end of the season in wildflower gardens and meadows, leave seedheads intact so they can dry and be distributed. Remove dormant growth early in the spring before new growth appears. Insect threats are the common spider mite and leafhopper. Potential diseases are powdery mildew, leaf spot, and sometimes aster yellows virus. Too much shade increases the chance of disease.

Landscape Merit
Use dwarf types for border plants. Gaillardia do well as filler plants for mid-level areas of the perennial bed. They are often used as wildflower or meadow garden plants. This durable native performs in containers and windowbox displays.

My Personal Favorite
G. aristate 'Fanfare' has quickly become my favorite with its colorful and unique shaped numerous flowers that continually bloom all summer long.

When, Where, and How to Plant

Plant seed in the spring or fall. Broadcast the seed on the surface and roll it with a sod roller to level the site and get contact with the seed. Do not cover the seed, however. Water it and keep the soil moist but not soggy until the seedlings emerge. Indian paintbrush is seldom sold as a container plant. *Castilleja* is hard to grow in containers because it is somewhat parasitic (hemiparasitic) or dependent on other companion plants in the wild for nutrition. Space plants about 1 foot from other companion plants. In the wild, Indian paintbrush is often found in sandy or sandy loam soils with crucially good drainage on elevated sites in full sun.

Growing Tips

The plants take several years to establish a large and showy colony, but once they are established, they are very drought tolerant. In a perennial bed, I suggest routinely fertilizing the transplants with a soluble fertilizer applied with water for the first several months until they have successfully attached their roots to other companion-type plants. Established Indian paintbrush responds favorably to supplemental feedings throughout the growing season.

Care

This wildflower native requires little care, other than remembering to allow the plants to mature and dry for reseeding themselves each year. Pest problems are seldom a concern.

Landscape Merit

Use this somewhat complex plant in wildflower or meadow gardens where it easily reseeds itself. In landscape perennial beds, it is more of a challenge but worth the effort, thanks to new research. It must be planted in close association with other host plants and allowed to grow in colonies. Some good companion plants are bluebonnets, dwarf ornamental grasses such as 'Little Bunny' pennisetum, or mondo grass.

My Personal Favorite

The Oklahoma native is mostly sold as seed; however, an orange flowering related species *C. integra* is sometimes sold as seedling transplants.

Although technically a reseeding annual, this Oklahoma favorite is in the perennial chapter because with luck it can perennialize in your landscape. This lovely, unbranched plant appears more frequently in sandy soils of the western and southwestern parts of the state. It is becoming common along Oklahoma roadsides, thanks to the Oklahoma Highway Beautification Program. Unfortunately, this herbaceous plant is tough to grow in cultivated landscape sites. It is perfect for the meadow or wildflower garden. The species typically found in Oklahoma have intriguing, bright, erect, red-orange flower spikes produced from April until June. The showy red-orange is actually colored leaves known as bracts. The flower is a creamy white to yellow found inside the colorful bracts. Western species grow to almost 3 feet and come in assorted colors.

Other Common Names
Texas Paintbrush, Scarlet Paintbrush

Bloom Period and Seasonal Color
Red-orange blooms in early summer.

Mature Height × Spread
8 to 24 in. × 4 to 6 in.

Cold Hardiness Zones
6a, 6b, 7a, 7b

Japanese Painted Fern

Athyrium nipponicum

Athyrium is a large genus of shade-loving ferns with assorted foliage colors. Although most of them are just green, they provide texture, filler, and background for any woodland design. Ferns need protection from the tough Oklahoma summers and require moist, shaded sites. In these conditions, the ferns thrive for years. Japanese painted fern offers variation in foliage color—a combination of gray-green, silver, and maroon. This color combination is perfect for brightening and softening the shade garden at the same time. They work well with other plants. Japanese ferns are relatively slow growing. 'Pictum' and 'Ursula's Red' have distinct tri-colored leaves. A primarily green fern is lady fern (Athyrium filix-femina), which is somewhat more tolerant of dry soils but not severe drought. Athyrium 'Cristatum' has delicate, crested fronds.

Other Common Names
Lady Fern, Glade Fern

Bloom Period and Seasonal Color
Season-long green foliage.

Mature Height × Spread
8 to 20 in. × 15 to 36 in.

Cold Hardiness Zones
6a, 6b, 7a, 7b

When, Where, and How to Plant
Plant bare-root plants in the spring. Set out container-grown plants in spring or early summer. Some ferns are started by tissue culture and later transferred to containers. Divide fern clumps in early spring as needed, usually every three to five years. Apply organic materials before planting time, and work them into the planting bed unless shallow tree roots exist. In that case leave amendments (no thicker than 6 inches) on the surface. Most ferns prefer slightly acidic soils with a pH of 5.5 to 6.5. Set bare-root plants slightly below the ground with the dormant foliage buds facing up. Place container-grown plants in holes wider than and the same depth as the rootballs. Space plants 1 to 2 feet apart.

Growing Tips
Most ferns in Oklahoma are deciduous, going dormant in the winter. Mulching around ferns with organic leaf mold and other products holds in moisture and provides slow-release nutrients. Avoid angling mulch up on the crowns. Ferns are light feeders, and in most cases organic or natural fertilizers are recommended because of their slow-release nature. If ferns are healthy and growing, there is probably no need to feed.

Care
Most ferns are relatively pest free, with occasional spider mites. Remove old, winter-burned fronds in early spring prior to the emergence of new growth typically in late February or early to mid- March.

Landscape Merit
The airy appearance softens harsher textures of coarse, broadleaf plants such as mahonia, hosta, and bergenia. Some of the taller selections are great background border plants. Use more compact versions in the front perimeter. Clump ferns in groups as filler. Fill the entire shade garden only with ferns for a bold, uniform appearance. Ferns work well in association with garden sculptures, rocks, and other hardscape items.

My Personal Favorite
'Ursula's Red' is absolutely stunning, and it may take a couple of years for the plant to mature into the iridescent burgundy and silver variegation.

Joe-Pye Weed
Eupatorium species

When, Where and How to Plant

Plant eupatorium from container-grown selections in the spring, summer, or fall. Root crown divisions in the spring. Start seed in the fall or early spring. Seed usually needs to be cold-stratified to encourage better germination. The plants have a tendency to spread by clumps, so divide every three years or so. Most named plants are sold by vegetatively propagated cuttings. This plant performs best in average, moist, well-drained soils. It accepts full sun or a half day of shade. Give the plants plenty of space to grow. Space them on 3- to 4-feet apart from center to center. Water and mulch them to keep the soil moist during the establishment period. As with most perennials, eupatorium gets better with age.

Growing Tips

Reduce frequency of watering to about four to six weeks after planting. Supplemental feedings are rarely needed unless the plants appear nutrient deficient.

Care

The plants can sometimes become leggy in rich soils. As the plants emerge in the spring, cut back the stems above a leaf node a couple of times to encourage more compact growth. Some selections require staking. Remove dormant plant foliage anytime in the winter or early spring. The plants are late to emerge from the ground—sometimes not until April or even early May. Pest problems occur in crowded sites with too much shade and include diseases such as powdery mildew, leaf spot, and rust. Potential insect threats are aphids, leaf miners, and spider mites.

Landscape Merit

Match the size of the particular selection with your growing location. Some are good background plants, others make late-summer hedges, and some of the more compact releases will work as mid-level plants.

My Personal Favorite

My favorite named cultivar is 'Chocolate' (*E. rugosum*) with beautiful white flowers and chocolate-purple foliage and stems.

Joe-pye weed dots the countryside, roadside, and forest edges from July through October with purple flowers atop elongated stems. The large flower clusters offer a color finale at the end of the season when other flowers have bitten the dust. This native is a great accent for any perennial garden. E. fistulosum, sold as giant Joe-pye weed, is the tallest species with reaching up to 12 feet. E. coelestinum with purple flowers is found near moist sites such as margins of lakes, streams, and ponds; it works well as a bog garden plant. E. purpureum is more often found in heavier shaded sites with pinkish-lavender blooms. Named cultivars include 'Alba' and 'Bartered Bride' (white), 'Atropurpurem' (purple), 'Gateway' (mauve), 'Cori' (pale blue), and 'Flore Plenum' (double pink).

Other Common Names

Eupatorium, Mist Flower, Hardy Ageratum, Snakeroot, Boneset

Bloom Period and Seasonal Color

Purple, white, and pink blooms in late summer.

Mature Height × Spread

3 to 8 ft. × 2 to 3 ft.

Cold Hardiness Zones

6a, 6b, 7a, 7b

Lavender

Lavendula angustifolia

Some herb plants also make wonderful perennials. Lavender has compact growth, brilliant flower display, and pleasant aroma. It thrives in heat and dry conditions. 'Twickle ('Twickle') Purple' is a compact, semi-evergreen plant with purple flowers and gray-green foliage turning a purple tint in winter. 'Hidcote' and 'Munstead' are probably the most popular and readily available. The dwarf 'Lady' is tough and flowers the first year of planting. Cultivars with feathery foliage are 'French Lace', 'Goodwin Creek', and 'Pinnata'. 'Fred Boutin' with lighter-colored foliage is good for cut flowers. 'Nana Alba' is white flowering, and 'Melissa' has almost pinkish-white flowers. 'Rosea', 'Jean Davis', and 'Hidcote Pink' are even darker pink. 'Provence' is known as a more rot-resistant selection that tolerates humidity and moister soils.

Other Common Names
English Lavender, Lavandin

Bloom Period and Seasonal Color
Purple, violet-blue, pink blooms in summer dependent upon the cultivar.

Mature Height × Spread
10 to 36 in. × 12 to 36 in.

Cold Hardiness Zones
6b, 7a, 7b (6a with protection)

When, Where, and How to Plant

Plant lavender in late spring or summer. These tough plants prefer full sun but tolerate a half-day of shade as long as the site has good drainage. The soils do not have to be overly fertile, but the plants like a sandy loam. Heavy, waterlogged soils kill this species fast. Most plants are container grown and planted the same depth as the rootballs. Planting slightly above soil grade is warranted in heavier soils. Start plants from seed in containers instead of directly in the ground. Space plants 1 to 3 feet apart, depending on the cultivar. Mulch after planting to keep weeds at bay; however, the mulch should not be too thick, especially near the plant stems. Water after planting to establish plants, but allow it to dry out between watering.

Growing Tips

After a couple of seasons, the plants are fairly drought tolerant. If the plants are healthy and actively growing, feeding is not necessary. Be careful not to apply fertilizer if the plants are declining or rotting since the roots may be stressed.

Care

Pruning typically consists of shearing off the old blooms to promote additional blooms later in the season. Shear winter-damaged foliage in early spring. Some cultivars of lavender need to be well established and will not bloom until the second growing season. Pests are not a problem; an occasional caterpillar or leaf spot affects plants in heavily shaded, humid, or damp sites. Root rot is the biggest concern in poorly drained soils.

Landscape Merit

The plants make a perfect border in the back or front of perennial beds. Some gardeners use them in rows as a small hedge. I have seen them in windowboxes and patio pots, and they are frequently grown in the vegetable or herb garden.

My Personal Favorites

I like the dwarf 'Hidcote' but have also found the taller 'Provence' to do well.

When, Where, and How to Plant

Plant ruellia in spring or summer (fall plantings are risky). Most plants are sold in containers. There is literally a species or cultivar for almost any landscape situation, whether in sun or partial shade. This plant likes humus-rich, moist soils. Dig a hole wider than and the same depth as the rootball. Space plants 1 to 3 feet apart, depending on the species. Mulch to keep weeds at bay and to retain moisture.

Growing Tips

This plant sometimes emerges late in spring or even early summer. Blooms start in late May or June and continue until frost. The plants go dormant in winter and come back in late spring from the crown or root. Mix slow-release fertilizers at planting and then scatter under mulch on a yearly basis. Side-dressing with water-soluble fertilizers can be beneficial, especially on plants that are chlorotic or not vigorous. The plants are not considered drought tolerant and thrive in moist sites. Supplemental irrigation is a must during prolonged drought periods. Reapply mulch as needed to retain soil moisture and squelch weed competition.

Care

Both the tall and the medium sized selections are self-cleaning. Prune only to keep plants in check. Occasionally remove some of the flowers on the dwarf types, especially after a rain. Pests are minimal, other than an occasional aphid in early spring. Many ruellia species that are not cold-hardy in the state make wonderful annual bedding plants for the summer.

Landscape Merit

The taller-growing species make great background border plants when they are allowed to spread. The compact cultivars mature at 10 to 12 inches for a border or edging plant. They work well in clusters. Use low-spreading types as a ground cover.

My Personal Favorite

The dwarf 'Katie' series, available in purple, pink and white, are nice compact plants with awesome spikey texture. 'Strawberries and Cream' is the same size but with speckled foliage and lavender flowers.

Ruellia works as a perennial from Oklahoma City to Sallisaw. Even if it were not hardy, I would grow it because of its large, colorful, petunia-like flowers. And the shiny-green, strap-like foliage creates splendid landscape texture. The plant thrives in soggy or dry soils, and I have used it in boggy sites. Ruellia brittoniana comes in dwarf or upright selections with narrower leaves. 'Katie' (also sold as dwarf, compact, or 'Nolan's Dwarf') is the smallest clumping form, maturing at 8 to 12 inches with a heavy set of purple flowers most of the summer. 'Bonita'((colobe pink) is a dwarf form. 'Strawberries and Cream' is compact with speckled cream, pink, white, and green variegation. The upright selections grow to 30 to 36 inches. 'Chi Chi' is upright and pink-flowering.

Other Common Names
Ruellia, Wild Petunia, Dwarf Ruellia

Bloom Period and Seasonal Color
Purple, pink, and white blooms in summer.

Mature Height × Spread
6 to 36 in. × 10 to 36 in.

Cold Hardiness Zones
7a, 7b (6b with winter protection)

Oregano
Origanum laevigatum

Oregano is an aromatic plant most widely known for its culinary use as an herb. O. laevigatum is also an excellent landscape plant with cold-hardy, showy, fragrant flowers. Because of its popularity with bees, plant it away from sidewalks and high-traffic areas. The cold hardiest and probably most popular floriferous cultivar is 'Herrenhausen' with pinkish-purple flowers on dense growth, maturing near 2 feet in height. 'Hopley's Purple', with its mauve-purple flowers, also has a bluish tint to the foliage but is best for Zones 7a and 7b in Oklahoma. 'Album' is a whiter-flowering cultivar. O. acutidens (Turkish oregano) has spicy, aromatic, mounding foliage that sends up arching flower stalks of pink flowers. O. rotundifolium is a clump-forming plant with whorls of flowers resembling hops.

Other Common Names
Marjoram, Ornamental Oregano

Bloom Period and Seasonal Color
Purple, pink, and white blooms in July through September.

Mature Height × Spread
15 to 30 in. × 15 to 36 in.

Cold Hardiness Zones
6a, 6b, 7a, 7b

When, Where, and How to Plant
Start ornamental oregano from seed in a container around midwinter. But it is easier to purchase container-grown plants in the spring and plant any time throughout the summer. This aromatic perennial prefers sites in full sun or with afternoon shade. In colder regions of the state, plant oregano in sheltered sites for winter protection. Well-drained soil is the most important factor to consider when growing oregano. Oregano tolerates more alkaline soils, typical of the western portions of the state. Fertile soils offer better conditions for vigorous growth and spread; however, ornamental oregano tolerates poor soils where it attains a more compact growth habit. Space plants 18 to 24 inches apart. Planting them diagonally instead of in a straight line clusters plants better.

Growing Tips
These plants do not tolerate wet sites. Be careful not to mulch too heavily or too closely to the plants, or rotting occurs near the stem base. Be careful with the high nitrogen fertilizers as well. Too much and you can burn the plants. Slow-release organic products are best. Do not confuse this species with the culinary type *O. vulgare*.

Care
Flowering occurs on the new growth of the season and starts in late summer, either in June or July, continuing into the fall. Any lag in flowering later in the season is rejuvenated by shearing the plants slightly below the flower stalks. Trim winter-damaged foliage in early spring as soon as new growth starts to emerge. Pests to watch for are mites, leaf spot, and stem rot.

Landscape Merit
Set out this lovely, free-flowing plant in a rock garden or allow it to cascade from a rock wall. Many cultivars do well in the perennial flower garden as mid-level or border plants. Planting ornamental oregano in groups creates more impact.

My Personal Favorite
'Kent's Beauty' has adorned my garden with its unique non-invasive spreading habit, hop-like flower pods, and small lavender florets.

When, Where, and How to Plant

Plant as a bare-root plant in early spring or as a container-grown plant in spring or summer. Garden phlox likes full sun or a half-day of shade. The plant prefers moist, but well-drained, fertile soils. Taking the time to prepare humus-rich soil nurtures vigorous green plants, rewarding you with tremendous color. Dig holes in loosely worked soil that are wider than and the same depth as the root-balls. Mulch between and around plants to hold in moisture and keep weeds out. Water after planting. Space plants about 18 inches apart for the best display.

Growing Tips

Water on a regular basis to keep the soil moist, but be sure it is well drained. These tall, dynamic plants are heavy feeders. Give them supplemental feedings a couple of times a year after the new growth emerges in the spring.

Care

The foliage typically goes dormant with the first freeze in the fall and emerges again next spring. Garden phlox blooms on new growth starting sometime in May or June. Trimming the spent blooms just below the flower head encourages more color later in the summer. If plants have a history of falling over, pinch the new growth a couple of times as it emerges in the spring. Doing this causes the plants to become more compact and bushy. It can also mean somewhat smaller blooms and a little later flowering, but I prefer both to using plant stakes or support hoops. Mildew is the most common pest problem. Disease resistant cultivars are the best answer.

Landscape Merit

Because phlox is tall, it offers dimension to the perennial landscape. Use garden phlox in the back of perennial beds or as a border plant. Group the plants in clusters of three or more, or plant them in diagonal rows for the best color effect.

My Personal Favorites

White 'David', pink 'Eva Cullum' and 'Blue Paradise' are tops in my garden especially when grown together.

Thankfully garden phlox has been greatly improved with many powdery mildew resistant cultivars. It is a good thing, too, because I do not know what a perennial garden would be without the towering stalks of refreshing summer blooms. If you are going to grow this old-time favorite in the Oklahoma heat and humidity, you almost have to start with disease-tolerant strains. 'David' is a disease-resistant white. 'Eva Cullum' (bright pink) is more tolerant but not always mildew proof. 'Red Magic', 'Flamingo', 'Miss Kelly', 'Elie', and 'Laura' are highly resistant cultivars. 'Norah Leigh' deserves a place in the garden, though afternoon shade causes mildew susceptibility. This beauty is grown for its unusual variegated foliage and light-pink blooms with dark centers. 'Harlequin' has somewhat narrower variegated foliage and lavender flowers.

Other Common Name
Garden Phlox

Bloom Period and Seasonal Color
Red and white blooms in summer.

Mature Height × Spread
3 to 4 ft. × 2 to 3 ft.

Cold Hardiness Zones
6a, 6b, 7a, 7b

Rosemary
Rosmarinus officinalis

This perennial does not offer large, spectacular flowers but should be included in the perennial border for no other reason than its prominent, pine-like fragrance. On windy days (plentiful in Oklahoma), the foliage brushes together, filling the garden distinctive aroma. When planted near the sidewalk, people brushing against it release its wonderful scent. Rosemary also has finely textured, attractive foliage and small blue-purple flowers, making a great package for any landscape. In Zone 7, the almost-velvety, dark-green foliage remains evergreen all winter. The most cold-hardy selection for Oklahoma is 'Arp' ('Madeline Hill') with dark-green foliage and light-blue flowers. 'Golden Rain' is not as winter-hardy but has variegated new growth. 'Huntington Carpet' and 'Irene' do well in southeastern Oklahoma and are more prostrate, with numerous blue blooms.

Other Common Name
Hardy Rosemary

Bloom Period and Seasonal Color
White or blue blooms in early to midsummer.

Mature Height × Spread
2 to 3 ft. × 2 to 3 ft.

Cold Hardiness Zones
7a, 7b (6b with winter protection)

When, Where, and How to Plant
Spring planting allows this perennial plenty of time to establish before the onset of winter. Rosemary tolerates full sun or partial shade. There should be at least four or five hours of sun. The most important factor to consider is well-drained soil since these plants easily rot in waterlogged or heavy soils. Fertile garden soils are perfect. If you do not have such a site, blend a complete fertilizer, peat moss, and other organic materials into the soil before planting time. Mulch to keep weeds out and grass from competing.

Growing Tips
Irrigate during prolonged dry spells. Water deeply to encourage deep roots but allow the plants to dry out between watering. Reapply mulch as needed. Supplemental feedings are typically not needed in good, fertile soils.

Care
Frequent shearing of the leaves and stems for culinary or aromatic uses keeps the plants more compact. Otherwise, prune winter-damaged growth, or prune to prevent branches from getting too woody. In colder climates the plants need protective mulch around the roots at least 4 to 6 inches deep, angled down to the stem. Do not cover the foliage or place the mulch thick on the stem, or it causes the plant tissue to rot, killing the entire plant. The top comes back from the soil crown as long as the roots do not completely freeze. Pests are highly unlikely in proper planting sites with good air circulation and appropriate soil. In stressed situations, insects, such as aphids and spider mites, and diseases, such as powdery mildew and botrytis, affect plants.

Landscape Merit
Use evergreen hardy rosemary as a background plant in the perennial garden. The solid backdrop of rosemary accentuates the brighter colors of other flowers. The stately growth habit works well as a hedge or border plant. Trailing forms freely cascade in rock gardens or along perimeters. Include a few in containers for the patio.

My Personal Favorite
'Arp' (a.k.a. Madeline Hill) is fragrant, decorative, and cold-hardy.

Russian Sage
Perovskia atriplicifolia

When, Where, and How to Plant
Plant Russian sage in spring, summer, or fall in full sun. These plants perform adequately in poor soils while rich, humus soils cause quite vigorous growth. Good drainage is important. Dig the planting hole at least 2 times wider than and the same depth as the rootball. Allow plenty of space between plants for good air circulation and growth. Space plants 3 to 4 feet apart. Mulch them to keep out weeds. Water after planting and as needed during the first few weeks to establish plants if rainfall is not adequate.

Growing Tips
Once established, Russian sage is quite drought tolerant. Fertilize only if the plants are lagging. Reapply mulch as needed.

Care
The blooms form in late June or July and continue through September and sometimes until the first frost. The flower production varies throughout the season and occasionally needs trimming to promote more growth. The plants receive various degrees of winterkill, depending on the severity of the temperatures. Shear dead growth in early spring. If no winterkill occurs, trim the foliage back to several inches from the ground to keep the plants more manageable. Doing this also forces new growth, which later produces the summer flower color. Pests are not a serious problem, although spider mites may appear.

Landscape Merit
The shrub-like growth of this plant requires plenty of background space and looks best in large perennial beds. The size seems out of place in smaller beds. The cool colors are nice for contrasting displays and seem to soften more dramatic, harsh textures. Combine the blue flowers and silver-gray, airy foliage with pink- or yellow-blooming perennials, hardy hibiscus, daylily, garden phlox, black-eyed Susan, and canna.

My Personal Favorite
'Little Spire' is shorter, around 2 to 2¹/₂ feet, with grayish foliage and lavender-blue flowers. It has a tendency to reseed pretty easily, so transplant or dig out seedlings as needed.

I needed a large plant with silvery foliage to fill in a big, sunny, perennial bed. I decided to give it a try. This one-gallon plant became a phenomenal specimen, blooming from July through September the first year. The pungent, silvery-gray foliage mixes with velvety, lavender flowers emerging from the upright, loosely grouped stems. Better yet is its resilience in poor soils, heat, and drought. Hybrid cultivars include 'Filigran', an improved selection with finer-cut foliage and lavender blooms; 'Longin', with narrow foliage, lavender-blue flowers, and distinctly upright growth; and 'Blue Haze', known for its pale-blue flowers. For darker, more-violet blooms, look for 'Blue Spire'.

Other Common Name
Azure Sage

Bloom Period and Seasonal Color
Lavender-blue blooms in summer.

Mature Height × Spread
3 to 4 ft. × 3 to 4 ft.

Cold Hardiness Zones
6a, 6b, 7a, 7b

Sage
Salvia species

If there is one plant that I always use in my personal gardens and landscape designs, it is hardy salvia. The biggest reason: it ignores summer heat and displays towering blooms of color throughout summer. It is always dependable and the perfect height for most perennial beds. Other selections are also hardy in Oklahoma. Lavender-blue selections include 'Blue Hill', 'East Friesland', 'Blue Queen', 'Purple Rain' (S. verticillata), and 'May Night'. S. azurea v. grandiflora is our native purple 'Pitcher's Sage', found in the eastern two-thirds of the state. Most of the hardy selections in Oklahoma are hybrids.

Other Common Names
Perennial Salvia, Meadow Sage, Hardy Salvia

Bloom Period and Seasonal Color
Purple, pink, and white blooms in summer.

Mature Height × Spread
2 to 3 ft. × 2 to 2^1/$_2$ ft.

Cold Hardiness Zones
6a, 6b, 7a, 7b

When, Where, and How to Plant
Plant salvias from container-grown stock in late spring or summer. They prefer full sun or partial shade with at least four to five hours of sun. Rich, humus soils that drain well are ideal for these plants. Incorporating organic materials into the soil before planting time is well worth the effort and investment. In loosely dug soil, set the plants in holes wider than and the same depth as the rootballs. Mulch to provide added organic nutrients, moisture retention, and weed control.

Growing Tips
Water regularly. Supplemental feedings are needed only when soils are depleted of nutrients, when plant foliage shows nutrient deficiency, or when growth is nonproductive.

Care
The flowers are produced on new growth, usually in late May and June. Cut the flower stalks back after the first flush of blooms to induce more compact growth and later flowering. Salvias usually go dormant in the winter. Cut the dead foliage off in early spring just as new growth begins to emerge from the ground. Some experts proclaim that cutting back the spent leaves and stems on sage in early winter allows moisture to get down in the hollow, square stems and freeze the root crown.

Landscape Merit
Hardy salvia quickly becomes an integral part of any colorful border. Use it in large island beds or next to the house. Grow these beauties in masses along borders and as fillers in the perennial garden. Plant them to complement mailboxes, rock walls, and other hardscape elements.

My Personal Favorite
I have a favorite for almost every species, but *S. nemorosa* 'Marcus^{TM}' has become my overall favorite due to its compact, 8 inch height and long bloom period.

When, Where, and How to Plant

Scabiosa can be planted in the spring, summer, or fall. It is relatively cold-hardy and thrives in many soil types. Fertile, organic soils that are well-drained provide the best growing conditions. Incorporate slow-release organic fertilizer products at planting. Make sure the planting holes are as wide as and the same depth as the rootball. Fill back the soil? and gently firm the soil around the rootball. Mulch for weed suppression and moisture retention. Water thoroughly for the first few days then weekly until the plants are established and sending out new growth.

Growing Tips

The plants are relatively drought tolerant except for prolonged periods. Supplemental irrigation should be provided during extreme dry periods to avoid complete shut-down of the plants. The plants respond well to supplemental fertilizing if not provided at planting time.

Care

Pruning should consist of deadheading the flower clusters as they turn brown. Blooms continue whether you deadhead or not, but it keeps the plants looking tidier. Plants occasionally spread and can be divided in the spring or fall. Pests are rare, but watch for spider mites, lace bug, and mildew.

Landscape Merit

Plant Scabiosa in large groups for the greatest display, whether in beds all by themselves or as border plants. They also work in container gardening displays due to their compact and continued bloom features. They can even be used individually worked in among perennial gardens when at the appropriate plant height.

My Personal Favorites

I frequently use 'Butterfly Blue' and 'Pink Mist' often together in combination plantings. The yellow flowering selection is a different species *S. ochroleuca*. Mix them all together for a festive spring color combination that lasts all summer long.

If you are in need of a low-growing border plant for you perennial garden, search no more. Scabiosa is perfect and has one of the longest blooming seasons of any perennial. If that is not enough, the flowers are favored by butterflies and provide an airy design to the landscape as they dangle above the compact bushy foliage. The color range is primarily pastels in pink, purple, yellow, and white. If you are still not convinced about growing this one, it also makes a great cut flower and was awarded the perennial plant of the year in 2000 by the Perennial Plant Association.

Other Common Names
Pincushion Flower, Cushion Flower

Bloom Period and Seasonal Color
Pink, purple, yellow or white blooms start early in March and continue through frost.

Mature Height × Spread
12 to 18 in. × 12 to 18 in.

Cold Hardiness Zones
6a, 6b, 7a, 7b

Solomon's Seal
Polygonatum odoratum

Solomon's seal is a delightful woodland plant for perennial shade gardens. This elegant, upright, arching plant has glossy leaves with spreading growth, offering a bold complement to more delicate textures. Once the stems and foliage emerge in the spring from their winter's rest, they quickly develop white tubular flowers gently dangling from the arching stems. Solomon's seal is available in solid-green foliage or variegated white, with fragrant flowers. In a couple of seasons, this hardy plant stakes its claim in the shade garden with its wonderful foliage display. There are quite a few species of Solomon's seal with various heights, spreads, foliage, and fragrances. If you need height with this type of landscape effect, some species mature at 6 feet tall while others are more compact at 6 inches.

Other Common Name
Variegated Polygonatum

Bloom Period and Seasonal Color
White blooms in late spring.

Mature Height × Spread
2 to 3 ft. × 2 to 3 ft.

Cold Hardiness Zones
6a, 6b, 7a, 7b

When, Where, and How to Plant
Solomon's seal spreads with underground rhizomes and is available either as dormant bare-root or container grown plants. Plant dormant bare-root selections in early spring, and plant container plants in the ground in spring or summer. Divide the plants every three or four years if planted in good soils. Divide in early spring or fall. Provide fertile, moisture retentive, and well-drained soil. Plant rhizomes slightly below the soil level, and plant container-grown selections in holes wider than and the same depth as the rootballs. Mulch with leaf mold or other highly organic materials to provide slow-release nutrients, hold in moisture, and minimize weed growth. If you are in a hurry to get instant coverage, plant with 18 inch spacing. Otherwise plant at 24 to 32 inches since the plants eventually spread.

Growing Tips
Remulch as needed, and water during drought conditions. The plants easily wilt and scorch during prolonged dry periods. Provide supplemental feeding only to push the growth for a quicker fill. Slow-release organic fertilizer is a great choice for incorporating at planting time or on a yearly basis as a topdressing when mulch needs to be replenished.

Care
The plants go dormant in the winter and emerge each spring from the rhizomes. Remove old, winter-damaged foliage as new growth begins to emerge. No other pruning is needed. As colonies fill in and need thinning, divide plants in the spring or early fall. Share extras with your gardening friends.

Landscape Merit
Depending on the height, *Polygonatum* can be a background or foreground border plant. Some of the species are somewhat aggressive as a ground cover, which is a nice feature in large, shaded gardens where a lot of filler is needed. The spreading is usually more prominent in moist, fertile soils. It generally has a noninvasive habit.

My Personal Favorite
The true dwarf form maturing at 10 inches is *P. hirtum*, with solid, deep green, shiny foliage and white drooping flowers in early spring.

When, Where, and How to Plant

Set out container-grown plants in late spring or summer. Fall planting is discouraged. These plants prefer full sun but accept two to three hours of shade. With too much shade, they have problems. I have seen these plants thriving in sandy, clay, rocky, or loamy soils. Good drainage and fertile soils are the important elements. Plant verbenas at the same depth that they were grown. Mulch to keep weeds from creeping through the spreading foliage. Water on a regular basis to establish the plants. Plant at 18- to 24-inch spacing for the best fill.

Growing Tips

These sun lovers tolerate drought after they are established, but they spread more quickly and bloom more profusely with consistent irrigation in well-drained sites. Provide supplemental feeding when new growth begins to emerge in the spring and maybe again after the first flush of heavy bloom. Fertilizing past July promotes new growth that is more susceptible to winter injury. Mulch around plant clumps as they spread to insulate roots and keep moisture in and weeds out.

Care

Prune to contain plants within their boundaries. When flowers stall out from stress, shear the plants just below the spent blooms to encourage more growth and later flowering. Leafminers are the biggest insect problem along with foliar mildew disease.

Landscape Merit

With their low-growing habit, verbenas go front and center in the flower bed. They show off their color planted as borders next to sidewalks or in front of the landscape bed. Their free-flowing form cascades over rock walls or from landscape slopes. They also make perfect windowbox or container plants.

My Personal Favorite

'Homestead Purple' seems to be the most reliable perennial selection in my garden.

I am a longtime fan of fragrant perennial or hardy verbenas. They are not picky about soil type, thrive in the summer heat, and are virtually pest free. They are low growing and spreading but not invasive. Some of my favorite hardy selections include 'Homestead Purple', 'Blue Princess', 'Kemerton', and 'Taylortown Red'. The 'Temari' series overwinters in milder winters. I have also found success with the lacy- or cutleaf-foliage types, including V. tenuisecta and a few others. These lacy types are more pest resistant with wonderful flower color. They bloom their hearts out in early summer and give two or three repeat performances, which typically last two to three weeks. 'Imagination' (purple), 'Tapien' (assorted colors) and 'Edith' (pink) are named cultivars. Cutleaf types come in white, lavender, and red.

Other Common Names
Hardy Verbena, Vervain

Bloom Period and Seasonal Color
Purple, pink, red, and white blooms all summer.

Mature Height × Spread
4 to 6 in. × 24 to 30 in.

Cold Hardiness Zones
7a, 7b (6b with winter protection)

Veronica
Veronica species

Veronica is often confused with perennial salvia because of the similarities in growth and flowering habits. Both require similar soil conditions and sites. The flowering times overlap, although some veronicas flower a couple of weeks earlier. The biggest difference is the greater variety in veronicas, which offer a few more growing habits and heights. Upright-growing, blue- or purple-flowering cultivars include 'Royal Blue', 'Blue Giant', 'Midnight', 'Blue Charm', 'Goodness Grows', and 'Crater Lake Blue'. Some cultivars with pinkish-violet flowers are 'Rosenrot', 'Heidekind', 'Spikata Fox' (more shade tolerant), and 'Minuet'. White-flowering selections are 'Icicle', 'Snow White', and 'Alpina Alba'. Ground cover or prostrate forms are 'Georgia Blue', 'Blue Carpet', 'Waterperry Blue', and 'Mann's'. 'Variegata' and 'Noah Williams' are white, variegated forms. 'Trehane' and 'Sunshine' have yellowish-golden foliage with occasional purple spikes.

Other Common Name
Speedwell

Bloom Period and Seasonal Color
Pink, white, and purple blooms in late spring and midsummer.

Mature Height × Spread
17 to 36 in. × 18 to 24 in.

Cold Hardiness Zones
6a, 6b, 7a, 7b

When, Where, and How to Plant
Plant container-grown speedwell in late spring or summer. Speedwell typically grows in a clump or mound, but there are spreading forms. As plants mature, divide to thin and rejuvenate the parent plants. Divide or relocate in early spring. Fertile, moist, well-drained soils are necessary for the success of this plant species. This plant prefers full-sun locations but tolerates shade for three or four hours. Plant them in holes wider than and the same depth as the container rootballs. Space plants 24 inches apart. Mulch and water plants as needed.

Growing Tips
Provide supplemental irrigation during drought conditions. On average the plants need 1 to 2 inches of water per week, including rainfall, depending on the time of the year. Fertilize if the plants are stunted or show signs of chlorosis, which is a yellowing of the foliage. Reapply mulch as it weathers or decomposes. Do not overfertilize in taller selections, or they will flop over. Slow-release fertilizers work best.

Care
The foliage of veronica goes dormant in the winter and reemerges in the spring. Leave the dormant foliage until new growth begins to emerge. Also prune after the first flush of flowers. Trim below the flower spikes to encourage compact growth and more flowering later in the summer or fall. There are few pest problems, but keep an eye out for aphids and powdery mildew.

Landscape Merit
These tough-growing herbaceous perennials are often used as border plants at mid-level or in the back of the bed, depending on the height. The more prostrate growers are used for ground covers or front border plants. They easily cascade over walls, on berms, and in rock gardens. Cluster them in groups for a more significant display of color when planting them for filler.

My Personal Favorites
I love the prostrate chartreuse leafed forms with striking purple flowers. The most commonly sold cultivars are 'Aztec Gold', 'Trehane', and 'Sunshine'. All will take full to part sun.

When, Where, and How to Plant

Plant artemesia in spring or summer. It likes full-sun locations; however, some prefer afternoon shade on with hot, windy sites. Artemesia is not picky about soil type as long as good drainage is provided. Waterlogged soils put a quick end to this plant. Place a container-grown plant in a hole 2 to 3 times the width of the rootball and the same depth. Mulch to keep weeds out. Water to settle the soil. Space plants 24 to 32 inches apart.

Growing Tips

Water as needed during the establishment year. Some species are drought tolerant but not nearly as drought tolerant as its cousin the "tumbleweed" *A. albus*. Minimal fertilizing is required.

Care

Since artemesia is grown for its foliage and not flowers, prune any time to keep plants bushy. Severely prune in early spring to remove winter-damaged branches and to promote new, vigorous growth. The biggest harm to artemesia comes from high humidity, which routinely occurs in Oklahoma. Planting with open spacing and air circulation somewhat alleviates this problem. Plants that tend to "melt down" during the summer can be moved the following spring to afternoon-shaded sites. Too much shade causes the foliage to lose its color. Pests include mildew and stem rot in poorly drained soils.

Companion Planting and Design

Wormwood is generally used as a border or "blender" plant. Its uniform growth makes it suitable for borders or hedges. The soothing color connects or emphasizes other colors in the perennial bed. Use it to divide or separate beds without using physical structures. Artemesia is an effective companion plant with coreopsis, salvia, veronica, Russian sage, and coneflower.

My Personal Favorite

I have variegated 'Oriental Limelight' in my garden. A word of caution: it spreads profusely with underground stolons. I have to battle it to keep it in bounds, but it offers brilliant foliage color.

Artemesia exemplifies what foliage offers in texture, color, and design. The eye-catching gray-green foliage softens or ties other colors together. There is a wide range of foliage textures, from coarse to fine. Artemesia has a pungent odor when the foliage is crushed or bruised. Artemesia offers all this and more, with dependability year after year and little to no care. 'Silver King' and 'Powis Castle' have lacy-type foliage. 'Huntington' and 'Valerie Finnis' have bolder, coarser foliage. For a more mounding growth habit, consider 'Silver Mound'. 'Silver Brocade' is often compared to a hardy dusty miller. A. lactiflora (white mugwort) is probably the most dramatic, and 'Guizhou' is purple stemmed, displaying white-flowering spires in late summer. A. versicolor 'Seafoam' has the airiest appearance and uniquely shaped, silver leaves.

Other Common Names

Artemesia, Sagebrush, Southernwood, Mugwort

Bloom Period and Seasonal Color

Silver gray foliage or variegated foliage from spring to fall.

Mature Height × Spread

2 to 4 ft. × 2 to 3 ft.

Cold Hardiness Zones

6a, 6b, 7a, 7b

Roses *for Oklahoma*

Everybody loves roses, but not everybody loves to grow them. I admire rosarians who spend countless hours spraying, feeding, and pruning their prized beauties. Rose growing is a passion with beautiful rewards. But I personally refuse to put that much time into any plant. Luckily, some rose selections perform acceptably with minimal care and provide summer-long displays of colorful flowers followed by showy seed or fruit—known as "rose hips."

Insects and Diseases

Be on the lookout for spider mites, aphids, thrips, and cane borers (after pruning). The best way to control these critters is to grow healthy plants. Having healthy soil, choosing a planting site with excellent circulation and full sun, inviting beneficial insects to your garden with a variety of plants, and spraying with the right product at the right time will aid you in the long run. A healthy plant will protect not only itself but your precious time, too; you'll be doing less in the long run maintaining a healthy plant than restoring an infected one. As a last resort, a severe infestation threatens the livelihood of your plant, apply a contact spray whether natural or synthetic.

Foliar diseases primarily include black spot and powdery mildew. Blackspot looks just like the name implies with nearly circular spots of various sizes and dark colors. As the disease spreads, the leaves start to yellow around the spots or the entire leaf. The unsightly foliage tends to drop prematurely, thus affecting the plant's overall vigor and health and eventually reducing the flower size and quantity. Another foliar scourge, powdery mildew, is recognized by a whitish coating on leaves, buds, and even stems. Severe outbreaks result in a stunted plant with curled leaves, closed buds, and misshapen flowers. Both blackspot and powdery mildew are most prevalent during warm, wet, humid conditions. Overhead watering that gets the foliage wet can also contribute to both diseases. If you see these on your roses, apply fungicides at the first site of infection and routinely thereafter during optimum weather conditions according to directions.

Treatment

There are numerous control products on the market, and there are home remedies that use household products. One popular disease control is made from one tablespoon baking soda mixed with two-and-one-half tablespoons of Sunspray Ultra-Fine Horticultural Oil™ per gallon of water. Mix two to four tablespoons dishwashing detergent with five tablespoons vegetable oil per gallon of water for insect control. Another natural product, Neem, has both disease and insect control benefits. These products should be rotated with other over-the-counter sprays and natural controls in order to avoid building pest resistance to the chemicals.

Climbing Roses and Daylilies

Soil Preparation

Properly prepare rose beds before planting time. Till rich, organic humus and fertilizer with phosphorus and potassium—and lime, depending on soil test reports—into the existing soil. Good drainage is crucial. I will never forget early in my career visiting the late rose expert C. W. Sturdivant in Muskogee. He literally had hundreds of dollars invested in his planting beds, and the end result was astonishing. He was notorious for his soil mix concoctions of alfalfa pellets, compost, fish emulsion, and who knows what else. The saying about "a $10 plant in a $50 hole" really did apply to his rose-growing techniques.

Fertilization

Healthy green foliage produces vibrant flowers and healthier plants overall. Getting beautiful blooms is the culmination of many preparatory steps, including fertilization. Just about any routine fertilizer combination will work as long as fertilizer salt deposits in the soil are visually monitored. The white, chalky fertilizer salt buildup along the rims of container plants can occur in overfertilized soils. Irrigating for long periods can flush salt residues below the root system. I know gardeners who prefer slow-release products; others like to pour on water-soluble fertilizers. Many swear by natural or organic products. Whatever the choice, I can assure you that the prevailing growers have properly prepared the soil ahead of time and practice routine feedings. On the flip side, too much tender loving care can cause floppy growth, fewer flowers, and more diseased foliage—especially with products high in nitrogen. I watch the plants and let them show me visually when it is time to fertilize based on vigor and healthy growth or lack thereof. I recommend slow-release or organic types applied in early spring.

Planting: Bare-root, Container-Grown, and Grafted Roses

Location of the rose bed is important. It should be in full sun for a minimum of four hours a day. Shade generally produces less foliage, a smaller number of blooms, and more disease. Proper spacing between plants creates better air circulation, which reduces pest problems. Soil preparation and site location are only preludes to proper planting, however.

Modern hybrid roses are usually packaged without soil and sold as bare-root plants. Bare-root plants should be planted in early spring while they are dormant. Dormant roses are packaged in assorted materials—most often sawdust to hold moisture around the roots—until they can be planted. Soak the bare roots in a bucket of water for several hours prior to planting to help re-hydrate the plant. Container-grown roses can be planted in spring, early summer, or even fall.

Typically, roses are grown and sold in two ways. Many hybrid selections are grafted or budded onto hardy, vigorous rootstocks. The area where the bud or graft is made is known as the bud union. If the top or grafted portion should ever die, sprouts may grow into a rambling vigorous rose. Other rose selections are typically propagated from cuttings and grow on their own rootstock.

After the soil beds have been properly prepared with a lot of organic matter, dig a hole two to three times wider than the root mass of the rose. For bare-root plants, mound excess soil in the shape of a pyramid in the bottom of the hole to drape and spread out the roots as well as support the plant at the appropriate height. Container-grown plants should be set the same depth as the rootball.

Budded or grafted roses are typically planted a couple of ways, depending on the growing climate. In milder zones, gardeners position roses so that the bud union (swollen area on the stem) is just above the soil level. In colder climates farther north, gardeners plant roses so that the union is about one inch below the soil surface to protect the graft from winter. In Oklahoma, most gardeners place the union above the ground but mulch around cold-sensitive hybrids for winter protection. The insulator mulch should be removed in late spring as new growth emerges.

Non-grafted varieties seldom need winter mulching since they are grown on their own rootstock and are typically cold hardy. Refill the planting hole without compacting the soil. Water deeply to settle the soil and soak the roots. Mulch to keep out weeds and hold in soil moisture. Compost, shredded leaves, cottonseed hulls, pine bark, and newspaper (not the slick stuff) are good mulch choices for roses.

Pruning

Pruning keeps roses more manageable and promotes new growth. Many gardeners make this task more difficult than it is. The best advice is to just prune! As a general rule, roses blooming on new growth—like many of the modern roses—can be pruned in late spring while they are still dormant. Pruning too early may force new growth that is susceptible to late spring freezes in Oklahoma. Pruning cuts should be made at an angle above rosebuds and covered with a pruning sealer to discourage cane borers. Note which direction the bud is facing. Pruning above buds pointing out will encourage more open growth and air circulation. Prune modern roses after each flowering period to keep the plants bushy. A new flush of growth will soon appear, followed by more blooms. At minimum, you must prune off faded blooms. Continue pruning until early fall. Landscape and shrub roses, which are gaining in popularity, can also be pruned this way although I in early spring and choose varieties that repeat bloom whether or not I prune during the growing season.

After each pruning, it is a good time to apply supplemental fertilizer, but no later than September. Water in the fertilizer especially during periods of drought. Avoid fall feedings, particularly ones high in nitrogen, which can potentially stimulate late-season growth that is more susceptible to winter injury.

Roses blooming on previous season's growth should be pruned after flowering. Climbers need a few canes removed each year to encourage good circulation and new shoots to train into new productive canes. Never prune a budded rose below the knotty-looking graft, or you will force unwanted growth from the rootstock.

Rose Types

Modern roses are breathtaking and are often classified as Hybrid Tea, Floribunda, Grandiflora, Polyantha, Miniature, Tea, and China roses. It is helpful to study the different types to learn how to work them into your landscape since each variety has distinctly different growth and flowering characteristics. But don't overlook some of the more steadfast selections like climbing, heirloom, rugosa, shrub, and species types that are just as colorful as "show type" flowers. Assess the amount of care you are willing to provide and select varieties that match your commitment. Some of my minimal care favorites follow:

Belinda's Dream Rose

Rosa × 'Belinda's Dream'

Belinda's Dream is a shrub or landscape rose that grows about 4 feet tall and 3 feet wide. It has large, fragrant, pink blossoms and gives its show of color from spring until frost. The bluish-green foliage is seldom bothered by disease, and the overall growth habit is upright and sturdy. This beauty even tolerates alkaline soils, making it a perfect choice for western Oklahoma.

Butterfly Rose

Rosa chinensis 'Mutabilis'

This China rose, also known as 'Mutabilis', rose is considered an "old garden" rose. Depending on your pruning and training choices, it can either be a climbing or shrub rose and reaches anywhere between 8 feet tall by 6 feet wide. It blooms primarily in the early spring with single blooms that dance in the wind, resembling butterflies. Depending on your pruning habits and summer temperatures, it occasionally reblooms in fall. The flowers go through a myriad of changes ranging from yellow to copper-orange and from pink to crimson, all happening at the same time. Butterfly rose is relatively disease tolerant; it occasionally yields to blackspot and mildew when prolonged periods of wet weather weaken the plant grown in excessive shade.

Carefree Wonder®

Rosa × 'Meipitac'

Carefree Wonder, also a shrub or landscape rose, is quite cold hardy and fights through our Oklahoma winters. It has semidouble pink flowers that give their best show in the spring and bloom throughout the growing season until the first frost. The plant grows about 3 to 4 feet tall by 4 to 5 feet wide. It has showy, glossy green foliage and produces autumn-like orange hips in the fall. Just like the name implies, it has great disease tolerance and is one that performs with minimal care. It was a 1991 All-America Rose Selections winner.

Fourth of July™

Rosa × 'Fourth of July'

In 1999, 'Fourth of July' was the first climbing rose to win the All-America Rose Selections title in twenty-three years. Like the name implies, it explodes with vibrant color in early spring with velvety red, white, and yellow striped fragrant flower clusters. Oklahoma gardeners are likely to get a couple more flushes of blooms, but nothing as exciting as the first. The canes grow 10 to 14 feet long and about 6 feet wide. The deep green foliage is fairly disease tolerant.

Flower Carpet® Yellow

Rosa var. 'Noalesa'

The Flower Carpet series is ideal for gardeners looking for tough ground cover with the beauty of specimen roses. The yellow selection was the sixth introduction into the series. It is quite cold hardy and exhibits great disease resistance. My particular plant tends to grow more upright (about 3 feet tall and 4 feet wide) than what I had imagined as a ground cover. It blooms profusely from late spring till frost. The semidouble yellow flowers fade as they mature.

Katy Road Pink

Rosa var. 'Katy Road Pink'

This rose is not that well known in the trade but gets my vote because it was found growing along the road near Katy, Texas. The shrub's open, graceful shape classifies it as a landscape or shrub rose. It has few pest problems and does not need a lot of fussy care. It provides continuous single to somewhat semi-double pink blooms throughout the season. An added treat is the nice large rose hips in the fall. I got my plant from a start sent to me from a gardening friend, but The Antique Rose Emporium out of Brenham Texas offers it for sale. See the Appendix for a list of nurseries with this plant.

Knock Out™

Rosa × 'Radrazz'

Knocked out and blown away was the way I felt when I first tried this rose. A 2002 AARS winner, this shrub rose exemplifes disease resistance and low maintenance care. Even in the wettest of conditions, it had had no obvious disease. I only prune it in the spring, and I get more flushes of growth and bloom from spring to frost than any other rose in my garden. The cherry red, fragrant, semidouble blooms are very showy throughout the season. As an added bonus, new foliage growth in between flowering is a beautiful burgundy. Look for Knock Out™ Pink, Blush, and Double.

Marie Daly

Rosa × polyantha 'Marie Daly'

'Marie Daly', a nearly thornless polyantha rose, likens floribundas with its small flowers on more compact plants. This selection is known for its continuous season bloom and very fragrant double pink flowers. Marie Daly has good disease and alkaline soil tolerance. The compact plants, about 3 feet tall by 3 feet wide, make great edging for borders edge or container specimens.

New Dawn

Rosa × 'New Dawn'

New Dawn is a classic old climbing rose. The canes can easily reach 10 to 12 feet high and produce glossy green foliage that is quite disease resistant. I've also seen this beauty successfully trained and grown as a large shrub rose. New Dawn's double, pale pink bloom clusters are best known for their spicy fragrance. Also, amongst the climbing roses, it is one of the best to flower consistently and repeatedly throughout the season.

Zephirine Drouhin

Rosa × 'Zephirine Drouhin'

Another climbing rose, 'Zephirine Drouhin', produces large clusters of fantastically fragrant rose-pink flowers. It, too, gives the best show of color in early spring and blooms throughout the season. In addition, this climber is thornless. The growth is fairly vigorous, reaching about 15 feet or more in height and 6 feet in width wide. Though touted as shade tolerant, you'd be safer planting it in full sun due to Oklahoma's humidity. 'Zephrine Drouhin' is prone to blackspot more than mildew. Proper pruning, abundant sun, and good air circulation minimizes most disease infestations.

Shrubs *for Oklahoma*

If trees are the pillars of the landscape, then shrubs are the framework. Shrubs provide filler, height variation, texture, color, and just about any presentation needed for a personalized design. Like all plants, shrubs have their specific growing preferences of sun or shade and soil type. Shrubs are categorized as woody plants, either evergreen or deciduous, ranging in height from inches to several feet. Some could even be considered small trees.

Homeowners frequently make the mistake of improperly spacing shrubs. Plant shrubs to allow them to reach their mature size. Give them plenty of room, especially when planting them near the foundation of your home. Allow widths of at least 5 to 8 feet in a bed design from the foundation according to the scale of your home or structure. In a couple of years shrubs will fill in all the open space. Cluster shrubs in groups to make a bigger impact. Use shrubs to form curves, provide background for other landscape plants, or divide areas of the landscape to make outdoor rooms.

Plant According to Soil

Planting shrubs is a little different from planting trees since they are more likely to be planted together in landscape beds rather than as single specimens. Group like-growing plants together, such as azaleas, loropetalum, and other acid-loving plants. If possible, prepare the bed before planting time by incorporating organic matter, complete fertilizers, whether synthetic or natural, and other amendments. Such preparation is especially important if lime, sulfur, potassium, or phosphorous is required; soil test results and the preferences of particular plants dictate this need. Mix the materials by tilling them into the soil. If the beds are in association with existing trees, skip the tilling process, or damage can occur to the shallow roots and shorten the lives of the trees. Never add more than 6 inches of soil on top of tree roots or it will create future problems. Plant a single shrub the same way you plant a tree by digging a wide hole and without adding organic backfill. Refill with the original soil, mulch and water thoroughly.

Loropetalum

Mulch Can Help

Mulch should be about 2 to 4 inches thick. Do not mulch the plant stems. Get it thick in between plants and angle it down to the base. Mulch will occasionally wash, blow away, and decay, so reapply it every two or three years.

Watering and Fertilizing

The preferred method for watering plants is to water deeply and infrequently. In other words, really soak the plants down to the root system and wait a few days before the next application. This encourages roots to grow deep. Watering every day for just a few minutes at a time encourages roots to remain shallow, making plants more susceptible to drought, freeze, and stress. In general, plants thrive on one to two inches of water a week, including rainfall. And don't

Lilac

forget that drought can occur in the winter months as well. Just because a plant is dormant doesn't mean it won't need an occasional soaking if rainfall is deficient. Plant roots are still functioning and active even during the winter. Lack of winter watering following fall planting can cause poor establishment and even death.

Supplemental feedings are beneficial. Simply broadcast fertilizers on the surface of the ground around the shrubs according to product directions. Split the application in early spring and summer. Adequate rainfall or supplemental irrigation is needed during these application times. Fall applications can potentially stimulate new growth that is more susceptible to freezing conditions unless a slow release organic fertilizer is used. A soil test should be done every couple of years to keep you up to date on any nutritional deficiencies or soil pH changes that may need correcting, especially with shrubs that prefer acidic soils like azaleas, hydrangeas, and loropetalum.

Pruning and Pests

Shrubs will occasionally need pruning and training to keep from overpowering other plants in the landscape. As a general rule, flowering shrubs should be pruned as soon as they have finished flowering. Tip shearing or directional pruning can be done at any time throughout the growing season to keep the plants in their desired shape and location. Avoid pruning however in severe heat, cold or drought. Plants with specific pruning times are noted in each corresponding plant entry. Also, remove any grass allowed to grow around and in shrubs. Not only does it look bad, but it competes with the shrubs for moisture and nutrients. Routine spot applications of glyphosate or glyphosinate herbicides are well worth the investment to keep weeds out, especially pesky Bermuda. Follow the label directions and keep any drift or splash off of the landscape plants.

Frequently scout for pests to shortcut epidemics. Spider mites, aphids, mealy bugs, caterpillars, lacebugs, and scale are the most common insects to watch for. Small populations identified early can be easily managed by determining whether beneficial insects are present and doing their job. Hand picking, high pressure water sprays, and organic products also work well on smaller populations. Healthy plants are less prone to pest problems. Place them in wide holes in their preferred site with plenty of air circulation; mulch and irrigate during drought.

I have included twenty-six selections of shrubs in this chapter and the cultivars that are generally considered low maintenance in the appropriate planting sites. There is something for sun or shade or just about any landscape situation.

Abelia
Abelia grandiflora

Abelia offers texture and color—with minimal care. The only attention it requires is occasional pruning of out-of-place suckers. The flowers bloom prominently during early summer; sporadic blooms continue until frost. The charming, bell-shaped blossoms are white, pink, or lavender, depending on the cultivar. The showy flowers are somewhat scattered but still beautiful—and hummingbirds love them. In southeastern Oklahoma, abelia is often evergreen, and farther north it is semi-evergreen. 'Compacta' and 'Sherwoodii' are dwarf, mounding cultivars, maturing to nearly three feet. Selections of variegated foliage types include 'Frances Mason' and 'Sunrise'. Hybrids are also available with more choices in flower color. 'Edward Goucher' is three to five feet in height with pink flowers. 'Purple Rain' is dwarf with a pale purple flower.

Other Common Name
Glossy Abelia

Bloom Period and Seasonal Color
White or pink blooms in May and June.

Mature Height × Spread
3 to 6 ft. × 3 to 6 ft.

Cold Hardiness Zones
6a, 6b, 7a, 7b

When, Where, and How to Plant
Plant abelia in the spring in western Oklahoma; plant it in spring or fall in eastern parts of the state. Abelia prefers rich, moist, well-drained, slightly acidic soil. Although it is hardy for most of the state, abelia is better suited for central and eastern Oklahoma. Plant abelia in a hole 2 to 3 times wider than and the same depth as the rootball. Water and mulch as needed. No amended backfill is necessary in a single planting hole unless materials were incorporated into the entire bed previously. Abelias grow an average of 5 feet wide, so allow plenty of space unless you choose a dwarf cultivar or commit to pruning routinely.

Growing Tips
Abelia responds to supplemental fertilization, but too much causes an overabundance of growth with minimal flowering. Abelia requires supplemental watering during drought periods but does not require pampering once it is established.

Care
Flowers typically occur on new growth of the season, so prune for shape in the fall or early spring before new growth emerges. The plants also respond favorably to frequent shearing to form into a hedge, but the flower display won't be quite as showy. Provide occasional pruning of suckers or shoots at any time throughout the growing season. There are no serious pests; however, powdery mildew occurs in too much shade.

Landscape Merit
Abelia makes a nice background plant since some of the cultivars grow in compact mounds while others are more upright. Match a cultivar's height according to your landscape needs. Some of the cultivars with colorful variegated foliage are good for mass plantings or as specimens. The compact growth habit of the dwarf selections are also ideal for slopes while the taller selections grow into a nice hedge.

My Personal Favorites
I particularly like the variegated foliage selections like 'Confetti', 'Silver Anniversary™', and 'Sunrise'. The foliage is just as showy as the flowers.

American Beautyberry
Callicarpa americana

When, Where, and How to Plant

Plant beautyberry in the spring or early fall in organic, moisture-retentive soils. Most varieties prefer afternoon shade or lightly filtered shade. Be careful not to place beautyberry in too much shade or the plants become straggly with poorer berry production. It sometimes accepts full-sun sites with wind protection and proper soil. Dig the planting holes the same depth as and 2 to 3 times wider than the rootballs. For a mass planting, space the plants 4 to 5 feet apart. Water after planting and on a regular basis until the plants are securely established. Mulch is crucial as it simulates a woody site, holding moisture, stabilizing soil temperatures during the summer, and providing slow-release nutrients.

Growing Tips

Supplemental irrigation is necessary during prolonged drought periods; otherwise, berry production (and the colorful fall show) will be diminished. Avoid excessive supplemental feedings, or overgrown, leggy growth occurs. Original, organic soil usually suffices.

Care

Pruning is needed only to train or control the size of the large shrub. Some gardeners prune beautyberries back 6 to 8 inches to keep them bushier and more compact. Dormant-prune in early spring before new growth emerges, removing dead, weak, rubbing, or damaged branches. Dormant-pruning also allows for fruit production, which occurs on new growth. Pests are of minimal concern. Seedlings may develop under and around the plants the following spring as a result of the fruit. Pull them up and share them with gardening friends.

Landscape Merit

Beautyberry makes a wonderful understory plant since its natural habitat is in rich, moist woodlands under tree canopies with partial sun. It is often found in thickets; mimicking this natural habitat in the landscape makes a brilliant fall display.

My Personal Favorite

Folks who do not think white is an attractive landscape color will think twice when they see 'Lactea' loaded with clusters of showy white berries in the fall.

This delightful shrub is native to the southeastern United States, including the southeastern locales of Oklahoma. There is not much to the deciduous plant early in the season, but it makes up in the fall with beautiful lavender berries. The pale-green foliage is somewhat aromatic, and leaves are arranged opposite each other on the long stems. By late June—and sometimes even later depending on the plant—the shrub flowers profusely. The bloom period can be prolonged into August and later. Showy clusters of fruit emerge in August through November, changing from translucent to a creamy greenish brown before they mature into a vibrant purple $1/4$ to $1/8$ inches in size. Use this lovely native as a colorful fall enhancer for the landscape and you will not be disappointed.

Other Common Names

Callicarpa, Sow Berry, Sour Bush, French Mulberry, Spanish Mulberry

Bloom Period and Seasonal Color

Lavender pink blooms in late summer.

Mature Height × Spread

3 to 8 ft. × 3 to 5 ft.

Cold Hardiness Zones

6b, 7a, 7b

Azalea

Rhododendron hybrids

Azaleas scream color for a couple of weeks in the spring, enticing gardeners to load up their landscape. But be careful, azaleas have a lot of specific needs. Evergreen or semi-evergreen types are the most common. 'Kurume' (Rhododendron obtusum) and 'Gable' hybrids are semi-dwarf and some of the most cold-hardy. 'Glenn Dale' hybrids are semi-dwarf with good hardiness and larger flowers. The 'Northern Lights' hybrids offer taller selections—reaching six to eight feet. 'Girard' hybrids are adapted to most of the state. Southern indicas are best for the southeastern counties, and Belgian types are the most dwarf. Satsuki azaleas are small in size and bloom later, extending the season. Underused azaleas include the deciduous or Exbury types. They come in many colors, even yellow, which is hard to find in the evergreen groups.

Other Common Name
Rhododendron

Bloom Period and Seasonal Color
Pink, red, white, and yellow blooms in April and May.

Mature Height × Spread
3 to 8 ft. × 3 to 6 ft.

Cold Hardiness Zones
6a, 6b, 7a, 7b

When, Where, and How to Plant
Though fall planting is feasible in milder parts of Oklahoma, you should plant azaleas in spring. They prefer filtered afternoon shade; full shade thins the plants, and full sun scorches them. Acidic soil with good drainage is a must! Design azalea beds slightly above soil grade for better drainage and for easier bed preparation. Use soil amendments such as soil sulfur and peat moss, pecan hulls, coconut coir, or other acid-based organic products. (Follow the directions the products give on their bags.) Mix organic materials into the existing soil to make a 50-50 mixture, 1 to 2 feet deep. When planting under trees, do not place soil amendments more than 6 inches above ground level; do not till it into the existing soil. Mulch using pine bark, pecan hulls, pine needles, or other acidic mulches.

Growing Tips
Provide routine feedings that include iron and sulfur after blooming. Stop fertilizing in June to encourage winter hardening. Supplemental irrigation during drought periods is a must.

Care
Prune azaleas as soon as they finish blooming. Buds for next season's bloom are in place by late summer. Severe infestations of lacebugs cause speckled or mottled foliage. When left untreated, these critters stunt and may even kill the plants. Monitor early in the season and spray under the foliage with the appropriate insecticide. Disease problems are occasional leaf spots and galls (abnormal tissue swelling). Pick the galls before they turn white and discard them somewhere off the property. Iron chlorosis is caused by high pH or alkaline soils. The preferred pH for azaleas is 4.5 to 5.5.

Landscape Merit
Good companions include loropetalum, hydrangea, blueberry, and epimedium.

My Personal Favorites
I tend to favor the Kurume series, particularly 'Coral Bells', which seems to take a little more sun. But I'm also smitten by the big golden flowers of the Exbury types.

Burning Bush
Euonymus alatus

When, Where, and How to Plant

Burning bush is a tough plant, adaptable to spring or fall planting. It tolerates just about any soil type as long as it is not waterlogged. Burning bush is commonly sold as a container-grown or balled-and-burlapped plant. Dig the hole at least 2 times wider than and the same depth as the rootball. Refill the hole with the original soil, but do not compact the soil during planting. Mulching is very beneficial when growing this plant. Water at planting to settle the soil and as needed thereafter.

Growing Tips

Burning bush develops a shallow, fibrous root system. Roots exposed to heat and cold cause stress and pest susceptibility. Mulch as often as the organic products decompose or wash away. Provide supplemental water during severe drought; the plants are fairly drought tolerant once established. The plants are considered slow growing, and reach 20 feet tall in optimum growing conditions in fifteen to twenty years.

Care

Prune anytime as needed to keep the height manageable or form a hedge. Pest and disease problems are minimal other than an occasional leaf spot and sunburn on foliage in full sun during a prolonged drought.

Landscape Merit

Use *Euonymus alatus* for a hedge or as a single specimen. I have seen it successfully used as a background landscape plant and as a foundation plant in conjunction with two-story homes. The flaming-red fall color complements evergreen companion plants. Consider planting it in perennial beds. The initial growth habit of burning bush is upright with a flat top, which is especially nice for hedges or background borders. The plants lose their colorful leaves in the late fall, but with their thick, greenish-brown branches they have an evergreen look in the winter. The growth becomes spreading as the plants mature.

My Personal Favorite

I use the dwarf varieties like 'Compactus' and 'Rudy Haag' that mature to around 4 to 5 feet in height.

Not only does this deciduous plant offer unique foliage that turns a glowing-red in the fall, but it has interestingly winged, corky twigs that add as much winter appeal as the foliage contributes to fall. On mature plants, you find capsule-like red berries in the fall. Burning bush lives up to its name in late fall with red foliage unmatched by any landscape plant. The wings and corky twigs are not as prominent on more compact selections, but the fall colors are traffic stopping. Mockingbirds and other nesting birds favor the open yet secluded growth habit for raising their families. The best news of all is that euonymus scale does not seem to be too interested in this particular species.

Other Common Name
Winged Euonymus

Bloom Period and Seasonal Color
Red fall foliage.

Mature Height × Spread
5 to 20 ft. × 5 to 10 ft.

Cold Hardiness Zones
6a, 6b, 7a, 7b

Butterfly Bush
Buddleia davidii

This plant is truly a magnet for attracting butterflies as well as bees and hummingbirds, thanks to its honey-scented blooms. The elongated flower clusters are showy and long-lived. Butterfly bush is deciduous and loses its leaves in the winter and is late to leaf out or break dormancy in the spring. In the colder areas of the state, butterfly bush freezes to the ground, but it comes back from the roots and can grow several feet in a season. It needs plenty of room to grow and can reward you with fragrant flowers all summer. The foliage is typically a gray or blue-green color. Most of the B. davidii selections reach six to ten feet in a season.

Other Common Name
Summer Lilac

Bloom Period and Seasonal Color
White, pink, purple, or yellow blooms in June through frost.

Mature Height × Spread
5 to 15 ft. × 5 to 10 ft.

Cold Hardiness Zones
6b, 7a, 7b

When, Where, and How to Plant
Plant butterfly bush in spring in fertile, well-drained soil. Heavy, poorly-drained soils amount to certain death. Avoid planting close to sidewalks or front doors because it attracts bees. Dig planting holes at least 2 feet wider than and the same depth as the rootballs. No soil amendments are needed in a single hole; however, prepare a complete bed with organic materials. Water deeply to soak the roots and settle the soil. Mulch to hold soil moisture and keep weeds in check. Space plants about 10 feet apart when planted en masse.

Growing Tips
The plants are often touted as drought tolerant, but I have lost many when I did not provide supplemental irrigation during dry periods. Flowers emerge from current-season growth, starting in early summer and continuing through frost. Thus, you should prune the shrub when it is dormant. Some folks even prune them back several inches from the ground to grow them more as herbaceous perennials. Others train them as a small tree.

Care
There are occasional lulls between flower spurts. Deadheading "spent" flowers encourages rejuvenation. Severely prune during the summer in years with ragged foliage or severe spider mite infestation. Spider mites are the biggest nuisance for butterfly bush, especially in areas with poor aeration. Watch for yellowing or speckling foliage. Spider mites typically suck the plant juices from the undersides of the foliage, which causes this mottling appearance on the tops. Tap the foliage on a white sheet of paper; if any of the specks start crawling, the plants have been invaded by these aggressive critters.

Landscape Merit
Most cultivars grow in an arching form and add texture to the landscape. It is often used as a specimen in the back of perennial or shrub beds, but mass plantings offer more color. Remember to give them breathing room.

My Personal Favorite
I like 'Nanho Blue' for its more compact growth.

Chaste Tree
Vitex agnus-castus

When, Where, and How to Plant

Plant chaste tree in the spring in northern and western Oklahoma. Plant it in spring or fall in the milder locations of the state. Although it tolerates poor soils, it performs better in well-drained, fertile soils. It is sold as a container-grown or balled-and-burlapped plant. Plant it as you would a tree, in a hole 2 to 3 times wider than and the same depth as the rootball. No organic backfill is required. Water deeply to settle the soil and soak the roots. Mulch to keep grass and weeds from competing during the establishment period.

Growing Tips

The plants are relatively drought tolerant once established. It is still a good idea to water during severe drought if you want to keep the foliage from scorching and the blooms developing. Mulch it as needed. Chaste tree responds to fertilizer during the growing season. Consider using slow release organic fertilizers for a gradual boost of nutrients and growth.

Care

The attractive blooms are formed on the current season's growth, so perform severe pruning while the plant is dormant. Trim flowers after the initial bloom to encourage more blossoms in the fall. I like to remove the lower branches on multiple trunk specimens to expose the elegant base. Pruning suckers growing along the trunk throughout the summer. Few pest problems are reported except spider mites in stressed situations. Fungal leaf spots can occur during prolonged periods of rain and cloud cover.

Landscape Merit

Chaste tree requires plenty of room and is most often used in lawns or the landscape as a specimen plant. The unique arrangement and shape of the foliage make it a great choice for texture in the landscape, and it is tough to boot.

My Personal Favorite

'Abbyville Blue' is quite showy with its violet blue flower spikes.

Chaste tree becomes quite tall, forming what is often thought of as a small tree. I have included it as a shrub because of its multiple trunk form and overall smaller, woody growth. It is occasionally nipped back by a severe winter but grows back readily. It should be used more often due to its drought tolerance and acceptance of poor soils after establishment. Chaste tree leaves are a dull gray-green with a slightly pungent aroma when bruised. The somewhat fragrant, showy flowers emerge on current-season growth. It is a good alternative for gardeners not having luck growing lilac. The growth habit is similar, but the highly fragrant lilac flower is missing. The species has blue flowers. 'Silver Spire' and 'Alba' have white flowers. 'Rosea' has pink blooms.

Other Common Names

Chase Tree, Hemp Tree, Indian Spice, Sage Tree, and Monk's Pepper

Bloom Period and Seasonal Color

Lavender, pink, and white blooms in summer through fall.

Mature Height × Spread

12 to 20 ft. × 10 to 20 ft.

Cold Hardiness Zones

6a, 6b, 7a, 7b

Crapemyrtle
Lagerstromia indica

I call this delightfully engaging shrub the "Summer Flowering Queen" of the state. The showy and fragrant flower blooms (depending on the cultivar) occur from midsummer to fall. Crapemyrtle is easy to grow and provides breathtaking autumn color. To top it off, it has dazzling golden-rose leaf color in the fall and unique exfoliating bark in maturity. Crapemyrtle offers various shapes for the landscape, depending on the cultivar. Some grow into small trees; others are more upright. Specimens are more likely to reach tree-size in milder parts of the state. Crapemyrtles are one of the last shrubs to break dormancy in the spring, sometimes in May. Several are considered dwarf, but choose your cultivar carefully since dwarf for crapemyrtle in the industry can be six to eight feet tall.

Other Common Name
Lilac of the South

Bloom Period and Seasonal Color
Red, pink, purple, or white blooms in summer to frost with golden-rose fall foliage.

Mature Height × Spread
1 to 25 ft. × 2 to 20 ft.

Cold Hardiness Zones
6a, 6b, 7a, 7b

When, Where, and How to Plant
Plant during spring in colder locations of Oklahoma and up to early fall in southeastern regions. They perform best in moist and well-drained soil. Dig the planting hole at least 2 feet wider than and the same depth as the rootball. No organic amendments are needed as backfill. Deeply water to settle the soil and adequately soak the roots. Spacing between plants depends on the particular cultivar's maturity size.

Growing Tips
Mulch as needed to retain soil moisture and keep weeds at bay. Fertilize in late spring or early summer to stimulate growth. Avoid feeding after July to encourage winter hardening. Though wonderfully drought tolerant, the plants need supplemental watering during drought.

Care
Prune during the winter or early spring to customize the size and growth habit. Flowers are set on current-season growth. Trimming spent flowers before they set fruit promotes a longer bloom period. In colder parts, crapemyrtle may succumb to a severe winter. Wait to see where spring growth emerges before pruning. When everything else is green and growing and some parts are not, prune what's been winter-killed. Though common, don't prune tree forms back into little sticks; knotty regrowth breaks during wind and heavy flower set. Look for powdery mildew in shady sites. Planting mildew-resistant cultivars in good circulation prevents this. Aphids sometimes feed on crapemyrtles and secrete a sweet substance called "honeydew" (which ants like to eat). Harmless, grayish-black mold known as "sooty mold" grows on honeydew. Beneficial insects like ladybugs feed on aphids.

Landscape Merit
Most often crapemyrtle is found as a specimen plant. Its mature height dictates its location; place taller plants in the back of your landscape beds. Use crapemyrtles as a screen or hedge. Plant them in groups of three when using the miniature selections for a bigger show of flower color.

My Personal Favorites
'Natchez' makes a beautiful small tree, but 'Pokomoke', a true dwarf cultivar, is my favorite.

Dwarf Fothergilla
Fothergilla gardenii

When, Where, and How to Plant

Plant fothergilla in spring or fall in filtered or afternoon shade under a tree or on the east-northeast side of a structure. Fothergilla must be in moist, well-drained, acidic soil. Before planting time, work peat moss or other organic material into the soil. Then dig the hole at least 2 times wider than the rootball and slightly above soil grade. Elevating the entire bed slightly above soil grade allows for better drainage. Mulching with acidic materials like pine bark or pine straw is highly recommended for these acid-loving plants. Space 3 to 5 feet apart depending on the variety.

Growing Tips

Minimal fertilization is needed with the appropriate soil preparation before planting, but the plants respond well to organic, slow-release fertilizers mixed into the soil and applied routinely each fall. Any synthetic fertilizers with acidic properties, iron, and sulfur used to correct this problem should be applied soon after flowering and watered in immediately.

Care

These eye-catching plants are often touted as trouble free—but only after the right environmental conditions are met. Prune after flowering since blooms are formed on the previous season's growth. In excessively alkaline soils, iron chlorosis occurs. Iron chlorosis turns a leaf yellow all over with green veins. Apply soil sulfur according to directions for a long-term fix and continue to mulch as needed. Foliar applications of iron chelates correct the problem only temporarily.

Landscape Merit

Fothergilla works well as a foundation plant or background plant in shade gardens. The plant's distinctiveness also affords it the opportunity to move front and center as a feature plant. The foliage and flower colors of fothergilla added to the assorted colors of azaleas are a goof-proof landscape match. Use as a companion plant for loropetalum, hydrangea, blueberry, and epimedium.

My Personal Favorites

'Mt. Airy' and 'Blue Mist' are the two most common dwarf cultivars and are perfect for any landscape.

If you are looking for a companion plant for azaleas, then look no further. Fothergilla is not well-known in Oklahoma, but it deserves more exposure, especially in the eastern and southeastern parts. The foliage and flowers spice up any dappled shade garden with season-long appeal. The white, bottlebrush flowers invigorate the air with a sweet fragrance. Deciduous foliage emerges with a soothing blue tint. The fall color, ranging from golden yellow to orange to scarlet red, is probably its best attribute. Just like azaleas, the plants must have the appropriate soil and site conditions or they will be a disappointing landscape addition. There are not too many varieties available, but size can vary based on the cultivar and species, ranging from three to six feet in height.

Bloom Period and Seasonal Color
White blooms in April or May.

Mature Height × Spread
2 to 6 ft. × 3 to 5 ft.

Cold Hardiness Zones
6a, 6b, 7a, 7b

English Boxwood

Buxus sempervirens

English boxwood is your basic, green foundation plant with minimal problems. I have found it to be more dependable than Japanese or littleleaf boxwood especially with afternoon shade. The foliage is a deeper green and somewhat pointed, where Japanese boxwood's leaf is rounded. The flowers are imperfect and inconspicuous. The female flowers occasionally set a green, capsule-like fruit. During the harshest winters, the lustrous, green foliage turns a brownish tint. Even though English boxwood is evergreen, do not be alarmed to see the plants shed older foliage at certain times throughout the year. Male dogs consistently visiting the plants have been known to burn the foliage. English boxwood seems more resistant to blights and leaf spots, although they are possible. There is an assortment of sizes, depending on the cultivar.

Other Common Name
Common Boxwood

Bloom Period and Seasonal Color
White blooms in early spring.

Mature Height × Spread
2 to 15 ft. × 3 to 6 ft.

Cold Hardiness Zones
6a, 6b, 7a, 7b

When, Where, and How to Plant
Plant English boxwood in the spring or early fall. It is available as a container-grown or balled-and-burlapped plant. I have seen plants in full sun, but protection from harsh summer winds would be beneficial for this plant. A site with afternoon shade is definitely preferred in Oklahoma's hot summers. English boxwood likes a good soil with some moisture retention and good drainage. Slightly acidic soil is an added bonus. Being planted in heavy, waterlogged soils shortens the lives of these shrubs. These plants are somewhat shallow rooted. Dig the holes wider than and at the same depth as the initial rootballs.

Growing Tips
Mulching and supplemental watering are necessities, especially during hot, dry conditions. Supplemental fertilizers speed up the growth somewhat, but the shallow roots are easy to burn when using frequent, high-nitrogen applications, especially during drought. Do not apply fertilizer after June, or the plants become more susceptible to winter injury. Organic slow-release fertilizer mixed in the soil bed before planting and then applied on a routine basis each spring or fall is ideal.

Care
English boxwoods respond well to shearing. The plants are considerably slow growing but have the potential to become quite large over time in optimum conditions. Pests include possible spider mites that suck on the plant foliage and fungal twig blights that kill back individual leaves and twigs. Mites are best controlled with oil-type products, and the disease can be pruned out sporadically to help prevent spread. In severe cases, fungicides are recommended.

Landscape Merit
Use English boxwood as a foundation shrub, a companion to neighboring deciduous plants, a hedge for screening purposes, or as topiary plants in formal gardens.

My Personal Favorite
I typically use the slow growing, dwarf, rounded selection sold as 'Suffruticosa' that seldom needs pruning.

Flowering Quince
Chaenomeles speciosa

When, Where, and How to Plant

Plant flowering quince in spring or fall. It prefers full-sun sites with good air circulation, but it accepts some morning-shade locations. This tough plant is not picky about soil type; it tolerates almost any soil as long as it drains well. Flowering quince is sometimes used as a substitute for early spring flowers. Dig the planting hole at least 2 times wider than and at the same depth as the rootball. Water to settle the soil and soak the root system. Mulch with pine bark, cottonseed hulls, compost, or any type of water-holding organic material.

Growing Tips

Flowering quince is considered a tough plant when it comes to drought tolerance and overall care. It responds to minimal feedings but requires no special formulations. As mulch decomposes or blows away, reapply it as needed.

Care

Flowers form on new wood that develops after pruning. Branches can be cut a few weeks earlier in February and forced to bloom indoors. Late freezes damage flower buds in some years. Prune the plants after flowering, just as you would azaleas. Potential pests include scale, aphids, and spider mites. These critters attack almost any plant in stressed situations.

Landscape Merit

Groupings of these plants offer the best color display. They are often used as back border plants in conjunction with evergreens. Flowering quince offers plenty throughout the rest of the season after they have bloomed; mix them with other showy plants that offer either flower or foliage color during the growing season.

My Personal Favorite

'Cameo' has a unique, apricot colored flower with few to no thorns.

This deciduous shrub has much to offer at times when there is little going on in the landscape. It is one of the earliest to flower from the previous season's growth in the spring. The flowers are quite showy and appear generally before the leaves emerge. As the leaves unfurl, there is a hint of burgundy color before turning a glossy green. Do not be surprised to see large, pear-like fruit develop. Although the fruit is bitter when eaten raw, it makes a great jelly or preserve when cooked. The shrubs may flower again later in the season. Flowering quince has made a name for itself in landscaping by discouraging prowlers near homes, thanks to their spines. Some cultivars offer a double flower.

Bloom Period and Seasonal Color
Pink, red, salmon, or white blooms in early spring.

Mature Height × Spread
4 to 10 ft. × 4 to 6 ft.

Cold Hardiness Zones
6a, 6b, 7a, 7b

Heavenly Bamboo

Nandina domestica

Nandina is one of my favorite landscape plants. It provides attractive foliage, flowers, and fruit. The enormous, compound, semi-evergreen leaves are feathery in appearance. The flowers are fairly showy. Bright-red fruit emerges in the late summer and fall. The foliage remains evergreen in milder winters but defoliates in severe cold spells. 'Royal Princess' grows five feet tall and spreads nearly six feet. 'Atropurpurea Nana' is a dwarf selection with twisted, yellow-green, and reddish-purple foliage, which is actually caused by a virus. 'Fire Power', another dwarf selection with the same brilliant color, has smoother foliage and is thought to be virus free. 'San Gabriel' is a dwarf selection with thin, feathery foliage but lacks cold hardiness and is best suited for protected areas. 'Plum Passion' has foliage that emerges as a purplish color throughout the growing season.

Other Common Name
Nandina

Bloom Period and Seasonal Color
White blooms in May or June.

Mature Height × Spread
2 to 10 ft. × 2 to 6 ft.

Cold Hardiness Zones
6a, 6b, 7a, 7b

When, Where, and How to Plant
Plant nandina in the spring or early fall. It tolerates rocky sites, heavy clay, sand, and most soil conditions as long as it does not stand in water. Most nursery plants are containerized. Plant in holes the same depth as but 2 to 3 times wider than the rootballs. Water on a regular basis to thoroughly soak the roots until the plants are well established.

Growing Tips
Overfertilization results in an overabundance of foliage and the plant's inability to set fruit. The plant is tough and often found growing in abandoned sites. It is quite drought tolerant, but like most plants in the landscape, it provides the best display of healthy foliage and color when given supplemental irrigation during severe drought.

Care
The most frustrating trait of the species or standard nandina is the tall growth habit and the increasingly woody quality at the base. When that happens, prune the top back each spring to force additional growth from the base. I have also seen them trimmed up from the base leaving a little foliage on the top that almost resembles a palm tree. Remove selected, older woody stems to thin plants and encourage more growth. Other than occasional foliage diseases in heavily shaded sites with poor air circulation, pest problems are very rare.

Landscape Merit
Use nandina as a background border plant, a hedge, or a foundation plant near buildings. It can be a single specimen plant placed just about anywhere, depending on the size of the cultivar. Compact varieties definitely make a better show as groups than as singles.

My Personal Favorite
My favorite is 'Harbour Dwarf' with the traditional species looking foliage and berry set but half the size.

Japanese Holly

Ilex crenata

When, Where, and How to Plant

Plant most hollies in spring, early summer, or early fall. Japanese hollies as a whole take full sun or partial shade. I have found over the years that they perform better when they get morning sun and afternoon shade—although I have seen some pretty incredible plantings in full sun when they are generally protected from hot summer winds. The plants are better suited for eastern Oklahoma but adapt as far west as Oklahoma City and at an angle down to Altus. Preferred sites are fertile, slightly acidic, well-drained soils, but they can tolerate some clay soils with descent drainage. Dig the holes at least 2 times wider than and the same depth as the rootballs. Water gently and deeply to settle the soil and soak the entire root system. Mulch with pine straw, pine bark, pecan hulls, or other acidic products.

Growing Tips

Supplemental watering and mulching are good practices. Fertilizing a couple of times throughout the growing season, preferably in late April and again in June, ensures vigorous plants. Later applications are not advised, for they increase the chance of winter damage.

Care

Japanese hollies respond to shearing and selective pruning. Pruning is typically done in early spring as new growth emerges; however, occasional maintenance pruning can be done throughout the season. Japanese hollies are inclined when stressed to succumb to spider mites, twig blight, and leaf spot. During the driest and hottest times, they sunburn when they are grown in full sun. Monitoring plants for these problems ensures quicker response to controls.

Landscape Merit

Japanese hollies are used most often as foundation plants and borders and in mass groupings. They can also be used to provide borders to separate different levels or rooms of the landscape.

My Personal Favorite

Without a doubt 'Soft-Touch' holly is my favorite with its limey green, delicate soft foliage.

Japanese holly is a frequently used evergreen in Oklahoma, and with its lustrous green foliage it is quite impressive all year long. It is a great substitute for Japanese boxwood. The foliage is a soothing deep green, which makes it a wonderful contrast plant in any landscape. Many of the varieties hold their green color better in the winter. Female Japanese hollies occasionally produce black berries late in the fall that may remain until spring. Most Japanese hollies are somewhat brittle and stiff. 'Soft Touch' Japanese holly, on the other hand, is a softer-feeling cultivar with more visual appeal. The most commonly available cultivars of Japanese holly are 'Helleri', 'Hetzii', and 'Compacta'.

Other Common Name
Box-leaved Holly

Bloom Period and Seasonal Color
Evergreen foliage.

Mature Height × Spread
4 to 6 ft. × 3 to 5 ft.

Cold Hardiness Zones
6a, 6b, 7a, 7b

Japanese Kerria

Kerria japonica

Shade gardeners, rejoice! Kerria is a great flowering shrub for such sites. The yellow flowers brighten up shady locations for several weeks in the early spring. Sparse flowering can occur later in the season. The upright-growing, deciduous shrub loses its foliage in the winter, but the remaining plant has an evergreen appearance, thanks to the green stems. The leaves are simple with serrated margins and provide texture to the landscape. I have used kerria in several of my landscapes through the years. The plants were perfect background plants in perennial shade gardens, especially in locations with adequate soil moisture. In addition to the bright yellow flowers, there are cultivars with variegated or chartreuse foliage. One of the most interesting cultivars is 'Pleniflora', with double, golden-yellow flowers. 'Albaflora' is a white-flowering cultivar.

Other Common Names
Japanese Rose, Gypsy Rose

Bloom Period and Seasonal Color
Yellow blooms in spring and early summer.

Mature Height × Spread
3 to 6 ft. × 6 to 9 ft.

Cold Hardiness Zones
6a, 6b, 7a, 7b

When, Where, and How to Plant
Plant kerria in spring, early summer, or early fall. This plant likes afternoon or dappled shade with humus-rich, moist soil. Heavy shade with poor air circulation promotes foliar diseases. The foliage scorches, and the flowers fade prematurely when planted in Oklahoma's full sun. Dig a hole at least 2 times wider than and the same depth as the rootball. There is no need for soil amendments in the hole unless the entire bed was prepared before planting time. Water at planting and as needed to establish plants. Mulching retains soil moisture, which benefits this shade-loving plant.

Growing Tips
The plants respond to supplemental watering during drought. Overfertilizing encourages weedy stem growth, less flowering, and potential root burn. To prevent this, I use organic or slow-release synthetic fertilizers that slowly provide nutrients over a longer period of time.

Care
Flowers originate from the previous year's growth, so prune them after flowering. Shear them back like a hedge to meet your height needs, or selectively remove canes to keep the shrubs more open and natural in their appearance. In loose fertile soils, the plants tend to send out underground shoots that are not aggressive in nature but can assist the plant in filling larger areas. The suckers can also be cut back to keep the plant in its landscape site. Occasional leaf blights and spots are possible but not severely enough to discourage more use of this unusual plant.

Landscape Merit
The narrow, elongated leaves are loosely arranged on the attractive stems, making for great texture. Because of its loosely upright and arching growth, use this plant for background borders. The plant has a tendency to spread over time (not aggressively). Plant it in large groups. The showy flowers are a real treat when used in color combinations of purple, yellow, and white.

My Personal Favorite
Japanese Rose 'Variegata' has grayish green and white foliage with single yellow flowers on a more compact plant.

Korean Lilac

Syringa meyeri

When, Where, and How to Plant

Plant lilacs anytime during the spring or fall when they are dormant. Korean lilac prefers full sun but accepts a half-day of shade. Too much shade causes sparse growth and few flowers. It likes good garden soil but tolerates poor soils as long as they have good drainage. Some cultivars are successfully grown in containers. Dig a hole at least 2 times wider than and the same depth as the rootball. Mulch the plant, and water it as needed.

Growing Tips

Lilac likes rich soil and occasional fertilizer side-dressings and will appreciate the nutrients you give. Slow-release organic fertilizers are a great choice because they provide several small spurts of nutrients over a longer period of time. Like the most common species, Korean lilacs are not really that drought tolerant and need supplemental water during prolonged periods of drought. Again, good drainage is key. Many plants die when planted in small holes with compacted soil.

Care

Flowers emerge from buds set on the previous year's growth. Late cold spells occasionally damage flower buds. Prune after flowering, although it is seldom needed with Korean lilacs because of their overall compact growth. Korean lilacs seem to be fairly resistant to mildew, but an occasional aphid might be found early in the spring. Korean lilacs flower early on in the season; the flowers emerge before the new leaves are fully developed.

Landscape Merit

Use this prized beauty as a single specimen plant, or show it off in groups of three. Using evergreen shrubs as a background promotes the beauty of these plants in the spring and winter.

My Personal Favorite

'Palibin' is a dwarf selection with lavender 4-inch-long flower panicles and nice orange-red fall leaf color.

As a kid, I remember fragrant lilac blooms at neighboring homes. As I developed my gardening interests, I learned that the common lilac (Syringa vulgaris) is more adapted to northern climates. After much searching, I have encountered another species of lilac that takes our heat and humidity. Korean lilac is a smaller-growing plant that provides fragrant flowers and healthy foliage. The species parent plant has a lavender flower with a pinkish tint. It typically grows as a small, bushy plant. 'Palibin' (Korean lilac) reaches four to five feet at maturity and displays fragrant, reddish-purple buds opening to a pinkish white. 'Miss Kim' (S. patula) is considered trouble free. Blooming occurs a little later than other lilacs, and the growth is compact. Cutleaf lilac (S. laciniata) is another great selection for southern Oklahoma climates.

Other Common Name
Meyer's Lilac

Bloom Period and Seasonal Color
Lavender or pinkish-red blooms in late April and May.

Mature Height × Spread
4 to 8 ft. × 4 to 7 ft.

Cold Hardiness Zones
6a, 6b, 7a, 7b

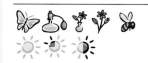

Loropetalum

Loropetalum chinense var. *rubrum*

Loropetalum is another great choice for acidic shade gardens. Because it is not very cold-hardy, it does better in southeastern portions of the state. Protect with mulch or, in more northern counties, plant on southeastern sides of a building. Planting fringe flower in Zone 6 will most likely lead to its demise from winter injury. The weeping growth habit and burgundy foliage are very appealing. As new growth emerges in spring, it is almost purple, changing to a reddish purple that remains throughout the season. 'Rubrum' ('Roseum') easily reaches ten feet under optimum growing conditions. 'Zhuzhou' is tall and more upright. 'Blush' matures at six feet with rose-colored leaves that turn olive green. A more compact, rounded cultivar is 'Ruby'. 'Monraz Razzleberri' and 'Pizzaz' are more compact weeping cultivars.

Other Common Names
Fringe Flower, Chinese Witchhazel

Bloom Period and Seasonal Color
Pink blooms in early spring.

Mature Height × Spread
4 to 10 ft. × 3 to 6 ft.

Cold Hardiness Zones
7a, 7b, 6b (with winter protection)

When, Where, and How to Plant
Plant fringe flower in early to late spring. This plant prefers afternoon shade or dappled shade. Soils must be acidic with a pH of 5.5 to 6.5. I have seen some plants tolerating afternoon sun in well-prepared, acidic, moisture-retentive soils. Till peat moss (or other acidic organic materials) and soil sulfur into the landscape bed before planting time. Do not damage existing tree roots nearby. Dig the hole at least 2 times wider than and the same depth as the rootball. If good drainage is not available, place the rootball slightly above soil grade. Mulching with pecan hulls, pine straw, or pine bark is imperative with acidic-loving plants to protect the shallow roots.

Growing Tips
Supplemental watering is needed during drought periods, but pay attention to good drainage. Mulch every couple of years to replace wind-blown, washed away, or decomposed mulch. Side-dress after flowering with acid-formulated fertilizers that contain sulfur and iron. The plants are vigorous growers, so use slow-release fertilizer products that provide smaller amounts of nitrogen over a longer period.

Care
The fragrant flowers are produced on the previous season's growth, so prune the plant after flowering if needed. The flowers will last two to three weeks if a late frost does not get them first. Pest problems are minimal.

Landscape Merit
Dwarf is one of those loosely used terms when describing lorepetalum since most are around 6 feet tall. Fringe flower is impressive when planted in groups but also works well as a single planting. Fringe flower, fothergilla, and perennial epimedium are great companion plants for azalea beds.

My Personal Favorite
Most of the time, freezes get the flowers, but at least 'Burgundy' will have sporadic repeat bloom periods. Its best attribute, however, is the burgundy-red color on the new leaves as they emerge. 'Burgundy' reaches 6 to 8 feet.

Oakleaf Hydrangea
Hydrangea quercifolia

When, Where, and How to Plant

Plant them in spring since younger plants are somewhat tender until established. Oakleaf hydrangea prefers afternoon or filtered shade and performs better in moist, fertile soil. A hole dug 2 to 3 times the width and the same depth as the rootball is recommended for most trees and shrubs. Oakleaf hydrangea establishes better with such planting conditions. Space plants 6 feet apart when planting in rows. Water deeply to settle the soil and on a frequent basis until plants are established. Mulching is beneficial.

Growing Tips

During drought conditions, supplemental watering and mulching are of utmost importance. Oakleaf hydrangeas prefer a somewhat acid soil, but do not expect to change the flower colors using aluminum sulfate to get blue or lime to encourage pink flowers as with the French types.

Care

Hydrangeas bloom at an early age and usually from terminal growth that occurred last season. Prune them after flowering. The plants send out root suckers and spread as they mature, although the growth is not considered invasive. The stems turn a reddish-gray color with exfoliating bark as they mature. Leaf spot and an occasional bout with powdery mildew occur in heavy shade.

Landscape Merit

Taller selections need plenty of room and do well as a background in shade or woodland gardens. They also make nice foundation plants on the east or northeast sides of multiple story structures. The season-long show and size also make them nice candidates for specimen plants. More compact cultivars can be used in perennial gardens.

My Personal Favorite

'Pee Wee' and 'Sikes' Dwarf' are the most compact selections reaching 2 to 3 feet and naturally fitting in the with the scale of woodland plants.

You must make room for oakleaf hydrangea in your landscape. This plant offers season-long interest for the shade garden or east-exposure landscapes. The new leaf growth starts with a grayish-purple tint at emergence, changing to a deep green during the summer and to a brilliant display of orange-red in fall. Sometime around May, the white flower spikes emerge. The perfect flowers later change to a pinkish-purple tint before turning a coppery brown. Both foliage and flower spikes remain on the plant well into the middle of winter. Similar in flower but different in foliage is H. paniculata (panicle hydrangea).

Bloom Period and Seasonal Color
White blooms in early summer with orange-red fall foliage.

Mature Height × Spread
4 to 6 ft. × 4 to 8 ft.

Cold Hardiness Zones
6a, 6b, 7a, 7b

Oregon Grape Holly
Mahonia species

I often hear gardeners complain that there are not enough shade-garden plants—mahonia is a great choice. Its lustrous, evergreen foliage, yellow flowers, and blue-black berries supply year-round interest. As new foliage emerges, tinges of red and purple brighten the display. The fruit forms late in the season and resembles a true berry. All mahonias have prickly foliage, so do not plant them in high-traffic areas. The leathery leaves turn a purplish color during the fall and winter. Leatherleaf mahonia (M. bealei) has bigger, more prominent foliage, making it a nice specimen plant. Leatherleaf is not as cold hardy as Oregon grape. Chinese mahonia (M. fortunei) has more delicate foliage, and though it is slightly prickly, it is a good choice for the southern areas of the state.

Other Common Name
Mahonia

Bloom Period and Seasonal Color
Yellow blooms in March or April.

Mature Height × Spread
3 to 6 ft. × 3 to 5 ft.

Cold Hardiness Zones
6a, 6b, 7a, 7b

When, Where, and How to Plant
Plant it in spring or fall. This foundation or shrub border plant requires partial shade; it prefers a somewhat acidic, moist soil. Dry soils and hot locations easily scorch most of the mahonia selections. It tolerates sandy and clay soils as long as they drain well. *M. repens* is a species that is typically stoloniferous in growth; that is, it spreads readily in moist, fertile landscape sites. Plant container-grown selections in holes 2 times wider than but the same depth as the rootballs. No amended backfill is needed. Water and mulch the plants.

Growing Tips
Slow-release organic fertilizers are also a good choice to keep allow slow amounts of nutrients over a longer period of time. Water as needed to keep thee soil moist.

Care
M. aquifolium sets foliage somewhat sparsely. The upright stems are more pronounced. Trim in early spring by tip-pruning the plant tops back about 6 inches or so to another leaf axis. Mature woody, dead, or diseased canes can also be trimmed back to the crown to stimulate new cane growth. Disease leaf spots occur in damp conditions with poor air circulation. Iron chlorosis develops in alkaline soils. In these cases, add soil sulfur at the recommended rate and mulch with pine bark or pine straw.

Landscape Merit
The prickly foliage is best used in the background of landscape beds and not close to sidewalks. I have not been impressed with this one as a specimen plant unless it is *Mahonia bealei* (leatherleaf mahonia) with its robust foliage. Otherwise, most other species work best in groups to provide massive evergreen color during the winter. The compound, thick, evergreen leaves add texture and provide consistent color to shade beds.

My Personal Favorite
'Arthur Menzies' is a more compact hybrid with bright green leaves, abundant yellow flowers, and prolific blue berries.

Possumhaw

Ilex decidua

When, Where, and How to Plant

Deciduous holly is available in container-grown or balled-and-burlapped choices that are easily planted in the spring or fall. Deciduous holly tolerates alkaline soils quite well and grows in central and western Oklahoma even though it is native to the slightly acidic soils of the eastern part of the state. Plant deciduous holly in a hole 2 to 3 times the width of the container and the same depth. No backfill with organic amendments is required. Water and mulch after planting and as needed thereafter.

Growing Tips

Most often you'll find deciduous holly in moist, partially shady sites. Once it is established in the landscape, possumhaw is more drought tolerant than one would expect. In severe prolonged drought, supplemental water is advised, but this plant does not need pampering otherwise. Do not overfertilize, or excess growth can occur with minimal berry set.

Care

The plants require minimal pruning, depending on how you want to train it. Possumhaw can be grown as a single trunk or multi-trunk plant. Most pruning has to do with broken, diseased, or competing branches. Structural pruning is best done during the dormant stage. Tip-pruning, which can be done anytime, guides the direction of plant growth and keeps suckers thinned out.

Landscape Merit

The plants need plenty of room; they work as a single specimen or in conjunction with evergreen backgrounds. In larger scaled plantings, I've seen them layered in front of taller evergreens acting as a windbreak. The winter berries viewed against the evergreen background was stunning. Most landscapes display the plant as a specimen.

My Personal Favorite

'Warren's Red' has profuse berry production and can be trained into an eye catching specimen.

Possumhaw is native to the southeastern part of Oklahoma. This large shrub or small tree is gaining popularity because of its brilliant berries in the fall. Deciduous holly generally has both male and female flowers on the same plant; therefore, additional pollinators are not required for fruit production. Fruit-set typically increases with age and is most often found on short spurs on the branches. The colorful red, orange, or yellow fruit persist on the branches most of the winter until possums or birds finish them off. The small, glossy, gray-green foliage drops late in the fall. The stems are usually a light-gray color. Both single- and multiple-trunk selections are available. 'Byers Golden' is a yellow-fruited cultivar, 'Council Fire' and 'Sundance' are orange-red, and 'Warren's Red' has red berries.

Other Common Name
Deciduous Holly

Bloom Period and Seasonal Color
Red, orange, or yellow berries fall through winter.

Mature Height × Spread
10 to 20 ft. × 6 to 15 ft.

Cold Hardiness Zones
6a, 6b, 7a, 7b

Southern Waxmyrtle

Myrica cerifera

Once established, Southern waxmyrtle grows in poor, dry soils in the full sun. The yellowish-green foliage provides an unusual color scheme. It is native to southeastern areas of our state but survives in the heavy soils of west-central Oklahoma. Southern waxmyrtle comes as a male or female plant (dioecious). The female plants produce a grayish berry late in the season. Both have pungent-smelling foliage. 'Emperor' has prominent, more serrated leaves. Compact M. pusilla (dwarf waxmyrtle) is not quite as cold hardy and does well in the sandy, piney woods of eastern and southern counties of the state or Zones 7a and 7b. It matures to five feet. Cultivars of dwarf waxmyrtle are 'Fairfax' and 'Georgia Gem'. 'Georgia Gem' has a more mounded growth form, reaching one to two feet tall by three feet wide.

Bloom Period and Seasonal Color
Evergreen foliage.

Mature Height × Spread
5 to 20 ft. × 5 to 20 ft.

Cold Hardiness Zones
6b, 7a, 7b

When, Where, and How to Plant

Plant southern waxmyrtle in early spring, early summer, or fall. It is probably risky to plant southern waxmyrtle in the Panhandle because of its vulnerability to severe cold. This plant is not picky about its soil type. Dig the hole 2 to 3 times wider than and the same depth as the root-ball. Deeply water immediately after planting to settle the soil and adequately soak the root system. Mulch at this time to ensure a slow, continual supply of nutrients.

Growing Tips

Continual mulching and occasional fertilizing turns this plant into quite a display. Slow-release organic products are ideal to provide small amount of fertilizer over a longer period of time without stimulating overabundant, lanky plant growth.

Care

Prune these trees as a hedge or "limb up" for a multi-trunk display. The bark is an attractive gray-green color. There are no reports of serious insect problems. In humid, poorly circulated sites, an occasional fungal leaf spot is detected. I have been told by gardeners that waxmyrtle naturally resists the deer that often feed in our gardens. Occasionally, root suckers are a problem in beds where the roots are disturbed. Trim the underground root suckers throughout the season.

Landscape Merit

The standard waxmyrtle is often too big for foundation plantings unless it is used in large beds in association with two-story homes. Use it as a feature plant in island bed designs, as a hedge screen, or as a specimen in lawns. A dwarf species does well as a foundation plant or small hedge. It is grown as a multi-trunk small tree and is the focal point of many landscape designs. The yellowish-green, contrasting foliage is a nice color to complement shades of purple companion plants.

My Personal Favorite

There are not really any improved selections. Remember to match the plant size to your particular landscape need.

Spirea
Spiraea species

When, Where, and How to Plant

Plant container-grown spirea selections in spring or fall. Spirea prefers full-sun locations or sites that receive shade in the afternoon. Too much shade, however, increases the chances of powdery mildew and other foliage diseases. Good, rich, garden soil provides the best growth, but spirea adapts to poor and heavy soils as long as they drain well. Digging a wide hole the same depth as the container root system is the most successful way to plant. Water to establish plants in their new home and mulch afterwards.

Growing Tips

They are somewhat drought tolerant once established. Spirea responds well to supplemental feedings, but do not overdo it because some plants can get too leggy and fall apart. Let the plant's appearance tell you whether or not added applications of fertilizer are needed. Slow-release products applied at planting time and on a regular basis are ideal. Reapply mulch as needed.

Care

Spirea generally flowers on new growth, so pruning during the dormant season or immediately after flowering is acceptable. Trimming spent blooms encourages regrowth and additional blooms in the fall. Thin any aged, overgrown canes to stimulate new growth. In addition to sunny locations, proper spacing with a little extra room between plants allows for more air circulation. This planting method minimizes the chance of foliar disease. Aphids occasionally appear in early spring, but ladybugs generally take care of the threat.

Landscape Merit

Spireas make great foundation plants, especially when used in combination with evergreens. Place the dwarf cultivars in front borders of landscape beds without blocking nearby companions. Taller selections can be used as background screens when used in combination with evergreens. The more compact cultivars can even be use intermittently in the perennial garden.

My Personal Favorite

I like the small growing, almost ground cover nature and chartreuse foliage of 'Golden Elf'.

Spirea tolerates many conditions. The soft, delicate, deciduous foliage provides texture and an explosion of fall color as the leaves turn a yellow-bronzy-red tint. The branches have a dense, twiggy growth habit, requiring minimal care. Spirea is a good substitute for the pickier azalea. Japanese spirea (S. japonica) has several colorful selections. Double reeves spirea (S. cantoniensis) is nice for southern areas of the state. Bridalwreath (S. prunifolia) and thunberg spirea (S. thunbergii) offer interesting features for landscapes. 'Magic Carpet', 'Alpina', and 'Norman' are very compact spireas. 'Goldmound', 'Goldflame', and 'Magic Carpet' are known for their chartreuse foliage. For a unique crinkled foliage, consider 'Crispa'. 'Shirobana' displays red, pink, and white flowers all on the same plant. 'Neon Flash' is a compact plant with bright-pink flowers. 'Dakota Goldcharm' is a dwarf, chartreuse-foliage selection.

Bloom Period and Seasonal Color
White, pink, or red blooms in May and June; yellow-bronze fall foliage.

Mature Height × Spread
2 to 6 ft. × 2 to 5 ft.

Cold Hardiness Zones
6a, 6b, 7a, 7b

Sumac
Rhus glabra

Most people overlook smooth sumac until the fall when it welcomes the season with an early burst of brilliant scarlet. The plants are dioecious and have showy, greenish-yellow flowers. The berries take shape in August or September, turning from a grayish green to deep, blood red in the fall and persisting into the winter. Related species ideal for the landscape are R. aromatica (fragrant sumac), Staghorn fern sumac (R. typhina), Chinese sumac (R. chinensis), and Flameleaf sumac (R. copallina). Contrary to belief, smooth sumac is not poisonous. Poison sumac, R. vernix (a.k.a. Toxicodendron vernix), is mostly found growing near wet areas. Its pairs of compound, glossy, velvet-like leaflets are arranged opposite one another and with seven to thirteen groups per stem with a single leaflet on the end.

Other Common Names
Smooth Sumac, Scarlet Sumac, Shoe-make

Bloom Period and Seasonal Color
Greenish blooms in summer; scarlet fall foliage.

Mature Height × Spread
6 to 15 ft. × 3 to 4 ft.

Cold Hardiness Zones
6a, 6b, 7a, 7b

When, Where, and How to Plant
Occasionally, the plants are started by cuttings to ensure uniformity among named selections. Homeowners do better starting sumac by purchasing container-grown specimens and planting them in the spring, early summer, or fall. Space plants 3 to 5 feet apart. Mulch and water them as needed. Sumac is not picky about soil as long as it drains.

Growing Tips
Sumac is quite drought tolerant once established. The foliage may scorch or even defoliate, but the plants recover nicely with rainfall or a deep watering. Fall color, fruit production, and overall plant vigor are best supported with supplemental irrigation during prolonged drought. Do not overfertilize sumac, especially with nitrogen-rich products. Slow-release organic fertilizers are best, offering slow amounts of nutrients over a longer period of time. Any fertilizer applications should be thoroughly watered in after applying.

Care
Sumac seldom needs pruning. Occasionally folks will get creative and try to train the larger species into nice specimens, but the overall growth habit of sumac lends itself to textural and architectural design features for the landscape. Continually prune root suckers to keep the plants in bounds. The plants are not considered invasive but will be more likely to colonize in fluffy organic soils. Pests and foliar diseases are minimal.

Landscape Merit
Sumac quickly covers ground on banks or disturbed sloping sites that need erosion control. Propagating suckering roots benefit a landscaper when trying to fill in harsh planting sites on a tight budget. The low-growing spreaders make great ground cover and filler plants for borders or fence rows, or for connecting tree specimens into island beds in partially shaded sites. Avoid planting them in foundation or landscape beds; managing them takes too much work.

My Personal Favorite
'Tiger Eyes'™ has deeply cut leaflets. The new growth catches the eye with chartreuse green, quickly changing to bright yellow. The leaf stems are fuzzy, purplish-pink and form a dramatic contrast with the lemon lime foliage.

Viburnum
Viburnum species

When, Where, and How to Plant

Plant viburnums in spring, early summer, or early fall. Species and cultivar selection determine sun preference and landscape use. Viburnums prefer slightly acidic, well-drained soils. Dig the hole 2 to 3 times wider than and the same depth as the root-ball. Organic backfill is not needed. If possible, prepare an entire with such materials before planting. Water at planting and as needed to establish the plants. Mulch is essential to keep the soil moist and acidic. Spacing depends upon the species; check the width listed on the plant tag.

Growing Tips

Watering is necessary during drought periods. Once the plants are established they don't require pampering. Reapply mulch as needed. Most viburnums respond to minimal feedings and like slow-release, slightly acidic organic products like pine straw or pine bark applied at planting and then on a yearly basis either in spring or fall. Reapply mulch as needed to hold in soil moisture and keep weeds at bay.

Care

Pruning is generally done to thin branches or to shape a specimen. Prune viburnums after flowering, depending on the cultivar; some berry loss will occur. Pests might include fungal leaf spots that are brought about by humid, rainy weather. Good air circulation between plants and removing disease-infected leaves minimize the problem.

Landscape Merit

Most are utilized as specimen plants in background areas because of their space requirements. In large turf areas, cluster the plants in groups of three to form island beds and combine with assorted perennials. Single specimens also work nicely, offering season long interest.

My Personal Favorite

Choosing a favorite viburnum is tough. I encourage folks to know what they are getting, whether it is fragrance, berry set, deciduous or evergreen foliage, and mature size. Other than that you cannot go wrong. They all have outstanding landscape attributes.

Showy, berry-producing plants are gaining popularity in home landscapes. Viburnums have flamboyant qualities, some being known for their fragrant flowers and others for their showy fruit. Some are evergreen while others are deciduous. 'Mohawk' is considered one of the most fragrant selections, with orange-red berries. 'Korean Spice' is fragrant with red fruit that turns black in the late summer. V. opulus 'Xanthocarpum' is a yellow-fruited selection that needs afternoon shade. 'Summer Snowflake', 'Shasta', and 'Mariessii' are double-file viburnums with attractive white flowers, later producing red fruit. 'Eskimo' is a compact specimen. Snowball viburnum is best known for its showy, white snowball flowers but is sterile and does not produce fruit. Leatherleaf viburnum is a semi-evergreen selection best used for its dark-green, coarse foliage; its flowers and fruit are not particularly showy.

Other Common Name
Cranberry Bush

Bloom Period and Seasonal Color
White blooms in April, May, or June.

Mature Height × Spread
3 to 15 ft. × 6 to 12 ft.

Cold Hardiness Zones
6a, 6b, 7a, 7b

Weigela

Weigela florida

Weigela is known for its distinctly dazzling early flowers that hummingbirds adore. It is pronounced "vie-ge-la" (after a German botanist), except of course in Oklahoma where the name has extra syllables. The medium-green foliage is fairly coarse and located on upright, gray-brown stems with noticable lenticels often mistaken for scale insects. The spring display is well worth the use of this plant in the landscape. The remainder of the season leaves much to be desired, however. Using weigela in combination with evergreen shrubs and ornamental grasses distracts from its unimpressive summer growth. The different types of weigela on the market are quite extensive ranging from dwarf selections, to those with assorted flower colors, to those with colorful foliage, or any combination.

Other Common Name
Cardinal Flower

Bloom Period and Seasonal Color
Pink, red, or white blooms in spring and early summer.

Mature Height × Spread
3 to 9 ft. × 3 to 12 ft.

Cold Hardiness Zones
6a, 6b, 7a, 7b

When, Where, and How to Plant
Plant weigela in the spring in a site protected by afternoon shade. Fall plantings are risky, especially in north and northwest Oklahoma. Plant it in a hole 2 to 3 times wider than and the same depth as the rootball. Planting weigela in heavy shade encourages mildew disease. Amend the soil with organic material to provide both nutrition and adequate drainage. Water after planting to settle the soil and thoroughly soak the roots. Mulch to hold in soil moisture and keep weed competition down.

Growing Tips
Weigela is not very drought tolerant. Without supplemental irrigation during drought conditions, the leaves scorch and the plant can die. At the same time, the plant will not withstand wet feet. Apply slow-release organic fertilizer in the fall. Or, as a second choice, apply fertilizers after spring blooming and follow with a good soaking of water. Avoid fertilizers in the heat of the summer, or the shallow roots can burn.

Care
Weigela blooms on the previous season's growth, so prune it after blooms fade but before flower buds set again. Occasionally, stems are damaged from severe winter spells, but there is no need to prune because they usually come back from the root system.

Landscape Merit
Weigela is often used for early color by gardeners who do not want to pamper azaleas. The most common flower colors are red and pink. Weigela is seldom used as a foundation plant. The dormant appearance is quite boring, so plant it in association with winter-attractive plants. The best display I have seen was weigela planted in an irregular row in the background of a landscape bed and dwarf yaupon planted in front of the weigela to add winter color and hide the barren stems.

My Personal Favorite
'Variegata' is easy to grow with afternoon shade and has variegated foliage that really compliments the early soft-pink flowers.

Winter Jasmine
Jasminum nudiflorum

When, Where, and How to Plant
Plant container-grown selections in either spring or fall. The plants grow and flower best in full sun, but they accept partial shade. Winter jasmine tolerates a wide range of soils. Plant it in a hole at least 2 times the width and the same depth as the rootball. Water after planting and as needed until plants establish. Mulch is very beneficial for all shrubs, but especially for winter jasmine. The plants will eventually grow together and touch at a 4-foot spacing.

Growing Tips
Initial plantings of winter jasmine have a tendency to send stems crawling along the surface of the ground where they root along the way. Tip-prune these stems to force more upright growth in the center of the crown. Share rooted runners with gardening friends or relocate them in the landscape. As the plants mature, they grow in a mounding, arching form. Winter jasmine is considered a fast-growing plant. Fertilizer applications are recommended in poor soils but seldom needed in rich, garden soils.

Care
Occasional pruning is needed to keep plants in their alotted space. Prune the plants after flowering, usually in late March. Many gardeners rate the flowers secondary to the remarkable green plant form. The flowers are some of the earliest to bloom in late winter or early spring. Although the flowers may succumb to freezing temperatures, this hardy plant is rarely harmed. There are seldom reports of pest problems.

Landscape Merit
Use winter jasmine as a foundation plant in areas at least 5 feet wide. Plant it for background borders and in combination with deciduous shrubs such as spirea. The texture tones down many coarse companion plants. Jasmine is a great choice for sites where the stems are allowed to cascade over a wall, slope, or berm. It also works well to offer evergreen-like color in the winter with its dark green stems.

My Personal Favorite
The standard species is the most common and works well in any landscape setting.

I first experienced this dependable plant as a horticulture student at OSU. Winter jasmine dotted the campus in full-sun and partial-shade locations. I was amazed by its display of bright yellow flowers in February, even as snow blanketed the ground. The deciduous plant masquerades as an evergreen, thanks to its dark-green, slender, arching stems. The mounded growth habit offers an uncommon presentation for landscape texture. Once a widely sold plant in the trade, winter jasmine is starting to make a comeback, thanks to its resilience. The dark-green species is the primary selection available; however, 'Aureum' is a lightly variegated form that is even more difficult to locate. Other jasmine species are available, but most are not as cold-hardy as J. nudiflorum featured here.

Bloom Period and Seasonal Color
Yellow blooms in February and early March.

Mature Height × Spread
3 to 4 ft. × 4 to 6 ft.

Cold Hardiness Zones
6a, 6b, 7a, 7b

Yaupon Holly

Ilex vomitoria

Yaupon holly is one of my favorite landscape shrubs. It is one tough cookie, taking all kinds of environmental abuse. The selections are phenomenal in height, texture, and berry set, and they truly fit any landscape design need. Throw in the toughness and tolerance of many environmental situations, and yaupon holly belongs at the top of your plant list. Pollination occurs from almost any nearby holly species; however, planting dwarf male types, such as 'Stokes' ('Schillings'), in close proximity increases fruit production. Dwarf types include 'Nana' and 'Bordeaux'. 'Bordeaux' has a more prominent purple hue on the new growth. 'Pride of Houston' is an upright, multi-trunk selection. 'Pendula' and 'Folsom's' are two excellent, tall, weeping forms that are not as cold-hardy and are suited more for southeastern areas of the state.

Bloom Period and Seasonal Color
Evergreen foliage.

Mature Height × Spread
3 to 20 ft. × 4 to 15 ft.

Cold Hardy Zones
6b, 7a, 7b

When, Where, and How to Plant
Plants are available as container-grown or balled-and-burlapped specimens. Plant yaupon holly in spring, early summer, or early fall. It favors full sun but tolerates partial shade. These tough plants grow in a multitude of soil conditions—dry or swampy. Even soil pH does not seem to matter too much. Winter damage is likely in the Panhandle. Widely dug holes at the same depth as the roots are the favored way to plant yaupons. Water them to settle the soil and then on a regular basis. Their fibrous roots make them a prime candidate for mulching.

Growing Tips
Once established, they are fairly drought tolerant. Reapplication of mulch every couple of years is beneficial. Supplemental feedings are optional.

Care
Since yaupons are used frequently as topiaries, they obviously respond well to shearing and pruning. Prune berry-producing varieties in early spring. Trim others any time throughout the growing season. Other than an occasional leafminer, pest problems are generally of no concern. In the far eastern part of the state, leaf-chewing caterpillars are common in early spring but are easily controlled. Yaupons are sensitive to frequent visits by male dogs and are likely to burn as a result.

Landscape Merit
Dwarf selections are great foundation or grouping plants because they naturally grow in a mounding form. Upright varieties make excellent single specimens or informal screens. Weeping yaupon also makes a nice specimen and can be allowed to grow to its mature size or trimmed to keep the weeping appearance more manageable. Yaupon holly is commonly used as a topiary plant because it responds well to frequent shearing.

My Personal Favorite
One of my favorite multi-trunk cultivars is 'Grey's Little Leaf', which is seldom found in Oklahoma garden centers but does exceptionally well here. The deep green leaves are more tightly clustered with short internodes. The red berry set is phenomenal.

Yew

Taxus species

When, Where, and How to Plant

Yews are typically planted in spring or fall, and they require very specific soils. Rich, fertile, moist, and well drained soils are a must for the best plant health. Yews tolerate sun, especially morning sun, as long as they are not planted in the direct path of sweeping winds. Dig a planting hole 2 to 3 times wider than and the same depth as the rootball. In poorly drained soils, plant them slightly above the soil grade. Remove the burlap from intact or firm rootballs. Otherwise set the plant in the hole and cut off burlap near the soil surface. Water immediately to settle soil and frequently during establishment. Mulching is of utmost importance.

Growing Tips

Reapply mulch occasionally to keep the roots cool and moist. Yews are not drought tolerant; deep soakings during drought conditions are a must. Do not overfertilize the tender roots. Apply slow-release, organic fertilizers at planting and again each fall.

Care

Yews respond well to shearing to keep plant forms intact. Detailed pruning is best done in early spring; keeping branches tipped and in check can be done anytime throughout the growing season to. Foliar diseases, such as needle and twig blight, are the most common. Root rot occurs in poorly drained soils. Needles burn in winters with severe temperature changes. Although yew is evergreen, older needles located in the center of the plants normally drop as the plants mature.

Landscape Merit

They are most often used as foundation plants or as background plants in partially shaded landscapes. Group plantings make better shows and are frequently used in association with deciduous plants requiring the same soil conditions. Taller cultivars make effective hedges and screens.

My Personal Favorite

'Emerald Spreader' ('Monloo') is a great low-growing cultivar that matures at around 18 to 24 inches tall with a slow growing width of 8 feet.

Yew is superior choice for shade gardens. There is nothing comparable in Oklahoma to the dark evergreen foliage display that yew provides in barren winter landscape. In addition, the lustrous, needled foliage is a soothing sight during the hot summers. This is an all-seasons plant with a wide range of textures and sizes to accommodate your landscape needs. Plants are male and female with seeds occasionally appearing on female plants. Consider height, width, and plant form when choosing the cultivar. Research cultivars to match your particular landscape site since some selections readily scorch in the Oklahoma summer winds, while others are more tolerant of sun.

Bloom Period and Seasonal Color

Non-showy flowers in the spring; more for evergreen foliage.

Mature Height × Spread

3 to 15 ft. × 5 to 10 ft.

Cold Hardiness Zones

6a, 6b, 7a, 7b

Trees *for Oklahoma*

Trees truly are the pillars of our landscapes, homes, and communities; and plant diversity is the key to dynamic and healthy environments. Think of trees as an investment for future generations and tree selection as the first step in successful community stewardship. Think of diversity as a way to add uniqueness to your landscape and neighborhood and to alleviate potential epidemic pest problems.

Unfortunately, there is no such thing as a perfect, no-maintenance, no-pest tree, but this chapter offers some of the best choices that thrive with minimal needs. These eighteen trees are by no means an all-inclusive list for Oklahoma. Other notable selections are listed in the Appendix. Additional choices with improved cultivars are sold in the nursery trade. But definitely think twice before considering silver maple, Lombardy poplar, tree of heaven, American elm, green ash, white poplar, and native cottonwood in your landscape. These trees are notorious for their shallow roots, weak wood, root suckers, diseases, and annoying seeds, although some improved selections are available.

When to Plant

Fall may be the best time to plant trees. The planting guidelines presented here reflect recently researched findings. For example, some eighty-five percent of a tree's roots are in the top twenty-four inches of soil. Roots grow wide, not deep, as was once believed. To accommodate a root-system's sprawling habit, dig a planting hole two to three times the width of the rootball and the same depth. Wider, loosely prepared soil means quicker establishment for horizontal root growth. Gently backfill the hole with the original soil. Adding peat moss and other expensive organic materials is not necessary. The tree has to grow in the original soil, and in most cases the soil provides some nutrition until the tree is established. It is definitely a risk to apply high-nitrogen fertilizers and excessive amounts of root stimulator in the planting hole. These items can burn the tender, new root growth when applied at excessive rates. Though soil amendment may encourage quick establishment and ssatisfy the impatient gardener, it will discourage the tree from sending its roots out into the natural soil. A weaker tree is the ultimate result.

Sweeping Branches of a Spruce

Water Deep Not Wide

Watering deeply and less often is the proper way to help get trees established and keep them healthy. It also encourages roots to grow deeper. Frequent shallow waterings encourages shallow roots that are more susceptible to drought, cold, and compaction. Building a shallow water basin with excess soil around the perimeter of the tree is imperative and helps in accomplishing this task. The ridge holds

Gingko

water and allows it to soak in around the roots. Otherwise, the water runs along the surface of the ground, never penetrating to the root system. The basin will need to be filled two to three times at each watering to help push the water down deeper. Newly planted trees should be thoroughly watered on a weekly basis pending rainfall until the tree is established. It takes a minimum of a year for trees to become established and sometimes even longer. During extreme drought, the amount of supplemental watering may need to be bumped up to twice a week.

A tall tree may be at risk of blowing over in a widely planted hole; stake a tree if necessary, but for no longer than a year. The staking method should not bind the tree trunk or penetrate the bark. Soft strapping material is best. Some movement of the tree is needed to develop strength. Leaving lower branches on for the first three years encourages a bigger, stronger tree trunk. Mulch the tree to keep weeds from competing with the tree roots and to prevent lawnmower or weed-trimmer damage.

The Need to Feed
Fertilizer applications can promote tree growth but are better applied after the tree is established. Fertilizer applications on lawns and landscapes are also probably sufficient for any adjoining trees since the roots grow well into these neighboring areas. Isolated trees not receiving indirect feedings or ones showing nutritional deficiencies need supplemental applications. Split the applications between early spring and fall according to product directions. Use granular, broadcast fertilizers.

The Importance of Pruning
Pruning and training the tree early on will reward you with a strong, long-lived specimen. Leave big pruning jobs to a professional, preferably someone trained and certified as an arborist. Topping or "coat racking" tree branches into stubs is not a proper pruning practice and can shorten the life of your tree. Instead, thin trees by cutting branches back to existing strong and properly angled branches to help relieve weight. Also, look for dead, diseased, and rubbing branches. No more than one third of the trees canopy should be removed at any one pruning. Significant pruning amounts are best done during the dormant season. Routine maintenance with a small limb or sucker can be done at any time throughout the year. A properly pruned tree is seldom obvious to passers-by. Pruning cuts should be made to the outside of the branch collar, especially on larger trees, and not flush with the trunk. Small cuts can be made any time of year. Oftentimes, improved selections of trees are budded onto the rootstocks of related tough species. Avoid letting suckers emerge from the lower rootstock.

Bald Cypress

Taxodium distichum

At first glance, this tree has the appearance of an evergreen with its needlelike foliage. Indeed, bald cypress is a conifer that forms rounded cones from female flowers in spring, but the leaves are deciduous. The fernlike growth emerges as a brilliant soft green, turning to a bright bronze-yellow in the fall before dropping. The small leaves easily break down in the fall with minimal raking. Bald cypress is also known for its distinctive reddish-brown, fibrous bark. The trees are fairly fast growers with strong wood. 'Monarch of Illinois' is a wider-spreading cultivar while 'Shawnee Brave' is more columnar. Pond cypress (Taxodium ascendens) is a smaller-growing relative of bald cypress. 'Nutans' pond cypress has a more pendulous growth. 'Prairie Sentinel' is a very tall and columnar pond cypress cultivar.

Other Common Name
Swamp Cypress

Bloom Period and Seasonal Color
Bronze-yellow fall foliage.

Mature Height × Spread
50 to 80 ft. × 20 to 30 ft.

Cold Hardiness Zone
6a, 6b, 7a, 7b

When, Where, and How to Plant

Plant bald cypress in early spring or fall. Bald cypress grows best in moist, deep, sandy loam soils. However, it tolerates poor soils or grows at the edge of water. I have seen this tough tree growing in swampy sites in eastern Oklahoma as well as in heavy clay in the western part of the state. Place the containerized or ball-and-burlapped tree in a hole dug 2 to 3 times the width and the same depth as the rootball. Refill the hole with its original soil, and water to settle air pockets. Mulch to retain moisture, control weeds, and keep weed trimmers away.

Growing Tips

Water during drought periods to fully establish the tree during the first two to three years. Continue to reapply mulch as needed. Supplemental applications of fertilizer accelerate the growth of bald cypress. Bald cypress sometimes grows "knees" known as pneumatophores, root tissue that emerges above the soil in soggy sites.

Care

Bald cypress requires minimal care. There are no prevalent pests, though you should regularly inspect for spider mites and bagworms. Restrict pruning to competing branches or central growing leaders. Leave the lower branches on the trunk to allow for thicker development, especially the first couple of years. Iron chlorosis on the foliage occurs in highly alkaline soils. Acidic mulches, such as pine needles, pecan hulls, or pine bark, and fertilizers containing sulfur and iron correct chlorosis.

Landscape Merit

Bald cypress requires a large space in the landscape and makes a majestic shade tree. Its diversity makes it ideal for those soggy locations with bog-type plants or in drier upland areas with ground cover and shade perennials. They make great trees for planting a grove or even lining estate drives.

My Personal Favorites

'Shawnee Brave' is a better choice for smaller landscapes due to its narrower growth habit. 'Cascade Falls' is a weeping form that makes a wonderful specimen plant.

Carolina Buckthorn

Rhamnus carolinianus

When, Where, and How to Plant

Set container-grown plants in the spring, early summer, or fall. Collect and start seed in the fall. When planting, do not remove too much growth since fruit is produced on one- or two-year-old wood. This large shrub or small tree naturally inhabits slightly acidic, moist, fertile sites. Plant container-grown selections at the same depth they were grown, in holes twice as wide as the rootballs. Water and mulch after planting.

Growing Tips

Deep, weekly watering will be needed for the first year if rainfall is not present to encourage roots, but it is relatively drought tolerant once established. The foliage will yellow and the inside leaves will drop if the plant gets to dry. Avoid overfertilization; too much stimulation encourages disease and weaker branching. Slow-release fertilizer or organic products are best.

Care

Insect pests are minimal but occasionally include fall webworms. There are potential canker dieback and wilt disease problems, especially in compacted, poorly drained soils. Routine pruning will have to be done to establish the shape of your plant. Watch for poorly angled and competing branches and remove them during the dormant season. As with any showy fruiting tree or shrub, seedling drop and potential germination is likely. In this case, birds help the seeding process. In mulched, fluffy soils expect notable seedling germination. Fortunately, the seedlings are easy to pull when they are small.

Landscape Merit

Use this beauty as a lawn specimen plant where the seed is harder to germinate in the adjoining turfgrass. Give it about 20 feet from any structure. Avoid planting it near sidewalks, or the fruit drop will cause problems. I have seen it best displayed in large island or background landscape beds combined with other bird-loving plants, birdbaths, and bird feeders. It can even be trimmed into a hedge.

My Personal Favorite

The native selection is ideal, but I also like the columnar design possibilities of a fruitless relative R. frangula 'Fine Line'™.

Do not let the name scare—this plant has no thorns. The real beauty of this plant is the berries that form in late summer or early fall. The fruit ripen in August to a red color that eventually turns black or metallic purple. When you get all colors in September and October, it really puts on a show. The plant is considered fairly fast growing and is somewhat weak wooded but not as weak as a silver maple. The younger twigs have a reddish-brown color, which enhances the winter appearance of the dormant, leafless tree especially since the birds eat the colorful fruit. The deciduous foliage has a very glossy appearance, which complements the brilliantly colored fruit. The perfect, creamy-green flowers are not showy.

Other Common Names
Indian Cherry, Alderleaf

Bloom Period and Seasonal Color
Creamy green blooms in summer.

Mature Height × Spread
15 to 30 ft. × 10 to 18 ft.

Cold Hardiness Zones
6a, 6b, 7a, 7b

Chinese Pistache

Pistacia chinensis

This stately tree exhibits brilliant color in the fall. Its leaves produce a distinctly pungent odor when they are bruised. Chinese pistache grows from one end of the state to the other and thrives in almost any soil, yet it is unknown to many gardeners. This superb tree has made the top lists of plants to use in Oklahoma and neighboring states. Pistache trees are dioecious (male and female flowers on separate trees). The female produces fruit that ripens to a metallic-red or blue color in October. Blue jays and mockingbirds occasionally disperse the small, round berries. As a result, a few seedlings might pop up in the landscape. Chinese pistache is related to the tree that produces pistachio nuts. Pistacia vera is a smaller tree, not cold-hardy this far north.

Other Common Name
Pistache Tree

Bloom Period and Seasonal Color
Gold, bronze, and red fall foliage.

Mature Height × Spread
30 to 45 ft. × 25 to 35 ft.

Cold Hardiness Zones
6a, 6b, 7a, 7b

When, Where, and How to Plant

Plant in spring or fall. Chinese pistache transplants well, whether in container-grown or balled-and-burlapped form. Like most trees, they grow larger in moist, well-drained, fertile soils. Dig the planting hole 2 to 3 times the width of the rootball and the same depth. Do not add organic backfill. Water thoroughly to settle the soil and deeply on a regular basis. Mulch to retain moisture, to discourage weeds and grasses, and to protect the trunk from mowers and trimmers.

Growing Tips

Chinese pistache, a fast-growing tree with exceptionally strong wood, is drought tolerant once established. Build a soil reservoir to hold water and help thorough watering down to the root zone. Staking may be necessary in younger trees to help guide a well defined central growing point or leader. Do not make the staking material too tight. It should be removed after a couple of years and checked regularly for any girdling as the tree increases in size.

Care

Chinese pistache needs selective pruning early on to form a good, straight crown. It is a good idea to leave lower branches on the tree for a couple of years to better establish a thicker trunk early on after planting. The tree has few pest problems, with the exception of an occasional webworm in the eastern part of the state.

Landscape Merit

I have seen them used as street trees in the western part of the state. Most often landscapers use them as specimen plants in yards. The brilliant fall color makes a nice companion to evergreen shrubs and trees. The sparse branching in the winter combined with late spring foliage makes it a nice companion for early flowering bulbs under its canopy.

My Personal Favorite

No improved cultivars are available to date, but the species is still an outstanding selection for Oklahoma landscapes.

Dawn Redwood
Metasequoia glyptostroboides

When, Where, and How to Plant

Plant dawn redwood in late spring. Dawn redwood prefers somewhat acidic, moist, well-drained soils. Dig the planting hole 2 to 3 times wider than and the same depth as the rootball. Use the original soil as backfill. Water the tree frequently and deeply. Mulch 2 to 4 inches thick for moisture retention, but avoid direct contact with the tree trunk. In optimum growing conditions, the tree can get very large and needs considerable spacing away from structures and other trees.

Growing Tips

In dry conditions, supplemental water is a must. Always water for a long period of time to encourage deep root growth. Do not apply fertilizers in late summer or fall to avoid delayed growth spurts and susceptibility to winter injury.

Care

Pruning is seldom necessary because of the tree's natural pyramidal shape and good branch angles. But remove competing or rubbing branches. Leave lower branches on for a couple of years to encourage quicker and stronger trunk development. Bagworms and spider mites are the most common pests.

Landscape Merit

The tree is a great choice for a park, golf course, or large yard. Dawn redwood requires plenty of room to mature and is a great shade or specimen lawn tree. Azaleas and other acid loving plants are nice companions favoring the same moist but well-drained soils. Keep plantings under the drip line to avoid root damage. Ground covers that spread and fill areas under the drip line are better choices.

My Personal Favorite

I'm intrigued by the Dawn redwood selection 'White Spot' and its speckled, creamy white foliage early in the season. Of course any of the Dawn redwood cultivars are impressive and reminiscent of the California Giant Redwood. The true Giant Redwood (*Sequoiadendron giganteum*) is not cold-hardy in Oklahoma, although southeastern Oklahoma gardeners might consider planting the giant redwood cold-hardy cultivar 'Hazel Smith'.

Yet another deciduous conifer well adapted to the eastern part of the state is dawn redwood. It is remarkably fast-growing with a soft evergreen appearance. It is a towering tree with an upright growth, often growing more than two feet a year under optimum conditions. Dawn redwood offers an airy, soft texture to any landscape. This historic tree was thought to be extinct until the 1940s when seedlings were found growing in China. Seeds were collected and brought back to the United States. I have seen the tree grown fairly successfully in poor, well-drained soils, even as a street tree. The bark is a beautiful reddish brown, exfoliating for an interesting display. 'Sheridan Spire' and 'National' are two upright cultivars in the trade with little variation from the parent species.

Other Common Name
Water Fir

Bloom Period and Seasonal Color
Reddish-orange fall foliage.

Mature Height × Spread
60 to 100 ft. × 25 to 35 ft.

Cold Hardiness Zones
7a, 7b

Eastern Redbud

Cercis canadensis

Making its way across the state with a burst of early-spring color from east to as far west as Woodward is our state tree—eastern redbud. The color is dramatic after a drab winter. The unique, heart-shaped foliage appears after the lovely blooms. 'Alba' is white-flowering with occasional tinges of pink. 'Oklahoma Alba' has pure white flowers followed by bluish-green foliage turning golden yellow in the fall. Cercis canadensis ssp. texensis has glossy leaves and purple-pink flowers opening later than most of the eastern selections. 'Traveller' and 'Covey' are weeping or pendulous selections. 'Oklahoma' is known for its glossy, thick foliage. Mexican redbud (Cercis canadensis ssp. mexicana) is a smaller tree or large shrub with wavy leaf margins and large, deep-purple flowers.

Other Common Name
Judas Tree

Bloom Period and Seasonal Color
Purple-red, white, and pink blooms in spring; pale golden yellow fall foliage.

Mature Height × Spread
25 to 45 ft. × 25 to 35 ft.

Cold Hardiness Zones
6a, 6b, 7a, 7b

When, Where, and How to Plant
Redbud transplants well in spring or fall. It is available as a container-grown, bare-root, or balled-and-burlapped tree. Redbuds can be multiple trunk specimens as well as single or pendulous selections, depending on the variety. In its native habitat, redbud is an understory tree that prefers filtered sun. Many of the newer cultivars grow in full sun. Too much shade causes thinning of the tree canopy. It grows best in moist, well-drained, fertile soils but tolerates a wide range of acidic or alkaline soil types. There is no need to amend the soil. Dig the planting hole 2 to 3 times wider than and the same depth as the rootball. Backfill the hole without compacting the soil. Water thoroughly, and mulch around the tree 2 to 4 inches thick.

Growing Tips
Encourage deeper roots with thorough watering. Apply slow-release or organic fertilizers after spring flowering. Replenish mulch on a regular basis as it breaks down to keep out competing weeds and grass. Staking may be needed on larger bare-root plantings.

Care
Remove the redbud branches to train the tree and reduce risk of splitting branches that grow with weak angles. Try to leave the existing lower branches on during early years to encourage a strong trunk. Prune regularly after the blooms fade. Unfortunately, leaf roller, leafhopper, and scale are potential insect pests. Canker problems arise in areas where the soil is poorly drained and compacted.

Landscape Merit
Use redbud as a specimen, or in groups next to structures or woodland gardens or underneath power lines. Redbud helps tie together shrubs and larger shade trees. The multi-trunk selections are a nice specimen even in perennial gardens.

My Personal Favorites
'Forest Pansy' is one of my favorites with intense purple foliage emerging in the early spring and later turning a purplish green. I am also very fond C. chinensis 'Don Egolf' that has prolific, rosy-mauve blooms and no seeds.

Flowering Dogwood
Cornus florida

When, Where, and How to Plant

Plant dogwood in spring or in early fall as a second choice. To protect dogwood from the intense sun and wind of western and central Oklahoma, plant it as an understory tree at least 20 feet from other trees. Plant in fertile, moist, and well-drained soil. Dogwoods are destined to fail in heavy, poorly drained soils. Just dig holes 2 to 3 times wider than and the same depth as the rootballs, adding organic mulch to keep the soil cool, moist, and fertile. Allow at least 20 feet from any structure.

Growing Tips

Irrigate dogwoods during severe drought conditions. Mimic forest settings and place organic fertilizer on top of the ground and under the mulch to slowly provide nutrition to the root system. Slow-release synthetic fertilizers will also work. Water-soluble products can burn the roots especially when the trees are already stressed in urban conditions by poor soils and heavy winds.

Care

Potential disease problems in Oklahoma are leaf spot and powdery mildew. The eastern United States is faced with a devastating disease called "dogwood anthracnose," causing the introduction of anthracnose-tolerant dogwood varieties. Borer insects attack stressed trees. Prune minimally to preserve flower buds. You may also prune to guide a strong central leader and eliminate any competing branches.

Landscape Merit

Dogwoods are extremely susceptible to damage by weed trimmers and lawn mowers, and they are not good selections for the harsh conditions of street trees. They make a great middle layer plant in a shade garden where there might be a large shade tree, shade loving shrubs, and herbaceous perennials.

My Personal Favorites

I like 'Ozark Spring' for its greater tolerance to urban sites even though it still needs protection. Look for disease tolerant selections that take heat and humidity like the Stellar series, a hybrid cross of the North American native and chinensis.

Dogwood is a plant for all seasons, starting with colorful blooms, followed by unusual foliage (some even variegated), and finishing the season with brilliant-colored seed and foliage in the fall. Dogwood is cold-hardy for the entire state of Oklahoma; however, it performs best in the eastern part where the soils are less alkaline and clayey. 'Ozark Spring' is more tolerant of exposed locations in the prairie states. 'Cherokee Chief' has a reddish-pink flower. 'Cherokee Brave' has a burgundy-red flower and larger, glossy leaves. 'Purple Glory' has a purplish tint to the foliage as well as ruby-colored flowers. Kousa dogwood (Cornus kousa) selections are more cold-hardy and better for the northern part of our state. 'National' is a kousa cultivar.

Other Common Name
Indian Arrowwood

Bloom Period and Seasonal Color
White, pink, and purple blooms in spring; red-orange fall foliage.

Mature Height × Spread
20 to 40 ft. × 20 to 25 ft.

Cold Hardiness Zones
6a, 6b, 7a, 7b

Fruitless Sweetgum

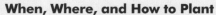

Liquidambar styraciflua 'Rotundiloba'

I rarely highlight a particular cultivar, but if you want to grow sweetgum in the landscape, fruitless sweetgum is the clear choice. Or maybe you like dealing with those prickly little balls? They've hurt my bare feet, clogged the gutters, and cracked windows ricocheting out of my lawn mower. That is why I like the fruitless sweetgum 'Rotundiloba'—few to no fruit balls! This cultivar, though the leaves are more rounded, has the same fragrant foliage turning yellow to reddish purple in the fall. 'Rotundiloba' is sometimes incorrectly called 'Obtusifolia'. There is another cultivar called 'Cherokee' or 'Ward'. It is said to be nearly seedless, but I have found it to have too many seed balls for my liking, even though it is more cold-hardy.

Other Common Name
American Sweetgum

Bloom Period and Seasonal Color
Yellow to reddish-purple fall foliage.

Mature Height × Spread
60 to 75 ft. × 40 to 60 ft.

Cold Hardiness Zones
6a, 6b, 7a, 7b

When, Where, and How to Plant
Plant sweetgum anytime in the spring or fall. Sweetgum is native to moist, fertile, bottomland sites, so it is better adapted to the eastern half of the state. If you plant it in heavy clay or alkaline soils, you are asking for problems. Plant it in a hole 2 to 3 times wider than and the same depth as the rootball. No extra soil amendments are needed. Watering is critical to establish the tree and to settle the soil. Mulch helps to mimic its preferred natural conditions.

Growing Tips
Sweetgum trees appear to just sit there after they are planted. Many times, the top growth does not start until the root growth is well established. Once the growth kicks in, they are considered moderate growers. They need plenty of supplemental water during drought conditions, and they respond to minimal fertilizations.

Care
Pruning is seldom needed. Leaving the lower branches on for the first couple of years after planting is a good practice to encourage bigger, stronger trunks. Potential pests are webworms, caterpillars, scale, and fungal leaf spot. Iron chlorosis is common when the trees are planted in alkaline soils. Mulch as needed to refurbish any that has decomposed or blown away.

Landscape Merit
Sweetgum requires plenty of space for the extensive root system and is not a good choice for a street or driveway tree. It does well as a lawn or park specimen. As a landscape shade tree, it needs at least 50 feet or more from any structure especially in good soils. Most urban soils are anything but good and are typically compacted, nutritionally deficient, and very shallow. so do not use this tree there.

My Personal Favorite
'Rotundiloba' has attractive foliage and is somewhat slow growing especially when not in a rich, well-drained soil.

When, Where, and How to Plant

Plant ginkgo in spring or fall. This adaptable plant tolerates adverse pH, drought, and wind. Sandy, deep, moisture-retentive soil with good drainage mimics gingko's natural habitat causing somewhat quicker growth. Dig a large planting hole as deep as the rootball and 2 to 3 times wider. Backfill with native (not amended) soil. Water to settle the soil and remove air pockets. Mulch to keep moisture in and weed trimmers away. Allow at least 25 feet from any structure to release its optimum potential.

Growing Tips

Provide supplemental water during drought conditions. Mulch to keep curb weed competition. Ginkgo, a slow grower, will speed up with fertilizer, but do not overdo it. Do not apply until after (at least) one year and the tree is established. Apply slow-release synthetic or natural organic fertilizers according to package directions either in spring or fall when grass competition is minimal.

Care

Drastic pruning is not necessary because the tree has strong wood and grows with good branch angles. Leaving the existing lower branches on for a couple of years promotes stronger trunk development. Ginkgo trees are typically free of pests. Occasionally, leaf scald can occur on the southwest side of the trunk due to sparse foliage. On smaller trees, protect the trunk with tree wrap (not too tight) or apply a reflective layer of white latex paint. The tree branches out better as it matures.

Landscape Merit

Because it is heat, pollution, and salt tolerant, it makes a good street tree, although it needs plenty of space. Use ginkgo as a shade or specimen lawn tree but just be patient. The fall color is majestic yet short lived since the leaves drop very quickly, almost overnight with a cold spell. The good thing is they are small and easy to rake or leave in the landscape bed.

My Personal Favorite

'Jade Butterflies' is a male selection which seems to have bigger and more vibrant green foliage.

Gingko has been growing on earth for more than 150 million years. It is often referred to as a living fossil. Though it can be hard to find at many local garden centers, it is well worth the extra time needed to find it and grow it. Plant named cultivars propagated from male selections. The female produces untidy and foul-smelling seed. Ginkgo becomes a distinctly pyramid-shaped, picturesque tree. The unique foliage resembles a silhouette of maidenhair fern leaflet. The fall color is a consistent golden yellow unless there is an early freeze and the leaves quickly drop. The smaller leaf means minimal fall cleanup. 'Autumn Gold' is a male selection with excellent fall color. 'Princeton Sentry', 'Fairmount', 'Magyar' are male cultivars more narrow in growth.

Other Common Name
Maidenhair Tree

Bloom Period and Seasonal Color
Golden yellow fall foliage.

Mature Height × Spread
40 to 60 ft. × 20 to 40 ft.

Cold Hardiness Zones
6a, 6b, 7a, 7b

Golden Raintree

Koelreuteria paniculata

Golden raintree adds intrigue to landscapes features with elaborate, showy yellow flowers in June. They later transform into a cluster of lantern-like seedpods with a golden color, continuing to tower above the foliage and remaining throughout part of the winter. The tree's small, rounded canopy fits in almost any landscape, and the compound leaves provide some shade. The uniquely shaped leaves provide color in the fall. 'Fastigiata' is more upright and narrow in growth. 'September', which is hard to find, blooms later in the fall. Koelreuteria elegans has yellow flowers and pinkish-rose seedpods. The tree is not as cold-hardy and is found more in the lower southeastern parts of the United States. 'Flamegold' is a selection with intense fall color.

Other Common Name
Panicled Golden Raintree

Bloom Period and Seasonal Color
Yellow blooms in June; orange-yellow fall foliage.

Mature Height × Spread
30 to 40 ft. × 20 to 40 ft.

Cold Hardiness Zones
6a, 6b, 7a, 7b

When, Where, and How to Plant
Plant it in spring or fall. This tough tree adapts to sand, clay, or rocky soils as long as they drains well. Dig the planting hole 2 to 3 times wider than and the same depth as the rootball to encourage root development. Supplemental amendments and nutrients are not needed at planting time. Water to gently settle the soil and remove air pockets. Mulch after planting to keep moisture in and weeds out. Reserve a space of 30 feet around the tree and allow it to fully mature in a landscape setting.

Growing Tips
Golden raintree is one of the easiest trees to care for. It is considered fast growing and responds well to fertilizer. Luckily, it uses the same fertilizers needed for lawns and landscapes. Water routinely after planting to ensure the tree's establishment. In a year, the tree will be more self sufficient and fairly drought tolerant.

Care
It seldom needs pruning. Leaving the lower branches on for the first couple of years encourages a bigger, stronger trunk. An annoying pest attracted to golden raintree frustrates homeowners more than the trees. These black, gray, and red critters are called box elder or red shoulder bugs. If the tree is planted nearby, they crawl from the tree to your eaves, shutters, windows, and doors searching for a place to overwinter.

Landscape Merit
Use golden raintree as a single specimen or in groups for a bigger flower display. It is not really tall enough for a shade tree but makes a great landscape accent plant. The showy flowers and compound leaves make this tree one of a kind for any landscape, especially if you like to use purple-and-yellow colors in your design.

My Personal Favorites
The cultivar 'September' blooms longer into the fall thus the name, but I really like a smaller selection known as 'Fastigiata' that is ideal as a taller specimen plant combined with other shrubs and herbaceous perennials.

Japanese Maple
Acer palmatum

When, Where, and How to Plant
Plant in spring or fall in a spot protected from the wind and hot sun. They prefer rich, moist soil and locations under trees or eastern- or northeastern-facing sites. Prepare beds with organic matter, but do not till if established trees are nearby. Japanese maples are frequently sold as balled-and-burlapped plants. Always remove the twine and burlap. Leaving the burlap slows and sometimes hinders root establishment. Dig the planting hole 2 to 3 times wider than and the same depth as the rootball. Water and mulch as needed.

Growing Tips
Scorching occurs from prolonged drought, so supplemental watering is necessary. Overfertilizing increases the green pigment in burgundy foliage selections. Mulching is a must with Japanese maples. Slow growing at first, they grow at a moderate rate after establishment.

Care
Prune to shape the appearance to fit your design and purpose. Do small pruning any time of year. Do drastic pruning for design (no more than one-third at a time) early in the dormant season. There are very few problems with insects or disease. Most leaf problems occur from exposure to scorching sun and wind. Japanese maples leaf out early and late-spring freezes occasionally damage the foliage.

Landscape Merit
Use as a single specimen, in a border, as an accent plant, or in groupings for a dramatic impact. Ground covers are nice companions, but they also compete for soil moisture with the shallow rooted maple. Japanese maple makes a great bonsai or espalier plant with intense pruning and design.

My Personal Favorites
There are literally hundreds of selections. I really like A. japonicum 'Aureum' when used in a dappled shade garden. In the spring, it emerges with a vibrant chartreuse color but unfortunately fades as the summer progresses. 'Tsumagaki' (yellow foliage with reddish edges) and 'Kasigiyama' (reddish/pink) are both breathtaking and expensive. And then there is Coral Bark 'Sangokaku' that has lime green foliage and really nice coral red branches in the winter.

If graceful is a term that can be used to describe a tree, it applies to the Japanese maple. The colorful foliage is very attractive and adds both color and texture to the landscape. Fall colors are quite intense and the unique bark is a nice attribute in the winter. Japanese maples are most often used as specimen plants because they offer unique upright, mounding, cascading, or textured features to a landscape design. Japanese maples are some of the priciest trees available. Trees range in the hundreds of dollars, depending on the species or cultivar and the size. Most are grafted or budded to a more resilient rootstock. There are literally hundreds of cultivars from which to choose. Select the appropriate ones for your particular site according to height and width.

Bloom Period and Seasonal Color
Orange-red to golden yellow fall foliage.

Mature Height × Spread
10 to 25 ft. × 10 to 15 ft.

Cold Hardiness Zones
6a, 6b, 7a, 7b

Kentucky Coffee Tree

Gymnocladus dioicus

Another native of Oklahoma is the Kentucky coffee tree. The large, compound leaves of this stately tree emerge with a pinkish tint and become a grayish green, providing sufficient shade. After the leaves drop in the winter, the tree's sparse branches permit sunlight. As a result, this tree is often promoted as an energy-efficient plant. The small leaflets are not a litter problem in the fall. There are male and female plants (dioecious). The female plant has fairly fragrant flowers. Soon after flowering, a beanlike seedpod develops, which is five to ten inchers long. There are three named male selections. 'Espresso' is a seedless male with upright branching growing about 70 feet tall by 40 feet wide in an elm-like form. 'Prairie Titan' (J.C. McDaniel), and 'Stately Manor' are other male selections.

Other Common Name
Coffee Tree

Bloom Period and Seasonal Color
Non-showy flowers in spring

Mature Height × Spread
60 to 80 ft. × 30 to 50 ft.

Cold Hardiness Zones
6a, 6b, 7a, 7b

When, Where, and How to Plant
Plant Kentucky coffee tree in the spring or fall. It is found in rich, bottomland soils or deep ravines with moist slopes. A moist, well-drained soil provides the best growth and display. It tolerates poor soils, however. Plant the tree in a hole 2 to 3 times wider than and the same depth as the rootball. Soil amendments, such as compost, peat moss, or root stimulators, are not needed. Add mulch after planting to simulate the moist, fertile conditions in nature in which the tree thrives.

Growing Tips
Water them during drought conditions and reapply mulch as needed. These potentially enormous trees respond to supplemental feedings. Fertilize once it is established about a year after planting. Fertilize in the spring or fall to avoid competition with grass fertilizer in the spring or fall. Trees planted in a fertilized lawn or landscape seldom need additional fertilizer except when nutritional deficiencies appear on the foliage.

Care
Young nursery seedlings are often tall and lanky with few branches; tip-pruning the main trunk slightly above a group of buds forces lower branches. Leave existing lower branches for the first couple of years to encourage a bigger, stronger trunk. Prune to develop strong branches that are not intersecting or rubbing. Kentucky coffee tree wood is fairly strong, even though the tree grows rather quickly. There are no major pest problems.

Landscape Merit
To fully reach its potential, this tree needs a large space. Plant it as a shade tree in a lawn or park setting. Its compound leaves and sparse branching make it a nice tree for the west side of a house or structure. It provides shade in the summer and allows plenty of sunshine in the winter when the large compound leaves drop.

My Personal Favorite
All of the improved male cultivars would make a nice addition to any landscape.

Lacebark Elm
Ulmus parvifolia

When, Where, and How to Plant

Plant lacebark elm in spring or fall in a site receiving at least six hours of sun. A hole of loose soil 2 to 3 times wider than and the same depth as the rootball encourages the roots to establish quickly. It will grow in a wide range of soil types conditions throughout the state. Water deeply to settle the soil and soak the roots. Mulch for added environmental benefits such as weed control, moisture retention, and protection from weed trimmers.

Growing Tips

Water during drought conditions. Lacebark elm is fairly drought tolerant once established. Elms respond to fertilizers, but do not overdo it. Rapid growth leads to week branches susceptible to storm damage. Lacebark elm blooms and sets seed in late summer or early fall.

Care

Chinese elm tolerates the elm leaf beetle and Japanese beetle that spread Dutch elm disease. In far eastern Oklahoma, beware a new critter known as the elm flea. About the time the leaves unfurl, the black, hopping beetle skeletonizes the leaves, making them unsightly. Fortunately, the trees put out another set of leaves. But as you can imagine, it monopolizes the tree's energy to produce two flushes of growth in a year. Slow-release or organic fertilization aids the tree after the beetles have finished their cycle.

Landscape Merit

Its relatively fast growth rate makes it a good choice for a shade tree in the landscape. Allow at least 15 to 20 feet from any structure to get the full value of its canopy. The unique bark pattern extends the season color display with brilliant winter interest. Trees and shrubs with fruit set in the winter like Possum Haw Holly make great companions.

My Personal Favorite

'Corticosa' Chinese Elm is a smaller growing selection to about 20 feet with really cool, corky bark. I have even seen it used as a bonsai tree along with numerous other dwarf cultivars. It also makes a nice specimen plant for any smaller landscape.

As you travel across our great state, you will see that elms like it here, too. The tree is quite elegant with its oval growth habit. As it matures, the bark exfoliates, creating a most unusual mottling of colors. To date, Chinese elm seems more resistant to Dutch elm disease. 'Athena' has a rounded growth habit, thick leaves, and consistent exfoliating bark. 'Allee' is more upright in growth habit with good fall color. 'Drake' has a more upright growth habit and likes the warmer climates of southeastern Oklahoma. 'Prairie Shade' likes western Oklahoma and the panhandle. 'Golden Ray' ('Rey's Golden') offers unique light green to yellow foliage during the summer with a combination of gray, orange, and brown exfoliating bark. This is just a small sampling of the many cultivars.

Other Common Names
Chinese Elm, Drake Elm

Bloom Period and Seasonal Color
Yellow, orange, and red fall foliage.

Mature Height × Spread
60 to 80 ft. × 30 to 50 ft.

Cold Hardiness Zones
6a, 6b, 7a, 7b

Pine
Pinus species

There are numerous pine species growing in our state, many of which are native. Pines offer ever-so-important green or bluish grey color, height, and texture to a drab winter landscape. Another benefit is the pine needle mulch to use under other shrubs and trees, especially azaleas, blueberries, and other acid-loving plants. Gardeners in the southeastern United States pay good money for bales of pine straw to use as landscape mulch. Other pines tolerant of Oklahoma conditions are pinyon, shortleaf, Austrian, limber, Japanese red, digger, and slash. Pines are often categorized and identified by the number of needles in a bundle whether two, three or five. The needles grow in clusters, "bundles," surrounded by a sheath that holds them together and attaches the bundle to the tree.

Other Common Name
Soft Pine

Bloom Period and Seasonal Color
Evergreen foliage.

Mature Height × Spread
5 to 100 ft. × 5 to 60 ft.

Cold Hardiness Zones
6a, 6b, 7a, 7b

When, Where, and How to Plant
Plant pines in the fall or spring throughout the state, except the Panhandle where spring is preferable. Pines like slightly acidic soil and absolutely cannot withstand waterlogged soils; drainage is a must (except for loblolly pine which tolerates wetter conditions). Towering pines need widely dug holes 2 to 3 times the width and the same depth as the container rootballs. In heavy soils, plant slightly above soil grade to help air get to the roots; always mulch pines planted above the soil. Mulching newly planted seedlings is a necessity, or weeds and grass overtake them.

Growing Tips
Excessive nitrogen fertilizer can kill a pine. Use slow-release fertilizers and/or organic mulches. Minimize heavy foot traffic over the shallow roots. Most pines prefer well-drained soils but respond to supplemental watering during drought.

Care
A healthy tree is less susceptible to pests. Pinewood nematode inhabits eastern Oklahoma (and really loves Scotch, Austrian, Japanese black, Japanese red, mugo, and long-leaf pines). Pine tip moth wreaks havoc by eating growing points of branches. Dispose of needles infected with needle or tip blight. Pine tip borer frequently disturbs loblolly and mugo pines. Prune pines in the spring before the candles start to elongate and needles form.

Landscape Merit
Pine looks naturalized when planted in groups of 3 or 5; this also simplifies needle gathering. With all the different species and cultivars, there is a selection for just about any landscape job. Match species size and cultivar to the scale of your home and landscape. Quick-growing pines can easily outgrow and tower above single story homes, leaving an awkward balance. Azalea, viburnum, and other dappled shade, acid-loving plants are great companions.

My Personal Favorite
You cannot beat the soft textured needles of Eastern White Pine, *P. strobus*, which is happier in eastern Oklahoma since it dislikes high pH and compacted soils.

Red Maple
Acer rubrum

When, Where, and How to Plant

Red maples are successfully planted in spring or fall; fall is the best time to ensure cultivar color. Maples thrive in moist, slightly acidic, deep soils with good drainage, though they will adapt to rocky sites or heavy clay with good drainage and supplemental moisture. Prepare the planting site 2 to 3 times the diameter of the rootball and the same depth. No organic backfill is recommended; just use native soil. Mulch and water thoroughly until the tree is well established; if it is persistently dry, water at least once a week.

Growing Tips

Reapply mulch as needed. Give your tree the gift of nutrition with synthetic or organic fertilizer. Manganese deficiency, with symptoms of yellow leaves and green veins, is a problem in alkaline soils. Minimize this with mulch, consistent watering practices, and a fall application of manganese sulfate or a spring application of manganese chelate to the foliage—both according to label directions.

Care

Occasional pruning promotes a straight central leader and better branch angles. Start pruning right away and always outside the branch collar. Do severe pruning in early winter, preferably December, and small pruning at any time during the growing season. Leave lower branches on for several years to encourage a strong tree trunk and protect from sunscald. Wrap or paint red maple trunks with white latex paint to reflect sun. Watch for anthracnose.

Landscape Merit

They make excellent specimen trees and have stronger wood than other fast-growing maples. Although not as bad as silver maple, red maple's roots can be somewhat shallow rooted. Get rid of the lawn grass and consider shade-loving ground covers if shallow roots do become a problem.

My Personal Favorite

The color of 'Red Sunet'® is breathtaking although somewhat later depending on your location of the state. Leaf scorch is possible without supplement irrigation during severe drought and in harsh urban settings with a lot of concrete and asphalt.

Red maple offers plenty to Oklahoma gardeners since it is native to our state. They take our cold as well as heat, growing somewhat quickly and providing beautiful fall color. They are fairly tolerant of many soil types. 'Red Sunset' holds its fall color longer. 'Autumn Flame' has early fall color. 'Drummond' has colorful seeds in addition to leaves. 'October Glory' has a more rounded growth habit. 'Karpick' has reddish twigs in addition to its fall color. 'Autumn Blaze' (A. × freemani) has brilliant fall color and is very fast growing but with somewhat weaker wood. Shantung maple (A. truncatum), trident maple (A. buergerianum), tatarian maple (A. tataricum), and hedge maple (A. campestre) are great choices for small- to medium-sized trees. 'Flame' has spectacular fall color.

Other Common Name
Swamp Maple

Bloom Period and Seasonal Color
Golden-yellow, orange, bronze, and red fall foliage.

Mature Height × Spread
40 to 80 ft. × 40 to 60 ft.

Cold Hardiness Zones
6a, 6b, 7a, 7b

Sassafrass

Sassafras albidum

Sassafrass is most often found in thickets in moist, somewhat acidic conditions, especially in eastern Oklahoma. In addition to the unique sassafrass aroma, there are the very exclusive shiny, mitten-shaped leaves. The yellow flowers emerge from terminal buds in March and April. The female trees later produce a greenish fruit, which changes to a metallic dark blue in the fall. The vibrant kaleidoscope of fall colors ranges from orange to red to purple. Compared to oaks and other majestic, long-lived natives, sassafrass is a fairly short-lived tree, particularly in improper planting sites. After twenty-five or thirty years the trees start to fall apart, losing branches and thinning. Occasionally, a variety of S. albidum, known as molle (silky sassafrass), is available in the South with slightly hairy twigs, buds, and foliage.

Other Common Name
Cinnamon Wood

Bloom Period and Seasonal Color
Yellow blooms in early spring; orange, red, and purple fall foliage.

Mature Height × Spread
25 to 40 ft. × 15 to 30 ft.

Cold Hardiness Zones
6a, 6b, 7a, 7b

When, Where, and How to Plant
Some native nurseries offer this picky tree, which can be transplanted from containers in spring or fall. This plant prefers full-sun or partially shaded sites with moist, somewhat acidic, but well-drained soil. Make the planting hole the same depth as and 2 to 3 times wider than the rootball. Mulch after planting, and water as needed; devise a soil reservoir around the rootball to hold water.

Growing Tips
Mulching under the drip line, watering uniformly and deeply, applying soil sulfur, and fertilizing with ammonium sulfate according to directions all help to manage iron chlorosis, whose symptoms are yellow foliage with green veins. Slow-release synthetic fertilizers or organic natural fertilizers are good choices to apply in the fall or early spring.

Care
Sassafras tends to sucker and form colonies of adjoining trees. Once the trees are established, avoid root disturbance, which promotes even more root suckering. The trees have a tendency to grow in a pyramidal form and seldom need pruning other than to remove older damaged, weak, or conflicting branches. Few insect and disease problems affect this plant in Oklahoma. Expect some foliage tattering not from wind but instead from the larval stage of a butterfly. Do not panic because the foliage will grow back and you get to enjoy the beautiful Spicebush butterfly as well as other butterflies and moths in the process.

Landscape Merit
Folks with large acreage and lots are more likely to find a home for this colorful native. Possible sites include the edge of woodland settings, naturalized locations, rough areas that are hard to mow, and an island bed in large lawn areas. It is not a good idea to try to incorporate sassafrass into the formal landscape in small areas because of the plant's suckering nature.

My Personal Favorite
Improved cultivars are hard to find, and the native offers many landscape attributes in the right location.

Shumard Oak

Quercus shumardii

When, Where, and How to Plant

Spring or fall planting is routinely done with either container-grown or balled-and-burlapped trees. Shumard oak is found naturally in rich, moist bottomlands. Fortunately, this tree adapts well to poor soils in dry conditions once it is established. The planting hole should be 2 feet wider than the plant root system and no deeper. It is no longer recommended to add organic backfill. Organic materials make great mulch, however. Water deeply to adequately soak the rootball.

Growing Tips

Apply commercial fertilizers and slow-release organic or natural fertilizers in the fall or spring before competing grass and weeds are growing. Supplemental nutrient applications are seldom needed in lawns and landscapes that are routinely fertilized. Without rainfall, water weekly for several months until they are well established and rooted. Mulch as needed.

Care

Pruning may be necessary to assist tree structure. Leave lower branches for two years for a bigger, stronger trunk. Oak trees are fairly resilient to pests, yet a few critters persist in our state. Insect galls harmlessly ornament our oak trees. Oak decline, on the other hand, is not as forgiving and is the slow death of trees. Little can be done to infected trees stressed by their environment. Hypoxylon canker is another disease that affects weakened, stressed, or damaged trees. Look for yellowing and wilting foliage and sloughing bark revealing grayish-white lining. There is no effective control other than removing and burning infected trees. Oak leaf blister occurs as a small, dark lesion sporadically located on the leaves. The fungus-causing pathogen usually occurs as a result of wet, warm weather as the leaves unfurl. Typically, no control is needed.

Landscape Merit

These large, towering trees need plenty of room in a lawn or park setting. They are occasionally used in urban street settings. The strong-wooded trees are moderately fast growers and make excellent choices for shade trees.

My Personal Favorite

The common species with its stately presence should satisfy everybody.

Oh, the mighty oak! It truly lives up to its name in our region. Just visit any part of the state and enormous oaks prevail, many of which are native. Oaks are quite drought tolerant after they are established, and they willingly take Oklahoma's notorious temperature variations. Not only do oaks make strong shade trees, but their acorns provide vital food for our native wildlife. One of the most suitable oak trees for the entire state is shumard. The size of acorns ranges from $^1/_4$ to 2 inches in diameter, depending on the variety. Consider potential litter problems from the acorns when planting trees near driveways and sidewalks. Shumard oak is a better choice for a landscape tree in alkaline soils and is tolerant of heavy clay soils.

Other Common Names
Spotted Oak, Texas Oak

Bloom Period and Seasonal Color
Unexceptional spring flowers; fall leaf color ranges from yellow bronze to a russet red. (Look for the orangey-brown acorns borne in shallow cups).

Mature Height × Spread
80 to 100 ft. × 50 to 60 ft.

Cold Hardiness Zones
6a, 6b, 7a, 7b

Southern Magnolia
Magnolia grandiflora

This Southern charmer is best known for its fragrant, showy flowers. Magnolias grow quite well in the eastern part of Oklahoma. In western Oklahoma, they can tolerate clay soils but cold-hardiness is more of a concern. The large leaves are an attractive component of this aristocratic tree, but also an occasional nuisance. The leaves may have a dark-cinnamon-brown or gray undersides, depending on the cultivar, which makes for an interesting color combination. Cold-hardy selections include 'Bracken's Brown Beauty', 'Edith Bogue', 'D. D. Blanchard', and 'Glen St. Mary'.

Other Common Name
Evergreen Magnolia

Bloom Period and Seasonal Color
White and cream blooms in early summer.

Mature Height × Spread
60 to 80 ft. × 30 to 50 ft.

Cold Hardiness Zones
6b, 7a, 7b

When, Where, and How to Plant
Plant magnolias in early spring to establish before harsh winters; choose protected sites since cold winds occasionally burn the foliage. Compensate for maturation and give magnolias plenty of room for the lower branches to develop and cascade down naturally. Choose a healthy container-grown or balled-and-burlapped tree. Plant it in a hole 2 to 3 times wider than and the same depth as the rootball. Make sure the soil is acidic with good drainage; amend it slightly with soil sulfur according to directions. Water thoroughly once a week if rainfall is not present. Organic mulches are necessities for these evergreen beauties.

Growing Tips
Supplemental applications of acid fertilizers pay big dividends in foliage and flower set. Winter organic mulches provide slow-release nutrients. Provide magnesium to the plant by applying Epsom salts at a rate of 1 pound per 10 feet of branch spread. Supplemental water is very beneficial during drought conditions especially in newly planted trees.

Care
Pruning is generally not necessary; however, tip-prune tall lanky trees to encourage lower branching. Flowers occur in early summer, followed by red, showy fruit on cone-like structures. Do not be alarmed if the leaves appear to wilt during the bloom time, the tree diverts energy to the beautiful flowers. Older leaves drop in the spring and are messy in certain landscape settings. There are essentially no serious pest problems, other than an occasional disease leaf spot.

Landscape Merit
I love to see magnolias planted in large spacious areas where the lower branches are left clear to the ground. The pyramidal look is majestic and makes an awesome backdrop for most any design, not to mention a great windbreak. In smaller landscapes, proper pruning can be done on the lower branches to allow for dappled light of adjoining acidic-loving plants like camellias, rhododendrons, and hydrangeas.

My Personal Favorites
'Little Gem' and 'Alta'™ are two compact tree selections suitable for smaller landscapes.

Sugar Maple
Acer saccharum

When, Where, and How to Plant
Plant maples in fall or spring. Caddo sugar maple prefers well-drained, moderately moist soil. Grow it in full sun for the best color. Dig a planting hole at least 2 to 3 times the width and the same depth as the rootball to encourage horizontal root establishment. Water deeply and then mulch.

Growing Tips
During dry summers, drought causes leaf drop. Leaf scorch from heat and wind is also typical. Water during drought to prevent stress and premature leaf drop. Mulch for moisture retention, cooler soil temperatures, and weed control. Slow-release commercial products or a natural organic fertilizers will stimulate growth since sugar maples are somewhat slow-growing trees. Apply in the fall or early spring when there is not much competition from weeds and grass. Mulch over the fertilizer when possible.

Care
Prune to encourage a well-trained tree. Make small directional pruning cuts throughout the year. Make larger cuts when the trees are dormant in December or January. Leave lower branches on the tree for the first couple of years to encourage a bigger, stronger trunk. Anthracnose fungal disease affects the foliage in early spring. Repeated heavy infections need preventative sprays early in the spring as leaf buds break dormancy.

Landscape Merit
Allow plenty of space for it to reach its optimum size as a shade tree. Most folks die to have that fall color in their landscape and forget about the space needed for these trees. Give it at least 20 to 30 feet from any structure. If space allows, plant them in the perimeters of your landscape where you can enjoy their view from inside the home as a background or framing plant.

My Personal Favorite
Most any cultivar will work. I choose my sugar maples from the nursery in the fall to see which ones have the brilliant color. Chances are better they will provide that same color at home with the right conditions.

As the name implies, sugar maple or hard maple is one of the strongest-wooded maples available. It is adapted to northern climates, but some varieties tolerate heat. Gardeners visit the New England states in the fall, see the breathtaking colors of sugar maple, and want to duplicate them at home. The typical sugar maple is generally short-lived in our climate. Never fear, though, Oklahoma has a native form of sugar maple, called Caddo. It is drought and heat tolerant after it is established. The fall color is a vibrant orange red. Moisture, temperature, and short days determine fall color, which can vary from year to year with each tree. 'Commemoration', 'Legacy', 'Green Mountain', and 'Summer Proof' are other sugar maple cultivars considered more heat tolerant and resistant to wind tattering.

Other Common Names
Hard Maple, Rock Maple

Bloom Period and Seasonal Color
Non-showy flowers appear in mid to late spring; brilliant fall color of yellow to scarlet red.

Mature Height × Spread
60 to 80 ft. × 40 to 60 ft.

Cold Hardiness Zones
6a, 6b, 7a, 7b

Vines *for Oklahoma*

Vines are perfect plants for offering height and individuality to the landscape. They create suspense by subdividing gardens into different rooms. Vines quickly become part of the welcoming ambiance when they are allowed to grow over entrance gate archways. Sun-loving vines grown on large arbors can create shade gardens below and outdoor areas for relaxation. They hide eyesores or add character to ordinary fences. If space is a concern, try growing vines in containers where they can climb up a trellis or an adjoining wall. The colors and textures of vines are numerous, with something for any gardener's particular interest.

Housing and Feeding the Locals

If you like providing habitats for wildlife, vines are a vital piece of the puzzle. Vines not only provide shelter for birds but also nesting sites in the intertwining of vines and tendrils. Many of the flowers of the vines featured in this chapter also provide a food source for hummingbirds, bees, and occasionally butterflies as noted by the appropriate icons.

How They Climb

Some of the vines discussed in this chapter are quite common. Others are unfamiliar to Oklahoma gardens. Some prefer shade, and others prefer sun—but all have minimal maintenance requirements. Although many of the vines are somewhat woody, the majority are deciduous; they lose their leaves in the winter. Vines typically have the ability to grow up a trellis or over nearby objects. Some are more aggressive than others. A few form aerial roots along the way, others are equipped with gripping tendrils, and some need a little help getting started by our weaving them in and out of their support system. Trellises and support systems must be strong and well built since many vines can become quite heavy as they mature. It may be frightening to read about the potential size of some vines, but height is often dictated by the size of the structure upon which they are grown. Many will grow as high as the structure is tall. Occasionally, you will see vines grown horizontally as a ground cover. It can be done with a fair amount of pruning and training. Keep an eye out for nearby plants, posts, and fences since the vines will quickly work their way up these objects.

Clematis

Planting and Pruning

In most gardening sites it is a good idea to prepare the soil in the landscape beds ahead of time by tilling or adding organic materials and slow-release nutrients before planting. This is not always the case when growing vines. Loose organic and nutrient rich soils means even more aggressive vines. Most vines will still perform in poor soils as long as they drain well. This also helps slow down the vigorous growth and can help keep them more manageable. In cases where you have the

198

space, time, and strong support systems, amending the soil with fertilizer and organic material may help provide quicker vine coverage.

Dig a hole two to three times the width of the rootball and the same depth, as with all planting procedures. Routine watering, mulching, and fertilizing are beneficial practices. Again, do not over do it with the tender loving care when growing vines. It has a direct impact on the vigor and aggressiveness of the plant. Slow-release or organic fertilizers are a good choice to provide steady nutrients over a longer period of time. Apply in early spring or as needed.

Pruning is a necessity when growing vines and is most often done for controlling height and width of aggressive vines. In newly planted vines, tip-pruning may be required to help encourage wider, bushy growth. Severe pruning should be done at the appropriate time of year to avoid reducing bud set for next season's flowers. The appropriate pruning time is highlighted in each plant entry. Some vines have a tendency to send

Coral Honeysuckle and Black-Eyed Susan

out suckers from their base along the surface of the ground. Others send out suckers underground. Both can be managed with a watchful eye and proper pruning to keep the suckers under control.

In addition to suckers, other pests to watch for are the normal spider mites and aphids or common diseases like mildew. Routine inspections of the plants and allowing natural predators to work help keep major problems under control. Plants that are stressed from drought, poor drainage, and compacted soils or plants that are planted in the wrong light conditions are more prone to pest problems.

Many of the vine selections described in this chapter are readily available through garden centers. Others may be ordered through specialty nurseries. The plants highlighted in this chapter are just a few of my favorites. I've listed more vines in the back that also work well in Oklahoma conditions.

Akebia

Akebia quinata

If you have not introduced yourself or your garden to this vine, put it first on your list. I grow this vine for its unique foliage, and the unusual flower color is bonus. The twining vine sends out palmate, compound foliage (that is, with leaflets like fingers). The purplish new growth matures to a glossy blue-green. The vanilla-scented, chocolate-purple blooms occur as the new growth emerges. In mild winters, the plants retain their leaves most of the season. Occasionally, fruit sets in the fall, developing into a violet-colored pod. 'Alba' is a white-flowering and fruiting cultivar. 'Rosea' has a lighter-violet-colored flower than the traditional species, and 'Shiro Bana' has white flowers with purple fruit. 'Amethyst Glow' has both bicolored dark and pale violet colored flowers on the same plant.

Other Common Names
Five-leaf Akebia, Chocolate Vine

Bloom Period and Seasonal Color
Chocolate-purple blooms in March or April.

Mature Height × Spread
To 30 ft. × 8 to 10 ft., or as permitted

Cold Hardiness Zones
6a, 6b, 7a, 7b

When, Where, and How to Plant
Plant containerized akebia in early spring, early summer, or early fall. The plants tolerate full sun or partial shade, and they are not picky about soil type or pH. Set the plant in a hole dug at least 2 times wider than the rootball and the same depth as the container. Place the plants 4 feet apart to become a screen or "wall." Mulch after planting. If possible, remove the stake and gently weave the vine in a support system.

Growing Tips
Reapply mulch as the initial applications weather or wash away. I do not fertilize vines unless they lack flowers or have chlorotic foliage. Too much tender loving care can push plants to outgrow their support structure. If plants do need some supplemental fertilizer, I usually go with slow-release organic or synthetic products at planting time and as needed. Water Akebia during drought periods or else premature leaf drop can occur.

Care
Tip-prune any time through the year to keep this fast-growing plant in bounds. This also promotes foliage growth along the lower stem, which cures the plant's tendency to favor the ends and leave the lower stem exposed. Watch for and cut off suckers or shoots that grow along the ground or under the mulch. There are no serious pest problems.

Landscape Merit
Use this fast-growing, twining vine on trellises, arbors, pergolas, or fences. It can also grow as a matted ground cover, but it chokes out adjoining plants. Use akebia singularly or massed as a hedge. I once grew akebia up a cattle panel fence among perennial coreopsis and daylilies. The purple flowers along with the unusual leaves made a perfect background for the yellow perennials.

My Personal Favorites
'Shirobana' or variegated Akebia (sometimes sold as 'Brookside') has splashes of gold in the foliage. Also unique is 'A. trifoliata' with three leaflets per leaf, and the hybrid cross A. pentaphylla has both 3 and 5 leaflets per plant.

Boston Ivy
Parthenocissus tricuspidata

When, Where, and How to Plant

Plant this vine in early spring, summer, or fall. It tolerates full sun, many soil types, and many environmental conditions, but it prefers afternoon shade and moist, fertile soils. Space plants 12 to 18 inches apart at the depth grown in its container in a hole 2 times the width of the rootball. Water to settle the soil. Mulch to keep moisture in and weeds out during the establishment period. If the planting site is near a wall, stake the planting hole until the vine attaches; routinely guide the vine. Boston ivy is fairly easy to start from rooted vines near the ground. Plant cuttings in a container or in moist, sandy soils.

Growing Tips

Supplemental feedings help establish the plant but afterwards cause excess growth. In drought periods, established vines will need a good soaking at least 1 to 2 times a week to avoid scorching and leaf drop. Reapply mulch as needed to help hold in valuable soil moisture.

Care

Boston ivy's only downside is lagging winter interest. The stems are a light-brown color and not showy during dormancy, and the deciduous foliage drops fairly early in the fall. Pruning is seldom needed, other than to keep the vine within its allotted growing space. Occasional leaf spot diseases occur in locations with too much shade. Watch for leafhoppers, spider mites, and scale (an infrequent problem).

Landscape Merit

Boston ivy grows up support systems, trees, or concrete walls. It also grows as a ground cover. I have seen on larger topiary displays where it was given ample water and frequently trimmed. Boston Ivy beautifully covers unsightly walls and camouflages eyesores. It also adds texture and color to multiple storied homes. On support systems like a trellis, the green foliage provides a nice backdrop creating a layered effect.

My Personal Favorite

There is just something about chartreuse color that brightens shady spots. 'Fenway Park' Boston ivy does just that with its lime green foliage intensified by the sun.

This deciduous vine has spectacular fall colors. In the spring the green, lustrous foliage unfurls, providing a thick cover to shade walls, fences, and arbors. The vining growth spreads by attaching small tendrils to its support system. This tough plant attaches to almost anything. The coarse foliage has three distinctive, dark, glossy-green lobes. There are several cultivars of this intriguing vine—some with purplish leaves throughout the growing season. 'Beverly Brooks' and 'Green Showers' have larger leaves and brilliant fall color. A smaller-leaved version is 'Lowii'. 'Purpurea' has predominantly purple-tinged foliage all summer, especially when grown in more sun, and 'Veitchii' has new growth emerging as purple and turning greener at maturity. A waxier, thick, green-leaved selection is 'Robusta', with orange-red fall color.

Other Common Name
Japanese Creeper

Bloom Period and Seasonal Color
Red or orange fall foliage.

Mature Height × Spread
20 to 30 ft. × 10 to 15 ft.

Cold Hardiness Zones
6a, 6b, 7a, 7b

Carolina Jasmine

Gelsemium sempervirens

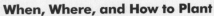

This early-flowering vine has sweet fragrant, funnel-shaped flowers that make quite a show. Its growth habit is a tangled mingling of wiry stems, which sounds worse than it appears. The predominantly evergreen foliage provides year-round, dark green color for southeastern Oklahoma. During the coldest part of winter in the rest of the state, the yellowish green foliage tinges with purple for a nice display during drab times. In severe winters, the foliage can burn and defoliate. This moderate- to fast-growing vine climbs as tall as its support or makes a mound if left alone. It grows better in Zone 7, but it grows in Zone 6 when planted in protected areas and mulched during the winter. 'Compacta' is a dwarf, mounding form that does not need staking.

Other Common Name
Carolina Yellow Jessamine

Bloom Period and Seasonal Color
Yellow blooms in early spring, March or April.

Mature Height × Spread
To 20 ft. × 5 to 6 ft.

Cold Hardiness Zones
6b, 7a, 7b

When, Where, and How to Plant

Plant it in early spring or summer. The best show of flowers occurs in full or partial sun, although the plant tolerates shade. It prefers moist, well-drained, slightly acidic soils, especially when planted in full sun. In scorching hot environments, afternoon shade is recommended. Carolina jasmine tolerates some alkalinity. The better the soil, the better the growth, which is the case with most plants. I have seen it growing quite well in alkaline soils, even though it is naturally found in slightly acidic soils. Dig a hole 2 to 3 times wider than and the same depth as the rootball. No organic backfill is necessary unless incorporated ahead of time into the entire planting bed. Mulch and water the plants as needed.

Growing Tips

With too much tender loving care, Carolina jasmine, like most vines, causes plants that outgrow their support structures. Slow-release products are best, whether organic or synthetic. Let the plants tell you when fertilizer is needed either by non-thrifty growth or chlorotic foliage. Reapply mulch as it weathers or washes away. The plants respond well to supplemental irrigation during drought. Otherwise, leaf scorch and drought are likely.

Care

Prune after flowering since it typically blooms on the previous season's growth. Occasional sporadic flowering occurs again in the fall. Carolina jasmine seldom has pest problems.

Landscape Merit

I have seen these beauties frequently growing up mailboxes and light poles. They are perfect for fences and trellises. Carolina jasmine is occasionally allowed to cascade as a ground cover, but it would need a site where it would not hide other plants or attach to other plants. Jasmine is also planted in large containers where it is allowed to fall over the sides or cascade over retaining walls.

My Personal Favorite

'Pride of Augusta' (a.k.a. 'Plena') is almost like a rose with its double canary yellow blossoms in early spring.

Chinese Wisteria

Wisteria sinensis

When, Where, and How to Plant

Plant wisteria in spring or early summer, giving the aggressive plants strong supports and plenty of room to grow. Wisteria love full sun and well-drained soil. Very fertile soils cause excess foliage and slow flowering. They tolerate partial shade and most soil types, but dense shade and extreme acidity foster diseases. Dig a planting hole at least 2 times wider than and the same depth as the rootball. Put phosphorus at the bottom of the planting hole and cover it with soil. Mulch after planting, and water.

Growing Tips

Wisteria is an aggressive grower, so fertilizing to promote blooms can actually backfire. Once the plants are established, they are fairly drought tolerant and don't require weekly watering unless there is prolonged drought that threatens next year's flower set.

Care

Wisteria's flowering habit, which occurs on year-old wood, frustrates gardeners. It is best to buy plants propagated from flowering wood or buy plants that are already flowering. Otherwise, root and stem pruning is suggested. Use a sharp shovel and cut sporadically into the roots, and prune vines to two or three buds. This stimulates more productive wood. Prune throughout the year to keep wisteria under control. Tip-prune throughout the growing season and after blooming. Prune when the vine is dormant to remove dead, diseased, or damaged wood. Pests are seldom a concern.

Landscape Merit

I have seen wisteria growing up telephone poles, trees, houses, and along fences. Plan your site carefully and tally the amount of time you plan on maintaining this vine. Training them into tree forms as a single specimen is quite eye catching in the landscape, especially with the weeping shape and breathtaking blooms. It also takes a lot of time.

My Personal Favorite

I tend to use the native *W. frutescens* 'Amethyst Falls' in my landscape. It is not quite as aggressive, blooms on younger plants, and can repeat bloom later in the season.

There is probably not a vine better known for its large, brilliant flower clusters. The violet-blue, pink, or white flowers are spectacular dangling from the vines. The deciduous, compound foliage is perfect for providing shade in the summer when wisteria is used on arbors. After the leaves drop, pods that are brown and velvety persist into early winter. Chinese wisteria blooms prior to foliage set and in some cases can rebloom in the fall. 'Alba' (white) and 'Caroline' (blue) are two of the most common Chinese types. Double-flowering cultivars such as 'Black Dragon' and 'Plena' are generally more erratic blooming but are still unique.

Other Common Name
Asian Wisteria

Bloom Period and Seasonal Color
Violet-blue, pink, or white blooms in April or May.

Mature Height × Spread
30 ft. or more × 15 to 20 ft.

Cold Hardiness Zones
6a, 6b, 7a, 7b

Clematis
Clematis species

Clematis has a spectacular range of flower colors. The deep, velvety shades brighten up anyone's day. Most gardeners are familiar with clematis and probably have tried growing them. In Oklahoma, growing them is not as simple as one would hope. Clematis grows in our hot, humid summers as long as mulch and shade are provided to the roots. Remember this rule—warm top (foliage), cool bottom (roots)—and you can enjoy clematis in your Oklahoma landscape. There are hundreds of cultivars from which to choose, with single or double blossoms generally grouped by flowering times. The bloom period is the key to pruning clematis to initiate continued growth and flowering. Most clematis are deciduous, but C. armandii is an evergreen species that is cold hardy only in Zone 7 of Oklahoma. Another unusual, hard-to-find plant is bush clematis (C. integrifolia).

Other Common Names
Vase Vine, Virgin's Bower

Bloom Period and Seasonal Color
Pink, purple, red, yellow, and white blooms in spring, summer, or fall.

Mature Height × Spread
5 to 8 ft. × 4 to 6 ft.

Cold Hardiness Zones
6a, 6b, 7a, 7b

When, Where, and How to Plant
Plant clematis in the spring in loamy, fertile, moderately moist, well-drained soils. Clematis prefers at least five to six hours of sun, sometimes best achieved in the morning. Equally important are mulching and root shading (preferably by another plant). Beware harsh sites, such as driveways where southwesterly winds can scorch foliage. Plant clematis in a hole that is wider than and the same depth as the rootball.

Growing Tips
Clematis take two years to fully establish before they start their spectacular flower show. Constant, consistent soil moisture is critical. I have found that the vines feed heavily and respond to organic fertilizers applied at planting and then yearly on the soil surface when mulch is reapplied. Water-soluble fertilizers also work well.

Care
Severe pruning is seldom needed unless plants become woody and nonproductive. Prune clematis for shaping purposes. Knowing the blooming time of your particular clematis is imperative. For example, some flower in June from the previous season's growth. The Jackman group flowers in June, July, and August. Therefore, pruning occurs in early spring when the plants are dormant. Early-spring-flowering types are pruned after flowering. Some bloom both in spring fall on both old and new wood. Prune these types only to remove dead and weak stems. Leaf spot, mildew, and stem rot are problems in heavily shaded sites with poor drainage. Other pests are of minimal concern.

Landscape Merit
These vines grow on rock walls, trellises, fences, mailboxes, and almost any structure where the tendrils and vines can attach. Plant clematis between shrubs and other perennials so it can tower above its companions. One of the most interesting plantings I have observed was clematis growing between and on dwarf yaupon holly.

My Personal Favorite
Choosing a favorite in clematis is just about as hard as choosing a favorite pansy. The color range is abundant, and all are spectacular. I tend to match the flower color with the particular landscape color design.

When, Where, and How to Plant

Plant crossvine in spring or early summer. It prefers full or partial sun, and too much shade reduces flowering. Crossvine tolerates poor soils but is most aggressive in moist, humus-rich soils. Dig the hole two times wider than and the same depth as the rootball. Soil amendments are not needed unless they are incorporated into the bed before planting time. Mulching and providing supplemental moisture quickly establish this underused vine. Crossvine may need help initially getting attached to its support structure by weaving the vines through the support. Once it gets a hold, it is self-clinging.

Growing Tips

This tough plant is drought tolerant when it is established, although the foliage scorches in hot sun with windy, dry conditions. Bignonia readily responds to occasional feedings when the plants seem chlorotic. Reapply mulch as needed to help retain soil moisture.

Care

Crossvine is considered a fast-growing vine, and it blooms on the previous season's growth in early spring. It sporadically reblooms on new growth later in the summer or early fall. Prune severely after flowering; however, tip-prune to keep plants in shape throughout the growing season. Crossvine seldom has pest problems. Occasionally, crossvine tends to send out suckers from the base of the vine that grow along the ground surface. Cut the suckers as needed to keep the vine upright and in its allotted location.

Landscape Merit

Use crossvine for fences, concrete walls, arbors, pergolas, and trellises. Crossvine works well with smaller or lightweight trellises because of its smaller vining size and diameter. This well-behaved vine is perfect to add vertical dimension to your perennial garden and block a view at the same time. It is also great to grow up a trellis to provide a softening effect to harsh hardscape structures.

My Personal Favorite

'Dragon Lady' has several advantages: it is fairly cold hardy, more floriferous than the species, and has more of a reddish tint to the flower color.

This tough vine needs more presence in our Oklahoma landscapes. Crossvine's unique semi-evergreen leaves assemble on the stems like a cross. Showy orange-red, chocolate-scented flowers emerge in early spring. Tendrils easily attach crossvine to its trellis system, and the height is determined by where it is allowed to grow. The foliage turns a bronzy color in the fall and remains on the vines during milder winters. Later in the season, a long, green, capsulated seedpod turns a brownish color but is not showy. 'Atrosanguinea' is a selection with tinged reddish-purple, narrower foliage, and reddish-purple flowers. 'Tangerine Beauty' is a yellowish-tangerine color, and 'Jekyll' is reddish; both have showier flowers than the native species. 'Helen Friedel' is thought to have the largest flowers to date.

Other Common Name
Quarter Vine

Bloom Period and Seasonal Color
Orange-red blooms in April; bronze fall foliage.

Mature Height × Spread
30 ft. × 4 to 6 ft., or as permitted

Cold Hardiness Zones
6a, 6b, 7a, 7b

Honeysuckle
Lonicera species

Honeysuckle gives most vines a run for their money as far as fragrance goes. As the name implies, the flowers are very sweet smelling. There are literally hundreds of species and hybrid crosses of honeysuckle. Decide whether fragrance or flower color is more important in your landscape and choose cultivars accordingly. Trumpet (same as coral or crimson) honeysuckle (L. sempervirens) has showy flowers in shades of yellow, red, and orange and produces colorful berries in the fall. It is not known for its fragrance. Japanese honeysuckle (L. japonica) is very twining in growth with either green or purple foliage and very fragrant blooms. Woodbine honeysuckle (L. periclymenum) has the best fruit set of any selection, which is an asset in wildlife landscapes.

Other Common Names
Honey Vine, Honey Bush

Bloom Period and Seasonal Color
White, coral, yellow, or pink blooms in early spring to summer.

Mature Height × Spread
6 to 30 ft. × 4 to 10 ft., or as permitted

Cold Hardiness Zones
6a, 6b, 7a, 7b

When, Where, and How to Plant
Plant honeysuckle in early spring, early summer, and early fall. Most selections prefer full-sun locations; however, a few like afternoon shade. Honeysuckle performs best in fertile, moist, well-drained soils. It is durable and tolerates most soil types. Dig the planting hole 2 times wider than and the same depth as the rootball. No amended backfill is required. Water and mulch as needed to establish the plants. When planting honeysuckle as a ground cover, space plants 3 feet apart.

Growing Tips
Fertility should be minimal, or excess growth occurs. The plants do not use water heavily, but supplemental irrigation is key during severe drought to keep foliage from scorching and minimizing next season's flower bud set. Mulch should be reapplied when needed to retain soil moisture and keep weed competition at bay.

Care
Honeysuckle is fairly care-free, other than an occasional pruning to keep plants in control. Prune early spring-flowering types after flowering. Prune plants that bloom in late summer or fall when they are dormant or in early spring before new growth begins. Cut back overgrown plants to the ground where they develop new growth. Pests include an occasional aphid and foliage leaf spot or powdery mildew in heavily shaded sites.

Landscape Merit
There is a species of honeysuckle to match almost any landscape situation, from mounding to vining. It is also a great plant to use for erosion control. Honeysuckle is typically used to grow up trellises or allowed to cascade over retaining walls. The bushy growth is a favorite for many birds, so honeysuckle is frequently planted in wildlife habitat landscapes for protection and nesting.

My Personal Favorite
I love the fragrant crimson and white flowers of 'Serotina Florida', which I was first introduced to while living in Florida. The red fruit is almost as showy. Grow this cultivar in afternoon or dappled sun in Oklahoma.

Hyacinth Bean

Lablab purpureus (Dolichos lablab)

When, Where, and How to Plant

Plant seed directly into the soil about ?? to 1 in. deep after the chance of frost. Planting indoors is not better than direct seeding. These vines will grow almost as tall and wide as the support system you plant them near. Well drained, organic soils produce the most vigorous vines, but they are not picky as long as there is good drainage. Mulch after the seeds germinate to hold in moisture and discourage weeds.

Growing Tips

The beans are legumes, and supplemental feedings are seldom needed unless planted in poor soils. In that case, side dress with a complete fertilizer or water-soluble type. Do not go overboard with fertilizing, however, or the plants will be all vine and no flowers or pods.

Care

Prune throughout the growing season by pinching or cutting to keep the plant growing within its support boundaries. Even though the vines are fast growing, they are not what I call aggressive like some of the woodier vines. Harvest seed pods once they shrivel and turn brown. Shell out the seed and keep them in the freezer in a freezer bag until next season. You can also store them in a cool, dry, dark location with good air circulation. Occasionally, you will have to remove seedlings.

Landscape Merit

I use the vines to provide a tall back drop for certain sections of my landscape. They also work on fences to hide eyesores. They will grow up most anything by weaving their vines around and through the support system, similar to pole beans. The flower and pod clusters make great cuts for fresh flower arrangements.

My Personal Favorite

Named cultivars are not common. There is some variation in the species however with some having white in the lilac flower and a purplish hew to the 3 leaflet foliage.

Talk about a good investment. I do not think I have ever grown a plant that provides as much show and interest for the expense of the seed as with hyacinth bean. It has been years since I bought my first seed for only a few cents. The black seed with a white line quickly germinated and grew on a nearby fence. The bean-like lilac flowers followed by the glossy purple three to four inch flat bean pods far surpassed both my expectations and the picture in the seed catalog. The flowers and pods emerge from the foliage as elongated clusters. Once blooming, it provided successive color from flowers and pods right up until the frost. Ever since, I save the pods for next year's planting and share them with gardening friends.

Other Common Names

Lablab Vine, Bonavist, Indian Bean

Bloom Period and Seasonal Color

Lilac-purple blooms followed by purple seed pods in midsummer and fall

Mature Height × Spread

6 to 10 ft. × as permitted

Cold Hardiness Zone

Grown as an annual in zones 6a, 6b, 7a, 7b

Malibar Spinach
Basella rubra

Ornamental and edible malibar is not a true spinach, but it is used just like spinach in cooking. Native to Eastern Asia and India, it is makes a vigorous annual vine. The glossy, dark green, fleshy leaves are attached to vines by showy red stems—thus the ornamental value of the rubra species. The flowers turn into small purple berries which later shrivel and fall to the ground. There is also a white stemmed species, B. alba, but it is not as showy. Malibar will grow in full sun or part shade and will make a ground cover if it does not have a support system. The plant is often listed as a reseeding annual since fallen seeds may germinate the following spring.

Other Common Names
Red Vine Spinach, Climbing Spinach, Ceylon Spinach

Bloom Period and Seasonal Color
Non showy blooms in late summer and fall.

Mature Height × Spread
10 ft. or as permitted × 1 ft.

Cold Hardiness Zone
Grown as an annual in zones 6a, 6b, 7a, 7b

When, Where, and How to Plant
The seed can be planted $^1/_4$ to $^1/_2$ in. deep directly into the ground in the spring after the chance of frost has passed. Get a head start by planting the seed in small containers indoors about three to four weeks prior to planting. It takes about 60 days from seeding until you can start harvesting some of the tender foliage and stems. Unlike regular spinach, which grows best in cooler temperatures in the spring or fall, this vine spinach thrives in the heat of the summer.

Growing Tips
Mulch after the seeds germinate and start to form true leaves. The mulch holds in soil moisture and keeps weed competition to a minimum. Avoid mulching up on the stem, instead get it about 2 to 3 inches thick in between or around the plants. Then angle it down to the base of the stem. The plants are not very drought tolerant. The thick foliage is most showy when it gets supplemental irrigation during drought periods. Side dressing with a granular vegetable fertilizer or periodically applying soluble brands will stimulate luscious growth. As with any plant, do not over apply too much fertilizer or the plant will quickly outgrow its support system.

Care
Trim the stems at any time throughout the growing season to keep the plant growing to your desired shape and space. Pests are rare, but watch for spider mites.

Landscape Merit
This heat loving annual vine hides unsightly areas or provides an upright back drop. It grows easily on adjacent fences and provides ornamental qualities in the vegetable garden. The plant can grow as a ground cover if no support system is provided. Only the young leaves are eaten. To prepare, boil and discard water. Or add the fresh, young leaves to a salad.

My Personal Favorite
The red stem cultivar is my favorite. The easy to grow plant has showy leaves and stems.

Passion Flower
Passiflora incarnata

When, Where, and How to Plant

Set out pot-grown plants in the spring or early summer. Start seed in containers in the late winter or early spring or plant in the ground in the fall, planting seed $1/4$ to $1/2$ inches deep. They prefer full sun and tolerate minimal shade. In a natural setting, maypops are found in average, moist soils in primarily eastern parts of the state. Soils with average fertility host this lovely plant. Place the plants at the same depth that they were grown, in holes 2 to 3 times the diameter of the rootballs. Space them 3 to 4 feet apart. Add mulch to retain soil moisture and minimize weed growth. Water on a regular basis.

Growing Tips

Rich, fertile sites rarely need extra care. Reapply mulch as needed, and water during extremely severe droughts to keep bloom consistent. Once established, the native species tolerates drought. It may look shabby during severe drought but readily comes back with rainfall.

Care

Winter almost always kills this vine back to the ground. Remove the vines and foliage in early spring. The new growth emerges in late April and quickly becomes a source of shade. Some of the species sucker underground. Keep an eye out and remove these as needed. Other than an occasional aphid, pests are not a concern.

Landscape Merit

Allow this beauty to scurry up just about anything or creep along as a ground cover. In many cases, passion flower and its tendrils will grow as tall as the support system. Maypop does well as a container plant when it is allowed to grow up a neighboring support system.

My Personal Favorite

Red Granadilla (*P. coccinea*) has scarlet crimson flowers and is free-flowering from midsummer to autumn, although it is only cold hardy in Oklahoma to Zone 7b.

This native looks almost too exotic to grow in our state. The large, astounding flowers, sometimes two to four inches in diameter, are colorful with unusually stringy leaf petals. The vines with lobed leaves emerge late in the spring and climb up neighboring support trellises or plants. In May, the lovely display of color and character begins and lasts throughout July. Later in the season, egg-shaped fruit emerge and are loaded with seed. Warning: there are reports of potential toxicity if they are not used appropriately. Ask experts and physicians about any health hazards. Passion flower is a pretty tough vine for most landscape settings. When using a passion flower for a perennial vine, check cold-hardiness guidelines. Some are more tropical and will not overwinter in the state.

Other Common Names
Maypop, Passion Vine, Apricot Vine

Bloom Period and Seasonal Color
Purple, white, and pink blooms in summer.

Mature Height × Spread
To 25 ft. × 2 to $2^{1}/2$ ft., or as permitted

Cold Hardiness Zones
6b, 7a, 7b

Porcelain Vine
Ampelopsis brevipedunculata

This vine has two selling points: unique foliage and dynamic fruit that is good for the ecosystem. Deciduous leaves variegated with shades of green and white intermingle with fragrant, commonplace flowers. Small, marble-like berries emerge green and later turn a glossy, metallic blue green to purple. The small berries last into the fall and are a favorite of cardinals, brown thrashers, wood thrush, and quail. The fragrant flowers are known to attract many insects and bees. It is well adapted to Oklahoma conditions with many related species native to our state. Monk's hood vine (A. aconitifolia) has finely cut foliage with nice landscape design features. A pesky native that is sometimes mistaken for poison ivy is Pepper Vine (A. arborea), which can also cause skin irritation for some folks.

Other Common Name
Porcelain Berry

Bloom Period and Seasonal Color
White blooms in spring to early summer with green to purple berries late summer to fall.

Mature Height × Spread
10 to 20 ft. × 6 to 10 ft., or as permited

Cold Hardiness Zones
6a, 6b, 7a, 7b

When, Where, and How to Plant
Plant this vine similar to the way that grapes are planted as a dormant plant in early spring or as a containerized plant in late spring or early summer. To get its best display of color, the ideal planting location in Oklahoma is afternoon shade. This native plant prefers fertile, humus-rich, moist, well-drained soil; however, it adapts to poor soils. Poor soils are sometimes even better to keep the plant more under control especially in the landscape. Plant porcelain vine in a widely dug hole the same depth that it was grown in the nursery. Mulch and water the plant as needed. Use caution when planting near walkways or entrances since the flowers attract wasps as well as bees.

Growing Tips
Few maintenance chores are associated with this plant. Stick it in the ground and let it do its thing. In rich soil with too much supplemental fertilizer, it can be quite vigorous. Feeding should be minimal so that excessive growth is not encouraged. Once established, it is fairly drought tolerant, only requiring supplemental irrigation during severe droughts to keep the foliage from scorching.

Care
Summer pruning to keep the vine within the confines of its support system is the only routine task. Just like the fruit of grapes, berries are produced on current-season growth from last year's wood. Dormant pruning should not include too much one-year-old wood or stems. Look for the occasional aphid and mildew when porcelain vine is in especially heavy shade.

Landscape Merit
Porcelain vine is not quite as woody as its grape cousin, but it spreads with gnarling tendrils attaching to its support system. Use it for arbors, fences, pergolas, and trellises. Grow this vine on a fence in the garden to attract birds and pollinators.

My Personal Favorite
The improved selection 'Elegans' is somewhat smaller growing with deeply lobed variegated leaves and shiny bright blue berries in the fall.

When, Where, and How to Plant

Plant trumpet vine in the spring, early summer, or fall. This tough beauty requires no special soil treatment and is very adaptable. In rich soils, the plant becomes aggressive. In poor soil, the plant still performs nicely and grows slower. Dig the hole 2 times wider than and the same depth as the rootball. Mulch for weed control, and water weekly when rainfall is not present for at least the first few months.

Growing Tips

After establishment, you could consider trumpet vine probably one of the most drought tolerant vines in the chapter. Severe drought results in leaf drop, but the vine sends out new growth once rainfall occurs. Supplemental feedings are needed only when nutritional foliar symptoms are present such as pale leaves or yellow chrolorsis. Over-fertilizing will trigger overly vigorous growth.

Care

The flamboyant flowers appear late in the summer on new season's growth. Prune any time through-out the growing season to keep vines under control, and tip prune the growing points when possible to keep growth along the base of the plant. Severely prune when the plant is dormant. Insect pest problems are usually not serious enough for control action. Foliar disease occurs in sites with too much shade.

Landscape Merit

Use this fast-growing plant as a screen on fences or stout trellises. I have seen it used to cover a dead tree kept in place for woodpeckers. It requires plenty of space and a strong support. Trumpet vine grows horizontally as a bushy ground cover when no support is available. Even as a ground cover, it manages to grow about 3 to 5 feet tall if left alone. Frequent pruning to keep the plants bushier is a must when trying to grow the plants horizontally.

My Personal Favorite

'Morning Calm' (*C. grandiflora*) has larger pastel peach colored flowers with yellow and red striped throats. It is fairly cold hardy (ideal for western Oklahoma) and is not quite as aggressive.

This showy native vine feels at home on larger support systems with plenty of space. The lustrous, green foliage is compound and changes to a yellow-green in the fall accompanied by a long seedpod. The perfect, trumpet-shaped flowers range from three to four inches long, and hummingbirds love them. Trumpet vine is very late to leaf out in the spring, sometimes not emerging until May. Once the buds emerge, the growth quickly takes off and provides summer-long color. 'Crimson Trumpet' has larger, red flowers with no orange. 'Flava' has showy, solid-yellow blooms, and 'Flamenco' has large, scarlet flowers with a more prominent golden fall color. 'Madam Galen' is a hybrid with huge, showy, coral-red flowers. A northern introduction from Canada is 'Indian Summer' with distinctly yellow flowers and orange-red centers.

Other Common Names
Trumpet Creeper, Trumpet Flower

Bloom Period and Seasonal Color
Orange, red, and yellow blooms in June through September.

Mature Height × Spread
40 ft. × 6 to 10 ft.

Cold Hardiness Zones
6a, 6b, 7a, 7b

Great Plains Plants *for Oklahoma*

Landscaping in Oklahoma's infamous no-man's-land can be quite a challenge. Just ask any gardener living in northwest Oklahoma and the panhandle, better known as the "red carpet" country, which is highlighted page 238. This area of the state is rich with history and plant material, but the gardening conditions are unlike other parts of Oklahoma. The growing season is shorter and drier, the winters are often colder, and the elevation is higher. The soils range from heavy clay to pure sand and often are very alkaline. Add consistently gusty winds and you have a whole new growing climate with distinct differences from the rest of the state.

Soil pH tends to be high, or alkaline, in many northwestern Oklahoma counties. Plants preferring slightly acidic soils (or a lower soil pH) oftentimes become chlorotic with yellowing leaves and green veins when planted in alkaline soils. This unhealthy and unsightly appearance over several growing seasons means that the plants are weakening and becoming more susceptible to drought and winter damage. Eventually, chlorosis stunts the plants and can even lead to death. Pin oak is a great example of a plant that gets chlorotic when grown in western Oklahoma. Its almost certain susceptibility to chlorosis in this region makes the shumard oak a better choice. The shumard oak resembles a pin oak but tolerates alkaline soils. Chlorosis problems can be managed by adding soil sulfur, fertilizing at the appropriate times with products that contain iron (Fe) and sulfur, and mulching particularly with pine straw, pine bark, or other slightly acidic products. This constant attention can become an expensive endeavor, so seek out plants that are specifically recommended for high pH soils.

If you want to push the limits and grow some plants that prefer acidic conditions, amend the planting beds ahead of time with a mixture of peat moss, compost, and soil sulfur. The peat moss and compost should be at a ratio of about one part peat, one part compost and two parts soil, or two parts

Pinyon Pine

peat to two parts soil. Apply soil sulfur according to directions per square foot. After planting, mulch to help hold in soil moisture and reapply mulch every couple of years as it weathers. Again, acidic mulches like pecan hulls, pine straw, or bark work best. A soil test is recommended every couple of years to see if additional changes are needed. Most often they will be because the soil pH tends to increase with time.

Gardening at the Crossroads

Oklahoma has been described as the ecological crossroads between eastern and western plant species, and the northwest region provides evidence to support this. Landscaping success starts with plants that tolerate a particular growing climate or region. Though this chapter is composed mainly of trees and woody shrubs, you'll find that plants such as perennials, annuals, and roses will also do well in northwestern Oklahoma. Throughout this book, any plant suitable for Zones 6a and 6b will do well in the "red carpet" region.

The plants covered in this chapter, however, are truly adapted for this region only and often do not perform well in the rest of the state. Colorado blue spruce, for example, is a favorite among many gardeners in the state thanks to its soothing blue color, evergreen foliage, unique landscape shape, and texture. Fortunately for gardeners in the panhandle and far northwestern Oklahoma, it grows quite well and provides years of enjoyment as do most cold-hardy conifers. In the south and eastern parts of the state, however, they are short lived and scorch in the heat and humidity of the summer.

General planting and maintenance guidelines are covered in more detail in other chapter introductions, depending on the plant category. Those recommendations also apply to the plants highlighted in this chapter, so be sure to check out the other chapters for good gardening tips and other plants for your area.

The challenging part will be finding some of these plants in the nursery trade. They are more likely to be available from southwestern or Great Plains states retailers or wholesalers. Many can be found through mail-order nurseries. If there is no interest in a particular plant, the nurseries are not likely to carry it. The key to getting a plant in your particular area is requesting it from the nursery and telling your friends to ask for it.

Alaska Cypress

Chamaecyparis nootkatensis

Alaska cypress is often considered a Pacific Northwest plant because it thrives in cool, moist climates. But that shouldn't discourage gardeners in the panhandle and northwestern areas of the state. This evergreen tolerates warmer and more humid sites as well. The biggest concern is the effect of frequent scorching winds. With careful placement next to a home or adjacent to other trees and shrubs, this medium-sized tree is a gorgeous plant for this part of the state. The foliage is a dark bluish or grayish green with long, weeping, flat sprays of color. The relatively slow overall growth is somewhat pyramidal, especially early on. 'Green Arrow' is an extremely upright columnar selection. 'Glenmore' and 'Compacta' are shrub forms, typically growing in a rounded habit up to 6 feet.

Other Common Names
False Cypress, Alaska Cedar, Nootka Cypress

Bloom Period and Seasonal Color
Evergreen bluish or grayish foliage.

Mature Height × Spread
20 to 40 ft. × 15 to 20 ft.

Cold Hardiness Zones
6a, 6b

When, Where, and How to Plant
Set out balled-and-burlapped Alaska cypress in spring or early summer. Partially shaded sites on the east or northeast side of structures provide protection from scorching summer winds. Dig the hole the same depth as and 2 to 3 times wider than the rootball. In heavy soils, set the rootball slightly above grade to improve drainage and aeration. Roll the burlap down to the base of the rootball once it's in the hole. If the burlap's contents stay put, you can remove the burlap. But if the contents fall off, leave the burlap on during planting to retain some soil around the roots; otherwise, you will stress the plant. Mulch at least 4 inches thick to hold soil moisture in and to keep weeds out. Water on a regular basis during the establishment period, especially during the first year.

Growing Tips
Provide supplemental irrigation during dry summers and supplemental feedings for nutrient-poor soils in early spring. Slow-release or organic type fertilizers applied in the spring provide gradual amounts of nutrition over a longer period of time. Broadcast the fertilizer on top of the ground and then cover it with your application of mulch. This helps the fertilizer stay in place and provides consistent moisture for better nutrient release.

Care
Small, directional pruning can be done any time throughout the year. Save larger pruning for spring. Leave the lower branches on to keep the plant more natural looking. This also encourages a bigger, stronger trunk and provides more wind protection. Potential pest problems include disease fungal blights, root rot in waterlogged sites, bagworms, and spider mites.

Landscape Merit
Alaska cypress functions as a windbreak, screen, foundation, or border plant. The downwardly weeping or cascading foliage is ideal as a single specimen or accent planting next to multiple-story homes. It does well in large island beds with other trees, which give the cypress some protection from wind in open lawn settings.

My Personal Favorite
'Pendula' is a wonderful selection with a distinct weeping form.

Arizona Cypress
Cupressus arizonica

When, Where, and How to Plant

Plant this evergreen in early spring to allow plenty of time for it to establish before winter. It is available as a container or balled-and-burlapped specimen. Plant Arizona cypress in full sun in well-drained sites. Heavy, waterlogged soils spell sure death for it. It is considered fairly fast growing. Place the plant in a hole the same depth as and 2 to 3 times wider than the rootball. Plant Arizona cypress slightly above grade to achieve better drainage in heavier soils. Always mulch in heavier soils to protect shallow roots. Water on a regular basis after planting, but allow the soil to dry between applications of water. Deep, infrequent watering encourages deeper roots, which in return promotes the plant's cold tolerance.

Growing Tips

The plants are fairly low maintenance. In some instances they become chlorotic (yellowish) in extremely alkaline soils, but the condition is corrected with applications of sulfur and mulch. In such cases, fertilizing with ammonium sulfate at a very low rate is beneficial. Never fertilize past June, or the plant will be more susceptible to winter damage. Refraining from feeding allows the plant to harden off for the winter. Reapply mulch as needed.

Care

Pests are not serious threats, but watch for bagworms, spider mites, and leaf blights (especially in more humid areas). Scout for pests, particularly bagworms early in the summer. The critters are much easier to manage when they are small. Pruning is seldom needed.

Landscape Merit

Use it as a single specimen, or plant it in groups for a windbreak or barrier. In the Southwest, it is used for erosion control

My Personal Favorite

'Blue Ice' has the most intense silver-blue color and is quite cold and wind tolerant.

If you like the shape of eastern red cedar but want color variety, consider Arizona cypress. It is found growing and thriving in northwestern areas of the state. Planting it in the panhandle is pushing it as far as its cold-hardiness will go, but it is worth trying, especially in the northwestern quadrants. The silver-gray tree has pyramidal growth with green needle foliage. The branching is open and loose. As the plants mature, the wood takes on more of a reddish brown hue, which complements the silvery-gray-blue foliage. Once established, it is very durable and somewhat drought tolerant. It is common in the Southwest where it prefers drier conditions. Humidity is the biggest adversary because it promotes disease. It is not an appropriate tree for the eastern parts of the state.

Other Common Names
Arizona Smooth Cypress, Pinte Cypress

Bloom Period and Seasonal Color
Inconspicuous blooms in spring with evergreen needles.

Mature Height × Spread
30 to 40 ft. × 20 to 25 ft.

Cold Hardiness Zone
6b

Cockspur Hawthorn
Crataegus crus-galli

Hawthorn is known for its showy flowers and brilliant-red fruit in the fall. Unfortunately, it often has thorns. Thanks to some exciting introductions, this lovely and resilient plant is now available with thornless selections. The overall growth habit is very dense, broad, and somewhat rounded. The deciduous foliage is a lustrous dark green, which later changes to a brilliant fall color. Around May, the showy, perfect flowers emerge with a hint of fragrance. In just a short few weeks, the blooms give rise to small, apple-like fruit, ripening to a vivid red sometime in September or October. The fruit persists into late fall and early winter. Hawthorn literally has hundreds of species and varieties, including small shrubs to large trees.

Other Common Name
Cock's Spur

Bloom Period and Seasonal Color
White to pinkish white blooms in summer with bronze, red, or purple fall foliage.

Mature Height × Spread
15 to 30 ft. × 15 to 25 ft.

Cold Hardiness Zones
6a, 6b

When, Where, and How to Plant
This tough plant is available in container or balled-and-burlapped forms. Plant it in early spring, summer, or fall. Cockspur hawthorn does not demand a particular soil type as long as it drains well. It thrives in poor, average, or rich garden soils, and it tolerates high pH soils. Plants do well in full sun, with good air circulation between them. Place the plants in holes at least 2 to 3 times the width and the same depth as the existing rootballs. Space plants on 15- to 20-foot centers when growing them in a group.

Growing Tips
Mulch the plants as needed and water during severe droughts, even though they are tolerant of dry soils. Mulching under these branches early on keeps weeds out and reduces the need to mow or use a weed trimmer under the branches. In severe droughts, the foliage can scorch and the fruit can drop prematurely. As with any plant, water slowly and deeply to encourage deeper roots.

Care
Pruning is seldom needed. Allow the plant to grow in its natural bushy form—leave the lower branches on for an even more brilliant bloom and fruit show. Hawthorn also tolerates heat and heavy, clay soils. The plants are quite prone to pest problems, and stressed situations make them more susceptible. Select disease-resistant cultivars. Watch for potential diseases such as bacterial fire blight, fungal leaf blight and spots, rusts, and powdery mildew. Insect problems include aphids, webworms, tent caterpillars, scale, and mites.

Landscape Merit
The thorny types should not be used in the landscape where children might play, but they are perfect for windbreaks, screens, or barriers when planted in groups. I have seen them used as a hedge where they were routinely pruned. The thornless selections are nice in the landscape, especially in lawn settings where they are allowed to grow in their natural form.

My Personal Favorite
C. crus-galli variety *inermis* is the thorn-less selection; it is sold under the cultivar name 'Crusader'.

Colorado Spruce
Picea pungens

When, Where, and How to Plant

Plant blue spruce in the spring or early summer in full-sun locations in the northwestern areas and afternoon shade in the rest of the state. Place the plants in rich, moist, well-drained soils in holes the same depth as and 2 to 3 times wider than the rootballs. Plant slightly above grade in heavy, poorly drained sites to help aeration and drainage. Mulch is especially needed with this planting method, but it is beneficial with this plant in any location. Water deeply and frequently to soak the entire root system until the plants are established. But be careful not to overwater. Allow the soil to dry slightly between applications of water.

Growing Tips

Provide supplemental irrigation during prolonged droughts. Heat and humidity are Colorado spruce's downfall. It tolerates dryness and drought more than most other spruces. Supplemental fertilization is seldom needed unless the tree is planted in a poor site. In that case, apply fertilizer in the spring.

Care

The worst thing a homeowner can do is to trim the lower branches. Leave this tree alone so that the natural pyramidal shape is enjoyed. The plant branches hold up well in snow and wind. Mulch past the branches and underneath to keep the weeds and grass out. Then you will not have to worry about trimming weeds and mowing under the tree. Insect pests are mites, aphids, and bagworms, and diseases include needle cast or rust.

Landscape Merit

Use as a single specimen to enhance a landscape design or structural feature. Use in groupings for a screen, windbreak, or wildlife cover. Probably the best use is in association with other forested plants and conifers where it is part of a naturalized setting.

My Personal Favorites

Some of my favorite cultivars include 'Fat Albert' (blue, wide, upright, and pyramidal), 'Argentea' (silvery white), 'Iseli Foxtail' (more heat tolerant with twisted new growth), 'Glauca Globosa' (round), and 'Glauca Pendula' (prostrate growth).

This lovely evergreen is often associated with the Rocky Mountain region. Gardeners in the panhandle and northwestern counties of the state are in luck, but those in the rest of the state are undertaking a risky venture to plant Colorado spruce. It thrives in upper elevations with milder summers, which characterize the growing regions highlighted in this chapter. The plants are known for their blue-gray foliage and pyramidal shape. They sprout new growth in late April or May and form oblong cones, which become scaly and yellow-brown when they ripen in August. Even in the right planting site, the trees grow slowly or moderately and are fairly long-lived. The plants hold up well in snow and wind. Heat and humidity are their downfall. Look for the numerous shape and color varieties.

Other Common Names
Blue Spruce, Silver Spruce

Bloom Period and Seasonal Color
Evergreen blue-gray foliage.

Mature Height × Spread
30 to 40 ft. × 10 to 20 ft.

Cold Hardiness Zones
6a, 6b

Giant Cedar
Thuja plicata

I'm not a fan of Arborvitae, particularly the common Eastern Arborvitae. They are overused in many landscapes, usually placed on each end of a home or adorning the front entrances. Furthermore, they fall apart in ice and snow and are a pest magnet. This particular species, however, is the exception to the rule. And one particular cultivar 'Green Giant' has some pretty big claims to live up to. Not only is this cultivar touted as deer resistant, disease and pest tolerant, snow and ice damage tolerant, it is even fast growing. I've been slow to join the bandwagon, but the ones I've grown over the past few years have won me over. The plant has wonderful evergreen foliage color and naturally grows a narrow pyramidal shape, thus living up to its many accolades.

Other Common Name
Western Red Cedar

Bloom Period and Seasonal Color
Small, inconspicuous, monoecioius flowers in the spring.

Mature Height × Spread
30 to 50 ft. × 10 to 12 ft.

Cold Hardiness Zones
6a, 6b, 7a, 7b

When, Where, and How to Plant
Thuja can be planted in the spring, summer, or fall. The plants will tolerate almost any soil type as long as it drains well. As with any plant, dig a hole 2 to 3 times the width of the rootball and the same depth. Fill with the original soil. Prepare a water-holding reservoir and mulch. Water to fill the reservoir several times to help settle the soil and ensure the entire rootball is soaked. Water at least weekly, unless rainfall is present, until the plant is established.

Growing Tips
The plant is fast growing, sometimes as much as 3 to 5 feet in height per year, and seldom needs supplemental fertilization. If anything, use slow-release organic products that release small amounts of nutrition over longer periods of time. Keep the area around the plant base free of grass, and mulch the area as needed. This holds in soil moisture and keeps weed competition down. As the plant grows, the broad thick base shades out most weeds. Supplemental irrigation is seldom needed once the plant is established.

Care
The plant seldom needs pruning. Instead allow the plant to grow in its natural pyramidal shape. Avoid trimming off the lower branches; allow them to grow down to the ground. In the rare case that branches are uneven, they can be sheared at any time to the desired shape. Pests are rare, but with any plant it is a good idea to frequently observe for problems on a routine basis. The plants are hardy to -25 ºF and don't need extra mulch or care in the winter

Landscape Merit
The plants are great alternatives to hemlock in the north and Leyland cypress in the south. They make great windbreaks. Their narrow growth habit and height also make them nice specimen plants for landscapes close to multi-story structures.

My Personal Favorite
'Green Giant' has caught my attention with its low maintenance attributes.

Korean Evodia

Evodia daniellii

When, Where, and How to Plant

Plant Korean evodia in the spring. Young seedling plants are somewhat more cold sensitive and at risk for winter injury with later-season plantings. The seeds of Korean evodia are about the size of buckshot and are fairly easy to germinate. It is most often found as a container plant. Like most plants, it performs best in well-drained, moist, fertile soils. It tolerates average or poor soils but has less growth. Plant it in full-sun locations. Dig the planting holes the same depth as and 2 to 3 times wider than the rootballs. Soil amendments and root stimulators are not recommended in the planting holes. Mulch the plants, and water them as needed.

Growing Tips

Provide supplemental irrigation during drought periods. Supplemental feedings are not usually needed in fertile soils.

Care

There are conflicting reports about the strength of the wood. Some say it is fairly weak, causing the tree to be short-lived, like an ornamental pear. Others refute such claims. Prune it during the dormant season to encourage stronger branches.

Landscape Merit

Use this small tree as a specimen plant in the lawn, or plant it in combination with other decorative small trees such as redbud and ornamental pear in their own island bed. The bed display then has a long season of bloom, fruit presentation, and fall color.

My Personal Favorite

The species is typically all that is available.

If you like trees with showy flowers and fruit like European mountain ash but want something easier to grow, consider Korean evodia. It tolerates heavy soils and higher pH. It has showy, white flowers forming on new season's growth around July or August. The flowers emit a discernable scent in large groupings. Capsule-like fruits turn reddish-black when they mature in fall. The lustrous, green foliage is compound and occasionally semi-evergreen. The tree is fairly fast growing, especially as a seedling. Approaching maturity, the tree develops bark with smooth texture and color. Because this underused tree is tolerant of heavy clay and alkaline soils, it is a perfect choice for western Oklahoma. In fact, its tolerance of a wide range of conditions makes it suitable for the entire state.

Other Common Names
Evodia, Bee Bee Tree

Bloom Period and Seasonal Color
White blooms in late summer.

Mature Height × Spread
20 to 30 ft. × 20 to 25 ft.

Mountain Ash

Sorbus species

This fast-growing tree is suited for northern climates, including the panhandle and northernmost parts of Zone 6b. The compound, deciduous foliage is dull, dark green on top and light gray underneath. Its early growth is erect and towering, but this tree later matures to a graceful, open specimen. The real show comes in summer with white flower clusters, which later form small, orange-red berries in fall. The fruit is a perfect match with the foliage. S. aucuparia, pictured above, is more prone to pest problems and is picky about acidic soil. Korean mountain ash is more pH adaptable with fewer pest problems. Arizona mountain ash (S. dumosa) is shrubby and more tolerant of heat and sandy soils. 'Coral Fire' (S. hupehensis) has red stems and bark, white flowers, and coral-red berries.

Other Common Name
Berry Ash

Bloom Period and Seasonal Color
White or red blooms in summer.

Mature Height × Spread
20 to 30 ft. × 15 to 20 ft.

Cold Hardiness Zone
6a

When, Where, and How to Plant
Many of the named selections are grafted or budded instead of seedling plants. Start the seed with a cold, moist stratification period of three to four months by planting directly in a container outside or by storing them in a refrigerator before planting. Plant container-grown or balled-and-burlapped ash in the spring, early summer, or fall. Moist, well-drained, fertile soils provide the best growth, especially when prepared before planting time. The European mountain ash prefers somewhat acidic soils. In high pH or alkaline sites, till and amend the soil with soil sulfur and peat moss before planting time. Do not backfill the planting hole; instead mix it into the soil of the planting site. Plant the trees in holes the same depth as and 2 to 3 times wider than the rootballs. Mulch and water on a regular basis.

Growing Tips
Keeping the soils moist during extreme drought is imperative and is best achieved with mulch in addition to supplemental watering. Slow-release fertilizer products are ideal and should be applied in the spring. Avoid late fall applications of fertilizer, which stimulate late growth spurts more susceptible to winter damage.

Care
This underused tree is fairly strong-wooded, especially when considering its fast-growing nature. The aging tree trunk develops a unique, smooth, grayish appearance that has the most seasonal appeal during the winter. Major pruning should happen early in the dormant season, around December or January. Potential pest threats include fire blight and canker disease or aphid and borer insects. The pests are more prevalent in poor sites with improper planting techniques.

Landscape Merit
Use mountain ash as a single tree specimen in lawns or in adjacent woodland borders. It is not a good choice for a sidewalk or street tree because of its fruit.

My Personal Favorite
Sorbus rufoferruginea 'Longwood Sunset' is more heat tolerant and disease resistant with nice fall color; it matures to about 30 feet.

Osage Orange
Maclura pomifera

When, Where, and How to Plant

Set out plants in the spring, early summer, or fall. The soil type is inconsequential and, in many cases, the poorer, the better as long as it is not waterlogged. Most often the new selections are budded varieties grown in containers. Dig the planting hole the same depth as the rootball and 2 to 3 times wider. Mulch to keep weed competition down and soil moisture in during the establishment period. Water at planting and on a regular basis for at least a year until the plants are well established

Growing Tips

Remember to provide supplemental irrigation during drought periods for the first year or so. Once the plants are established, they are quite drought tolerant. They respond well to light applications of supplemental feedings. Slow-release or organic fertilizers are ideal and provide minute amounts of nutrients over a longer period of time.

Care

These fairly fast-growing trees are strong wooded. Pruning during the dormant season is required in landscape settings to train and direct branch growth. When these trees are used for barriers or windbreaks, pruning is rarely needed. Pest problems are not serious, although a few fungal leaf spots have been reported with certain selections.

Landscape Merit

The new and improved medium-sized trees work well single-specimens in lawn settings. They are effective windbreaks because of the branches' weeping nature. Plant in groups in alternating rows or in combination with other rows of trees. This resilient plant tolerates pollutants and is being planted in urban street setting where it thrives amidst city grime.

My Personal Favorite

'White Shield' is a male, thornless cultivar with lustrous green leaves. The male flowers are not showy and don't produce fruit.

Osage orange tolerates drought, wind, heat, and cold more than almost any tree in Oklahoma. Perhaps the female's thorns and messy fruit have kept it from becoming a favored landscape plant. The large, round, yellow-green fruit formed on female trees has a brain-like rind; fruits are a smelly mess once they rot. Thanks to selective propagation, the plant is now available with male, thornless cultivars perfect for the landscape. Aesthetically, the Osage orange offers a distinctive yellow-colored bark; shiny, thick foliage; and yellow fall color. The wood of this long-lasting tree is very hard. Many of the thornless types are from the variety inermis. 'Whiteshield' is a favored, male, thornless introduction. 'Wichita' is thought to be the most thornless overall, and 'Double O' is a male form with more upright growth.

Other Common Names
Horse Apple, Hedge Apple, Bois d'Arc, Yellow Wood

Bloom Period and Seasonal Color
Yellow fall foliage.

Mature Height × Spread
20 to 40 ft. × 20 to 30 ft.

Cold Hardiness Zone
6a, 6b, 7a, 7b

Pinyon Pine
Pinus cembroides

Pinyon pine has a lovely, dark gray-green color with a stiff, upright growth habit. It is often found growing naturally in sandy loam sites in higher elevations in the western parts of the state. The pinecones are distinctly different as well, maturing in late summer with large, edible seed. The plants make great landscape and lawn choices for most of northwestern Oklahoma, including the panhandle. P. cembroides is a rather bushy, small tree with needles primarily in clusters of three per bundle (rarely two). Another small-growing pine, sometimes confused with Mexican nut pine, is P. edulis (Colorado pinyon pine, which is shown above). This pine has thicker needles usually in bundles of two (rarely three). Otherwise both are similar in growth, care, and use, and both thrive in drier, elevated sites.

Other Common Names
Mexican Nut Pine, Mexican Pinyon

Bloom Period and Seasonal Color
Evergreen dark gray-green needles.

Mature Height × Spread
15 to 20 ft. × 10 to 15 ft.

Cold Hardiness Zone
6a, 6b

When, Where, and How to Plant
Plant in early spring or summer. It prefers full-sun sites with well-drained, sandy, loam soils. Amend heavy, waterlogged soils before planting time with a sandy organic mix, and till it into the ground. Do not apply these products in the planting hole as fill, or root growth will be restricted to the amended area. Dig the planting hole the same depth as and 2 to 3 times wider than the existing roots. Place the plants slightly above soil grade in heavy soils to make sure there is good drainage. Mulch to keep weeds out. Water on a regular basis, but allow plants to dry slightly between applications.

Growing Tips
Avoid excess fertilizer. The plants are relatively drought tolerant as most pines are, but supplemental irrigation is beneficial during prolonged drought. Mulch under the drip line and the tree will be easier to maintain. Avoid tilling or planting around the roots, weed-trimmer or lawn mower damage to the trunk, and any other stress-related actions.

Care
This particular plant is more attractive when the lower branches are left alone. Dead branches may occur with age; remove these at any time. Excess pruning or stress increase the risk of pests and diseases, such as borers, fungal needle diseases, sawflies, pine moths, and pinewood nematodes. Do not be alarmed by brown needle drop in the late summer or fall, especially if it occurs from older needles toward the center of the trunk. This is a normal drop of two- or three-year-old needles, a common practice even on evergreen conifer plants.

Landscape Merit
Use this lovely plant as a single specimen or or group several in the lawn. It is frequently used in windbreak plantings as a background or mid-level plant. Foundation plantings are not as common but occur occasionally in combination with evergreen and deciduous plants.

My Personal Favorite
The species is most common.

Plains Zinnia

Zinnia grandiflora

When, Where, and How to Plant

Plant in full sun in well-drained soil. Plains zinnia adapts to most soil types and tolerates drought extremely well. Water logged soils, however, means certain death. The plants are best planted in the summer or fall from container grown plants. They can also be started from seed directly into the landscape or garden, but germination is typically low. Special seed treatments are needed and are most easily done by professional nurseries.

Growing Tips

The plants seldom need fertilization. High nitrogen fertilizers can readily burn the plants. If fertilizer is needed, use composted organic fertilizers. Water is most important for a few weeks after planting until the plants are established. Don't overwater or allow the plants to dry in between watering. Once established, they thrive in drought conditions.

Care

Once the plants are established, they can be divided in the spring to share with friends or to increase the numbers in your landscape. The plants are notorious for coming up late. They need the warm soil temperatures characteristic of spring in the spring; you may not see new growth until late May. Pest problems are rare when planted in the right growing conditions. Powdery mildew is occasionally a problem if zinnia is planted in too much shade or in humid areas of the state. Poor drainage causes the plants to die. This plant is truly a low maintenance favorite.

Landscape Merit

Space the plants 15 inches apart to achieve a ground cover effect. The small growing plants are best used as border plants or lower level plants in a perennial garden. Be sure to match the plant's growing conditions with other similar plants when growing them in perennial gardens. Perennials that need a lot of water are not a good companion for plains zinnia. Their colorful, long blooming display also makes them a nice choice for island beds out in full-sun locations of the landscape or lawn.

My Personal Favorite

The native species is most common.

One of the few herbaceous perennials highlighted in this chapter, plains zinnia deserves the spotlight. This native uplands prairie plant thrives in some of the most adverse terrain imaginable. It has remarkable blooming power and show, as well as extreme drought tolerance. It blooms non-stop from mid summer to fall and is adapted to sandier soils of the panhandle and western Oklahoma. It does not perform well in the humid locales of eastern and southeastern counties in the state. When planted close together, its low growing, clumping growth habit simulates a ground cover with a show of color like no other. Zinnia grandiflora is often used as a xeric (drought tolerant) plant throughout Arizona, Mexico, and Colorado, which makes it a perfect candidate for the gardens of northwestern Oklahoma.

Other Common Names

Little Golden Zinnia, Rocky Mountain Zinnia, Paperflower, Prairie Zinnia

Bloom Period and Seasonal Color

Yellow orange flowers from June to October.

Mature Height × Spread

4 to 6 in. × 15 to 18 in.

Cold Hardiness Zone

6a, 6b

Rocky Mountain Juniper

Juniperus scopulorum

Look around the state and you'll see that junipers do well in Oklahoma, especially in the west-central and northwestern counties. There are many species, but J. scopulorum (Rocky Mountain juniper) is one of the best. Its early pyramidal growth eventually becomes more rounded; there are low spreading and rounded forms also. The foliage color for Rocky Mountain juniper ranges from dark green to blue or yellow green, depending on the selection. Rocky Mountain juniper grows through Zone 7 of the state but prefers northwestern areas because of lower summer humidity; it does better the farther west you go. It is more naturalized in higher elevations and thrives in sandy, rocky, or heavy soils. It also provides shade and wind protection in the hot western Oklahoma counties.

Other Common Name
Colorado Red Cedar

Bloom Period and Seasonal Color
Evergreen dark green, blue, yellow-green needles.

Mature Height × Spread
20 to 40 ft. × 5 to 15 ft.

Cold Hardiness Zones
6a, 6b

When, Where, and How to Plant
Rocky Mountain juniper is often available as a container-grown or balled-and-burlapped specimen. Plant in the spring or summer. Fall planting is somewhat risky since the roots will not be well established by winter and the plants will succumb to winter winds. The trees prefer poor to average soils, though they accept rich, fertile well-drained soils. Place the plants in the planting holes the same depth as and 2 to 3 times wider than the rootballs. Avoid organic backfill and use only the natural soil. Mulch to conserve moisture and keep weeds at a minimum. Water on a regular basis for the first several months to establish the roots. Allow it to dry a bit between irrigations instead of keeping the soil consistently moist.

Growing Tips
Once established, the species is drought tolerant. However, it will respond to supplemental irrigation during prolonged dry periods, especially the first couple of years after planting. The plants respond well to slow-release or organic fertilizers applied in early spring because these fertilizers provide slow amounts of nutrients over a longer time period.

Care
The tree needs pruning only to make an occasional directional cut or to remove damaged branches. The species is more beautiful if the lower branches are left intact and allowed to form its natural growth habit. Potential pests are spider mites, phomopsis fungal blight, and it is a host for cedar apple rust. Most of the pest problems occur more frequently farther east because of increased moisture and humidity.

Landscape Merit
The trees are valued for their background color as well as for their use as barriers, screens, and hedges. They work nicely in foundation plantings, in group plantings, or as specimens. There are numerous cultivar variations, one to fit almost any landscape need.

My Personal Favorites
There are numerous upright, shrubby, and even ground cover selections. My favorite is 'Wichita Blue' with wonderful shape and color, but 'Fairview' is also a nice and more tolerant of cedar apple rust.

When, Where, and How to Plant

Plant soapberry in the spring, early summer, or fall. Container-grown and balled-and-burlapped specimens will transplant the same as bare-root tree seedlings. Trees planted in lawn areas are less to likely to produce seedlings than those planted in mulched landscape beds. They like full-sun locations. Soil type is not as crucial as good drainage. The trees naturally thrive in dry, poor soils and grow even bigger in moist, humus-rich sites. Avoid planting them near sidewalks or driveways because of the potentially messy fruit. Dig the planting hole the same depth as the rootball and 2 to 3 times wider. Mulch to keep moisture in and weeds out. Water on a regular basis for a couple of years until the plants establish.

Growing Tips

Water during prolonged drought periods, especially the first couple of seasons after planting. Once established, they are quite drought tolerant. Reapply mulch as needed to help preserve moisture and to supply the tree with slow nutrients. Supplemental feedings are beneficial but should be done rarely—every three or four seasons if that.

Care

These care-free trees hardly ever need pruning. Occasionally prune to direct growth or to help in branch development. It is a good idea to leave the lower branches on the first two to three growing seasons to encourage a bigger, stronger tree trunk. Pests are minimal, other than occasional box elder or soapberry bugs.

Landscape Merit

This tree works nicely in the landscape as a lawn specimen because it creates wonderful shade. Soapberries planted in groups act as barriers, windbreaks, or groves.

My Personal Favorite

Most commonly sold in the nursery trade are the seedling species.

Western soapberry is often touted as the tree for all seasons, offering beautiful spring flowers, attractive summer fruit, colorful fall foliage, and picturesque winter bark. That list is enough to encourage gardeners to use them more in the landscape, but do not forget about their resilience to heat, drought, cold, alkaline soils, and wind. It is close to being the perfect tree, especially for western areas of the state. It is native to the arid Southwest and thrives in limestone or sandstone soils. Soapberry grows in a shape similar to an umbrella with a large canopy. The tree offers great shade because of its compound, deciduous leaves, which are a medium-green color. You cannot go wrong with this tree that grows at a moderate pace and is long-lived.

Other Common Names

Indian Soap Plant, Soap Tree

Bloom Period and Seasonal Color

Creamy white blooms in late spring.

Mature Height × Spread

25 to 50 ft. × 25 to 30 ft.

Cold Hardiness Zone

6a, 6b

Planning and Starting a New Lawn

Site Survey

Lawns and landscapes are, unfortunately, an afterthought for many building contractors and even many homeowners. Heavy clay and other aggregate materials are often hauled in and packed down to prepare for the structure's foundation. There also may be leftover piles of sand, burned debris, roofing materials, limestone, concrete, wire, nails, and sack lunches. Grass is tough, but it is asking a lot for any plant to grow and thrive in such conditions. Dig a few holes in the area you want to plant, and see what you find. If the soil is full of debris or so compacted it is difficult to penetrate, you have a few problems to correct.

Removing compacted fill and debris in the lawn and landscape area, then bringing in good topsoil, is the best approach if at all possible. Garden topsoil is a sandy loam containing a lot of organic matter. It is neither too sandy nor mostly clay, but somewhere in between. Ideally, apply the good topsoil 12 to 18 inches deep, but certainly no less than 6 to 8 inches to allow for strong, drought-resistant root growth. Grade the soil gently so it drains away from the foundation of your home.

If bringing in good topsoil is not an option, incorporate as much organic matter as possible into your existing soil. Organic matter includes decaying plant materials or manures that enrich and loosen soil, improve the drainage of clay soils, hold water and nutrients in sandy soils, slow down erosion, and provide a favorable environment for earthworms and beneficial microorganisms. As it decays, organic matter releases small amounts of nutrients back into the soil for plants to use. Peat moss, manure, and compost are some of the most common forms of organic material. Adding just a few inches of these products and working them in with a tiller can make a huge improvement in any poor, nutrient-deficient soil.

Soil Testing

Take your soil seriously. Poor infertile soil means poor non-productive plants. A healthy lawn is a result of fertile, healthy soil. Since turfgrass receives its primary nutrition from the soil, having your soil tested is a must. Otherwise you are "growing by guessing," and that can be costly financially, nutritionally, and environmentally. A soil test will measure the fertility of your soil and tell you what needs to be added.

Collect ten to fifteen samples of soil from a depth of 4 to 6 inches throughout your lawn area, then mix them together, and fill a pint jar with the mixture. Take the sample to your Cooperative Extension Service, which will send it to their state lab for analysis. Typically there is a small fee for the service. In a few weeks, test results will be sent back with your soil's nutritional data along with adjustment recommendations and guidelines. Many of the soil nutrients and pH adjusters that may be needed are best worked into the soil prior to planting. While waiting for the soil test results, calculate your total lawn

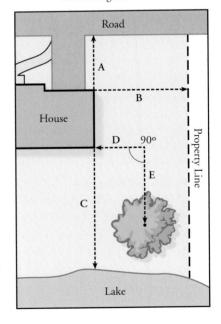

Calculating Lawn Area

Lawns not only provide recreational space and accent landscape beds, they also control erosion, reduce glare and noise, absorb air pollution, and trap dust particles.

area (minus any structures) in square feet, which is length multiplied by width. This is important information to use later in determining the amount of seed, sod, fertilizer, soil additives, or other materials needed to establish and care for your lawn.

Cool or Hot, Shade or Not

Matching your grass selection to your growing zone and site is a key factor in developing a good lawn. There are two broad categories of turf that grow in the Southern United States—cool-season and warm-season grasses. The line between the areas where these two categories of grass do well is often called the transition zone. It falls along the northern boundaries of the southernmost states as seen on the Southern States Grass Zones map in the Introduction.

Cool-season turf is more cold hardy and grows best during the cooler fall, winter, and spring months of the year. These grasses typically remain green most of the winter but can occasionally brown or burn during extreme cold spells. Because they don't acclimate well to heat and drought, they can be grown somewhat successfully in partial shade.

Cool-season grasses usually grow in clumps that do not spread. Therefore, to keep a nice thick lawn, routine reseeding is needed, sometimes as often as once a year. This is best done either in the fall or spring. Fescue, Kentucky bluegrass, and ryegrass are cool-season grasses. They are usually successful in the Upper South, but they are not as commonly used in the Deep South because they cannot take the summer heat and drought. Supplemental irrigation, whether by hand or an automated sprinkler system, is a must to keep cool-season grasses from going dormant or dying completely in the heat of the summer.

Warm-season grasses, on the other hand, thrive in the South's summer heat. In the winter, they naturally go dormant, turning brown in the coldest of conditions. These grasses green up in the spring—sometimes late spring—as soil temperatures rise. All warm-season grasses can suffer some winter damage depending on how cold the temperatures become and how much soil moisture is available during the cold spell.

Bermudagrass, centipedegrass, St. Augustinegrass, and zoysiagrass are the most common warm-season grasses. Bahiagrass, buffalograss, and carpetgrass are also grown but not as widely. All these warm-season grasses spread by stolons (aboveground stems) and rhizomes (underground stems), eliminating the need for routine reseeding. Overall, warm-season grasses are more drought tolerant than cool-season grasses. They will also recuperate better if they should go dormant during extended dry periods.

Avoid combining permanent plantings of warm-season and cool-season grasses, such as ermudagrass and fescue. They have distinctly different growing periods, textures, mowing heights, and management requirements. Combining the two will just create twice the amount of work and will result in a patchy-looking lawn during most seasons of the year.

Observe shading patterns in your yard before selecting a grass. Most lawn grasses perform best with full sun all day. Partial or dappled shade (with shade four to six hours per day) limits the type of lawn you can plant. Don't even try a lawn grass in heavy shade (more than six hours a day) unless you are willing to do some tree work. Thinning trees or removing lower branches can increase the light and make grass a possibility even in fairly shady situations.

Prepare the Planting Site

Before planting grass, eliminate all undesirable weeds or grasses either mechanically or chemically. Mechanical techniques for removing weeds include digging, hoeing, and smothering. Covering the soil with black plastic for three to five months prior to planting prevents sunlight from reaching the ground, smothering existing weeds and grasses, while generating ample heat to kill weed seed. Tilling to remove existing vegetation will not work with plants that form underground stems, such as bermudagrass. The rhizomes and stolons scatter, then later root and grow. Tilling also brings more weed seeds to the surface where they will germinate.

Be awqre of sunlight patterns in your yard. An area with dappled shade will limit the type of lawn you can grow there. Tall fescue and Kentucky bluegrass are the most shade tolerant of the turfgrasses.

Chemical approaches that include very specific herbicides are often the most complete eradication methods. Use a non-selective herbicide like glyphosate (the active ingredient in herbicides such as Roundup®) or glufosinate-ammonium (the active ingredient in the herbicide Finale®) according to label directions to kill any existing vegetation. Non-selective means the herbicide kills anything the spray reaches. But non-selective herbicides don't sterilize the soil, so you can replant once the existing vegetation is completely dead. Spraying herbicides should be done a few weeks, even months, before planting to allow the chemicals time to kill the entire plant, roots and all. Persistent weeds or grasses such as bermudagrass may require more than one spraying. Mixing an indicator dye (typically blue), available at turf or farm supply businesses, with the herbicide allows you to see where you have sprayed.

Remove large rocks, pebbles, or soil clods that may interfere with seed establishment. Large pieces of wood, tree branches, and bark should also be removed since they can contribute to a perplexing problem in lawns called "fairy ring," discussed in detail in Chapter Seven.

Once all vegetation is killed or removed, lightly work the top inch or so of soil just prior to planting by tilling very shallowly or raking by hand. Working the soil too deeply will stir up more weed seeds.

Other Considerations

If you live in a drought prone part of the South, which is pretty much all of the South, you should think about an irrigation system. A 5,000 square foot lawn can transpire about 3,000 gallons of water on a hot summer day, helping cool the area around it. But some of that water will need to be replaced or drought stress will occur, and the benefits of cooling will be lost. Irrigation is an investment that can pay for itself in a couple of years in water and time saved.

How do you like your lawn grass—coarse or fine? Some folks just prefer the look and feel of fine-textured grasses such as bermudagrass or zoysiagrass to coarser types such as St. Augustine or fescue. And some grasses are assumed to be higher maintenance (zoysia, for example, although I have found that it doesn't necessarily need more mowing or fertilizing than other grasses). Categorizing lawn grasses according to maintenance is very subjective and depends on what you imagine a lawn should look like—sometimes it's a case of being more realistic in your expectations.

Seed, Sprig, Plug, or Sod

Most lawn grass varieties have several specific named cultivars from which to choose. The specific cultivar will dictate the method of planting depending on whether the grass is available as seed or strictly in vegetative form. Look for turfgrass with "certified" on the label for extra insurance that you are getting what you want. The planting bed should be prepared as described earlier whether you are seeding, sprigging, plugging, or laying sod. Specific seeding and vegetative planting rates are covered in Chapter Six.

Grasses available only in vegetative form either have no flowers or the flowers are typically sterile, so the grass must be reproduced by sprigs, plugs, or sod. Grasses available as seed are reproduced by pollination and seed collection.

When purchasing seed, read the label of the container to find the best purity ratings, which is a nice way of saying percentage of weed contamination. Generally, purchase grass seed with no more than 10 percent weed contamination. The germination rate of the grass seed should be around 85 percent.

Seed Application Pattern

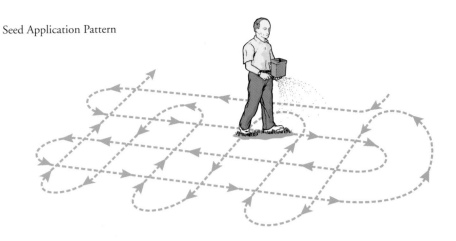

After planting, make sure the seed comes in contact with the soil by lightly raking it to cover the seed at a depth of about ¹/₈ inch. Firm the planting site, and provide even more soil-to-seed contact by tamping or rolling with a weighted roller. For more uniform coverage, apply half the seed in one direction and the remaining half at right angles to the first. Hand, drop, or rotary seeders are most commonly used, although drill seeders are also available. Small seed can be mixed with dry sand in about a 50/50 mix to make spreading easier.

Mulching with weed-free grain straw (oat, wheat, or barley) at a thickness of about 1 to 1¹/₂ inches is optional, but it does help retain soil moisture and minimize erosion. Typically one bale of straw, weighing between 60 to 80 pounds, will cover about 1,000 square feet. Grain seed present in the straw may also germinate but usually dies out with mowing or increased summer temperatures. Do not use grass hay as mulch, or additional weed seed will be introduced. Hydro-seeding using machines that mix seed with water, and sometimes even mulch, is another option for establishing a lawn, especially on steeply sloping sites.

If you are planning a bermudagrass, zoysiagrass, or St. Augustinegrass lawn, you can find some cultivars in sprig form. Planting with sprigs is the least expensive of the vegetative planting methods. Sprigs are stems or runners with two or four nodes, or joints, and few to no roots. A node is the location on the stem where roots and shoots emerge. Rates and spacing vary depending on the type of grass, but sprigs are typically planted at a depth of about 1 to 2 inches. Sprigs are available commercially or can be harvested from existing turf or pulled from sod. One square yard or 9 square feet of sod can yield approximately one bushel of sprigs. This works out to be approximately 2,000 bermuda or zoysia sprigs and 500 St. Augustine or centipede sprigs. The sprigs can be furrowed into the soil, or they can be broadcast on the surface and topdressed with a light covering of topsoil or organic material. Whichever method you use, the sprigs should have good soil contact. The ideal placement is to leave one-quarter of

Plug Spacing	Number of Plugs/ 1,000 sq. ft.	Yards of Sod Required
6 inches	4,000	12+
8 inches	2,250	7
12 inches	1,000	3+

the sprig sticking out of the ground. The closer together the sprigs are placed, the faster they will cover the area.

Plugs are nothing more than small, cut pieces of sod usually 2 to 4 inches across, with a thickness of 2 to 3 inches of soil and roots. Unlike sprigs, plugs are seldom available commercially, but you can cut your own from either an existing lawn or a pallet of sod. In some regions of the country, grasses are available in flats, similar to flats of flowers, with individual containers of grass, also known as plugs. It takes three to ten times more material to plant a lawn with plugs than with sprigs. The following chart will help you determine the amount of sod to purchase if you are going to cut plugs. One square yard of sod yields approximately three hundred twenty-four 2-inch plugs. Plugs are not recommended for cool-season, clumping grasses, such as fescue.

Plugging can be done with both warm- and cool-season grasses. The plugs may be round or square depending on the plugging tool or machine. Plugs establish faster than sprigs because they are already well-rooted, but like sprigs, the more closely they are spaced, the quicker they will fill an area.

Sod is harvested turf, roots and all, cut into assorted sizes, then stacked or rolled on a pallet. Sod creates an instant lawn and is therefore more costly than any other method. But research shows that sod lawns are fifteen times more effective in controlling runoff than seeded lawns, even after three years. The planting bed should be prepared ahead of time even when laying sod. The roots establish faster in a prepared bed than on an unprepared site. Snugly fit the sod pieces together in an alternating pattern so the seams do not line up. Avoid stretching the sod when you are laying it since it will shrink as it dries a bit and settles, causing voids in the lawn (although you should avoid letting the sod dry out). Most sod is sold by square yards per pallet with 50 yards per pallet being the norm. There are 9 square feet in a square yard of sod, so if you have 3,500 square feet of lawn to plant, you will need to order at least 388 yards of sod (3,500 ∏ 9 = 388). Roll or tamp the sod, (sprigs and plugs also) to ensure good soil contact, eliminating air pockets and leveling the soil. Roll at right angles to the direction the sod was laid.

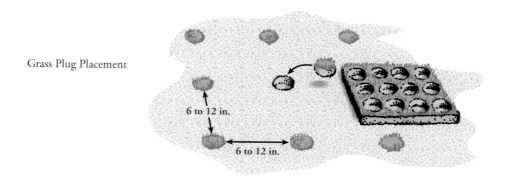

Grass Plug Placement

6 to 12 in.

6 to 12 in.

Mixing sprigs with areas of plugs and sod can cause a slightly uneven lawn. Sprigged lawns seldom grow to the thickness of sod, so expect the surface to remain uneven, even years after planting. The unevenness can be detected when mowing or walking across the lawn surface.

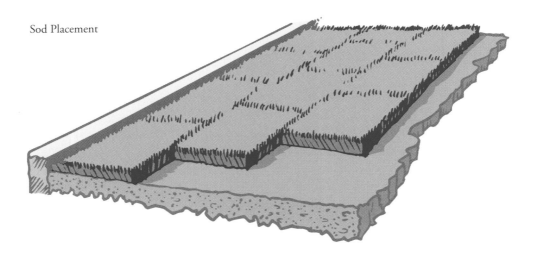

Sod Placement

When to Plant Your Lawn

Seed, sprig, sod, or plug at the appropriate times of year. For warm-season grasses, that means the soil temperatures need to be approaching 70° F. A good guide is to plant when other warm-season grasses start to green up and grow. There must also be at least two months allowed for warm-season grasses to become established before winter. April through July is the ideal planting time for warm-season grasses assuming you have adequate rainfall or supply supplemental irrigation. Dormant sodding of warm-season grasses is sometimes done, but the chances for winter-kill are much greater since the roots have not penetrated the soil for extra protection.

Cool-season lawns can be planted in the very early spring between late February and early April or in the fall during September or October. Fall planting is preferred in order to give the grass a longer time to get established before the onset of the summer heat and drought. Cool-season lawns are usually started by seed although some varieties are available as sod. The sod squares are not as tight as the warm-season, rhizomatous grasses, so they are more likely to fall apart.

Post-Establishment Care

Gently water after planting, and keep the newly planted lawn moist but not soggy for at least ten to twenty-one days. Never allow seedlings, in particular, to dry out completely. This is best accomplished by daily light waterings. On windy, sunny days you may need to water two or three times per day depending on your soil type. Less irrigation will be needed if straw mulch is used. As the turf becomes more established, water deeply and less often.

Mow as soon as the grass, whether from seed, sprigs, plugs, or sod, reaches a height 1/3 greater than the recommended mowing height for your particular variety. (Specific mowing guidelines are found in Chapter Six.) This will promote lateral spread and deep rooting. Do not mow when the grass is wet. Wet leaf blades are more likely to mat together or tear, and pull the plant, roots and all, out of the ground.

If you prepared your soil properly, any needed phosphorus, potassium, and lime were added prior to planting. These materials do not move readily through the soil and are best worked in at the root zone. If fertilizer was not applied before planting, a complete blend of nitrogen (N), phosphorus (P), and potassium (K) can be applied three to four weeks afterward. It will just take longer for the P, K, and lime to work. Any fertilizer mixture you use should be less than 10 percent nitrogen since a higher analysis can burn newly emerging seedlings.

On newly planted lawns it is best to pull or hoe any weeds. Frequent mowing, proper fertilization, and correct watering will also help. Any maintenance practices that help the grass cover the ground more quickly will also help shade out germinating weed seeds. Herbicides should be a last resort on a new lawn. If you decide to use one, read the label carefully since few are recommended for new lawns.

Renovating a Lawn

"Renovation" is the term for trying to get poorly performing lawns reestablished and back into shape. There are different levels of renovation. Partial renovation may be a simple process of seeding over thinning grass. Complete renovation is the most extreme form, and it basically means starting over from scratch. Some form of renovation is usually required when a lawn becomes thin and spotty or overgrown with undesirable weeds or grasses.

First find the cause of your lawn's problem. If the issue is pests, then properly identify them and treat the lawn accordingly. Pests are covered extensively in Chapter Seven. Many thinning, weed-infested lawns are the result of improper management or cultural practices. Take a soil test to determine if the problem is poor soil nutrition or improper pH. If the soil is compacted from heavy foot traffic or repetitious mowing patterns, then aerating the soil may be needed. This is covered in Chapter Four.

If correcting these problems does not help reestablish your existing grass, then replanting may be required. Choose the appropriate turfgrass cultivars for your site and growing conditions. Replanting can be done in localized areas or can encompass the entire lawn depending on the extent of the problem. In either case, use the same procedures described earlier to prepare a planting bed. Kill all the existing vegetation before replanting, especially if another invasive lawn species has encroached into the preferred lawn grass.

What Can Go Wrong When Planting a Lawn

Over-Watering	Under-Fertilization
Under-Watering	Compacted Soil
Cold Temperatures	Seed Blew or Washed Away
Hot Temperatures	Damping-off Disease
Seed Planted Too Deep or Too Shallow	Site Too Steep, Poor Water Penetration
Poor Soil Contact	Dog Spots
Improper Weed and Feed Applications	Birds
Use of Pre-emergent Herbicide	Insects
Over-Fertilization	

United States Ecoregions

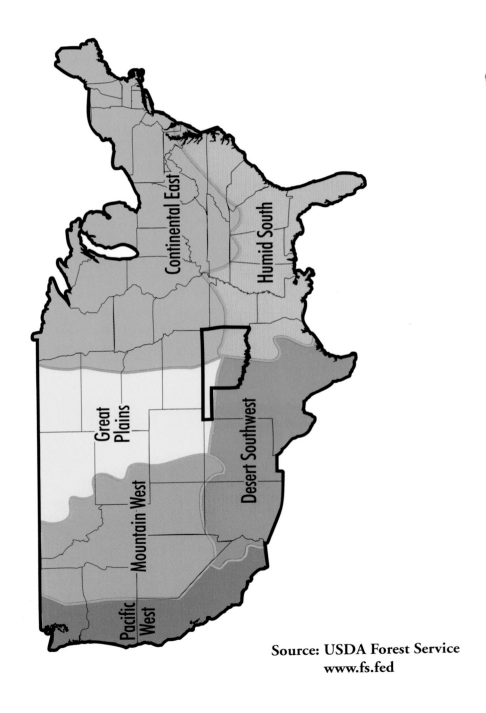

Continental East

Humid South

Great Plains

Mountain West

Desert Southwest

Pacific West

Source: USDA Forest Service
www.fs.fed

Oklahoma Frost-Free Map

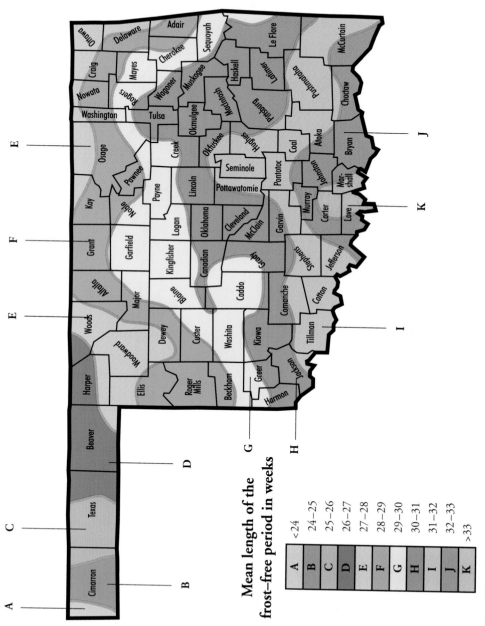

Mean length of the frost-free period in weeks

A	<24
B	24–25
C	25–26
D	26–27
E	27–28
F	28–29
G	29–30
H	30–31
I	31–32
J	32–33
K	>33

Source: Oklahoma Climatological Survey: www.ocs.ou.edu

Oklahoma Freeze Map

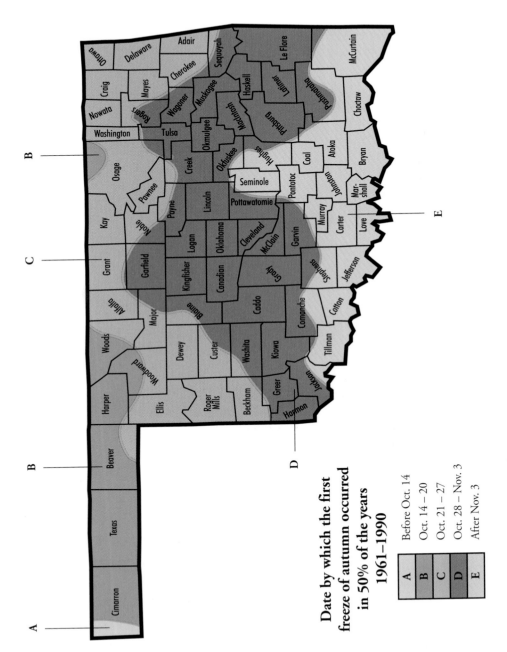

Date by which the first freeze of autumn occurred in 50% of the years 1961–1990

A	Before Oct. 14
B	Oct. 14 – 20
C	Oct. 21 – 27
D	Oct. 28 – Nov. 3
E	After Nov. 3

Source: Oklahoma Climatological Survey, www.ocs.ou.edu

Oklahoma Precipitation Map

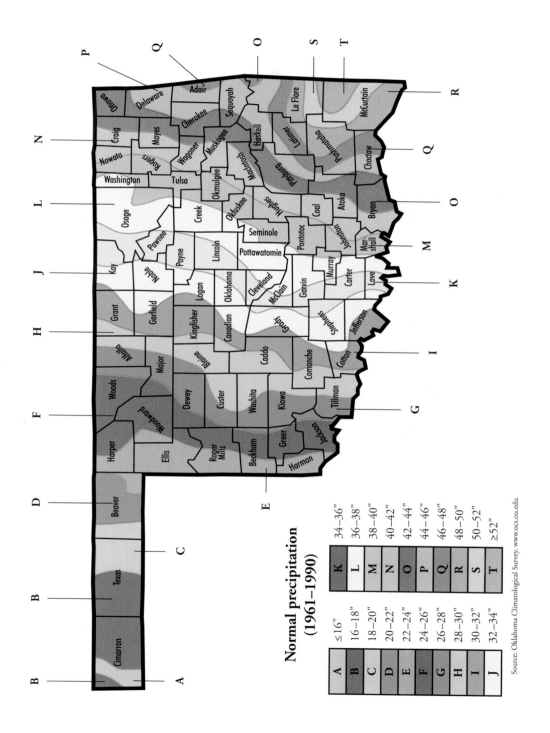

Normal precipitation (1961–1990)

A	≤16"
B	16–18"
C	18–20"
D	20–22"
E	22–24"
F	24–26"
G	26–28"
H	28–30"
I	30–32"
J	32–34"
K	34–36"
L	36–38"
M	38–40"
N	40–42"
O	42–44"
P	44–46"
Q	46–48"
R	48–50"
S	50–52"
T	≥52"

Source: Oklahoma Climatological Survey. www.ocs.ou.edu

Oklahoma Northwestern Counties

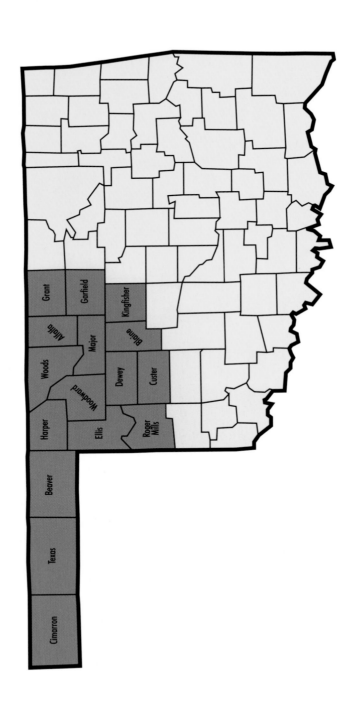

Perennial Ground Covers as Lawn Alternatives

For Shade

Common Name	Other Name	Botanical Name	Cold Hardiness Zones	Comments
Ajuga	Bugleweed	*Ajuga reptans*	4-9	
Asiatic Jasmine	Confederate Jasmine	*Trachelospermum jasminioides*	7b-10	
Barren Strawberry		*Waldsteinia ternata*	6-10	
Barrenwort		*Epimedium* species	3-8	acidic soils
Bishop's Weed		*Aegopodium podagraria*	3-9	can be invasive
Bloodroot		*Sanguinaria canadensis*	4-8	
Bromeliads		*Billbergia* species	8-10	
Bunchberry		*Cornus canadensis*	2-6	sensitive to heat
Cast Iron Plant		*Aspidistra elatior*	8-10	
Coontie		*Zamia integrifolia*	8-10	
Creeping Charlie		*Pilea nummulariifolia*	7-10	can become lawn weed
Creeping Fig		*Ficus* species	8-10	
English Ivy		*Hedera helix*	4-9	can be invasive
Euonymus	Wintercreeper	*Euonymus fortunei*	5-9	can be invasive
Ferns		(assorted species)	4-9	
Foam Flower		*Tiarella cordifolia*	5-8	
Ginger		*Asarum canadense*	4-7	
Japanese Spurge	Pachysandra	*Pachysandra terminalis*	4-8	
Lamium	Archangel	*Lamium maculatum*	4-9	
Leadwort	Plumbago	*Ceratostigma plumbaginoides*	5-9	
Lilyturf	Monkey Grass	*Liriope muscari*	6-10	
Mazus		*Mazus reptans*	5-9	
Mondo Grass		*Ophiopogon japonicus*	6-10	
Moneywort	Creeping Jenny	*Lysimachia nummularia*	6-10	acidic soils
Moss		(numerous genera)		
Partridge Berry		*Mitchella repens*	8-10	acidic soils
Peacock Moss		*Selaginella uncinata*	6-10	
St. John's Wort		*Hypericum calycinum*	5-8	
Sweet Woodruff		*Gallium odoratum*	4-8	
Vinca	Periwinkle	*Vinca minor/major*	4-9	
Wedelia		*Wedelia trilobata*	8-10	
Woodland Phlox		*Phlox stolonifera*	3-8	
Wandering Jew		*Tradescantia zebrina*	8-10	

Beneficial Insects

Beneficial Insect	Feeds On
Ant Lion (Doodlebug)	Caterpillars, aphids, and many other soil insects
Assassin Bug	Assortment of insects, but can bite you also (Wheel Bug)
Big-eyed Bug	Chinch bugs, assorted insect eggs, small larvae, and soft-bodied insects
Damsel Bug	Aphids, assorted insect eggs, small larvae, and many other soft-bodied insects
Earthworm*	Doesn't feed on insects but good for the soil, although too many can make the soil level lumpy. Verti-cutting the soil can help with this rare problem.
Earwig	Can also feed on plants, but is typically a predator and eats chinch bugs, webworms, and other soil insects
Green Lacewing (Aphid Lion)	Small caterpillars, aphids, mites, thrips, mealybugs, soft bodied insects, and insect eggs
Ground Beetle	Feeds on almost any soil insect, particularly cutworms, armyworms, sod webworms, and small mole crickets
Ladybug Beetle (Ladybird Beetle)	Adults and larvae feed on small, soft-bodied insects such as aphids, mites, scale, and insect eggs

Beneficial Insects

Beneficial Insect	Feeds On
Minute Pirate Bug	Thrips, spider mites, and assorted insect eggs
Nematode	Beneficial nematodes (Steinernema and Heterohabditis species) can feed on assorted caterpillar larvae or grubs, and flea larvae
Predaceous Stinkbug	Feeds on many assorted insects including caterpillar larvae
Praying Mantis	Feeds on almost any other insect. including other beneficials
Rove Beetle	Aphids, nematodes, most soil inhabiting larvae
Spined Soldier Bug	Fall armyworm and other caterpillar larvae
Spider*	Feeds on an assortment of pests, including beetles, caterpillars, leafhoppers, and aphids
Syrphid Fly (Hover Fly)	Larval stage feeds on soft-bodied insects such as aphids
Parasitic Wasp	Crickets, caterpillars, and aphids

*not technically insects, but beneficial nonetheless

Learn to recognize good bugs in all their stages—a ladybug beetle larva doesn't look at all like a ladybug.

Other Plants for Oklahoma

Annuals

Common Name	Botanical Name	Comments
Angel Wing Begonia	*Begonia × hybrida*	afternoon shade, up to 3 ft. tall
Black Leaf Shooting Star	*Pseuderanthemum atropurpureum*	darkest purple/black foliage I've seen
Celosia	*Celosia argenteas plumosa* hybrid	'Fresh Look' Series
Dwarf Impatiens	*Impatien × hybrida*	tiny flower/plants; Firefly and Pixie series
Evolvulus	*Evolvulus* 'Blue Daze'	powder blue flowers all summer long
False Dracaena	*Cordyline australis* 'Red Sensation'	purple dracaena look a like
Peek-A-Boo	*Spilanthes oleracea*	reseeding annual, unusual yellow flower
Pigeonberry	*Duranta erecta*	awesome chartreuse or variegated foliage
Snowbush	*Breynia disticha* 'Roseo-picta'	variegated pink, green and white foliage
Perilla 'Magilla'	*Perilla × hybrida*	coleus look alike, full sun, part shade

Bulbs

Common Name	Botanical Name	Comments
Alocasia	*Alocasia* species	shiny leaf elephant ears
Blackberry Lily	*Belamcanda chinensis*	showy flower and seed
Blue-Eyed Grass	*Sisyrinchium angustifolium*	carefree, dies back after bloom and foliage
Crocus	*Crocus* species	dainty, naturalizes
Fritillaria	*Fritillaria imperialis* 'Aureomarginata'	cool variegated foliage, orange flower
Hardy Amaryllis	*Hippeastrum × johnsonii*	hardy to zone 7
Pineapple Lily	*Eucomis* 'Sparkling Burgundy'	pineapple like flower on burgundy foliage
Snowdrop	*Galanthus* species	fragrant, early spring woodland plant
Snowflake	*Leucojum aestivum* or *vernum*	summer flowering, spring flowering
Striped Japanese Iris	*Iris ensata* 'Variegata'	bog plant, moist sites, afternoon shade

Grasslike Plants

Common Name	Botanical Name	Comments
Blue Love Grass	*Eragrostis elliotii*	readily reseeds
Carex Sedge	*Carex* species	part shade, moist sites
Hakonechloa	*Hakonechloa macra*	nice cascading habit, afternoon shade
Ornamental Millet	*Pennisetum glaucum*	allowing seedling to get potbound stunts growth
Palm Grass	*Setaria palmifolia*	ribbon like foliage, annual
Pony Tail Grass	*Stipa (Nasella) tenuissima*	airy featherlike foliage and plumes
Tufted Hair Grass	*Deschampsia caespitosa*	part shade, moist sites
Yellow Stripe Grass	*Dianella tasmanica*	annual, bold green and yellow stripes

Ground Covers

Common Name	Botanical Name	Comments
Annual Dichondra	*Dichondra argentea*	silver foliage, 2 in., annual
Chameleon Plant	*Houttuynia cordata*	invasive, plant in contained sites
Creeping Thyme	*Thymus* species	look for cold hardiness
Euonymous	*Euonymous fortunei*	'Kewensis' tiny evergreen
Mazus	*Mazus reptans* or *radicans*	needs moist shady sites
Pink Skullcap	*Scutellaria suffrutescens*	drought tolerant groundcover
Woodland Phlox	*Phlox stolonifera*	part shade, slow growing

Perennials

Common Name	Botanical Name	Comments
Amsonia	*Amsonia hubrectii*	spring flowers, awesome fall color
Armeria	*Armeria* species and hybrids	dainty plant, early blooms
Brunnera	*Broonera macrophylla*	afternoon shade, wind protection, moist
Bush Clover	*Lespedeza thunbergii*	great fall bloom
Campanula	*Campanula* species and hybrids	assorted heights, colors and foliage
Chinese Indigo	*Indigofera kirilowii*	18 in. tall and slowly spreads, part shade
Euphorbia	*Euphorbia* species	dry well drained sites
False Solomon's Seal	*Disporopsis pernyi*	evergreen, spreads

Perennials (continued)

Common Name	Botanical Name	Comments
False Sunflower	*Heliopsis* species	assorted heights, colors and foliage
Gold Leaf Tansy	*Tanacetum vulgare*	chartreuse foliage, yellow flower
Hardy Geraniums	*Geranium* species and hybrids	assorted heights, colors and foliage
Helleborus	*Helleborus orientalis*	early flowers, tough, underused
Himalayan Indigo	*Indigofera heterantha*	4 ft. tall, full sun, flowers all summer
Hosta	*Hosta* hybrids	wind, afternoon sun protection
Lysimachia	*Lysimachia punctata*	'Golden Alexander', not invasive
Peony	*Paeonia* hybrids	showy flowers, numerous selections
Poker Plant	*Kniphofia uvaria*	dry well drained sites
Prairie Clover	*Dalea purpureum*	prarie plant for northwest, 'Stephanie' cultivar
Rumex	*Rumex sanguineeus*	red/purple foliage, afternoon shade
Spiderwort	*Tradescantia* species and hybrids	'Sweet Kate' is to die for
Stoke's Aster	*Stokesia laevis*	compact plant, large flowers
Variegated Comfrey	*Symphytum* × *uplandicum*	'Axminister Gold' awesome
Variegated Horseradish	*Armoracia rusticana* 'Variegata'	variegation comes with age

Shrubs

Common Name	Botanical Name	Comments
Barberry	*Berberis thunbergii*	Deciduous, 'Bonanza Gold' my favorite
Button Bush	*Cephalanthus occidentalis*	Bog shrub, round flowers, native
Cotoneaster	*Cotoneaster* species	Great groundcover
Forsythia	*Forsythia intermedia* hybrids	Look for variegated foliage selectiosn
Inkberry	*Ilex glabra*	Native, underused
Juniper	*Juniperus* species	Watch for mites and blight problems
Leucothoe	*Leucothoe* species	Nice foliage
Mock Orange	*Philadelphus coronarius* hybrids	White showy flower in spring
New Jersey Tea	*Ceanothus americanus*	Dry soils, white flowers
Red/Yellow Twig Dogwoods	*Cornus alba* hybrids	Wonderful winter color stems

Shrubs (continued)

Common Name	Botanical Name	Comments
St. John's Wort	*Hypericum* species	Herbacous and groundcover types also
Stephanandra	*Stephanandra incisa*	Tall and compact selections
Witch Hazel	*Hamamelis × intermedia*	Early spring flowers, acid soils
Yucca	*Yucca* species	'Colorguard' has variegated foliage

Trees

Common Name	Botanical Name	Comments
American Linden	*Tilia americana*	nice choice for eastern Oklahoma
Black Gum	*Nyssa sylvatica*	native, prefers wet sites
Bur Oak	*Quercus macrocarpa*	large acor, stately tree
Deciduous Magnolia	*Magnolia soulangiana* hybrids	Awesome flowers
Desert Willow	*Chilopsis linearis*	summer blooms, small tree
Fringe Tree	*Chionanthus virginicus*	spring bloom, small tree
Hackberry	*Celtis occidentalis*	leaves pest prone, but great tree dispite
Ninebark	*Physocarpus opulifolius*	small tree, look for purple foliage types
PawPaw	*Asimina triloba*	great foliage, flower and fruit
Sawtooth Oak	*Quercus acutissima*	moderate grower, nice foliage
Seven Sons Flower	*Heptacodium miconioides*	small tree, late season flower and color
Shantung Maple	*Acer truncatum*	smaller tree, heat tolerant
Swamp White Oak	*Quercus bicolor*	large tree, wet or dry sites
Tulip Poplar	*Liriodendron tulipifera*	moderate grower, unique foliage
Water Oak	*Quercus nigra*	train when small
Willow Oak	*Quercus phellos*	moderate grower, nice form

Vines

Common Name	Botanical Name	Comments
Bowtie Vine	*Dalechampia dioscoreifolia*	annual, purple flower
Climbing Hydrangea	*Hydrangea petiolaris*	needs lots of space
Variegated Kiwi	*Actinidia kolomikta*	variegation comes with age

Natives as Ornamentals

Gardeners have shown an active interest in using native plants within the landscape. Just drive across the state and you will see Oklahoma's beautiful and diverse native or naturalized habitat - everything from pines to blackjacks, wildflowers to prairie grass. Native plants are plants that grow without cultivation and are indigenous to an area without being artificially introduced. Naturalized plants are those that have been introduced but have escaped cultivation and continue to thrive and reproduce.

In either case, the plants grow well on their own in the wild without assistance from gardeners. This characteristic is usually interpreted to mean that natives are tough, low-maintenance plants. This is only true if they are in the proper growing conditions. Native or naturalized plants flourish in very specific sites. If you love a particular native plant, mimic its natural habitat in your yard. You'll be pleasantly surprised how your soil can produce the same thriving plants that natural spaces do. For example, dogwoods are native to the state in moist, loamy sites where they are understory trees in filtered shade. Plant this native in full sun next to a hot concrete driveway in heavy soil, however, and dogwood will not readily survive. But put it in shade with soil conditions similar to its choice spots in nature and you will enjoy its beauty indefinitely.

A collection of native plants is often controversial among gardeners. Major concerns are that plants may become extinct or that some plants may become invasive threats when introduced into cultivated locations. It is best to buy propagated plants from reliable nurseries specializing in tried-and-tested native plants. You may be surprised to learn that many plants already in the nursery trade are "Oklahoma originals." Some mail-order companies specialize in native plants, but you need to do your homework in selecting plants that adapt to your particular region. Native plant organizations, nurseries and nature preserves are great places to get more info about native plants.

Alabaster Caverns State Park and Nature Trail
Rt. 1, Box 32
Freedom, OK 73842
(580) 621-3381
http://www.woodwardok.com/parks/
    alabastercaverns.htm

Chickasaw National Recreation Area and Park
P.O. Box 201
Sulphur, OK 73086
(580) 622-3165
http://www.nps.gov/chic/

Clear Creek Farms and Gardens
P.O. Box 89
Peggs, OK 74452
(918) 598-3782

Forest Heritage Center
Beavers Bend Resort Park
P.O. Box 157
Broken Bow, OK 74728
(405) 494-6497
http://www.beaversbend.com

Martin Park Nature Center
5000 W. Memorial Rd.
Oklahoma City, OK 73142
(405) 755-0676
http://www.martinpark.org/

Oklahoma Native Plant Society
c/o Tulsa Garden Center
2435 South Peoria
Tulsa, OK 74114
http://www.usao.edu/~onps/

Oklahoma Wildscape Certification Non-game Wildlife Program

Oklahoma Department of Wildlife Conservation

1801 N. Lincoln

Oklahoma City, OK 73105

(405) 521-4616

http://www.wildlifedepartment.com/
watchabl.htm

Oxley Nature Center and Red Bud Valley
Nature Preserve

5701 E. 36th Street North

Tulsa, OK 74115

(918) 669-6644

http://www.tulsawalk.com/parks-
places/tulsaparks-mohawk.html

Sunshine Nursery and Arboretum

Rt. 1, Box 4030

Clinton, OK 73601

(580) 323-6259

http://www.sunshinenursery.com/

Tallgrass Prairie Preserve / Nature Conservancy

Box 458

Pawhuska, OK 74056

(918) 287-4803

http://nature.org/wherewework/northamerica/stat
es/oklahoma/

Wichita Maintains National Wildlife Refuge and Nature Trail

Rt. 1, Box 448

Indiahoma, OK 73552

(580) 429-3222

http://www.nps.gov/chic/textver.htm

Oklahoma Public Gardens

Bivens Garden
P.O. Box 154
Shidler, OK 74652
(918) 793-4011
http://www.thebivingarden.com

Cann Memorial Gardens
Ponca City, OK
(405) 767-0430
http://www.poncacitynews.com/community/
attractions/cann

Garrard Ardeneum
501 N. 5th
McAlester, OK 74502
(918) 423-5492
http://www.lasr.net/leisure/oklahoma/pittsburg/
mcalester/att8.html

Hambrick Botanical Garden
National Cowboy Hall of Fame
1700 NE 63rd Street
Oklahoma City, OK 73111
(405) 478-2250
http://www.cowboyhalloffame.org

Honor Heights Park
641 Park Drive
Muskogee, OK 74403
(918) 684-6302
http://www.cityofmuskogee.com/
Template0.asp?pg=24

Jo Allyn Lowe Park
Price Road and Locust Road
Box 699
Bartlesville, OK 74005
http://home.okstate.edu/Okstate/dasnr/hort/
hortlahome.nsf/toc/joallyn

**John E. Kirkpatrick Horticulture Center
and Gardens**
900 N. Portland Avenue
Oklahoma City, OK 73107
(405) 945-3358
http://www.osuokc.edu/agriculture/

Kerr Arboretum and Botanical Area
P.O. Box 577
Talihina, OK 74571
(918) 567-2326
http://www.fs.fed.us/oonf/oklahoma/nra/kerr.html

Lendonwood Gardens
1310 W. 13th Street
Grove, OK 74344
(918) 786-2938
http://www.lendonwood.org

**Myriad Botanical Gardens and
Crystal Bridge**
301 W. Reno
Oklahoma City, OK 73102
(405) 297-3995
http://www.myriadgardens.com

**North Oklahoma Botanical Garden
and Arboretum**
1220 E. Grand Avenue
Tonkawa, OK 74653
580-628-2220
http://home.okstate.edu/Okstate/dasnr/hort/
hortlahome.nsf/toc/noc

**Oklahoma City Zoo and Botanical
Garden**
2102 NE 50th Street
Oklahoma City, OK 73111
(405) 424-3344
http://www.okczoo.com

Oklahoma Heritage Center Gardens

201 N.W. 14th Street
Oklahoma City, OK 73103
(405) 235-4458
http://www.oklahomaheritage.com

Omniplex Gardens and Greenhouse

2100 N.E. 52nd Street
Oklahoma City, OK 73111
(405) 602-6664
http://www.omniplex.org

OSU Botanical Garden

3415 W. Virginia Street
Stillwater, OK 74078
http://www.okstate.edu/ag/asnr/hortla/

Overstreet-Kerr Historical Farm

Rt. 2, Box 693
Keota, OK 74941
(918) 966-3396
http://www.kerrcenter.com/overstreet/index.html

Philbrook Museum of Art

2727 S. Rockford Rd.
Tulsa, OK 74114
(918) 749-7941
http://www.philbrook.org

Gilcrease Museum and Gardens

1400 N. Gilcrease Museum Rd.
Tulsa, OK 74127
(888) 655-2278
www.gilcrease.org

Tulsa Zoo and Living Museum

5701 E. 36th N.
Tulsa, OK 74115
(918) 669-6600
http://www.tulsazoo.org

Will Rogers Horticulture Gardens and Arboretum

3500 N.W. 36th
Oklahoma City, OK 73112
(405) 297-2356

Woodward Park, Rose Gardens, and Arboretum

Tulsa Garden Center
2435 S. Peoria
Tulsa, OK 74114
(918) 746-5125
http://www.tulsagardencenter.com

Woolaroc Museum, Wildlife Preserve, and Gardens

Rt. 3, Box 2100
Bartlesville, OK 74003
(918) 336-0307
http://www.woolaroc.org

Reference Publications of Interest

Antique Rose Emporium
9300 Lueckmeyer Rd.
Brenham, TX 77833
(800) 441-0002
www.antiqueroseemporium.com

Arborvillage
P.O. Box 227
Holt, MO 64048
(816) 264-3911
www.arborvillagellc.com

Avant Gardens
710 High Hill Rd.
Dartmouth, MA 02747
(508) 998-8819
www.avantgardensne.com

Brent and Becky's Bulbs
7900 Daffodil Lane
Gloucester, VA 23061
(877) 661-2852
www.brentandbeckysbulbs.com

Burpee Co.
300 Park Avenue
Warminster, PA 18991
(800) 888-1447
www.burpee.com

Forestfarm
990 Tetherow Rd.
Williams, OR 97544
(541) 846-7269
www.forestfarm.com

Heronswood Nursery
7530 NE 288th St.
Kingston, WA 98346
(360) 297-4172
www.heronswood.com

High Country Gardens
2902 Rufina Street
Santa Fe, NM 87507
(800) 925-9387
www.highcountrygardens.com

Logee's Greenhouses
141 N. Street
Danielson, CT 06239
(888) 330-8038
www.logees.com

Old House Gardens
536 Third St.
Ann Arbor, MI 48103
(734) 995-1486
www.oldhousegardens.com

Park's Seeds
1 Parkton Ave.
Greenwood, SC 29647
(800) 845-3369
www.parkseed.com

Pine Ridge Gardens
P.O. Box 200
London, AR 72847
(479) 293-4359
www.pineridgegardens.com

Plant Delights Nursery, Inc.
9241 Sauls Rd.
Raleigh, NC 27603
(919) 772-4794
www.plantdelights.com

Singing Springs Nursery
8802 Wilkerson Rd.
Cedar Grove, NC 27231
(919) 732-9403
www.singingspringsnursery.com

Siskiyou Rare Plant Nursery
2825 Cummings Road
Medford, OR 97501
(541) 772-6846
www.srpn.net/index2.shtml/

Song Sparrow Farm
13101 East Rye Rd.
Avalon, WI 53505
(800) 553-3715
www.songsparrow.com

Stokes Tropicals
P.O. Box 9868
New Iberia, LA 70562
(800) 624-9706
www.stokestropicals.com

Wayside Gardens
1 Garden lane
Hodges, SC 29695
(800) 845-1124
www.waysidegardens.com

White Flower Farm
P.O. Box 50
Litchfield, CT 06759
(800) 503-9624
www.whiteflowerfarm.com

Backyard Living Magazine
5925 Country Lane
Greendale, WI 53129
(800) 344-6913
www.backyardlivingmagazine.com

Better Homes and Gardens Magazine
P.O. Box 37449
Boone, IA 50037
(800) 374-4244
www.bhg.com

Birds and Blooms Magazine
P.O. Box 984
Greendale, WI 53129
(800) 344-6913
www.birdsandblooms.com

Country Living Gardener
P.O. Box 7335
Red Oak, IA 51591
(800) 777-0102
www.cl-gardener.com

Fine Gardening Magazine
The Taunton Press
P.O. Box 5506
Newtown, CT, 06470
(800) 477-8727
www.taunton.com

Garden Design Magazine
460 N. Orlando Ave., Suite 200
Winter Park, FL 32789
(407) 628-4802
www.gardendesignmag.com

Garden Gate Magazine
P.O. Box 842
Des Moines, IA 50304
(800) 341-4769
www.gardengatemagazine.com

Horticulture Magazine
98 North Washington Street
Boston, MA 02114
(877) 436-7764

Oklahoma Gardener Magazine
State by State Gardening
P.O. Box 13070
Ruston, LA 71273
(318) 255-3149
www.okgardener.com

Oklahoma Horticulture Society Newsletter
PO Box 75425
Oklahoma City, OK 73147
www.okhort.org

Southern Living Magazine
P.O. Box 62376
Tampa, FL 33662
(800) 272-4101
www.southernliving.com

The American Gardener
7931 E. Boulevard Drive
Alexandria, VA 22150
(703) 768-5700
www.ahs.org

Glossary

Alkaline soil: soil with a pH greater than 7.0. It lacks acidity, often because it has limestone in it.

All-purpose fertilizer: powdered, liquid, or granular fertilizer with a balanced proportion of the three key nutrients—nitrogen (N), potassium (K), and phosphorous (P). It is suitable for maintenance nutrition for most plants.

Annual: a plant that lives its entire life in one season. It is generally determined to germinate, grow, flower, set seed, and die the same year.

Balled and burlapped: describes a tree or shrub grown in the field whose soilball has been wrapped with protective burlap and twine when the plant is dug up to be sold or transplanted.

Bare root: describes plants that have been packaged without any soil around their roots. (Often young shrubs and trees purchased through the mail arrive with their exposed roots covered with moist peat or sphagnum moss, sawdust, or similar material, and wrapped in plastic.)

Barrier plant: a plant that has intimidating thorns or spines and is sited purposely to block foot traffic or other access to the home or yard.

Beneficial insects: insects or their larvae that prey on pest organisms and their eggs. They may be flying insects, such as ladybugs, parasitic wasps, praying mantids, and soldier bugs, or soil dwellers such as predatory nematodes, spiders, and ants.

Bract: a modified leaf structure on a plant stem near its flower that resembles a petal. Often it is more colorful and visible than the actual flower, such as in dogwood.

Canopy: the overhead branching area of a tree, usually referring to its extent including foliage.

Cold hardiness: the ability of a perennial plant to survive the winter cold in a particular area.

Composite: a flower that is actually composed of many tiny flowers. Typically, they are flat clusters of tiny, tight florets, sometimes surrounded by wider-petaled florets. Composite flowers are highly attractive to bees and beneficial insects.

Compost: organic matter that has undergone progressive decomposition by microbial and macrobial activity until it is reduced to a spongy, fluffy texture. Added to soil of any type, it improves the soil's ability to hold air and water and to drain well.

Corm: the swollen energy-storing structure, analogous to a bulb, under the soil at the base of the stem of plants such as crocus and gladiolus.

Crown: the base of a plant at, or just beneath, the surface of the soil where the roots meet the stems.

Cultivar: a naturally occurring form of a plant that has been identified as special or superior and is purposely selected for propagation and production.

Deadheading: a pruning technique that removes faded flower heads from plants to improve their appearance, abort seed production, and stimulate further flowering.

Deciduous plants: unlike evergreens, these trees and shrubs lose their leaves in the fall.

Desiccation: drying out of foliage tissues, usually due to drought or wind.

Division: the practice of splitting apart perennial plants to create several smaller-rooted segments. The practice is useful for controlling the plant's size and for acquiring more plants; it is also essential to the health and continued flowering of certain plants.

Dormancy: the period, usually the winter, when perennial plants temporarily cease active growth and rest. Some plants, such as spring-blooming bulbs, go dormant in the summer.

Established: the point at which a newly planted tree, shrub, or flower begins to produce new growth, either foliage or stems. This is an indication that the roots have recovered from transplant shock and have begun to grow and spread.

Evergreen: perennial plants that do not lose their foliage annually with the onset of winter. The term refers to needled or broadleaf foliage that persists and continues to function on a plant through one or more winters, aging and dropping unobtrusively in cycles of three or four years or more.

F1 hybrid: the first-generation result of a hybrid cross.

Foliar: of or about foliage. It usually refers to the practice or spraying foliage, as in fertilizing or treating with insecticide; leaf tissues absorb liquid directly for much faster results, and the soil is not affected.

Floret: a tiny flower, usually one of many forming a cluster that comprises a single blossom such as a lilac or spider flower.

Germinate: to sprout. Germination is a fertile seed's first stage of development.

Graft (union): the point on the stem of a woody plant with sturdier roots where a stem from a highly ornamental plant is inserted so that it will join with it. Roses are commonly grafted.

Hardscape: the permanent, structural, nonplant part of a landscape, such as walls, sheds, pools, patios, arbors, and walkways.

Herbaceous: plants having fleshy or soft stems that die back with frost; the opposite of woody.

Hybrid: a plant that is the result of intentional or natural cross-pollination between two or more plants of the same species or genus.

Low-water-demand: describes plants that tolerate dry soil for varying periods of time. Typically, they have succulent, hairy, or silvery-gray foliage and tuberous roots or taproots.

Mulch: a layer of material over bare soil to protect it from erosion and compaction by rain, and to discourage weeds. It may be inorganic (gravel, fabric) or organic (wood chips, bark, pine needles, chopped leaves).

Naturalize: (a) to plant seeds, bulbs, or plants in a random, informal pattern as they would appear in their natural habitat; (b) to adapt to and spread throughout adopted habitats (a tendency of some plants that are not native).

Nectar: the sweet fluid produced by glands on flowers that attract pollinators such as hummingbirds and honeybees for whom it is a source of energy.

Organic material, organic matter: any material or debris that is derived from plants. It is carbon-based material capable of undergoing decomposition and decay.

Peat moss: organic matter from peat sedges (United States) or sphagnum mosses (Canada) often used to improve soil texture. The acidity of sphagnum peat moss makes it ideal for boosting or maintaining soil acidity while also improving its drainage.

Perennial: a flowering plant that lives over two or more seasons. Many die back with frost, but their roots survive the winter and generate new shoots in spring.

Perennialize: When a reseeding, hardy perennial spreads out over an extended period of time from its original planting.

pH: a measurement of the relative acidity (low pH) or alkalinity (high pH) of soil or water based on a scale of 1 to 14, 7 being neutral. Individual plants require soil to be within a certain range so that nutrients can dissolve in moisture and be available to them. Philadelphia-area soil is typically slightly acidic, measuring about 6.3.

Pinch: to remove tender stems and / or leaves by pressing them between thumb and forefinger. This pruning technique encourages branching, compactness, and flowering in plants, or it removes aphids clustered at growing tips.

Pollen: the yellow, powdery grains in the center of a flower. A plant's male sex cells, they are transferred to the female plant parts by means of wind or animal pollinators to fertilize them and create seeds.

Pond liner: a molded fiberglass form or a flexible butyl or poly fabric that creates an artificial pond for the purpose of water gardening.

Rhizome: a swollen energy-storing stem structure, similar to a bulb, that lies horizontally in the soil, with roots emerging from its lower surface and growth shoots from a growing point at or near its tip, as in bearded iris.

Rootbound (or potbound): the condition of a plant that has been confined to a container too long, its roots having been forced to wrap around themselves and even swell our of the container. Successful transplanting or repotting requires untangling and trimming away of some of the matted roots.

Root flare: the transition at the base of a tree trunk where the bark tissue begins to differentiate and roots begin to form just prior to entering the soil. This area should not be covered with soil when planting a tree.

Self-seeding: the tendency of some plants to sow their seeds freely around the yard. It creates many seedlings the following season that may or may not be welcome.

Semi-evergreen: having functional and persistent foliage during part of the winter or dry season.

Shearing: the pruning technique whereby plant stems and branches are cut uniformly with long-bladed pruning shears (hedge shears) or powered hedge trimmers. It is used in creating and maintaining hedges and topiary.

Slow-acting fertilizer: fertilizer that is water insoluble and therefore releases its nutrients gradually as a function or soil temperature, moisture, and related microbial activity. Typically granular, it may be either organic or synthetic.

Sucker: a new growing shoot. Underground plant roots produce suckers to form new stems and spread by means of these suckering roots to form large plantings, or colonies. Some plants produce root suckers or branch suckers as a result of pruning or wounding.

Tuber: a type of underground storage structure in a plant stem, analogous to a bulb. It generates roots below and stems above ground (example: dahlia).

Variegated: having various colors or color patterns. The term usually refers to plant foliage that is streaked, edged, blotched, or mottled with a contrasting color, often green with yellow, cream, or white.

White grubs: fat, off-white, wormlike larvae of Japanese beetles. They reside in the soil and feed on plant (especially grass) roots until summer when they emerge as beetles to feed on plant foliage.

Wings: (a) the corky tissue that forms edges along the twigs of some woody plants such as winged euonymus; (b) the flat, dried extension of tissue on some seeds, such as maple, that catch the wind and help them disseminate.

Your Garden Plans

Garden Notes

Garden Notes

Garden Notes

Garden Notes

Bibliography

Ajilvsgi, Geyata. *Butterfly Gardening for the South*. Dallas, TX: Taylor Publishing Co., 1991.

Bender, Steve and Felder Rushing. *Passalong Plants*. Chapel Hill, NC: The University of North Carolina Press, 1993.

Dirr, Michael. *Manual of Woody Landscape Plants*. Champaign, IL: Stipes Publishing Co., 1983.

Masters, Ron, John M. Dole, Steven H. Dobbs, and Stephanie Smith. *Landscaping and Gardening for Birds*. Stillwater, OK: OSU Extension Fact Sheet 6435. 1996.

McCoy, Doyle. *Roadside Trees and Shrubs of Oklahoma*. Norman, OK: University of Oklahoma Press, 1981.

McCoy, Doyle. *Roadside Wild Fruits of Oklahoma*. Norman, OK: University of Oklahoma Press, 1980.

McCoy, Doyle. *Wildflowers of Oklahoma*. Lindsay, OK: Doyle McCoy Publisher, 1987.

Schopmeyer, C.S. *Seeds of Woody Plants in the United States*. Washington DC: USDA Forest Service, Ag Handbook 450, 1974.

Still, Steven. *Manual of Herbaceous Ornamental Plants*. Champaign, IL: Stipes Publishing Co., 1994.

Smith, Stephanie, Ron Masters, Paul Mitchell, Ken Pinkston, Don Arnold, and John M. Doyle. *Landscaping to Attract Butterflies, Moths, and Skippers*. Stillwater, OK: OSU Extension Fact Sheet 6430. 1996.

Vines, Robert. *Trees, Shrubs, and Woody Vines of the Southwest*. Austin, TX: University of Texas Press, 1990.

Welch, William C. *Perennial Garden Color*. Dallas, TX: Taylor Publishing Co., 1989.

Welch, William C., and Greg Grant. *The Southern Heirloom Garden*. Dallas, TX: Taylor Publishing Co., 1995.

Whitcomb, Carl E., Ph.D. *Know It and Grow It, II*. Stillwater, OK: Lacebark Publications, 1983.

Woods, Christopher. *Encyclopedia of Perennials*. New York, NY: Facts on File, 1992.

Young, James A., and Cheryl G. Young. *Seeds of Wildland Plants*. Portland, OR: Timber Press, 1986.

Catalogs

Bluebird Nursery Wholesale Catalog. Clarkson, NE, 1998, 1999.

Bluemel, Kurt, Inc., Wholesale Nursery Catalogue. Baldwin, MD, 1998, 1999.

Glasshouse Works. Mail Order Catalog. Stewart, OH, 1998.

Greenleaf Nursery Wholesale Catalog. Park Hill, OK, 1999.

Green Leaf Ent., Inc., Wholesale Starter Plants Catalog. Leola, PA, 1998-99.

Logee's Greenhouses. Mail Order Catalog. Danielson, CT, 1998.

Monrovia Wholesale Catalog. Azusa, CA, 1998.

Plant Delights Nursery, Inc. Raleigh, NC, 1998, 1999.

Siskiyou Rare Plant Nursery. Mail Order Catalog. Medford, OR, 1998.

Wayside Gardens, The Complete Garden Mail Order Catalog. Hodges, SC, 1999.

White Flower Farm, The Garden Book. Mail Order Catalog. Litchfield, CT, 1998, 1999.

Mesonet

AgWeather is a cooperative project between Oklahoma State University, the University of Oklahoma, and the Oklahoma Climatological Survey. This professional team works together to provide Oklahoma citizens with the Oklahoma Mesonet, one of the finest weather data collection and reporting systems in the world. On the AgWeather web site, you can access Oklahoma weather information updated every 15 minutes. It's like having a 24-hours-a-day, 7 days-a-week weatherman in over 110 locations across Oklahoma. The Mesonet towers have been collecting data for every 5 minutes every day of the year since 1994. This service provides valuable decision-making information, such as air and soil temperatures, soil moisture, rainfall, wind speeds, live weather radars and much more for agriculture producers and natural resources management professionals. As home gardeners, our outdoor activities also revolve around the weather. Home gardeners can also use this service as a record keeping tool as well as a planning tool to coordinate their gardening and landscaping activities.

Oklahoma Mesonet / Ag Weather
http://agweather.mesonet.org
405-224-2216
405-325-3231

Photography Credits

Tom Eltzroth: 12, 22, 23, 24, 26, 29, 30, 33, 34, 35, 36, 38, 40, 42, 43, 44, 46, 47, 48, 49, 52, 59, 60, 64, 65, 66, 67, 68, 69, 74, 75, 77, 95, 103, 110, 112, 113, 116, 119, 120, 122, 125, 126, 127, 132, 135, 136, 137, 138, 142, 143, 147 (top), 150, 152, 157, 158, 162, 164, 167, 168, 170, 177, 181, 182, 183, 186, 188, 191, 192, 195, 198, 201, 202, 210, 217, 221

Jerry Pavia: 10, 25, 32, 39, 41, 45, 50, 53, 55, 62, 71, 72, 94, 97, 99, 102, 105, 106, 107, 108, 117, 123, 128, 130, 131, 139, 141, 144, 149 (middle and bottom), 156, 159, 161, 163, 169, 171, 172, 173, 184, 190, 194, 199, 207, 211

Liz Ball and Rick Ray: 58, 76, 98, 111, 114, 115, 118, 124, 154, 174, 178, 179, 180, 185, 187, 189, 193, 197, 203, 214, 216, 219

Steve Dobbs: 28, 51, 73, 147 (bottom), 148 (top), 148 (all), 208

Pam Harper: 104, 133, 146, 147 (middle), 153, 160, 175, 205, 206

Felder Rushing: 8,13, 31, 54, 61, 151

Bill Adams: 37, 96, 121, 166, 176

Charles Mann: 15, 16, 63, 101, 134, 220

Andre Viette: 11, 17, 18, 140, 155, 204

Karen Bussolini: 165

Mike Dirr: 129

Greg Grant: 149 (top)

Lorenzo Gunn: 196

Dency Kane: 209

Peter Loewer: 14

Judy Mielke: 215

Park Seed Company: 208

John Pohly: 224

David Winger: 222

University of Oklahoma: 225

Plant Index

Meet Steve Dobbs

Steve Dobbs

Steve Dobbs is an award-winning horticulturist, garden writer, and lecturer. He was host and producer of the popular television show, *Oklahoma Gardening*, from 1990-1995, selected in 1992 as the Best TV Gardening Program in the Nation by the Garden Writers Association. He is also author of *The Perfect Oklahoma Lawn*.

Since his graduation from Oklahoma State University and the University of Arkansas in horticulture, he has worked in the retail and wholesale greenhouse business as a grower, in landscape design, installation, and maintenance, and in education as an Extension Horticulturist in both Oklahoma and Florida. For fourteen years he worked with the Extension Service equipping gardeners to better solve horticulture problems and answer questions.

In 2002, Steve started as Director of Grounds and Landscape at the University of Arkansas - Fort Smith where he is helping develop a botanical garden and arboretum. Under his direction, the University was awarded the Grand Award for the Best Maintained Landscape in the Nation by the Professional Grounds Management Society in the school and university category in 2003.

This vast array of experience has uniquely qualified Steve, as one of the leading horticulturists in the two-state area.

Dobbs and his wife Jo Alice have two children, as well as dogs, horses and cats - all residing on their family farm (Morning Star Farms) in Eastern Oklahoma near Sallisaw where they enjoy gardening and raising tiger-stripe cattle.